His Majesty's Indian Allies

British Indian Policy in
The Defence of Canada, 1774–1815

Robert S. Allen

His Majesty's Indian Allies

British Indian Policy in The Defence of Canada, 1774–1815

Robert S. Allen

Dundurn Press
Toronto & Oxford
1992

Editing: Diane Mew
Printing and Binding: Gagné Printing Ltd., Louiseville, Quebec, Canada

Dundurn Press wishes to acknowledge the generous assistance and ongoing support of The Canada Council, The Book Publishing Industry Development Program of the Department of Communications, The Ontario Arts Council, The Ontario Heritage Foundation and the Ontario Publishing Centre of the Ministry of Culture and Communications.

Care has been taken to trace the ownership of copyright material used in the text, including the illustrations. The author and the publisher welcome any information enabling them to rectify any reference or credit in subsequent editions.

J.Kirk Howard, Publisher

Canadian Cataloguing in Publication Data

Allen, Robert S.
  His Majesty's Indian allies

Includes bibliographical references and index.

ISBN 1-55002-175-3 (bound). – ISBN 1-55002-184-2 (pbk.)

1. Indians of North America - Canada - Government relations - To 1830.* 2. Indians of North America – Government relations – To 1789. 3. Indian of North America – Wars – 1750–1815. 4. Great Britain. British Indian Dept. – History. I. Title.

E92.A58 1992   323.1'197071   C92-095300-X

Dundurn Press Limited
2181 Queen Street East, Suite 310,
Toronto, Ontario
M4E 1E5
Canada

Dundurn Distribution Limited
73 Lime Walk
Headington, Oxford
England
0X3 7AD

CONTENTS

PREFACE

This study was initiated several years ago as a doctoral dissertation at the University of Wales (Aberystwyth). Its aim was to redress or balance the historiographical ledger pertaining to the events of 1774 to 1815 on the Great Lakes frontier by focusing on the "old" province of Quebec. Sources for this period, both printed and unpublished, are numerous, with new studies continually appearing. But apart from the writings of A.L. Burt some fifty years ago, most notably his *The United States, Great Britain and British North America*, and the more recent scholarship of such historians as Jack Sosin, Reginald Horsman, and George F.G. Stanley, the majority of scholars engaged in this subject tend to concentrate on such themes as American Indians, the fur trade, United States Indian policy, military campaigns, American westward expansion, and Anglo-American diplomatic relations. The constant among them is their failure to assess in any great detail the central importance for Great Britain during these critical four decades of preserving and defending Canada. The analysis which follows therefore is not a retelling of events, but a reinterpretation of the strategies and policies devised by crown officials to secure, largely through the military use and assistance of Indian allies, the survival of Canada, and thus the continuation of a British political and economic influence and empire in North America.

Within the text, three points relating to definition or terminology require brief explanations. First, the territorial limits of Canada as defined in the documents between the years 1774 to 1815 meant and included in general terms only the lands which now constitute the southern portions of the provinces of Quebec (including the Eastern Townships) and Ontario from the Gulf of St. Lawrence to Montreal, and west along the north shores of the upper St. Lawrence, Lake Ontario and Lake Erie to the Detroit River. The northern limits were vaguely defined, but stopped at Rupert's Land, a vast area which by royal charter in 1670 granted the Hudson's Bay Company the exclusive trading rights and ownership to all the lands drained by the rivers flowing into James Bay and Hudson Bay. For the purposes of this study, therefore, Canada excludes the present Atlantic provinces, the prairie provinces, British Columbia, and the North.

Second, for general clarity and easier identification, Indian tribal names and personalities have been anglicized. For instance, Ojibwa and Six Nations Confederacy of Iroquois rather than Anishnabwe and Ho-dé-no-sau-nee or their derivatives will be used. As for the names of prominent Indian leaders, wherever possible when first introduced, the person will be identified by the anglicized name followed in brackets by a form of the real or traditional name. Thereafter, only the anglicized version will be employed. Thus, Joseph Brant (Thayendanegea) or Black Hawk (Ma-ka-tai-me-she-kia-kiak) will be referred to thereafter as Joseph Brant or Black Hawk.

Third, the expression in common usage during the period of this study to identify a person from Scotland was Scotch, and since even Robbie Burns applied the term to his countrymen, I have chosen to use Scotch in the text rather than the later and now more popular English affectation of Scots or Scottish.

During the research and preparation of this study, I received every courtesy and assistance from my colleagues in Ottawa at the Department of Indian and Northern Affairs Canada, the staffs of several archives, museums, and libraries in Canada, the United States, and Great Britain, and from friends. To all these people I extend my sincere thanks and deep sense of gratitude. In particular, at Indian Affairs, I would like to thank Dr. Katie Cook, ex-director of the Corporate Policy Branch, and Lizzie Fraikin, ex-director of the Comprehensive Claims Branch, for supporting me in this undertaking. Also at Indian Affairs, thanks are due to John F. Leslie and Jack Stagg for valuable comments made on draft chapters; to Hélène Lanthier, Susan Mongrain, Julia Finn, and Karla Weys of the departmental library for always responding in an efficient and good-natured fashion to numerous requests and queries over the years; and to my colleagues at the Claims and Historical Research Centre for covering for me.

In Canada and the United States, I acknowledge and thank the staffs at the National Archives of Canada (Ottawa), and especially David Hume, Lisa Patterson, and Mary Jane Commanda, all experts on Records Relating to Indian Affairs; and to the Ontario Archives (Toronto), the Metropolitan Toronto Library, the McCord Museum Archives (Montreal), Harry Bosveld at Fort Malden National Historic Park (Amherstburg), and Carl Benn at Old Fort York (Toronto). My appreciation is also extended to the staffs at the National Archives (Washington, DC), the Library of Congress (Washington, DC), the Detroit Public Library (Burton Historical Collection) and the Bureau of Indian Affairs (Washington, DC).

In Great Britain the primary documentation germane to this study is rich and voluminous, and I profited immeasurably from my research efforts in both London and Wales. In this regard my appreciation and thanks are extended to the staffs at the British Library (Department of Manuscripts), especially for the abundance of Additional Manuscripts made available from the Haldimand Collection, the Public Record Office (Kew) where the little-used Audit Office "Declared Accounts" of senior officials in the British Indian Department in North America were canvassed, the House of Lords Record Office which provided relatively untapped information through a series of Main Papers detailing the Burgoyne and St. Leger campaigns of 1777, the National Register of Archives and the Historical Manuscripts Commission, the Institute of Historical Research, the National Army Museum and the library of the Royal Commonwealth Society.

In Wales the staff at the Welch Regiment Museum (Cardiff) greatly facilitated my research endeavours by allowing me unlimited access to materials, of which a rare, hand-written account of the War of 1812 entitled "The War in Canada" proved especially valuable. At Aberystwyth, the National Library of Wales houses among its collections the Tredegar Park Muniments, of which the John Bradstreet Papers were found to be a useful source of information; and at the Hugh Owen Library of the University of Wales, Mrs. Chadwick and Mr. Brinkley provided reference assistance and showed me every kindness, for which I extend personal thanks.

In the preparation of the maps and in the gathering and selection of the illustrations and appendices, I received the assistance and advice of a number of people. To Ronald French (Okwaho), a skilled cartographer who drew the maps and printed the place names, all of which were devised by the author and relate solely to the events detailed in this study, my grateful thanks. I would also like to thank the Picture Division of the National Archives of

Canada for permission to reproduce several of the illustrations in the text, and especially to Jim Burant who alerted me to the two rare paintings recently acquired by the archives through a private purchase – "Two Ottawa Chiefs" and the "Deputation of Indian allies from the Mississippi Valley." In addition, I thank the following organizations: the Public Record Office for the Audit Office Declared Accounts of Daniel Claus Esq., the Montreal Museum of Fine Arts for the Great Indian Council, the Ontario Archives for the list of Indian warriors in 1812, the Chicago Historical Society for the rarely viewed oil painting of Black Hawk, and the McCord Museum of Canadian History both for Fort McKay and the previously unseen "Speech of Robert Dickson Esq. to Indian tribes in January 1813," which was carefully photocopied for me.

To my Mohawk friends, Kahn-Tineta Horn and Ronald French of Kahnawake, Don Maracle of Tyendinaga, and Phil Monture of Ohsweken, "Nia: wen Agwekenh." Equally, "tansi" to Sidney Fine Day, Plains Cree elder of Treaty Six, for allowing me a glimpse of Indian spiritual life.

To Wendy Pickard and Marianne Moore, both of whom successfully undertook the onerous task of deciphering and processing all the rough notes and words, I extend heartfelt thanks and gratitude. Their mastery of the technical complexities of the Wordperfect 5.1 system remains a bewildering and remarkable accomplishment to a Luddite like me.

To my tutor Dr. Boyd Stanley Schlenther, senior lecturer in the Department of History at the University of Wales, my most sincere thanks for the academic council and guidance provided to me during the research and writing of this study.

I would also like to thank Kirk Howard and the staff of Dundurn Press for their professional guidance, and Diane Mew, editorial consultant, who almost convinced me that revising could be a pleasant experience.

Last, because she always gets the last word, an abiding and affectionate thanks to my wife Karen, a woman of extraordinary patience and understanding who stayed the course.

PART ONE

British-Indian Relations in
Colonial America to 1774

CHAPTER 1

FORGING THE CHAIN OF FRIENDSHIP

Sir William Johnson, His Britannic Majesty's "Sole Agent for and Superintendent of the Affairs of Our faithfull Subjects and Allies the six united Nations of Indians and their Confederates in the Northern Parts of North America," died in the early evening of 11 July 1774 at Johnson Hall in the Mohawk Valley of the British province of New York.[1] From 1755 to 1774, this self-interested yet devoted servant of the crown had directed with energy, skill, and success the affairs of the Indians in the Northern District. Prior to the pivotal influence of the Johnson regime, Indian affairs in the American colonies had been marked by a long, vexing, and generally rudderless period of imperial salutary neglect. Inter-colonial land rivalries and wrangling disunity had only further complicated British-Indian relations, which fluctuated between the benign and the intolerable. But by the 1750s the looming and final conflict with France for paramountcy in North America turned British vacillation into resolve. The appointment by royal commission of a single crown official for the administration and management of Indian affairs was therefore a sensible if long overdue imperial initiative. Finally, after 150 years of permanent British settlement along the eastern shores of the "new world," a formal and centralized policy for the aboriginal or native people had emanated from Britain.

The vehicle for implementing the policy directives was the British Indian Department, the forerunner of the present Department of Indian and Northern Affairs Canada. For the next sixty years, until the end of the War of 1812, the fundamental tenet of that policy was to court and maintain the allegiance of the native people to the royal cause. As a result, and especially in the post-1774 years against the common enemy – the Americans – an enduring and symbiotic relationship evolved between the native people and the British crown in North America which was rooted in the mutual need and desire for protection and survival.[2] British Indian policy from 1774 to 1815 was thus geared primarily to ensuring the preservation and defence of Canada through the military use and assistance of His Majesty's Indian allies.

Among the Eastern Woodland Indian tribes of the Great Lakes region, the Mohawk of the Ho-dé-no-sau-nee or People of the Longhouse, were the earliest and staunchest allies of the British crown.[3] Like all native tribes in the Americas, the Longhouse people possessed a strong spiritual bond with the land and the natural environment. Through the teachings of the Creator (the Great Spirit), they revered all living things, from plants and animals to the forests, rivers, lakes, and mountains. Communal sharing of the sacred land through the sustainable development of resources was traditionally practised, and the concept of individual ownership was unknown or unthinkable. The native people considered themselves to be the custodians or stewards of the land, and as such honour-bound to protect it for the benefit of the next generation. The arrival and settlement of Europeans, therefore, who felled and burned the trees, polluted the waters, and fenced vast areas was akin to the raping of Mother Earth. These two diametrically opposed beliefs concerning the natural environment – preservation versus progress and settlement – with the resultant and ongoing clashes over land issues and land claims, have remained the dominant feature of Indian-white relations, certainly in North America, from the moment of contact until present times.

Prior to the arrival of Europeans, the Longhouse people, according to their oral traditions, were organized by Dekanahwideh (the Heavenly Messenger) and Hiawatha, into the League of the Iroquois. The league was initially composed of five nations – the Mohawk, Oneida, Onondaga, Cayuga, and Seneca – but about 1721 a sixth nation, the Tuscarora, was admitted, thus forming the Six Nations Confederacy of Iroquois. The confederacy functioned under the Great Law of Peace, a political system granting the autonomy of each nation over local interests whilst deciding general confederacy matters, such as foreign and military policy, through a "grand council." This form of federalism was strengthened by the clan system which threaded through the whole confederacy and linked the various nations to each other. The Mohawk possessed only the Turtle, Wolf, and Bear clans, but there were others belonging to other nations, including Heron, Hawk, Eel, Snipe, Deer, and Beaver. Within the clan system, a Mohawk of the Turtle clan would be linked, for instance, with a Cayuga of the same clan, and indeed, the bonding between clan members was often stronger than the loyalty an individual might have for his or her particular nation.[4]

Fundamental to the operation of the confederacy was the fact that Iroquois society was based on matrilineal descent and an extended kinship in which all individuals and nations of the confederacy were one family, symbolically living together in one longhouse. This practice and principle gave women, especially the matrons or clan mothers, a special position of influence in the policies and decision-making of the confederacy, since they alone appointed or removed the clan chiefs of the grand council. There were fifty of these civil chiefs or sachems, known as royaneh (translated as "lord"). Their titles were hereditary within the clan, and a chief could only inherit through the lineage of his clan mother. War chiefs were also selected by the clan mothers, but again only the eligible sons of the female families holding the hereditary titles would be considered as appropriate heirs. Finally, the confederacy chiefs, from time to time, could elect a man who had proven to be wise, honest, or worthy to sit with them in the grand council. These honoured individuals, know as Pine Tree or "merit" chiefs, had no authority to name a successor, and the title was not hereditary.[5]

Issues affecting the whole confederacy were discussed in the grand council in a formal and ritualistic manner. A particularly distinguishing feature of the councils, common throughout the Indian world, was the use of tobacco and the extensive and significant importance of prayer. Among the Six Nations Confederacy, there were several sacred rituals, medicine societies, harvest dances and ceremonials. The "Roll Call of the Chiefs," for instance, comprised one of the rites of the condolence council, a time to honour the dead and "raise up" a new chief.[6] The Onondaga, as the confederacy "Keepers of the Fire," also became "the Keeper of the Wampum." By custom, the wampum – coloured beads woven into belts – provided an archive or record of important statements, treaties, or events in confederacy history. It was also used as gifts. The value of wampum to the Iroquois and other Indian tribes soon prompted the Europeans to establish wampum "factories" to produce sufficient quantities both for the Indian demand and as a form of currency among the whites.[7] To the Indians, wampum became so popular and prized that it became a major item of exchange in the fur trade. Indeed, for the European traders, "wampum was the magnet which drew the beaver out of the interior forests."[8]

For all Indians of the Americas, the most significant disruption of their lives (whether recorded on wampum or not) was the arrival of the newcomers - the Europeans. This encounter between two worlds awakened the native people from the long pristine isolation of their dreamtime to a dawn of a new era which would break upon them. As the eastern door of Iroquoia, whose traditional lands included most of the Finger Lakes in what is now upper New York, the Mohawk were the first nation of the Iroquois confederacy to make contact with these technologically dominant European newcomers. They were Dutch, and in about 1643 an unrecorded treaty of trade and peace was concluded with them by the Mohawk in which apparently an "iron chain" or alliance was forged against their common enemies.[9]

This agreement is known among the Iroquois as the Two Row Wampum treaty. The wampum belt consisted of two parallel rows of coloured beads sewn on a white background. The agreement purportedly stipulated that both the Mohawk (representing the Six Nations Confederacy) and the Dutch were separate but equal, with the two discrete rows of beads symbolizing that neither nation would interfere with the integrity of the other's culture, language, laws, or religious and political systems. When the British displaced the Dutch in the Hudson Valley of New York in 1664, the precedents established in Dutch-Mohawk relations were generally assumed. Yet in two subsequent agreements in 1677, the iron chain was replaced by a symbolic "Silver Covenant Chain of Friendship" which enhanced the significance of the alliance. Silver was chosen, perhaps by both the Mohawk and the British, as it was more durable and beautiful and would be easier to polish and brighten when the chain needed to be renewed. The Two Row Wampum and the more encompassing and well-documented concept of a Silver Covenant Chain of Friendship symbolize for the Mohawk and the Six Nations Iroquois their status as a sovereign nation. For the British, the chain of friendship - eventually extended to include almost all the tribes of the Great Lakes - was the foundation of the British-Indian military alliances.[10] The purpose to 1763 was the defence against New France; the intent from 1774 to 1815 was the defence of Canada.

In securing the chain of friendship with the Iroquois, whose lands lay between New France and New York and Pennsylvania, the British had constructed "a wall unto us both by night and day" to protect their trade and settlements against the French.[11] Thomas Dongan, governor of the royal colony of New York, was fully aware of the importance of the British-Iroquois alliance as a barrier of frontier defence, observing that the Iroquois "are a bulwark between us and the French and all other Indians." Further, "those five nations are very brave and the awe and Dread of all ye Indyans in these parts of America and are a better defence to us, than if they were so many Christians."[12] The great fear, however, was that if the Iroquois, who for a time held the military and economic balance of power between France and Britain in North America, decided to switch their allegiance to New France, the French would certainly dominate and control all of North America. In their relations with the Iroquois, therefore, British colonial officials were instructed to use "all faire means to keep them firme and steady to the Covenant Chaine," and "to make them sensible, that as they are and have always been, the subjects of the King of England, they are therefore under the care and protection of the Great King of England."[13]

The British assertion that the aboriginal or native people (in this case the Iroquois) were subject to the king was a general concept shared by Britain's European rivals for empire in the new world. English claims in North America were based on discovery, symbolic possession (the planting of a cross or flag), and actual possession (the founding of a colony or settlement). In Virginia, for instance, the English declared: "Wee seeke Dominion." But this dominion had to be "absolutely good agaynst ye Naturall people."[14] English rights in North America, therefore, became linked to the act of discovery, which apparently and unilaterally justified the sovereign crown acquiring the fundamental, but blurred, jurisdictional and territorial rights of *imperium* (the right to rule) and *dominium* (the right to private property).[15] These self-declared English claims and rights were duly solidified by a number of royal charters or "speculative grants" to various individuals and companies interested in the promotion of settlement, the Christian religion, and the profits of commercial trade.

As for aboriginal rights, the English acknowledged that the Indians had a "natural title" to the land which sprang from the right of soil or prior occupancy. But since they were considered a wild and heathen people "that live up and downe in troupes like heards of Deere in a Forrest," the English rationalized moral and legal justifications for dispossessing the Indians.[16] To leave the tribes in possession of their country was to leave the new world a wilderness. The English, therefore, could either relinquish their claims and abandon the country, or enforce those claims against "the fierce savages, whose occupation was war" by the use of the sword and by "the adoption of principles adapted to the condition of a people with whom it was impossible to mix, and who could not be governed as a distinct society."[17] For the English and their European rivals, therefore, the Indians of North America could thus be allies or enemies. If they were to be enemies and disrupt the progress of a Christian and European "civilization," war and conquest were deemed justified. Precedents for this method of dealing with aboriginal people were found in the previous practices of English sovereigns. In 1109, for instance, Edward I had granted Gilbert de Clare "all the land of Cardigan, if he could win it from the Welsh."[18] Although the purchase of Indian lands became a useful device in the American colonies (and later in Canada) for peacefully pushing aside the tribes in the face of the advancing frontier, the settlers placed minimal legal importance to these treaty agreements, and the conditions established by Edward I more closely reflected the conduct of British-Indian relations in colonial America to 1774.

For the Six Nations Confederacy of Iroquois, however, these British territorial and sovereignty claims to areas which included, for instance, Mohawk traditional lands, were not viewed by the sachems as a particularly dangerous threat. In large part, this lack of concern was the result of a fundamental misunderstanding between the Iroquois and the British. For nearly one hundred years the Iroquois had been engaged in a state of alternate peace and war with the French in North America, as both sought to control the fur trade with the "western" tribes of the Great Lakes and Ohio Valley. In the 1640s the Iroquois smashed and dispersed the Huron (Petun) and other tribes north of Lake Ontario, and subdued some of the Ohio tribes. The French and their Indian allies invaded Iroquoia in the 1680s, but succeeded only in "Warring on the cornfields." Yet, in the years following, the Ojibwa people ventured south from the upper lakes, and in a series of bloody engagements ranging from Georgian Bay and Lake Huron, through to Lake Simcoe, the Rice Lakes, and along the northern shore of Lake Ontario from the "Carrying Place" (Toronto) to the Bay of Quinte, drove the Iroquois from their recently established and temporary stockaded villages in vacated Huronia, and pushed them back to their traditional castles in the Finger Lakes district of upper New York.[19]

By 1700 the Iroquois Confederacy, although still formidable, was tired, battered, and depleted. In the summer of that year alone, sachems complained to the British that "wee Sinnekes [Seneca] have lost forty of our people" to the "Dowaganhaes" (Ojibwa) from Canada who had struck them "hard by ye Sinnekes Castles."[20] Frustrated by these French-encouraged Indian attacks against them, the Iroquois agreed at Albany, New York, in August "to cleave firm to our resolution to be instructed in the Protestant Religion and also that we shall be firm to the Covenant Chain and dutifull subjects to the Great King of England."[21] In July of 1701 the confederacy further strengthened the alliance with the British (or so it thought) by signing over a "Deed in Trust" to the King of England. As allies and subjects, the Iroquois, who had suffered losses in the defence of Britain's northern colonies against New France, decided at this time of crisis to place their beaver hunting grounds, which they had conquered some fifty years before, under the protection of the English crown. The sachems intended only that the King "might be their Protector and Defender."[22] There was never any thought that the deed represented a surrender of territory or sovereignty.

The British, however, regarded the deed as an extinguishment of Iroquois title to them of a vast tract of land which stretched west and north into areas claimed or coveted by the French in Canada. Here was the fundamental and grievous misunderstanding. Yet, the British also contended that the Iroquois Confederacy, "being the most warlike in these parts of the world, held all their neighbouring Indians in a manner of Tributary subjection, they went sometimes as far as the South Sea [Pacific Ocean], the North West Passage and Florida to war, and extended also their conquests over that part of the Country, now called Canada."[23]

Although this assessment was an exaggeration, particularly after the "Grand Alliance" of 1700–1701 when the Iroquois agreed to remain neutral in any future conflicts between France and Britain in North America, the confederacy indeed remained the most powerful military alliance of tribes in the Great Lakes region.[24] Therefore, since the Iroquois had voluntarily placed themselves and their lands under the care and protection of the English crown, the British were quite content to acknowledge and promote Iroquois claims of territorial sovereignty over huge and nebulous areas of land. The straightforward and calculated British reasoning was based on the understanding (or misunderstanding) that as subjects, yet allies, of the English crown, all Iroquois lands were under the jurisdiction of Britain. Consequently, any French attempts to expand their interests west or south towards the Ohio Valley and Mississippi River could be construed as a violation of British territorial and sovereignty rights. The perpetuation of the notion of an "ambiguous Iroquois empire," therefore, at least until the French were eliminated from Canada, suited British imperial and territorial interests in North America perfectly well.

Throughout the period of the British-Iroquois alliance against the French and their Indian allies in New France, trade, religious conversion, and military defence "against ye Common Enemy" were the elements of mutual interest that linked them together under the Silver Covenant Chain of Friendship.[25] But trade was the most important commodity in keeping the alliance intact. Both sides profited and benefited from the bartering and exchanging of beaver furs for trade goods. From the moment of contact, the Indians were willing and capable partners in fur. The Montagnais in eastern Canada, for instance, told the Jesuit Fathers in 1634, that "the beaver does everything perfectly well, it makes kettles, hatchets, swords, knives, bread, and in short, it makes everything."[26] Over one hundred years later, the secretary to Sir William Johnson echoed this continuing theme by noting that in regard to British-Iroquois relations, "trade was the foundation of their Alliance or Connexions with us, it is the chief Cement whch binds us together. And this should undoubtedly be the first Principle of our whole System of Indian Politics."[27]

The Ojibwa war, King William's War, and the peace treaties concluded at Albany and Montreal in 1701 in which the Iroquois agreed to remain neutral in any future conflict between the British and the French, weakened the confederacy's domination of the fur trade. But the sachems were not content to remain idle, sitting on their mats and smoking their pipes. Instead, they devised economic and diplomatic strategies that attempted to uphold the league's power by luring the western tribes, and even the Ottawa to the north, into trading with the British at Albany, under the auspices of the confederacy. Although the sachems frequently visited Albany "to renew the Covenant Chain" and pledge "allegiance and fidelity" to the British crown, "the faithful Mohawks" and others of the confederacy were decidedly more interested after 1701 in maintaining their strategic position of holding the economic and military balance of power between Britain and France in North America, in order to preserve a durable peace and prosperity for Iroquoia.[28]

But in 1726-27 the carefully constructed plan of the sachems crumbled with the intrusion into Seneca and Onondaga country of both the French and the British who built forts at Niagara and

Oswego.[29] Thereafter, confederacy policy was transformed into ensuring the protection and security of Iroquois lands. With the outbreak of King George's War in 1744, the threats to the league became even more severe, particularly as Iroquois neutrality was compromised by their participation in the war on behalf of the British. Yet the sachems continued to insist that they were "desirous to remain at peace with the french and English," and that they were "not subjects of England" nor had they "ceded to any one their lands, which they hold only of Heaven."[30] The British, however, maintained that Iroquois territory had long since been solemnly submitted to the crown, and further, that by both the Treaty of Utrecht and by the Treaty at Aix-la-Chapelle, the Iroquois were subjects of Great Britain.[31]

By the 1750s the economic lifelines and territorial parameters of Iroquoia were being squeezed ever tighter on all sides by the British, the French, and the western tribes of the Ohio, who were becoming stronger and more confident in defying the increasingly naked pretensions of Iroquois superiority. Angry and frustrated, a delegation of Mohawk met in council with the British at Fort George in the city of New York in June 1753. The respected sachem Hendrick (Theyanoguin), speaking for the Mohawk, scolded the British for their "indifference and neglect" and complained that Albany remained defenceless, thus leaving the Six Nations Iroquois without assistance and "exposed to the enemy" who held "a knife over our heads to destroy us." Hendrick had come "to remind you of the ancient alliance agreed on between our respective Forefathers." But with such apparent British apathy, the Mohawk sachem could only surmise that "we were united by a Covenant Chain and it seems now likely to be broken not from our Fault but yours." Therefore, he concluded, "as soon as we come home, we will send up a belt of Wampum to our Brothers the 5 Nations to acquaint them the Covenant Chain is broken between you and us."[32]

The words of Hendrick startled New York and the Board of Trade and Plantations in London. The importance of preserving the British-Iroquois alliance was considered vital to the security of Britain's northern colonies. In consequence, the Board ordered the holding of a general congress at Albany by the several colonies in order to resolve any differences between the British and the Six Nations Confederacy. In part, the result of this directive was the Albany Congress of June and July 1754 and the "Plan of a proposed Union of the several Colonies ..., for their mutual defence and security, and for extending the British Settlements in North America." But at the same time a major council was held at Albany with the Iroquois. Hendrick again harangued the British and colonial representatives by demanding that they open their eyes and "look about your Country and see, you have no Fortifications about you, no not even this City, 'tis but one Step from Canada hither, and the French may easily come and turn you out of your doors."[33] Yet, in spite of Iroquois bitterness and unresolved grievances, the sachems were reconciled to the idea of accepting a renewal of the British-Iroquois Covenant Chain of Friendship, based on mutual protection and survival.

Although the Albany plan for a proposed union was stalled by both the individual colonies and the Board of Trade and Plantations (and was eventually to collapse), the Board was resolute in recommending that the management of Indian affairs be placed under one central administration, which would be supported at the general expense and in the interest of the whole. A centralized British Indian policy was indeed sensible and long overdue. French Indian policy had proven to be eminently successful under a unified, coherent, single chain of command in which even the French officers of the regular troops were obliged to take their tours among the Indians. Whilst the British, the Iroquois, and the factionalized Thirteen Colonies were attempting to reach some degree of organization and cooperation, their collective security and interests in the west were dealt a further blow by the confirmation of French dominion in the Ohio Valley with the defeat of the young Virginian George Washington and his probing force at the Great Meadows, ironically enough on "the Fourth of July." Into this chaotic atmosphere of competing empires and tribal alliances emerged a figure who would become the most influential and powerful British crown official for the management of Indian affairs in North America – William Johnson.

CHAPTER 2

SIR WILLIAM JOHNSON AND THE INDIAN DEPARTMENT

Willian Johnson was born of Anglo-Irish parentage in 1715 at Smithstown, County Meath, Ireland. He came to America in 1738 to oversee the Mohawk Valley plantation of his wealthy and influential uncle, Vice-Admiral Sir Peter Warren.[1] Before too long, Johnson began to purchase lands in upper New York, initially with capital provided by his uncle. So as to be better situated for the Indian trade, Johnson also moved north of the Mohawk River where he established residences – Mount Johnson, Fort Johnson, and finally in 1763, the impressive Johnson Hall. In addition to real estate, Johnson aggressively pursued the profitable fur trade, and opened a road to Oswego, the principal British fur-trade post in the northern colonies. He also contracted with local farmers to supply the trading posts and Indian settlements, and among other business ventures established a trade in imported English goods. The fact that he traded directly with the Indians endeared him to George Clinton, the governor of New York. Clinton was trying to stop the monopoly of the Dutch houses and merchants of Albany who had been in concert for years with French middle-men in a lucrative smuggling trade with Montreal. As Johnson was decidedly a King's man, he received appointments to the New York council and as a colonel of militia, thus becoming publicly active in the fractious rivalries of the colony's economic and political activities.[2]

Although Johnson had become one of the most successful businessmen and entrepreneurs in colonial New York, his relations with Indian people were the central features of his personal and professional life. Soon after his arrival in the Mohawk Valley, he made contact with the neighbouring Mohawk and others of the Six Nations Confederacy of Iroquois. A review of the historical documents gives the impression that the Irishman was an earthy, robust, and physical man who had little difficulty relating to the wilderness life of the Iroquois. Johnson liked Indian people, and the feeling was mutual. He seemed at home with them, and especially among the Mohawk. Johnson frequently visited their "castles," shared food in the traditional communal manner, generously offered gifts, laughed with them, attended their ceremonies and rituals, sat through their lengthy councils, joined their dances, queried the sachems and clan mothers on their thoughts and attitudes, and generally became acquainted with Iroquois culture.[3] In recognition of their respect for him, the Iroquois gave Johnson the name "Warraghiyagey," roughly translated as "he who does much business."

With the outbreak of King George's War, he was "undefatigable among the Mohawks; he dressed himself after the Indian Manner, made frequent dances, according to their Custom when they excite to War, ... and engaged many of the young Men to join the Army against Canada." At Albany on 8 August 1746 he "put himself at the Head of the Mohawks, dressed and painted after the Manner of an Indian War-Captain; and the Indians who followed him were like-wise dressed and painted, as is usual with them when they set out in War."[4] Less than three weeks later, and at the urging of the confederacy sachems, Clinton appointed William Johnson "Colonel of the Forces of the Six Nations of Indians."[5] Although Johnson quitted the position in 1751 because he was not being reimbursed, as promised, for considerable personal expenses incurred during the war, the appointment was the foundation for the future creation of a single crown official to superintend the affairs of the Indians in Britain's northern colonies.

Yet the importance of Johnson to British imperial interests in North America rested to a considerable degree on his ability and success in courting and maintaining the loyalty of the Six Nations Confederacy. This achievement, however, tended to be the result of frequent and intimate connections between Johnson and agreeable Iroquois, mostly Mohawk, women. Miscegenation (not to be considered a pejorative here) was a sensitive subject in the American colonies, with proponents of the Old Testament warning against the wickedness of "marrying strange wives," meaning "heathen peoples" or those with "dark complexion."[6] Even the well-known marriage of John Rolfe and Pocahontas in April 1614 at Jamestown, Virginia, which resulted in a secure and quiet peace for several years between colonists and Powhatan's Confederacy, was only considered acceptable by the English because Pocahontas converted to Christianity and changed her name to Rebecca (Rebecka). At the beginning of European-Indian contact in the new world, however, the native people urged intermarriage, suggesting that the English were not their friends if they refused it. In time, the method of obtaining Indian allies and lands by "reclaiming them from barbarity, and that is, charitably to intermarry with them, according to the modern policy of the most Christian King in Canada and Louisiana" was undeniably successful. Although there was no formal consensus on this tactic, a general feeling eventually prevailed in the British colonies in America that in order "to embrace this prudent alliance ... a sprightly Lover is the most prevailing Missionary that can be sent among these, or any other Infidels."[7]

William Johnson would have agreed with that sentiment; certainly he gave new meaning to the word dedication in the pursuit of a policy. Although he had three children by a German indentured servant woman who lived with him until her death in 1759, he also engaged over the years in sexual relations with Indian women and he fathered several children (accounts vary) who remained at the villages of their mothers.[8] To suggest, however, that Johnson's activities among the Mohawk and other Iroquois women contributed in large part to his success in Indian affairs is not supported by extant documents. Nevertheless, there is no doubt that Johnson was astutely aware of the nature and significance of matrilineal descent in Iroquois society, which provided the clan mothers with great power and influence in the decision-making of the confederacy councils. As a consequence, his more enduring relationships were with Mohawk women of prominence within the clan circles.

There is some indication that he was linked for a time with Caroline, niece of the prominent sachem and orator Hendrick. After 1759 Molly or Mary Brant (Konwatsi'tsiaienni) became his "prudent and faithful Housekeeper."[9] They produced eight children, and Johnson treated his Mohawk family in accordance with their status and connections among the Iroquois, showing them every respect and courtesy, furnishing them with comforts benefitting an upper-class family, and providing generously for all of them in his will. Molly was unquestionably of inestimable value to Johnson during his often difficult negotiations with the confederacy sachems. In fact, "one word from her [was] more taken Notice of by the Five Nations than a thousand from any white man without exception."[10] In terms of equality and status, Iroquois women were far in advance of their non-native sisters in the society of eighteenth-century colonial America or Europe. For William Johnson, therefore, his relations with Iroquois women were based on a potent mixture of passion and political expediency. In the pursuit of a policy, his stamina at council and in the longhouse proved helpful in the conduct and success of British Indian policy in the defence against the French in Canada. When he was appointed to manage the affairs of the Six Nations in 1755, the council minutes reflected the reality of this post more accurately than anyone realized in declaring Johnson "the fittest person for that purpose."[11]

At Alexandria, Virginia, on 15 April 1755, Johnson was duly appointed to "the Sole Management & direction of the Affairs of the Six Nations of Indians & their Allies" in order that "the said Indians may be heartily engaged in & attached to the British Interest."[12] To facilitate the recruitment of Indian allies, Johnson was provided with funds for gifts and provisions. The appointment was made under the military authority of Edward Braddock, "Major General of Our Forces, and whom we have appointed General and Commander, of all and singular Troops and Forces, that are now in North America."[13] The arrival of Braddock and two regiments of British regulars was prompted by the new and aggressive French policy of constructing a line of frontier posts to connect Lake Erie with the Ohio River. With the completion of Fort Duquesne on the Monongahela, followed almost immediately by the defeat of George Washington at the Great Meadows (Fort Necessity), French supremacy in the Ohio Valley was confirmed, thus blocking the northernmost of the Thirteen Colonies from expanding their trade and settlement westward.[14] In London these activities angered and alarmed cabinet ministers and senior crown officials who complained that the French "are daily Encroaching upon us, and erecting Forts upon the Continent of North America so as to reduce us to a bare narrow Possession on the Sea Coast; And for This they think We will not Venture a Rupture."[15] Britain was indeed prepared to fight, but the President of the Board of Trade and Plantations reasoned in "Methods of Disappointing French Encroachments in North America" that if there was to be a military campaign, the Ohio must not be the solitary objective, for neither the colony of New York nor the Six Nations would participate in such a scheme unless other French forts were also subdued. This point was clarified by noting that

the great Improbability of any Indian auxiliary Force, if the design is confined to the single attempt of dispossessing the French from their present establishment on the Ohio, for the Indians in that part are already lost and intimidated, and the Five Nations upon the back of New York will it is feared hardly be brought to act at such Distance from their own Residence, while the Forts Niagara, Frontenac and Crown Point are left to subsist upon their Backs.[16]

Therefore, in his "Secret Instructions," Braddock was to coordinate a general plan which would remove the French from those key frontier areas which threatened British imperial and territorial interests in North America. His own task was to drive the French from their posts upon the Ohio. But in conformity with the recommendations put forward by the Board, expeditions were also organized against Fort Niagara and Fort Saint-Frédéric at Crown Point on Lake Champlain.[17] In the expedition against Fort Duquesne, Braddock and his sizable army, which consisted of British regulars, American provincials, but, most revealing of all, only eight Indians, marched into the wilderness. They were slaughtered along the Monongahela River on 9 July by a small French force, strengthened by mostly Ottawa and Potawatomi allies.[18] As for the effort against Fort Niagara, the expedition collapsed en route at Oswego. Only the campaign to take Crown Point, therefore, remained undecided.

William Johnson, commissioned major-general of provincial forces in New York, was to command the Crown Point expedition. In preparation for this military adventure, he held a major Indian council at Mount Johnson between 21 June and 4 July in which over eleven hundred chiefs and warriors assembled from the Six Nations and the "western Indians." During the proceedings, an agreement was reached "to renew, to make more strong and bright than ever the Covenant Chain of love and friendship."[19] The Iroquois sachems were especially pleased with Johnson's mastery of traditional forms of council rituals, and pledged that "by this [wampum] Belt we acknowledge the Great King of England our Father is the Master of our confederate Nations and we put our trust in him."[20] Yet when the expedition moved towards Crown Point, only the Mohawk accompanied it in any considerable numbers from among the Indian allies.

Whilst still some distance from the objective, the vanguard of Johnson's army was attacked by the French and their Indian allies, who were all in motion in New France towards Crown Point. Hendrick was killed in this action and Johnson immediately positioned his provincials and Indians behind a hastily constructed breastwork of trees, wagons, and batteaux to await the advancing enemy. According to Johnson, a "warm engagement" ensued which was accentuated by "heavy firing" as the French regulars, all resplendent in white uniforms and with "bright and fixed bayonets," conducted a spirited frontal assault against his laagered encampment. When the charge withered before the accurate musket fire of the defenders, "our men and Indians jumped over the breast-work, pursued the enemy, slaughtered numbers, and took several prisoners, amongst whom was the baron de Dieskau, the French general of all regular forces, lately arrived from Europe." [21] Thus concluded the battle of Lake George, fought on 8 September 1755.

Johnson neither hounded the retreating enemy nor moved to secure Crown Point. In a military sense, therefore, his campaign was inconclusive. But, for British imperial and territorial aspirations in North America, Johnson's successful defence against the French at Lake George, following only two months after the Braddock disaster, carried considerable significance. Johnson's "victory" had prevented the complete disintegration of the British-Iroquois fragile alliance. In frequent subsequent councils, Johnson struggled to maintain the affections and loyalty of the Six Nations to the British cause. This effort was made even more difficult owing to a series of successive French victories under the command of the Marquis de Montcalm at Fort Bull (March 1756), Oswego (August 1756), Fort William Henry (August 1757), and Ticonderoga (July 1758).[22] Therefore, although the Mohawk remained steadfast, the league factionalized over how best to preserve and defend the lands of Iroquoia, with the result that the confederacy wavered throughout the war between neutrality, support for the French, and support for the British. Nonetheless, the battle of Lake George had sufficiently impressed the sachems to the point that there was no wholesale Iroquois defection to the French in Canada.

The appointment of a single crown official responsible for the administration, management, and policy directions of Indian Affairs in Britain's northern colonies in America had been formalized with the king's approval on 13 March 1756. William Johnson, powerful and influential in the society and politics of colonial New York, respected among the Iroquois, and recently successful at Lake George, was recommended and accepted as the obvious choice for the position. In consequence, he was granted a royal commission as "Colonel, Agent and Sole Superintendent of the affairs of the Six Nations, and other Northern Indians," with a salary of £600 per annum. As well, Johnson received a patent of baronet, "having passed the great Seal in the usual form," and a reward of £5,000 for long and faithful service in North America.[23]

His immediate responsibilities were to assemble the several

Indian tribes and tell them of His Majesty's steady resolution to support and protect them, as his allies, and to invite them to renew and strengthen the chain of friendship against the French. In addition, Johnson was to inform the Indians that the king had ordered the prohibition of settlements upon their paternal lands, and to promise redress for tribal complaints and grievances regarding past and future land encroachments. These instructions, and the establishment of a crown-appointed superintendent for Indian affairs, were the direct result of the critical military situation which confronted Britain and her fractious colonies in America during the first years of the last great war for empire between France and England in North America. Notwithstanding, Johnson worked with energy and skill to obtain the desired results according to his instructions, which on the question of Indian land redress were a precursor of the Royal Proclamation of 7 October 1763.

Two months after Johnson's royal commission and awards, Edmond Atkin was appointed as "Agent for, and Superintendent of the affairs of the several Nations of Indians upon the Frontiers" of the southern colonies.[24] Atkin, who would be replaced as Indian superintendent by John Stuart in 1762, was to cultivate His Majesty's interest and to secure the cooperation and alliance of the Creek, Cherokee, Chickasaw, Choctaw and other tribes of the colonial south. [25] These two royal commissions therefore sensibly divided the general plan and system for the imperial administration and management of Indian Affairs in colonial America into a "Northern District" and a "Southern District."[26] The northern superintendency marked the formal beginnings under crown prerogative of the British Indian Department, and after 1774, of British Indian policy in the defence of Canada against the rebellious American colonies.

By 1758-59 the tides of war in North America were shifting in favour of Britain and her American colonies. The early French victories were the result of their initial superiority in military organization and preparedness, which was largely dependent on the dedication and wilderness knowledge of their colonial officers, actively and efficiently supported by the Mission Indians (mostly Mohawk) around Montreal, and the Ottawa, Potawatomi, Huron, Abenaki and other tribal allies. The problem for the French in Canada was not the lack of manpower, foodstuffs, clothing, or military supplies, but rather the inability or unwillingness of the homesick regular army (officers and men) to maintain the *esprit de corps* necessary to prosecute the war successfully. In the final analysis, low morale and poor generalship caused the loss of Canada for imperial France.

In contrast, British strategy and generalship showed a slow but steady improvement over the years of the war. The capture of Louisbourg on Ile Royale (Cape Breton Island) in July 1758, the attack on Fort Frontenac in August 1758, the successful negotiations with the Indians at the Treaty of Easton in October 1758 which "signalized the beginning of the end for the French in the Ohio," along with the creation of irregular units such as Rogers' Rangers, which at one point struck deep into New France and destroyed the Abenaki village of Saint-François-de-Sales (Odanak), attested to the growing confidence and commitment of the British and America colonials to winning the war.[27]

The British military successes encouraged and allowed Sir William Johnson to propose an expedition against the French at Niagara. In his opinion,

> commanding the Navigation of Lake Ontario & destroying Niagara, would I conceive oblige & indeed incline the 5 Nations to declare & act heartily in our favour, and by the means of a well conducted Trade would draw the Western Indians into our Alliance & Interest, and I think shake the whole French Indian Interest to the Center & disconcert if not totally subvert their whole system of Indian Trade & Power upon the Continent.[28]

After years of struggling merely to "hold fast the Covenant Chain," Johnson was now actually able to secure the active participation of the Iroquois in a military campaign.

In July 1759, therefore, Johnson, as second-in-command, led more than nine hundred Iroquois allies in a major British and American colonial offensive against the impressive French fort and stone "castle" of Niagara. With the place soon under siege, the senior British officer was killed, owing to the fact that one of his gunners "carelessly fired a Cohorn [coehorn mortar] & shot his head to pieces," thus leaving Johnson in command.[29] Four days later, on 24 July, a large French relief force, rushing from the Ohio, was engaged by the British near the fort in the wilderness battle of La Belle Famille. According to Johnson, "the action Begun about half after nine; But they were so well Received by the Troops in front & the Indians on their Flank that in an Hours time the whole was Completely Ruined & all their Officers made Prisoners.... I cannot ascertain the Number of the killd, they are so dispersed among the Woods, But their Loss is Great."[30] In fact, however, apart from the Mohawk, Britain's Indian allies "would not fire one Gun" until the battle had been decided, at which time the warriors recklessly pursued and slaughtered the fleeing

French troops. Nonetheless, the outcome of the battle sealed the fate of the garrison, and the next day Fort Niagara surrendered, the French troops marching out under arms with drums beating.

Although no doubt somewhat disappointed, even concerned, at the initial recalcitrance of the Iroquois allies in the battle, the siege of Niagara and the battle of La Belle Famille were the crowning achievements for Johnson and British Indian policy in the war against New France. In the late summer and autumn, the Ohio tribes and upper lakes Indians, most of whom had been loyal allies of the French, assembled at Fort Pitt (the site of the old Fort Duquesne), and in two separate conferences smoked the pipe of peace and declared "the War Hatchet is now buried."[31] The fall of Quebec in September 1759, and the capitulation of Montreal in September 1760, thus concluded the last great war for empire between France and England in North America.

The "reduction of Canada," however, as noted later by Sir William Johnson, afforded "us a connection with many [Indian] Nations, with whom before we had no intercourse; it became necessary [therefore] that we should cultivate a good understanding with them, for the security of, and the safety of the public." This new dimension in the management and administration of Indian Affairs necessitated in part an increase in the personnel of the British Indian Department. As a result, Johnson, with just a dash of nepotism in an age of preferment, proceeded to sprinkle the department with appointments of family and friends. In particular, he retained his trusted friend George Croghan as deputy on the Ohio, appointed Guy Johnson, his nephew and son-in-law, as deputy for the Six Nations in New York, and Daniel Claus, his son-in-law, as "Deputy Superintendent of Indian Affairs for Canada."[32] Various interpreters, assistants, clerks, storekeepers, and blacksmiths were also subsequently added to meet the demands of the broader duties.

Among the Ohio and upper lakes tribes now under the authority of the northern superintendency, Johnson regarded the Huron of Detroit (Wyandot/Wendat) as "the most polished and sensible people ... who had much influence over the rest."[33] But the Shawnee, Delaware, and Miami Confederacy in the Ohio Valley region were strong and defiant; and the "Far Indians" - namely the Ojibwa, Ottawa, and Potawatomi, along with the Sauk, Fox, Winnebago, Menominee, Kickapoo and other tribes scattered throughout the upper lakes and upper Mississippi - were numerous, if still rather inaccessible to British and American colonial trade and land encroachments.[34]

The Seven Nations of Canada, whom Johnson described as "chiefly Emigrants from the Mohocks and the other Five Nations" in New York, lived at the French mission villages of Sault-Saint-Louis or Caughnawaga (Kahnawake), Lac des Deux-Montagnes or Oka (Kanehsatake) and Lac de Saint-François or St. Régis (Akwesasne), all in the general area of Montreal.[35] The St. Régis group was later joined by some of the Oswegatchie Onondaga who had settled for a time at the mission of La Présentation (Ogdensburg, NY). At Oka, Algonquin and Nipissing resided with Mohawk. As well, Huron, refugees from the destruction of their villages in the 1640s, lived at Ancienne-Lorette (Loretteville) near Quebec; and two Abenaki mission villages were located at Saint-François (Odanak), south of Quebec, and Bécancour, across from Trois-Rivières on the south side of the St. Lawrence River.

The Seven Nations were thus composed of three groups of Mohawk, one of Algonquin, one of Nipissing, one of Huron, and one of Abenaki (with an attendant smaller village at Bécancour). These tribes were all loyal to the French throughout the half-century of conflict and were considered formidable by the British. In September of 1760, safe-conduct passes were issued to the Huron, as requested, and every effort was made to calm the fears of the Canadian Indians during the difficult period of transition in Canada from French to British rule. In fact, the Articles of Capitulation surrendering Montreal and Quebec specifically provided in article XL that "the Savages or Indian allies of His Most Christian Majesty [France] shall be maintained in the lands they inhabit, if they choose to reside there; they shall not be molested

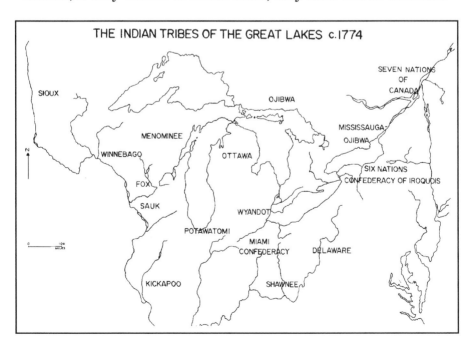

THE INDIAN TRIBES OF THE GREAT LAKES c.1774

on any pretence whatever for having carried arms and served His Most Christian Majesty; they shall have, as well as the French, liberty of religion, and shall keep their missionaries."[36]

By the early 1760s the western tribes rightly believed that the generosity and respect the British afforded the Mohawk and Indians of Canada were not being extended to them. Within months of the defeat and expulsion of the French from the Ohio Valley, Ottawa, Shawnee, Delaware, Wyandot, and even some Six Nations people told senior British officers and George Croghan at Fort Pitt that they were now dependent upon British government stores for supplies. But Sir Jeffrey Amherst, major-general and commander-in-chief of the British forces in North America, although instructed to "cultivate the best Harmony & Friendship with the Chiefs of the Indian Tribes [and] keep a constant Correspondence with Sir William Johnson," devised a personal plan to subjugate the frontier by reducing Indian expenses.[37] He considered the costs of the Indian Department to be excessive, and in consequence ceased the traditional practice of gift-giving, "for it is not my intention ever to attempt to gain the friendship of Indians by presents."[38] Amherst also reasoned that a scarcity of supplies, shot, and powder among the tribes would be the most secure way to keep them quiet.

For the western Indians, the reduction of Canada, followed by the termination of the customary presents and the immediate encroachment upon their ancient hunting grounds by American colonial backwoodsmen and traders who employed "every Low Trick and Artifice to Overreach and cheat those unguarded ignorant People," alarmed and provoked them.[39] In July 1761 George Croghan uncovered a Seneca plan in which the Indians around Detroit were to seize and murder the British traders and garrison and make all the plunder they could. Further, all the Indian tribes settled between the Ohio and Lake Erie were to attack the posts between Pennsylvania and Fort Pitt. The Indian hostility soon became more intense, widespread, and spontaneous, particularly with propagated reports that the French were returning.[40] At Fort Michilimackinac on the upper lakes, near the confluence of Lake Huron and Lake Michigan, British fur trader Alexander Henry was told in very clear terms that

> although you have conquered the French, you have not yet conquered us! We are not your slaves. These lakes, these woods, and mountains, were left to us by our ancestors. They are our inheritance; and wee will part with them to none. Your nation supposes that we, like the white people, cannot live without bread – and pork –

and beef! But you ought to know, that He, the Great Spirit and Master of Life, had provided food for us, in these spacious lakes, and on these woody mountains.[41]

By the spring of 1763 rumours and reports of a general Indian uprising were widespread.

Yet the aggressiveness of the American colonials, combined with the apparent arrogance of Amherst, was not matched by the enthusiasm or military preparedness of the British garrisons at the scattered and isolated frontier posts. The troops assigned for frontier defence were drawn almost exclusively from the fairly new 60th Regiment of Foot (the Royal Americans) which was largely recruited from German and Swiss Protestants within the American colonies. Life at the posts was dreary, with few diversions. Although Amherst was in the process of establishing a supply system to provide the garrisons with necessaries, the soldiers in the spring of 1763 were subsisting mainly on "flour and pease-soup." These generally poor conditions proved dispiriting for both the officers and men. Indeed, some of the officers expressed a decided lack of confidence in the determination or physical ability of the troops under their command to withstand any sort of military contest. At Ligonier, for instance, a small post southeast of Fort Pitt, Ensign Schlosser reported that "my garrison consists of Rodgers, unfit for any kind of fatigue, Davis, improper to be entrusted on any duty, Shillem, quite a little boy, my servant, an inactive simple creature, and one more. Two stout fellows would beat the whole five of them."[42]

The uprising began in May, with the Ottawa chief Pontiac investing Detroit.[43] Within a few weeks, the Indians had taken "all the Posts round Detroit, the Garrisons chiefly murdered in a manner too shocking to mention with hundreds of the Frontier Inhabitants Scalp and thousands of Families ruined." To the consternation of Sir William Johnson and senior British officers, the Seneca of the Six Nations Iroquois, "our friends as they are called," took an active part in the uprising, as they massacred the garrison at Venango and "cut to pieces" a column of troops and waggoners near Fort Niagara.[44] But not all the posts fell; Detroit, Niagara, Fort Pitt, and a few others, including, surprisingly enough, Ligonier, withstood sieges or attacks. Amherst, if nothing else a solid military administrator, began to organize and direct the movement of troops, supplies, and transport to combat the uprising. He also wondered whether it could "not be contrived to send the Small Pox among those disaffected tribes of Indians? We must on this occasion use every stratagem in our power to reduce them."[45] Whether this early method of germ warfare was actually tried remains unclear.

The general result of these mixed countermeasures, however, was the battle of Bushy Run, fought near Fort Pitt on 5-6 August 1763, in which the Shawnee, Delaware, Ottawa, Wyandot, Miami, and Mingo (Ohio Seneca) were dispersed.[46] In the following months Sir William Johnson held a number of Indian councils at Johnson Hall, where he succeeded in persuading the Six Nations (minus the Seneca) and the Caughnawaga Mohawk to brighten the chain of friendship. For the hostile tribes to the west, already discouraged and tired after Bushy Run and months of warfare, the thought of a fresh British-Iroquois force in alliance against them dampened the last of their fighting spirit. In the summer and autumn of 1764, therefore, several peace agreements were concluded with these western tribes at Niagara, Johnson Hall, and throughout the Ohio country.[47]

The uprising of 1763, like all Indian wars, was primarily a struggle by an increasingly desperate people to preserve their traditional lands and cultural values against interlopers and the steady advance of the frontier. But in 1763 the pro-French tribes of the Ohio Valley and upper Great Lakes also fought in the vain belief that they could facilitate the return of the *ancien régime*. In this sense, the failure of the Indian uprising of 1763 was the final heartbeat of imperial France in Canada. At the same time, therefore, the war signalled the end of the British-Iroquois military alliance in the defence against the French in Canada.

From 1763 to 1774 British-Indian relations in colonial America were centred around attempts to establish a general and centralized plan for the management of Indian affairs and trade through the enactment of a number of imperial regulations. The plan was intended to reduce Indian expenses in the postwar years whilst at the same time to provide for the orderly and peaceful flow of western settlement.[48] In this regard, the signing of the Treaty of Paris (10 February 1763) in which France officially ceded Canada to Britain, followed by the Indian uprising in the Great Lakes region, hastened but did not cause the passing of the first and most significant of these imperial regulations – the Royal Proclamation of 7 October 1763.[49]

The Royal Proclamation was in part concerned with "establishing New Governments in America," of which the boundaries, government, and place of the new colony of Quebec within the British empire was fundamental. Yet, the proclamation also considered "it just and reasonable, and essential to Our Interest and the Security of Our Colonies, that the several Nations or Tribes of Indians, with whom We are connected, and who live under Our Protection, should not be molested or disturbed in the Possession of such Parts of Our Dominions and Territories as, not having been ceded to, or purchased by Us, are reserved to them, or any of them, as their Hunting Grounds." In effect, the proclamation was a consolidation of British Indian policy that was intended to satisfy both imperial and trading interests, and the expansionist ambitions of the colonies. The proclamation therefore established a frontier or boundary line between Indians and whites, and forbade any unauthorized entry into areas in which the Indian "interest" in land had not been formally surrendered.

The decision to create a boundary line was both sound and necessary, as "great Frauds and Abuses have been committed in the purchasing Lands of the Indians, to the great Prejudice of Our Interests, and to the great Dissatisfaction of the said Indians." In an effort "prevent such Irregularities for the future, and to the End that the Indians may be convinced of Our Justice, and determined Resolution to remove all reasonable Cause of Discontent," crown officials at Whitehall devised a formal mechanism for obtaining the extinguishment or surrender of Indian lands. The methods required that "no private Person do presume to make any Purchase from the said Indians of any Lands reserved to the said Indians, within those Parts of Our Colonies where We have thought proper to allow Settlement; but that if, at any Time, any of the said Indians should be inclined to dispose of the said Lands, the same shall be purchased only for Us, in Our Name, at some public Meeting or Assembly of the said Indians."[50] In other words, where the Indian interest in land still existed, only the crown (through purchase), could obtain the formal surrender of those lands. These measures were adopted in the hope of bringing some form of imperial control to the prevailing turmoil along the wilderness frontier.

Further to this hope, the Lords of Trade, following the recommendations put forward by Sir William Johnson, on 10 July 1764 introduced a plan for the "Future Management of Indian Affairs in America."[51] The plan placed the sole management of Indian affairs and the regulation of the Indian trade in the administrative care of the superintendents and their agents in the Northern District and the Southern District. Through them, trade was to be licensed, regulated, and confined to designated frontier posts. But the traders flaunted the licensing requirements and violated the post restrictions by bartering directly with the Indians at their villages. American backwoodsmen and land speculators also ignored the Indian boundary line and the general provisions of the Royal Proclamation to the point that the thirst for Indian lands became almost universal.

With royal authority in America being blatantly defied, Sir William Johnson was instructed to extend the western limits of the boundary line in order to meet the demands of the settlers and to prevent the possible renewal of an Indian war. To this effect, Johnson, who was not only the royal superintendent of Indian Affairs for the Northern District, but also an entrepreneur and opportunistic New York land speculator, negotiated, under the authority of the king, a huge land settlement with the Six Nations Iroquois at Fort Stanwix in November of 1768.[52] By the terms of the treaty, in which Johnson had exceeded his instructions but personally profited in subsequent land deals, the boundary line was stretched west to the Ohio River.

For the Six Nations, the treaty temporarily deflected settlement away from the lands of Iroquoia. But, in a manner similar to surrendering their "deed" to the nebulous beaver lands in the north to the crown some seventy years before, the desperate confederacy once again disposed of lands over which in reality they no longer exercised authority. In the Southern District, the Cherokee decided on a similar policy and ceded territory to their north. As a result, American migrants from both north and south converged into the Kentucky lands of the Shawnee, who were thus sacrificed by both the Iroquois and the Cherokee in an effort to delay the destruction of their traditional lands. Nonetheless, the pledge at the Treaty of Fort Stanwix that the Ohio River would be forever the boundary line between Indian and whites was to become a major and combative issue between them for the next thirty years.

The efforts by crown officials at Whitehall and in America to resolve the difficult and chaotic conditions in the west were compounded by the rise of civil insurrection among the Thirteen Colonies along the eastern seaboard, who were protesting vigorously over a series of import duties imposed upon them by Parliament to help defray some of the costs of frontier defence. Reports that "the Stamp Duty makes a great uproar in America," along with the subsequent levying of further duties, produced increasingly passionate debates in England and the colonies over taxation without representation and the political-constitutional legality of the supremacy of Parliament over the colonial assemblies.[53] As this colonial resistance to external authority continued to mount in volume and intensity, crown officials at Whitehall retreated from the imperial policies and regulations prescribed in the immediate post-1763 war years.[54] No longer able to maintain its authority on the frontier, the crown decided in 1768 to reject the now impracticable and inoperative plan of 1764, return Indian affairs and the regulation of trade to the colonial legislatures, vacate the interior posts, and confine royal authority to the volatile eastern seaboard. The decision, although prompted by a desire to reduce American expenses, represented an abdication of imperial responsibility towards native people.

Throughout the period of colonial control (1768–74) over Indian affairs and matters of trade and settlement, the aged and increasingly fatigued Sir William Johnson continued to hold numerous meetings and assemblies with the various tribes, soliciting their friendship and goodwill in the face of the continuing and irregular land encroachments practised on the frontier by the competing colonies and provinces. Although he decried the "disorderly behaviour of the [American] frontier inhabitants," he nonetheless continued to counsel peace in the name of the king.[55] At Johnson Hall on 11 July 1774, and in the midst of attempting to convince the sachems of the Six Nations to remain neutral in Lord Dunmore's War against the Shawnee in Kentucky, Johnson "was taken Suddenly ill with a fainting and sense of suffocation which notwithstanding all the Assistance afforded by his Nephew Dr. [John] Dease, & others carried him off in two hours."[56]

With Johnson's death, royal government in the American colonies lost an effective and loyal subject whose "greatest Abilities, and singular Disposition, enabled him to acquire and hold a greater Influence among the Indians than any other English Man ever had."[57] Much of Johnson's success had been based on the symbiotic relationship he had developed with the Six Nations Iroquois, the most powerful collection of tribes in the Great Lakes region. In all his dealings with them he had demonstrated a practical leadership in the management and conduct of Indian affairs, and never pretended to assume the bearing of an administrator or a bureaucrat.

This lack of concern for administrative details showed in the Indian Department, which was as haphazardly managed and maintained as any other part of the loosely organized eighteenth-century British colonial system. In fact, Johnson's "Declared Accounts" indicated that between 1755 and 1774 he received from the crown a total of £146,545.15.3 for expenses (salaries, presents, contingencies, and sundry incidentals) in the general management of Indian affairs. Johnson provided no "written Vouchers" and the accounts were never audited, but the "Said Account [was] Allowed."[58] Not surprisingly, during his regime Johnson, very much a product of an age of profit and preferment and therefore hardly immune from the temptations of acquiring wealth through business ventures and land speculation, used patronage, favours, and the power and influence of his office to ensure his personal fortune. As first superintendent, and therefore the father of the department, Johnson set the standards which in one form or another over the next hundred years and more were emulated by successive superintendents and senior officials responsible for Indian affairs.

But most significantly, Johnson had succeeded in organizing a group of departmental officers who, after twenty years of apprenticeship, were experienced and capable of influencing and manipulating the tribes. This condition was the result of Johnson gaining the trust of the influential Six Nations, and subsequently using them as a fulcrum to establish and extend his power and prestige to include the western tribes. By scattering agents throughout the Indian villages, Johnson was also able to maintain direct contact with the pulse of native feeling. By the summer of 1774, therefore, with the threat of a civil war and rebellion erupting in colonial America, the long, calculated, and successful efforts of Johnson in managing Indian affairs under the auspices of the crown encouraged Whitehall to expect the military cooperation of Indian allies against the potentially common enemy. To this extent, although there has been a suggestion that imperial policy in North America was in some state of "bankruptcy" at the time, British Indian policy, within the larger framework, by comparison, appeared quite creditable.[59]

PART TWO

Rebellion and Resistance,
1774–1796

CHAPTER 3

THE AMERICAN REBELLION
AND THE FRONTIER

T he death of Johnson in July of 1774 caused a general
uneasiness among the Indian tribes of the Great Lakes
region, and especially with the Six Nations Confederacy of
Iroquois who "expressed the utmost confusion and doubt" that
peace and stability could now be maintained on the frontier.[1] At
Johnson Hall, the confederacy sachems conducted a "ceremony of
condolence" to honour the passing of a man with whom they had
enjoyed a long and mutually profitable courtship for nearly thirty
years. In conformity with the tradition of a condolence council,
the sachems also called for the "raising up" of a new chief. In fact,
in April the ailing Sir William Johnson had recommended his
nephew and son-in-law, Guy Johnson, to be his successor. This
choice was also agreeable to the tribes, and was thus suggested
officially so as to satisfy the Indians that "I have fulfilled their
desire."[2] With the death of Sir William, therefore, Guy Johnson
was duly appointed as acting Superintendent of Indian Affairs for
the Northern District, at which time it was noted that he had "for
some time transacted most of the Indian Business," and in consequence was considered "capable and fit for the Employment."[3]

For Guy Johnson and the British crown in America, however,
the death of Sir William was an especially severe "Public Loss ... at
this Juncture, when the Frontier People of Virginia particularly,

have taken so much Pains to bring on an Indian War. They have slaughtered a Number of Indians so wantonly and cruelly that we might reasonably expect every Tribe would rise upon us."[4] Although Guy Johnson possessed neither the style nor the skill to manage and influence the Indians in the practised manner of Sir William, he nonetheless made every effort over the next several months to promote peace, to restrain the tribes from taking revenge, and to retain the allegiance of the still powerful Six Nations Iroquois.[5]

Guy Johnson's immediate concern, however, was Lord Dunmore's War in the western parts of Virginia, which was provoked by the encroachments onto Shawnee lands of American backwoodsmen contrary to the signed and mutually agreed terms of the Treaty of Fort Stanwix in 1768. The conflict was further complicated by the fact that, in spite of imperial directives forbidding settlement in the area, Lord Dunmore, the governor of Virginia, supported the frontier people and western expansionism. Throughout the summer and autumn of 1774, therefore, Guy Johnson, in cooperation with John Stuart of the Southern District, worked to neutralize the other tribes and prevent a general Indian confederation in support of Shawnee resistance. The British Indian Department, under the direction of the two active superintendents, was reasonably successful in pacifying most of the sachems and chiefs.[6] As a result, the war became a local affair which ended along the Kanawha River on 10 October 1774 with the defeat of the Shawnee under the leadership of Cornstalk (Keigh-tugh-qua) at the battle of Point Pleasant.[7]

Although victorious in the war, Lord Dunmore had defied the authority of the king. Under reprimand, the governor defended his conduct and actions, explaining that

> the established Authority of any government in America, and the policy of Government at home, are both insufficient to restrain the Americans; and that they do and will remove as their avidity and restlessness incite them. They acquire no attachment to Place: But ... for ever imagine the Lands further off are Still better than those upon which they are already Settled ... Proclamations have been published from time to time to restrain them ... But ... they do not conceive that Government has any right to forbid their taking possession of a Vast tract of Country, either uninhabited, or which Serves only as a Shelter to a few Scattered Tribes of Indians. Nor can they be easily brought to entertain

any belief of the permanent obligation of Treaties made with those People, whom they consider, as little removed from the brute Creation.[8]

Dunmore's letter, which could be applied with some accuracy to almost any period in the history of Indian-white relations in America, represents a classic statement of the philosophy and attitude of a people who were determined to push the frontier ever westward. This process began with the arrival of Europeans to the new world and continued until about 1890. The history of the American frontier, therefore, was a history of continuous conflict over land between Indian people and white interlopers.

In the case of Dunmore's War, the repercussions were long-lasting and significant for the American frontier and for British-Indian relations. Although the Shawnee were annoyed with the officers of the Indian Department for successfully counselling the other tribes to remain neutral in the war, they were furious with the Americans for encroaching onto their lands and killing their people. Thereafter, and for the next forty years (until their military strength and capability dissipated), the Shawnee waged a war of attrition on the frontier people which drove the tribe into a ready alliance with the British during those few occasions when both were fighting the common enemy – the Americans. As a consequence, the efficient, defiant, and warlike Shawnee, who produced great military leaders such as Cornstalk and Tecumseh (Tech-kum-thai), became, next to the Mohawk, the most consistent and effective of Britain's Indian allies in the defence of Canada.

But in 1774 the disorder and violence was not confined to the western frontier. Along the eastern seaboard of the Thirteen Colonies the populace was becoming even more vociferous in its opposition to external authority. The increased agitation and civil insurrection were provoked by the British imposition of a number of so-called "Intolerable Acts" which the recently formed first Continental Congress declared to be unconstitutional.[9] Further, the Quebec Act, which extended the boundaries of the province of Quebec in two stages to include the coveted lands between the Ohio and Mississippi rivers, was viewed, logically enough by the American colonies, as a blow against their ambitions for westward expansion, and too reminiscent of the tactics of imperial France in the Ohio during the early 1750s. Finally, the American colonies reacted with perverse anger over the religious toleration clause in the act which granted Roman Catholics, meaning largely their old French-Canadian enemies, the free exercise of their faith.[10]

By the end of 1774 the first Continental Congress had adopted a "Declaration of Rights and Grievances" which summarized the colonial arguments of protest and denied Parliament's jurisdiction over the affairs of the American colonies, except for the regulation of commerce and matters of strictly imperial concern. In addition, the approval of an economic boycott on the import and consumption of British goods crippled the trade of Britain with her American colonies by the spring of 1775. With the organization of Minute Men companies, along with the general appeal to take up arms in defence of "American liberty," an uninterrupted march of folly towards civil war and rebellion in colonial America seemed destined.

The most unfortunate and unnecessary series of events which led to the deterioration and final collapse of Anglo-American relations were in large measure the result of the longstanding British colonial policy of salutary neglect. Apart from some periodic administrative regulations and trade restrictions under the general mercantile system which emanated from the Lords of Trade and Plantations in London, the character and direction of the individual colonies had evolved through internal initiative and energy. But after 1763, with the removal of the threat from imperial France in Canada, a self-conscious American spirit rapidly developed, particularly when they looked west and saw the rich potential of a vast continent. However, the last great war for empire between France and England in North America, which had been fought and financed largely by the people and government of Britain on behalf of the Anglo-American nation and in defence of the British colonies in America, had left Britain staggering under the weight of a huge war debt.[11]

British ministers and crown officials at Whitehall therefore reasoned that in order to reduce expenditures, the American colonies should be at least willing to help defray the costs of colonial administration and frontier defence. Without consulting the American colonial assemblies (a courtesy considered constitutionally unnecessary), import duties were placed on specific items such as glass, paint, and tea entering colonial ports. This unilateral decision to raise revenue by taxing the colonies ignited the already smouldering ideological passions of some of the colonial elite who argued forcefully against "taxation without representation." The political-constitutional debate was further inflamed by the crown's insistence that the colonies were duty-bound to honour the sovereignty of the king and the supremacy of the British parliament.

Although often motivated by personal gain and economic profit, the eloquent and clever political rhetoric of the militant colonial leaders nonetheless convinced significant and volatile elements of the population to grasp the cause of American liberty and independence by throwing off the burdensome and restricting yoke of external authority. The final and tragic result was the outbreak of hostilities between British regulars and American colonials at Lexington and Concord in April 1775.[12] In spite of the fact that the causes of the colonial rebellion were complex and pluralistic, British intransigence on parliamentary supremacy formed the keystone of the ideological and constitutional conflict, and the inability or unwillingness of the crown officials at Whitehall to resolve the admittedly difficult problem of reconciling the aspirations of colonial autonomy with imperial authority and unity signalled the abject failure of eighteenth-century British statesmanship.

In the months following the confrontations at Lexington and Concord, both the British and the American colonial rebels endeavoured to secure the assistance of Indian allies. As early as September of 1774, Lieutenant-General Gage in Boston had written Guy Carleton, governor of Quebec, inquiring "whether a Body of Canadians and Indians might be collected, and confided in, for the Service of this Country, should matters come to extremities."[13] By June 1775 Gage had been placed under siege by American rebels, who had also captured Ticonderoga and Crown Point, thus controlling the strategic Lake Champlain–Richelieu River route to Canada. For the harried Gage, matters indeed had come to extremities, and in consequence he urged Dartmouth at Whitehall to sanction the military use and assistance of Indian allies in the defence of the crown in America. Gage promoted and encouraged the policy by reporting that the "Rebels [were] Solliciting the assistance of the Indians, and had actually a Body of them in their camp before Boston."[14]

The Gage correspondence and general events in America prompted Dartmouth to prosecute the rebellion with increased vigour. As a result, Gage received a despatch from Whitehall which commented in part that "the Steps which you say the Rebels have taken for calling in the Assistance of the Indians, leave no room to hesitate upon the propriety of our pursuing the same Measure." For this purpose, a letter was also enclosed for Colonel Guy Johnson "containing His Majesty's Commands for engaging a Body of Indians." The crown's commitment to this policy was demonstrated by the delivery of "a large Assortment of Goods for presents" which were to be conveyed "to the Colonel."[15] The instructions, which included a justification for employing the warriors, noted that the time might possibly come when the King, relying upon the Attachment of his faithful allies, the Six Nations of Indians, might be under the necessity of Calling upon them for their Aid and Assistance in the present State of America. The unnatural Rebellion now raging there, calls for every Effort to suppress it and the Intelligence His Majesty has received of the Rebels having excited the Indians to take a part, and of their having actually engaged a body of them in Arms to support their Rebellion, justifies the Resolution His Majesty has taken of requiring the Assistance of his faithful adherents the Six Nations.16

Johnson was therefore ordered to "lose no time in taking such steps as may induce them to take up the Hatchet against His Majesty's Rebellious Subjects in America." How best to achieve this, whether by separate negotiations with the sachems or in a general council, Dartmouth prudently left to the judgment of the officers of the Indian Department.17

By the time Guy Johnson received his formal instructions from Whitehall on the conduct and direction of the Indian Department, the process of recruiting and organizing the Six Nations and other tribes as military allies on behalf of the crown was already advanced. Although both the British and the Americans attempted to win the allegiance of the Indians, most of the tribes who were actually engaged in the rebellion eventually gravitated toward the British, for as Thomas Gage observed, "the Indians well know that in all their landed disputes the Crown has always been their friend."18 This assessment was quite untrue, of course, but in comparison to the increasingly aggressive acts and encroachments onto traditional tribal lands by the American backwoodsmen, the generally protective nature of British Indian policy, especially in the sensitive area of aboriginal land rights, convinced the chiefs and warriors that to support the crown would be the lesser of two evils.

Nonetheless, Guy Johnson experienced considerable difficulties and some failures in convincing the tribes to demonstrate their active and consistent support for the king. In part, the reasons for his lack of uniform success was the effective efforts of various representatives (official and unofficial) of the Continental Congress. In May of 1775, for instance, Ethan Allen sent a letter from Crown Point to the Seven Nations of Canada requesting a meeting "to treat with you in our behalf in friendship" and urging the Indians not to "fight on either side."[19] At German Flats and Albany in Sir William Johnson's beloved Mohawk Valley, American Indian commissioners held conferences with the Six Nations Iroquois in August and early September and impressed upon the confederacy sachems that the rebellion was "a family quarrel between us and old England."[20] After some discussions involving trade and the retention of the missionaries, but with no resolution of Iroquois land grievances, the sachems pledged neutrality in the upcoming struggle. This success for the Americans was particularly galling to Guy Johnson, especially when the Oneida and Tuscarora subsequently supported the cause of the Continental Congress, thus splitting the confederacy and ending for ever the traditional British-Iroquois chain of friendship which was the strength of the general alliance.[21] Finally, the Americans managed "to cultivate Peace and Friendship" between the most recent enemies of the frontier people, the Ohio tribes, for "so long as the Sun shall Shine."[22]

Thus faced with "uncommon trouble and various Difficulties" in the increasingly hostile environment of the Mohawk Valley, Guy Johnson and a sizable party of Loyalists left their homes for Canada in late May of 1775. At Fort Ontario (Oswego), en route, he managed to assemble "1485 Indians and adjusted matters with them in such a manner, that they agreed to defend the Communications, and assist His Majesty's Troops in their operations." Upon reaching Montreal in mid-July, Johnson convened a second body of Indian allies "to the Amount of 1700, and upwards" who also agreed to serve in the interest of the British crown.[23] Indeed, Carleton reported that "the Indians upon the Borders of the River St. Lawrence had promised their Assistance and together with some Messages from Lake Ontario had done duty with the Troops ever since the 18th June."[24] In just three months, therefore, Johnson had achieved a notable success in collecting and organizing significant numbers of Iroquois allies, both from the Six Nations and the Seven Nations. Of particular interest was that these warriors were largely pro-British Mohawk and pro-French Mohawk from the last war, who were now formally united on behalf of the British crown and in the defence of Canada.

During the course of the summer, however, Johnson was frustrated by Carleton's instructions, which refused to allow the Indian allies to campaign beyond the borders of the province of Quebec. With reports in early August of an enemy force in the vicinity of Pointe-au-Fer at the northern end of Lake Champlain in the province of New York, Johnson experienced particular difficulties in restraining the warriors.[25] But at the end of August a major colonial rebel army moved out of Ticonderoga and pushed north up the Richelieu River towards Montreal, thus initiating the American invasion of Canada.[26] By early September, the Americans began landing in a swamp and woody area about one mile below the British fort of St. John (Saint-Jean-sur-Richelieu), which blocked the route to Montreal. At this critical juncture, about one hundred Caughnawaga Mohawk, without support from the regular troops, sallied out and engaged the Americans in the woods with "so warm a reception that after being twice repulsed they [the rebels] retired with precipitation," and considerable loss.[27]

Following their defeat, the Americans decided to conduct a careful siege campaign against St. John, and in the process forced the surrender of Chambly, which was a vital communication link between the besieged garrison and Montreal. Finally, after a stubborn resistance on the part of the British, the fort of St. John surrendered on 2 November 1775.[28] Two weeks later, confronted with only token opposition, the Americans occupied Montreal. But most significantly, the resolve of the Indian allies during the 1775 campaign, and especially the spirited attack of the Caughnawaga Mohawk at St. John, along with the subsequent and stiff resistance of the British garrison at that post, had critically delayed the American advance on Montreal. This lengthy disruption forced some of the Americans into winter quarters around Montreal, and stalled the linking with a second invasion force now besieging Quebec. In consequence, the final result was the utter defeat of the isolated and outnumbered Americans before the well-prepared British and Canadian outer defences of Quebec at Sault-au-Matelot and Près-de-ville on the last day of the year. This outcome virtually ended the 1775 American invasion of Canada.

Although the Americans remained at Montreal and continued to huddle around Quebec in a symbolic siege for the duration of the winter, the arrival of the Royal Navy with reinforcements and provisions in early May 1776 scattered the ragged and near-starving remnants of those American invaders still before Quebec. In mid-May a combined British-Indian strike force from Oswegatchie, a post on the south side of the upper St. Lawrence, advanced to the relief of Montreal. Spearheaded by about 160 Seneca, Cayuga, and Mississauga Ojibwa allies, who came "skiping and runing out of the woods," a much larger American force, frightened at the sights and sounds of the war whoops and musket fire, surrendered almost without resistance.[29] A detachment of rebel reinforcements moving into the area was also overwhelmed. By the end of June, after suffering another defeat at Trois-Rivières, mid-way between Montreal and Quebec, the last of the American invasion forces scrambled out of Canada and retreated along the Richelieu River to Crown Point and Ticonderoga, pursued rather too leisurely by a cautious or compassionate Governor Carleton.[30]

The successful defence of Canada in 1775 and 1776 was to a considerable degree determined by the effective assistance of Iroquois (mostly Mohawk) and other Indian allies. Guy Johnson had managed to assemble sufficient numbers of warriors whose military abilities and willingness to serve and engage the enemy at such places as St. John and the Cedars had ultimately forced the colonial rebels to abandon their goal of absorbing the French province, as the fourteenth colony, into the newly formed united American states. Yet the defence of Canada was marred for several months in 1775 by an increasingly nasty dispute between Johnson and Carleton over the methods of employing the warriors. Whereas the humane and moral-minded, if idealistic, Carleton instructed that the Indians were to be used only as scouts and in defence, the more realistic Johnson stressed that the warriors would be much more effective in suppressing the revolution by acting as raiders in frequent and devastating strikes against the rebel back settlements of New England, New York, and Pennsylvania.[31] The controversy was further intensified by Carleton's dislike of the monopoly hold the Johnson family possessed over appointments in the Indian Department. Therefore Carleton replaced Johnson and Daniel Claus (who had been deputy agent to the Canadian Indians for fifteen years) with his own appointed officials.[32] By November 1775 the situation in the management and administration of Indian affairs in the Northern District had become so confused and untenable that Guy Johnson took passage for England in order to clarify the scope of his superintendency. He was accompanied by Daniel Claus and the Mohawk war chief Joseph Brant (Thayendanegea).

Born at Cayahoga in the Ohio wilderness about 1742 or 1743, Joseph Brant was a member of a prominent Mohawk family and the brother of Sir William Johnson's companion Molly Brant.[33] This fortunate combination provided Joseph with some considerable degree of power and influence in both the Indian and white worlds. As a boy he settled at the Mohawk castle of Canajoharie, near Fort Johnson. During the wars against the French, Joseph experienced his first military action at Ticonderoga in July 1758, where the young warrior "was seized with such a tremor when the firing began that he was obliged to take hold of a small sapling to steady himself – but that after the discharge of a few vollies he recovered the use of his limbs and the composure of his mind, so as to support the character of a brave man, of which he was extremely ambitious."[34] The following month Brant served as a volunteer in the Bradstreet expedition against Fort Frontenac, and he subsequently participated in the campaigns of 1759 and 1760 at Niagara and Montreal under Sir William Johnson.

The determined character and intellectual potential exhibited by Joseph soon made him the favourite of his brother in-law. As a result, and at the conclusion of the war, Sir William Johnson sent the young Mohawk to Moor's Indian Charity School in Connecticut (the forerunner of Dartmouth College) for religious and educational instruction. At school, Brant was described as "a considerate, modest, and manly spirited youth."[35] The Indian uprising under Pontiac in 1763, however, provided the young Mohawk warrior with the opportunity to return to his first love, the battlefield. As such, he took part in the British-Indian campaign against the Ohio Valley tribes and again in 1764 against the western Indians as a volunteer in the Bradstreet expedition. Brant never returned to the New England school following these events, but instead spent the next ten years at Canajoharie where he assisted in translating a number of religious works, including a concise history of the Bible and the Gospel of St. Mark, into the Mohawk language. His proficiency in languages (he spoke English and three of the Six Nations languages) proved very valuable to Sir William Johnson, who used him as an interpreter and a translator of speeches at the Iroquois councils. Brant's services and talents were formally recognized in 1775 with his appointment to the Indian Department as "Interpreter for the Six Nations Language" at an annual salary of £85.3.4.[36]

With the outbreak of the American Revolution, Brant declared for the king, but he desired assurance from the British crown that Six Nations military assistance would be compensated by some determined action on the part of Britain to resolve Iroquois grievances regarding lands and encroachments. To obtain these assurances, Brant sailed for England in November 1775 with another and more elder chief, along with Guy Johnson and Daniel Claus.

Brant, attired in the full regalia of a Mohawk war chief, was a sensation in the fashion-conscious London social circles. He was introduced to a number of influential crown officials and some of the more notable individuals of the arts and literature. He was inducted into the Lodge of Freemasons and had his portrait painted by George Romney in the romantic tradition of the eighteenth-century "noble savage" from the wilderness of America. Yet these pleasant diversions did not detract from the vital reason for his visit to England. After meeting with Lord George Germain, the new secretary of state for the colonies, and explaining Iroquois land grievances and expectations for Six Nations military assistance, the Mohawk leader was assured "of every Support England could Render Them," after the suppression of the rebellious American colonials.[37] The promise appeared to satisfy Brant, who became convinced that for the future protection and survival of the Indian people, a military alliance with Britain against the America colonies was essential.

By the autumn of 1776, therefore, he had returned to the New York frontier and with a mixed force of Indians and white Loyalists was leading forays against American back settlements. Although Brant had "as many enemies among the Six Nations as friends with us," and was outranked by a number of other sachems and chiefs, notably the Seneca Sayenqueraghta (Kaien'kwaahton) or Old Smoke, who was more respected and influential within the Iroquois Confederacy, the Mohawk war chief during the course of the rebellion became acknowledged by the British as the leader of the Six Nations.[38] This recognition was strengthened after 1784 owing to his leadership in settling the Mohawk and others of the Six Nations Iroquois at Grand River and as a result of his prominence in Ohio Valley Indian affairs which had a direct impact on the defence of Canada.

During the winter of 1776–77, a general plan for the campaign of 1777 to suppress the rebellion in America was developed by Whitehall and approved by the king. The essentials were drawn from a number of sources, and the plan, which was not particularly new or innovative, was decidedly a collective responsibility. As to Canada specifically, Lieutenant-General John Burgoyne, a veteran of the Boston events in 1775 and second-in-command to Carleton in the slow and frustrating chase of the colonial rebels in 1776, offered a document in late February 1777 entitled "Thoughts for Conducting the War from the Side of Canada."[39] After consultation and analysis, Germain supported the plan in a slightly modified form. In its execution, the plan called for an army of about 11,000 officers and men (regulars, Canadians, and Indians), under the independent command of Burgoyne, to advance south from Canada along the Lake Champlain–Hudson River route to Albany and thence to link with Lieutenant-General Sir William Howe in New York.[40] The intention was to sever New England from the rest of the American colonies, thus providing the British with the opportunity by land and sea to suppress the two rebellious areas more easily by preventing any full concentration of rebel forces which might muster against them. This apparently simple plan did not take into account the degree of rebel resistance, the extent of the loyalty of the Canadians and Indians, the harsh reality of transporting a large and cumbersome army through dense wilderness terrain, the timing and cooperation to effect a junction between Burgoyne and Howe, or even whether Howe understood his role in the general campaign.

Curiously enough, Howe had submitted a plan of his own at the end of November 1776 for the orderly conquest of the rebellious colonies, which he predicted would "finish the War in one year."[41] His strategy was to campaign in New Jersey and Pennsylvania, with the capture of Philadelphia being the principal objective. Unbelievably, Germain approved this plan as well. By the early summer of 1777, therefore, whilst Burgoyne was marching south from Canada, Howe was in effect going in the wrong direction by sailing south from New York. Where was the logic and cooperation in these simultaneous military manoeuvres? With both armies heading south, a reasonably sound deduction could be made that there would never be a linking of the two commands, unless, of course, Burgoyne's force marched at an accelerated rate of speed and caught Howe's rearguard. In reality, Germain expected that Howe would take Philadelphia quickly and then extend his lines north to join Burgoyne. But there was a considerable amount of vagueness on all sides as to the precise meaning of cooperation and junction. Howe was aware of Burgoyne's campaign, but had only agreed to "facilitate in some degree the approach of the army from Canada."[42] The final result of this British muddling was that, although Howe enjoyed victories in September and October at Brandywine Creek and Germantown near Philadelphia, the isolated and trapped Burgoyne was forced to surrender on 17 October 1777 at Saratoga, several miles north of Albany.

The details of the Burgoyne campaign have been well documented in a number of sources.[43] The army, numbering only 7,300 officers and men, assembled on 20 June 1777 at Cumberland Point, a clearing near the River Bouquet on the west side of Lake Champlain. The next day Burgoyne held a council with about four hundred Indian allies, the vast majority from the Seven Nations of Canada. The general urged the warriors to "strike at the disturbers of public order, peace and happiness, destroyers of commerce, parricides of the state." But, he cautioned, they must fight with restraint, and in particular the Indians were strictly forbidden to take scalps from "the wounded or even dying." Following this oration, the warriors were "regaled by liquor and other refreshments." The festivities were finally concluded with a spirited war dance.[44]

In spite of Burgoyne's instructions, the warriors fought in

their traditional manner. This is hardly surprising, particularly since they were led by Luc de La Corne, a seigneur and veteran officer of Indians for New France during the last war, now in the service of the British crown, who considered that "il faut lâcher les sauvages contre les misérable Rebels, pour imposer de terreur sur les frontiers; ... qu'il faut brutaliser les affaires."[45] As a result, the Indian allies in 1777 proved to be more of a hindrance than an asset. Nonetheless, the warriors intrigued the British officers, one of whom wrote that "their appearance came fully up [to] or even surpassed the idea I had conceived of them." At Skenesboro on the southern edge of Lake Champlain, for instance, a war party of Ottawa entered Burgoyne's camp in July, and were described as surpassing "all others I had before seen in size and appearance when assembled in Congress, which was well worth seeing, they being painted in their usual stile and decked out with feathers of a variety of birds, and skins of wild beasts slain by them, as trophys of their courage."[46]

But the allure wore thin as the Indians generally "walked freely thro our camp and came into our tents without the least ceremony wanting brandy or rum, for which they would do anything, as their greatest pleasure is in getting beastly intoxicated." As well, the war dance was regarded as "curious and shocking, being naked and painted in a most frightful manner." As for the war whoop, "they appear more like infernals, than of the human kind."[47] The annoyances increased as the campaign progressed through Crown Point, Ticonderoga, and towards Albany. Reports of Indian plundering and scalping culminated in the murder of Jane McCrea, a young woman engaged to a Loyalist officer – an event which was exploited effectively by the Americans for propaganda purposes to arouse the frontier inhabitants against Burgoyne.[48] The deterioration in the relationship between the British and the Indian allies became increasingly worse, and in consequence, following the battle of Bennington in which Burgoyne exhibited a callous indifference towards the Indian dead and wounded, the warriors deserted almost en masse. For Burgoyne, his fate would be decided two months later at Saratoga.[49]

In his "Thoughts," Burgoyne had also envisioned a secondary force which would strike along the Mohawk River, thus creating a diversion for his army. This part of the plan was also approved, and in consequence a mixed force of about fourteen hundred British regulars, Hessians, Loyalists, and Indian allies (the latter composed of between six and eight hundred warriors drawn mainly from the Six Nations Iroquois), all under the command of

Lieutenant-Colonel Barrimore Matthew (Barry) St. Leger, left Montreal on 21 June 1777 for Oswego and thence to the Mohawk Valley.[50] The Indian allies were easily recruited through the efforts of the reunited Johnson clan. The returned Daniel Claus was put in charge of the warriors for this expedition and given command of the Six Nations in Canada; Sir John Johnson, son of Sir William, raised a two battalion Loyalist provincial corps (the Royal Regiment of New York or Royal Yorkers); Joseph Brant mustered the Six Nations; and John Butler (agent at Niagara), raised another Loyalist provincial corps (Butler's Rangers), which served throughout the rebellion on the frontier in concert with Indian allies.

By early August this force was engaged in a siege operation against the colonial rebels at Fort Stanwix (Rome, NY). On the afternoon of the 5th, Molly Brant sent word from Canajoharie that an enemy column of about eight hundred officers and men were advancing to the relief of the fort. The next day, at Oriskany, some six miles east of Fort Stanwix, they were "surprised, briskly attacked, and after a little resistance repulsed and defeated, leaving upwards of 500 killed on the spot, among which were their principal officers and ringleaders." But in spite of this decisive and largely Indian victory, St. Leger expressed grave disappointment at the lack of discipline on the part of the warriors. In part, he reported that "the impetuosity of the Indians is not to be described, on the Sight of the Enemy, forgetting the judicious Disposition formed by Sir John, and agreed to by themselves, which was to suffer the attack to begin with the Troops in Front, while they should be on back, Flank and Rear, they rushed in, hatchet in hand, and thereby gave the Enemy's Rear an Opportunity to escape."[51]

Nonetheless, St. Leger admitted that the victory was complete, and would probably have an even greater consequence since those individuals who escaped would only serve to spread the panic wider among the frontier people. In the battle, which was one of the most bloody and hard-fought of the American Revolution, the Indian losses were considerable by their standards, and especially among the Seneca. In total, thirty-three Indian were killed, including some of their favourite chiefs and confidential warriors. Two weeks later, with his Indian complement largely vanished, St. Leger lifted the siege and returned to Canada.

The duration of the civil war and rebellion on the frontier was marked by an increasingly bitter internecine rivalry between Loyalists and rebels, and by desperate, slashing attacks on American settlements by Britain's Indian allies, who fought a near hopeless war to prevent the usurpation of their lands by the relentless westward advance of the backwoodsmen. The chiefs and warriors cared little with whom they formed alliances, as long as they could obtain military and other assistance in their struggle for protection and survival. In this regard, the Indian desire for help fitted in with the general plan of operation devised at Whitehall, which was to secure "the affection and assistance of our old friends and allies, the Indians of the Six Nations," and by extension, the "western Indians."[52] British Indian policy was thus to be fixed firmly on the objective of using Indian allies "to worry the enemy; destroy their Fields of Corn and Cattle; all their Bridges, ferry Boats or others and Mills ..., rendering the Fordable places impassable ... [through] incessant incursions into all quarters."[53] For the Indian tribes, however, the American rebellion on the frontier was merely an opportunity to strike another blow in their long fight to defend their traditional lands and culture against white interlopers.[54]

By the autumn of 1782, Britain's Indian allies had raided and fought along the frontier for more than six years. The warriors had won some stunning victories during this time, most notably at Oriskany (August 1777), Wyoming Valley (July 1778), Cherry Valley (November 1778), Minisink (July 1779), Mohawk Valley (May 1780), Schoharie Valley (October 1780), Lochry expedition (August 1781), Mohawk Valley (October 1781), Sandusky (June 1782), and Blue Licks (August 1782).[55] They had also suffered defeats, the Six Nations, for instance, had lost their ancient castles throughout the Finger Lakes of upper New York as a result of the Sullivan expedition of 1779; and at Gnadenhutten in the Ohio Valley, more than one hundred Christian (Moravian) Delaware men, women, and children were slaughtered by rebel forces.[56]

The British government was fully aware of the military contribution of the tribes on behalf of the king and had expended considerable sums of money to promote and maintain the affections of the Indian allies.[57] Indeed, a grateful Frederick Haldimand, governor of Quebec from 1778 to 1784, reported to Whitehall that in combating Sullivan "the fidelity of these Indians [Six Nations] has alone preserved the Upper Country."[58] Joseph Brant was especially tireless and effective in fighting the Americans, and in recognition of his efforts he received a royal commission as captain of the northern confederate Indians. The resilience and determination of the Six Nations was also evidenced the year after Sullivan's destructive campaign when they renewed their raids under Sir John Johnson and "took fourteen rebel officers and 316 men, and destroyed 714 houses and granaries full of grain, six small forts and several mills, which afforded the rebels the most convenient supplies."[59] To the west, the Ohio and upper lakes tribes fought equally well, and won two successive and decisive battles against the Americans in the summer of 1782 at Sandusky and Blue Licks (where Daniel Boone was among the routed).[60]

But the surrender of Cornwallis at Yorktown, Virginia, in October 1781 which virtually ended the southern campaign and the long war in America, convinced the British government, confronted and burdened as it was European enemies, that peace negotiations with the Americans was the only practical course of action. The news of the proposals of peace caused a general alarm and discontent among the Indian allies, however, who feared the possible loss of their lands and, if isolated, American retaliation. Haldimand was particularly concerned, reporting that "the Indians are Thunderstruck at the appearance of an Accommodation So far short of their expectations from the Language that had been held out to them, and Dread the idea of being Forsaken by us, and becoming a Sacrifice to a Vengeance which has already in many Instances been raked upon them."[61] For Haldimand, the preservation of the British-Indian alliance was critical for the security and defence of Canada. Therefore, the governor instructed Sir John Johnson to devote his energies to cultivating "the Private Friendship and confidence of the chiefs of greatest note."[62]

Yet in spite of the earnest endeavours of Sir John Johnson and other Indian Department officials, along with British post commanders, to allay the fears of the tribes,

> the Indians from the surmises they have heard of the Boundaries, look upon our conduct to them as treacherous and cruel: they told me they never could believe that our King could pretend to cede to America what was not his own to give ... That they were the faithful Allies of the King of England, but not his subjects ... they would defend their own Just Rights or perish in the attempt to the last man, they were but a handfull of small People, but they would die like men, which they thought preferable to misery and distress if deprived of their Hunting Grounds.[63]

At Niagara, the post commander, Allan Maclean, was incensed at the Americans for sending messages and private emissaries among the Indians, explaining that they were not only allies, but "part of our family." Although the British affection was genuine enough, what really concerned the officers was a general fear that the Indians, embittered by the treaty and a sense of betrayal, might take their revenge, "Pontiac fashion," by attacking the British garrisons at Niagara, Detroit, Michilimackinac, and elsewhere. The Treaty of Paris, signed on 3 September 1783, only confirmed the worst fears of the crown officials in Canada, for by its terms the British totally abandoned the Indian allies, who were not even given a mention.

Joseph Brant was absolutely furious at the treaty provisions and the blatant British betrayal of native interests, exclaiming that the king had "sold the Indians to Congress."[64] But Haldimand hurriedly devised a frontier and Indian policy which would form the basis of British thinking in North America for more than a decade. In a lengthy report to Lord North, the British prime minister, he explained his plan:

> The Indians know that no infringements of the Treaty in 1768 can be binding upon them without their express concurrence and consent. In case things should proceed to extremities, the event no doubt will be the destruction of the Indians, but during the contest not only the Americans but perhaps many of His Majesty's subjects will be exposed to great distresses. To prevent such a disastrous event as an Indian war ... cannot be prevented so effectually as by allowing the posts in the upper country to remain as they are for sometime ... The intermediate country the limits assigned to Canada by the provisional treaty of 1782 and those established north-west of the River Ohio in the year 1768 should be considered entirely as belonging to the Indians.[65]

Here was the crucial proposal to retain the western posts indefinitely and to preserve the Ohio Valley as some sort of Indian barrier between Canada and the new republic of the United States. The intention had little to do with commercial or fur trade interests, but rather was to retain a British imperial and territorial presence in the region south of the lakes, contrary to the treaty terms, in order to allow at least for a time the unhindered establishment of the Loyalist settlements in the western parts of the province of Quebec. The final and hopeful outcome was to mollify the Indian allies (thus possibly saving lives) and to provide for the general security and defence of Canada by retarding the advance west and north of American settlement. British Indian policy in the defence of Canada after 1783 was thus based on fear and necessity.

CHAPTER 4

THE STRUGGLE FOR THE OHIO VALLEY

The decision to retain the western posts, a policy reached in 1784 after two years of studied deliberation by His Majesty's government in consultation with senior crown officials in Canada, preserved the tenuous British-Indian alliance and checked the expansion west and north of the American frontier. The immediate effect of these results provided time for the fledgling Loyalist settlements along the upper St. Lawrence, the Bay of Quinte, and at Niagara and Amherstburg to develop and prosper under "the Government and Laws of England."[1] By thus restricting the dangerous influx of new settlers from the United States, who would no doubt bring with them strong republican sentiments, the evolving character of the upper province of Quebec (later Upper Canada) became imbued with the Loyalist ideals. Fundamental to these ideals was a steadfast loyalty to the king and the unity of the empire, and an abiding respect for British political and legal institutions which were based, not on a restrictive American-style written constitution, but on the traditions and flexibility of custom and usage. The retention of the western posts, therefore, was motivated primarily by a desire to preserve and defend Canada, that northern remnant of the British empire in North America.

The continuance of a British presence south of the lakes, which was contrary, of course, to the terms of the international treaty signed at Paris in September 1783, barely appeased the Indian allies of the king. At several councils, officers of the British Indian Department followed instructions and attempted to placate the warriors with rhetoric, presents, and an assurance to these "unfortunate People, that they will find an Asylum within His Majesty's Dominions, should they be inclined to cross the Lakes and put themselves under our Protection."[2] Only a few of the Algonkian-speaking or "western" tribes of the Ohio Valley opted to move to Canada, notably the Christian Delaware survivors of the horror of Gnadenhutten, who found refuge along the Thames River and established a settlement which they called the Moravian Town. A generation later, this place would be the site of more violence and brutality in another bloody war.

But the Six Nations Confederacy of Iroquois, who had been dispossessed of their traditional lands and ancient castles along the Finger Lakes of upper New York, especially as a result of Sullivan's campaign in 1779, accepted this gesture with some relief, as their status had been reduced to refugees stranded at Lachine, outside Montreal, and at Niagara. In particular, Haldimand showed a special concern for the welfare and resettlement of the Mohawk whom he considered to be "the first nation deserving the Attention of Government." It was, therefore, with "great cheerfulness" that reasonable assistance was provided in order that "a fertile and happy Retreat for them," could be obtained.[3] For this purpose, lands were considered along the Bay of Quinte and in the Niagara peninsula, north of Lake Erie on the Grand River.

With the transplanting of the Loyalists and Indian allies to Canada, the British government began the process of obtaining the formal cession or surrender of the Indian interest in their traditional lands from the Ottawa River at Pointe-au-Baudette, and west along the northern shoreline of the upper St. Lawrence and the lower Great Lakes to Lake St. Clair. These land surrenders, which allowed for the rapid settlement of Loyalists and non-native migrants, continued unabated for years throughout the province and followed the process established by the Royal Proclamation of 1763.[4] Among the native people, apart from the Christian Delaware, it was two major groups of Mohawk, with some others of the Six Nations, who were the chief beneficiaries of the grants of land set aside for them as partial compensation for services rendered and losses suffered on behalf of the king during the colonial rebellion.

One group of Mohawk Loyalists under John Deserontyon (Deserontyou) settled at Tyendinaga on the Bay of Quinte, west of Cataraqui (Kingston).[5] A second and larger contingent of Mohawk and other tribes under Joseph Brant was established on "a Safe and Comfortable Retreat" along the Grand River in a settlement subsequently called Ohsweken.[6] In addition to land, the Mohawks, like the other Loyalists in the province, received His Majesty's royal bounty of provisions, clothing, and tools which materially assisted in further alleviating the plight of the families during the first few difficult years of resettlement. Both Mohawk communities fared well in their new surroundings, but Grand River was considered especially fine. Within three years of its founding, and with a population of two thousand of whom one-third were Mohawk, the settlement consisted of several houses, a grist mill, a school and a "neat little church."[7]

Travellers to Grand River were impressed with the growth and prosperity of the community. Joseph Brant hospitably entertained a number of guests who were lavished with an abundance of quality spirits, and teas served in the handsomest China plate. Beds with sheets and English blankets, equally fine and comfortable, were all provided in an atmosphere exuding refinement and contentment. Brant was considered a "renowned chief" and his Mohawk people, a warlike tribe of handsome young warriors. Indeed, the Iroquois men were observed to be "remarkably tall and finely made and walk with a degree of grace and dignity," which prompted Anne Powell, gentlewoman, author, and wife of a future chief justice of Upper Canada to exclaim, "I declare our Beau's look'd quite insignificant by them."[8] Most significantly, however, for the conduct and direction of British Indian policy after 1784, was that these warlike, and finely made loyal warriors and their descendants along the Grand River could provide a valuable future force of skilled fighting men in the defence of Canada.

Although the Mohawk and others of the Six Nations Iroquois had found sanctuary in Canada, the condition and status of the predominantly Algonkian-speaking tribes to the south of the lakes was not nearly as safe or secure in 1784. Following the American Revolution, the indigenous tribes of the Ohio Valley were shocked to learn that the lands upon which they had lived "since time immemorial" had been ceded by the king to the Americans at the Treaty of Paris. These Indians were therefore now residing within the territorial and political jurisdiction of the United States. Worse, by fighting as military allies alongside the British between 1775 and 1783, the tribes, according to the Americans, had forfeited their aboriginal title to the land. As a consequence, these Indian lands were considered as conquered and surrendered territory.

This logic was incomprehensible to the tribes of the Ohio Valley. In the summer of 1782 they had won two decisive victories over the Americans at Sandusky and Blue Licks and had never been overrun or conquered. As well, the British appeared to remain firmly in possession of the western posts. How then, reasoned the Indians, could the king surrender the Ohio lands (which the tribes regarded as their own) to the Americans? Yet the tribes were made to understand that as a result of an international treaty, negotiated solely between Great Britain and the United States, all Indian lands south of the lakes had been surrendered to the Americans.

The tribes of the Ohio Valley had not been totally abandoned by the British. Those crown officials responsible for the conduct of Indian affairs were fully aware of the advantages in preserving the military and commercial British-Indian alliance.[9] Haldimand, for instance, who was determined to provide for the future security of the province of Quebec, regarded the continued loyalty of the Six Nations and the warriors of the western tribes now residing in the United States as the cornerstone of his defensive strategy. In mid-November 1784 the governor returned to England. Within a few months of his arrival in London, he presented a lengthy report on public matters in the province of Quebec for the consideration of the minister responsible for colonial affairs, Lord Sydney, secretary of state at the Home Department.

A key element of this report was "Means Suggested as the Most Probable to Retain the Six Nations and Western Indians in the King's Interest."[10] In part, Haldimand urged that the Grand River settlement "should meet with every Indulgence and Encouragement of Government, not only in consideration of Their past Services, but in proportion as it shall be thought necessary to preserve the Friendship and Alliance of the Indians in general, whose Conduct is always governed by that of the Six Nations." Haldimand, of course, was off the mark in thinking that the Iroquois still possessed a dominant control over the Algonkian or western tribes. Nonetheless, he believed that if the Mohawk were "comfortably established and experience the Sweets of the King's Protection," their traditional loyalty, fighting prowess and persuasive influence in the decision-making at united tribal councils would significantly contribute to maintaining "possession of the Upper Country and the Furr Trade" – in other words, Canada.

As for the Indian tribes of the Ohio Valley, whom Haldimand regarded as "infinitely a more numerous People" but who "will always be influenced by that of the Six Nations," the governor considered that "some Presents and marks of Friendship are nevertheless due to Their past services, and should be, from time to time, dispensed amongst Them." But Haldimand also regarded the expense of these donations as excessive and reckoned that "with a prudent management" the distribution of the presents could be gradually reduced "without alarming or distressing the Indians." In spite of his almost enamoured view of the Mohawk, his overstated emphasis of the influence of the Iroquois over the Algonkian tribes and his coldly practical approach in lessening Indian expenditures, Haldimand was genuine in his desire to promote the welfare of the Indian allies in both Canada and the United States. He remained faithful to this mission, and his "suggestions" were probably more than the British government anticipated, expected, or wanted. Nonetheless, for the next decade Haldimand's report significantly influenced the course of British Indian policy in Canada.

The efforts to maintain a form of the British-Indian military and commercial alliance for the future security and benefit of Canada did not deter the United States from pushing ahead with an agenda for Indian affairs which would surely alienate the tribes. Following two committee reports in the autumn of 1783 and spring of 1784, the Continental Congress inaugurated an Indian policy which was based on a set of assumptions and one firmly fixed objective. The first assumption was that by the terms and conditions of the Treaty of Paris, all lands south of the international boundary line belonged solely to the new and sovereign republic. The second was that the Indian tribes inhabiting these lands were a conquered and subdued people and therefore subject to the wishes of the United States. The third was that in consequence of the foregoing assumptions, the Congress would be justified in compelling the Indians to withdraw either north to Canada or west toward the Mississippi.[11] In formulating this policy, the Congress chose to ignore the British colonial precedents of acknowledging and recognizing the aboriginal "right of prior occupancy," and that, consequently, the extinguishment of land title should be accomplished through formal negotiations and purchase. But the young and confident United States was determined to set and implement its own national priorities. A peaceful accommodation with the tribes was of some importance, but the exclusive and overriding objective of American Indian policy in the years following the Revolution was to obtain the acquisition of all Indian lands from the Ohio to the Mississippi.[12]

The American quest for Indian lands in the Ohio Valley was formally enunciated with the issuance of a congressional ordinance which forthrightly repudiated the Ohio River boundary and demanded that the tribes in the region promptly retire beyond the Miami and the Maumee, two rivers considerably to the west of the Ohio. In order to achieve this result, American Indian commissioners began by assembling the influential Six Nations Iroquois at Fort Stanwix, with the intent of negotiating a settlement. But the Iroquois chiefs protested that no treaty could be concluded without the participation of the Algonkian tribes. This stance was an effort to honour the pledge of Indian unity against American territorial ambitions which had been made by Joseph Brant and other Indian leaders at the Sandusky conference in September 1783.

The commissioners, however, sternly dismissed the plea by reminding the Iroquois that the king had surrendered all Indian lands and that by right of conquest the Americans could "claim the whole." The British provided a rejoinder to this interpretation by denying that the king had forfeited Indian lands by the terms of the Treaty of Paris. Rather, insisted various crown officials, what had been transferred to the United States was the exclusive right to purchase, for instance, Indian lands in the Ohio Valley which had been guaranteed to the tribes by several prior treaties, but especially by the 1768 Treaty of Fort Stanwix. After debating the alternatives, the assembled Iroquois, consisting only of Mohawk, Onondaga, Cayuga, and Seneca (the pro-American Oneida and Tuscarora remaining secure in possession of the lands on which they were settled), accepted the peace offer of the commissioners which included a guarantee that the United States would "receive them into their protection." By the terms of the Treaty of Fort Stanwix of 22 October 1784, the Six Nations Iroquois in part ceded to the United States their ancient claims to much of the land west and north of the Ohio River.[13] More important to the Americans was the knowledge that this action freed the Algonkian tribes of the Ohio Valley from Iroquois domination. For the Continental Congress, the door was now open to terminate land claims with the western Indians, tribe by tribe, a strategy reminiscent of the old British policy of "divide and rule."

So, apparently abandoned by the British in 1783, and now sold out in 1784 by their old rivals, the Six Nations Iroquois, the Algonkian tribes of the Ohio Valley assumed a new resolve to treat formally and independently with the United States. At the Treaty of Fort McIntosh on 21 January 1785, although only a few minor chiefs from the more pacifistic factions of the Wyandot, Delaware, and Ojibwa were present, the American commissioners repeated the process begun a year earlier at Fort Stanwix and dictated a

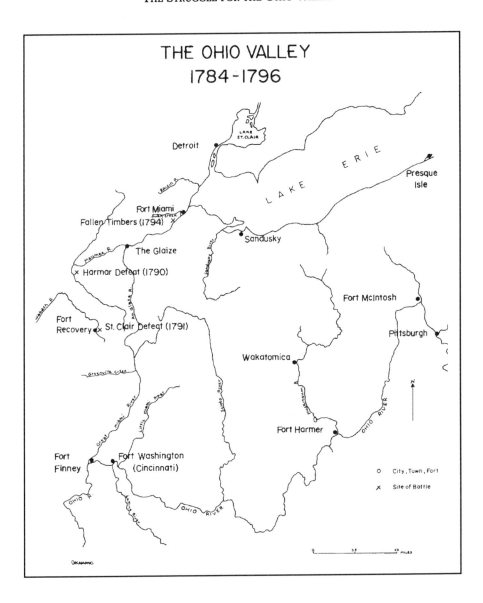

THE OHIO VALLEY
1784-1796

treaty. After mustering some token verbal objections to the terms, the chiefs acknowledged the protection of the United States and ceded specified land north of the Ohio River.[14] But in spite of this embarrassing episode for Indian unity, most of the Algonkian chiefs and warriors were determined to resist any further encroachments.

Nonetheless, the treaties of 1784 and 1785 had weakened the spirit and sense of unity among the Indians. The cession of 1784 naturally angered the western tribes, who complained that the Iroquois had no right to give away the traditional Ohio Valley hunting grounds of the Algonkian people. As for the 1785 treaty, most of the tribes, including the militant and influential Shawnee, had not even been in attendance. Yet even before these two treaties were ratified, the confused and frustrated tribes were forced to respond to additional pressures, as American backwoodsmen swarmed down and across the Ohio River and into "so fine a country my eyes never beheld."[15] The attempts by congressional forces to remove these settlers from unceded Indian lands proved futile, for the "white banditti" were numerous, organized, well armed, and steadfast in the belief that they had a right to rove and settle on what to them was vacant forest lands.

Divided and somewhat shaken at the land cessions in the recent treaties, the Indians were nonetheless still prepared to contest the advance of the backwoodsmen. At Wakatomica, a Shawnee village at the eastern end of the Ohio Valley, for instance, Captain Johnny (one of their chiefs) warned the Americans that "you are drawing close to us, and so near our bedsides, that we can almost hear the noise of your axes felling our Trees and settling our Country ... The Boundary is the Ohio River, ... but it is too clear to us your design is to take our Country from us ... [We are] determined to act as one man in Defence of it. Therefore be strong and keep your people within Bounds, or we shall take up a Rod and whip them back to your side of the Ohio."[16] The resolution of the Indians to defend their country was no mere bravado. Settlers who continued to glide down the Ohio River in their flatboats were repeatedly attacked by increasingly frustrated and angry bands of warriors.

Various Indian leaders tried to explain their actions to British agents located throughout the Ohio country by restating that the tribes had no idea that the Americans looked upon them as conquered people until so informed by the commissioners. Chiefs and warriors also reminded the British that the tribes had never asked for peace and had listened to the Americans only because they were so advised by the king. Whilst these events were transpiring, the peace faction of the Shawnee was summoned by the commissioners to assemble at the mouth of the Miami. In return for a promise that hostilities would cease, the Shawnee delegates agreed to the terms of the Treaty of Fort Finney on 31 January 1786 and acknowledged that the United States was "the sole and absolute sovereign of all territory ceded by Great Britain in the 1783 treaty."[17] As well, the chiefs signed away Shawnee claims to lands east of the Miami River.

The treaties of 1784, 1785, and 1786, based solely on the idea of conquest, violated the previous treaties, proclamations and acts of 1758, 1763, 1768, 1774, 1775, and 1778. But this consideration had little or no effect on the moral conscience of Americans, for land was the young nation's most treasured commodity in the first fifty years of the republic, and the effort of men to acquire it was probably the dominant force of the period. More important to the Congress was that, as a result of these treaties, the Indians had been forced into relinquishing all their lands along the northwestern frontier to the United States. But the surrendering of their territory did not mean that the Indians were pacified. In fact, the haughty manner in which the treaties had been conducted, along with the continued influx of settlers, so incensed the tribes, especially the Shawnee, that the warriors renewed their raids along the Ohio River.

In a effort to bring some security to the chaotic frontier, two expeditions under George Rogers Clark of Vincennes fame and Benjamin Logan, both independent of congressional authority, were organized by Kentucky. The Clark campaign against the Miami and upper Wabash tribes failed miserably owing to a lack of supplies and to desertion. Logan performed rather better by surprising the Shawnee on 6 October 1786 and burning their two principal villages of Maycockey and Wakatomica (where Captain Johnny had uttered his defiant speech a year earlier). Simon Girty reported on these events, noting that "Maycockey town raised the 'Yanky' colours but to no purpose, as the army destroyed the town, proceeded to Wakitumikie and destroyed it and burned the houses of Alexander McKee and Blue Jacket."[18]

In the midst of these several events, Joseph Brant sailed for England in late 1785. Among his intentions was to present Mohawk compensation claims for losses during the rebellion and petition for a personal half-pay pension. Most important, however, Brant wanted to obtain assurance that the Indians were still considered by the British government "as His Majesty's faithful allies, and have that support and countenance such as old and true friends expect."[19] In a lengthy letter of introduction to Lord

Sydney, the Mohawk leader reminded the minister of the military role and contribution of the Six Nations on behalf of the crown during the American Revolution. He continued by expressing the Indian astonishment that the British had apparently forgotten them at the 1783 peace treaty. Furthermore, he informed Sydney, the Americans were now violating the British-Indian agreement of 1768 by encroaching on Algonkian lands in the Ohio Valley. With these considerations in mind, concluded Brant, would the king support the tribes in the event of a war with the United States?

Sydney provided a formal and diplomatic reply three months later, on 6 April 1786. The letter, carefully crafted and deliberately vague, offered that the "liberal Conduct on the part of His Majesty, He trusts will not leave a doubt upon the Minds of His Indian Allies that He shall at all times be ready to attend to their future Welfare." Further, "His Majesty recommends to his Indian allies to continue united in their councils, and that their measures may be conducted with temper and moderation; from which, added to a peaceful demeanour on their part, they must experience many essential benefits, and be most likely to secure to themselves, the possession of those rights and privileges which their ancestors have heretofore enjoyed."[20]

This response seemed to suggest that the tribes could expect some assistance from the British government in the event of "serious consequences" developing over the continued American encroachment on Indian lands in the Ohio Valley. Somewhat encouraged, and pleased with his success in securing his pension and £15,000 for the Mohawk people, Brant returned to Canada and the forests of America.

Yet in a secret despatch to Henry Hope, lieutenant-governor and administrator of the province of Quebec, written on the same day as the reply to Brant, instructions were issued by Sydney to avoid any open assistance to the tribes, although the home secretary considered that it was neither "consistent with justice or good Policy entirely to abandon them, and leave them to the mercy of the Americans, as from motives of resentment it is not unlikely that they might hereafter be led to interrupt the Peace and Prosperity of the Province." For Sydney, who mirrored British Indian policy in the defence of Canada during the immediate post-rebellion years, "the flourishing state of the new [Loyalist] Settlements" was a source of great satisfaction.[21] He was fully aware, however, that with the weak state of the army both in the province and in garrison at the western posts, the security and welfare of the Loyalist settlements and Canada was largely dependent on the continued allegiance of the Indian tribes.

With these considerations in mind, Sydney could only offer the opinion to Hope and his successor that "It is utterly impracticable for his Majesty's Ministers to prescribe any direct line for your Conduct should matters be driven to the extremity, and much will depend upon your judgement and discretion in the management of a Business so delicate and interesting, in which you must be governed by a variety of Circumstances which cannot at this moment be foreseen."[22] Although Sydney was vague, his Indian policy for Canada was sufficiently flexible to allow local crown officials and field officers to use their own discretion according to the exigency of the time and circumstance. Whitehall, of course, could then condemn any such action that proved harmful to the delicate balance of Anglo-American diplomatic relations.

The return of Sir Guy Carleton (now Lord Dorchester) to Canada in October 1786 as captain-general and governor-in-chief provided continuity in Indian policy. His instructions, apart from sections 31 and 32 which forbade the establishment of settlements "beyond the Boundaries ascertained to the different Posts among the Indian Nations" and made "the Peltry-Trade of the interior Country" free and open to all British subjects, were similar to those sent to Hope.[23] Upon his arrival, and as the senior crown official in Canada, Dorchester immediately conveyed the message to the Indians that the king was at peace with the United States and was neither prepared nor wished for war. In a despatch to Sir John Johnson, the governor cautioned that "all promises [to the Tribes] not intended to be fulfilled must be avoided."[24]

Indeed, the escalation of violence along the Ohio frontier so alarmed Dorchester that he was prompted to write a letter to Sydney and elaborate on the reasons for his concern: "The Americans have made an inroad on the Shawanese country west of the Ohio, burned some of their villages and carried off some women and children as prisoners. The town where the Indian Congress was to assemble was also laid in ashes. The alarm [is] increased by the report that parties are moving up the Rivers which fall into the Ohio River from the North and leads to Detroit."[25]

The distinct possibility of a prolonged war between the Indians and the United States meant that the preservation of the British-Indian alliance for the defence of Canada was never more vital. Without the loyalty and determination of the warriors, little hope could be entertained for the continued retention of the western posts or indeed for the survival of the new and near-defenceless Loyalist settlements in the upper province. Therefore, to bolster Indian loyalty and confidence, the British government began to increase the amount of supplies and gifts to the tribes. Lord Sydney even suggested that the issuance of shot and powder to the Indians might be advisable so that they could better defend themselves against the Americans.[26]

The self-interested British policy of promoting and strengthening the Indian cause was given a boost in December 1786 when Joseph Brant, buoyed by his recent trip to England, assembled a grand council of all the tribes near the mouth of the Detroit River. The Mohawk leader opened the conference with a passionate speech in which he reminded the Indians that they were "Lords of the Soil, and that all the White People are intruders or Invaders."[27] Brant was furious that his brother Iroquois had broken their pledge at Sandusky in 1783 by sacrificing Algonkian interests at Fort Stanwix a year later. He pleaded successfully for strength and unity among the tribes and the council unanimously denounced the treaties of 1784, 1785, and 1786. After further discussions, the "United Indian Nations," as they now called themselves, sent a message to the Congress which demanded that the Americans stop encroaching on the Algonkian lands of the Ohio Valley and that a meeting take place between the United Indian Nations and the United States in order to negotiate a new general treaty of friendship and understanding.[28]

The accomplishments of Brant at the Detroit conference in obtaining a loose confederacy of the tribes had dealt a blow to the American Indian policy of divide and rule. But Indian unity was shaky at best. The grand council became divided over the concession of lands north of the Ohio River by the terms of the Treaty of Fort McIntosh. The Wyandot and Delaware, some of whom lived in the eastern portion of the Ohio Valley and who would in consequence bear the brunt of an American attack, were prepared to compromise. But the Shawnee and other tribes, located in the less threatened western regions of the valley, were determined to stand firm on the 1768 line as the absolute limit of white expansion.

The constant fluctuations and alarms in the Ohio Valley, and along the American frontier generally, convinced Dorchester that an official inspection of the western posts would be useful for the information of Lord Sydney. The governor therefore assigned Robert Matthews, his military secretary, to undertake the mission in the spring of 1787. In the course of his travels, Matthews wrote to Brant a personal summation of his findings and views on British Indian policy. In part, Matthews confided to his friend:

> [The king] cannot begin a war with the Americans, because some of their people encroach and make depre-

dations upon parts of the Indian country; but they must see it is his Lordship's intention to defend the posts ... On the other hand, if the Indians think it more for their interest that the Americans should have possession of the posts, and be established in their country, they ought to declare it, that the English need no longer be put to the vast and unnecessary expense and inconvenience of keeping posts, the chief object of which is to protect their Indian allies, and the loyalists who have suffered with them.[29]

The tone of the letter suggested a certain frustration and uncertainty in the application of British Indian policy, especially as to the retention of the western posts in American territory. To a degree, Sydney echoed this thought. In correspondence with Dorchester he felt constrained to justify the decision to retain the posts by arguing that the British treatment of the Indians had always been liberal, and "considering that the security of the Province may depend on their loyalty, supplies may be augmented rather than leave them discontented."[30] His analysis reflected the consistent theme in British Indian policy for North America after the Revolution, which was to provide for the defence of Canada through the preservation of a British-Indian alliance, rooted south of the international boundary.

For the United States, the continued existence of the British-Indian alliance, combined with the rather surprising and militant resolve of the tribes in contesting American advances into the Ohio Valley, forced the weak and financially depleted central government to rethink some of the basic assumptions previously held regarding land and Indian affairs. Although the acquisition of Indian lands remained the goal, appeasement and moral good conduct toward the tribes were now the focus of a new policy. This attitude was evidenced with the passing of the Northwest Ordinance of 13 July 1787, providing for the creation of three to five new states between the Ohio and Mississippi rivers. But article three of the ordinance stated categorically:

The utmost good faith shall always be observed towards the Indians; their lands and property shall never be taken from them without their consent; and in their property, rights and liberty, they shall never be invaded or disturbed, unless in just and lawful wars authorized by Congress; but laws founded in justice and humanity shall from time to time be made, for preventing wrongs

being done to them, and for preserving peace and
friendship with them.[31]

How "justice and humanity" could be compatible with the continued and unwanted American intrusion onto Indian lands was left
unexplained.

In spite of the stated desire of the United States to demonstrate
"the utmost good faith" towards the Indians, Arthur St. Clair,
appointed by the Congress on 27 October 1787 as the first governor of the Territory Northwest of the River Ohio, was told not to
"neglect any opportunity that may offer of extinguishing the
Indian rights to the westward as far as the river Mississippi."[32]
Although there was to be no significant departure from the former
treaties of 1784, 1785, and 1786, the Congress had voted some
money for acquiring Indian lands. Thus slowly, and possibly
reluctantly, the United States shifted towards the old British policy
of obtaining the extinguishment of aboriginal land title through
formal negotiation and purchase.

St. Clair reached the Ohio in early July 1788. After making all
the necessary arrangements with various tribal delegates for holding an Indian council, he waited patiently at Fort Harmar, a post
on the Muskingum, just north of the Ohio River. In response to
the governor's call, the chiefs of the confederation assembled at
the Maumee to plan strategy and discuss the feasibility of going to
Fort Harmar. Some of the more remote tribes, immune from the
pressure of American expansion, saw no need for another treaty.
Brant, however, counselled a policy of moderation and suggested
that the Muskingum-Venango line would provide a reasonable
compromise to the Ohio River boundary, especially since some
American settlements had already been established there. This
compromise proposal badly divided the tribes, and the Shawnee
and Miami angrily left the meeting, but not before vowing that
they would tolerate no white settlements north of the Ohio.
Although the rest agreed to attend the St. Clair meeting, Brant was
so upset with the factionalism and lack of Indian unity that he
refused to participate in the separate tribal negotiations with the
American governor.

In January 1789 the tribes of the United Indian nations, with
the notable exception of the Shawnee, Miami, and Brant's
Mohawks, assembled at Fort Harmar. After some bickering and
posturing over insisting on the Ohio line, the Indian leaders somewhat reluctantly agreed to negotiate two separate and dictated
treaties. The Six Nations Iroquois accepted terms on 9 January

which merely reaffirmed the boundary provisions of 1784. But on this occasion the Americans paid the Iroquois $3,000 for the ceded land. A second treaty was concluded on the same day with the Algonkian tribes. Similarly, the 1785 boundary provisions were renewed; and the Indians in turn received a total of $6,000 in presents and goods.[33]

The treaties of Fort Harmar ended the Indian policy devised by the Continental Congress. The early assumptions that the United States possessed an absolute and sovereign right to all lands between the Ohio and Mississippi by reason of victory over Great Britain and the terms of the Treaty of Paris infuriated the Indian tribes to such an extent that their subsequent, effective resistance to American expansion into the Ohio Valley rendered the policy inoperative. Four months after Fort Harmar, the Senate of the first congress under the constitution formally noted that "the Indians are greatly tenacious of their lands, and generally do not relinquish their right [of soil], excepting on the principle of a specific consideration expressly given for the *purchase* of the same."[34] But the decision to adopt the old British policy of purchase came too late. The treaties of 1784, 1785, 1786, and even 1789 had humiliated the Indians and stained their honour. By the summer of 1789, the tribes were seething for revenge and preparing themselves to fight the Americans in defence of the lands of the Ohio Valley. Ironically, the United States, moving rapidly towards a policy of peace and purchase, was forced to wage a desperate and costly five-year Indian war for which the new republic initially had neither the means nor the desire.

The Shawnee, Miami, and Wabash tribes, all of whom had refused to attend the Fort Harmar negotiations, were particularly determined to prevent American settlements on the north side of the Ohio River. Throughout the summer and autumn of 1789 the warriors repeatedly struck at selected targets in Kentucky and along the Ohio River. The attacks became so serious that George Washington, recently selected by the new Congress as the first president of the United States, requested the "immediate intervention of the General Government." As a consequence, an American expeditionary force under the command of Brigadier-General Josiah Harmar was mustered the following year at Fort Washington (Cincinnati) on the lower Ohio.[35]

In the autumn of 1790 Harmar advanced against a group of Miami towns clustered between the Maumee and Wabash rivers. He met little opposition and barely fired a shot, as the Indians burned their houses and cornfields and slowly retired before him. Harmar was satisfied, as he had completed his assigned mission of destroying the Miami settlements. But Colonel John Harden of the command was disappointed at the lack of action and received permission to make a reconnaissance in force in the hope of goading the retreating Indians into fighting. In two separate engagements on 20 and 23 October the impetuous Harden was attacked and severely mauled by Miami, Shawnee, Delaware, and Potawatomi warriors under the leadership of the Miami chief Little Turtle (Michikinakoua).[36] In the first action the Americans suffered three hundred killed; and in the second confrontation the Indians drove the troops into a swamp and slaughtered two hundred more, mostly with spear and tomahawk. Nothing, apparently, "could equal the intrepidity of the Indians on this occasion."[37]

In early November 1790 Little Turtle and Blue Jacket, a principal chief of the Shawnee, visited the British at Detroit to recount their recent victories and request food for the distressed Indian families who had suffered during the Harmar campaign. The two chiefs stressed that war had resulted solely because of American encroachments on lands north of the Ohio River, and that the tribes were bound and determined to defend their traditional hunting grounds. The lands of the Ohio Valley, they reiterated, had always belonged to the Algonkian people, and by former treaties, especially that of 1768, the Ohio River was considered the permanent boundary between the Indians and the whites. There would be no compromise, asserted the chiefs, regarding this border.[38]

Later that month the Delaware echoed this theme during a council at the Maumee with officers of the British Indian Department by indicating that they would soon be "going off to the [American] Forts on this Side of the Ohio River to see what we can do in defence of our Lands." The war chiefs were most enthusiastic and proclaimed that "we are all upon our feet ready to protect our Country." But at the same time other Delaware leaders recalled that the British had not only encouraged the Indian alliance "to make ourselves as one," but had "always told us, if We took your advice We should not want for any thing." Therefore, they continued, "we hope to get all Necessaries for fighting from our Father."[39] The several and ongoing Indian demands that the British provide appropriate supplies and general assistance in their struggle to defend the Ohio Valley was hardly surprising, and reflected the traditional and mutual rapport and cooperation which existed and characterized the British-Indian alliance against the Americans.

Since the Indian defence of the Ohio Valley was so intrinsically entwined with the survival of Canada, the British naturally and readily provided the necessaries to assist the chiefs and warriors. Thus, confident in their relationship with the British and emboldened by their success against Harmar, the Indians increased their raids along the Ohio frontier. At the Home Department, Lord Grenville, who had replaced Sydney, expressed alarm at the report of Indian outrages and urged Dorchester to seek some resolution to calm the situation in the Ohio country. The governor had anticipated the request. Even before the despatch arrived from Whitehall, he had instructed Sir John Johnson to "learn the nature and extent of the specific terms on which the Confederated Indian Nations would be disposed to establish a great tranquillity and friendship with the United States."[40] But all attempts that spring by the Indian Department to convince the tribes gathering at the Miami to consider a favourable termination of their troubles with the Americans ended in failure. The mood of the Indians was highly optimistic and they decided to continue with their war preparations.

The Indian spirit for continuing the struggle left the financially overburdened and less than enthusiastic United States little option but to organize a second expedition to restore peace and order on the frontier. Following the Harmar disaster, St. Clair was appointed commander-in-chief as well as governor, and throughout the summer and autumn of 1791 at Fort Washington, he collected and trained an army of militia and regulars, whilst overseeing minor military operations. In May and July, for instance, American army strikes against the Wabash tribes, apart from destroying some villages, only succeeded in heightening Indian-American contempt and bitterness in which the desire for retaliation was mutual.

By the late summer of 1791 the tribes, under the general leadership of Little Turtle, had assembled in full force at the foot of the Miami rapids. They agreed to renew the confederacy and defend their lands by stopping the Americans at the Ohio River. They had been provisioned from the British stores at Detroit and further bolstered by the presence of Alexander McKee, Matthew Elliott, Simon Girty and other notables of the Indian Department who acted as advisers. In council with the British, the chiefs stated that they were "very thankful to their Father for the seasonable delivery of their Annual supplies, but earnestly entreat, he will consider the distressed situation of their families who are now obliged to abandon their villages and [corn] fields."[41] Yet in spite of some hardships and sufferings, Simon Girty reported that the Indians were never in better heart and were determined to drive the Americans to the Ohio and to starve their posts.

At sunrise on 4 November 1791 the Indians under Little Turtle and the Americans under Arthur St. Clair finally clashed in a major field of battle to the south of the Wabash. The struggle was fierce, desperate, and bloody, and ended with the rout of the American army. Indian losses were about one hundred warriors. But American casualities, both among the militia and regulars, exceeded one thousand.[42] The St. Clair battle was the greatest and most important Indian victory since the Braddock disaster of 1755. In an anonymous letter from Niagara, written three weeks after the engagement, the details and potential implications of the battle on Indian, British, and American interests in the Ohio Valley were generously presented:

> The American Army of which no doubt you have this summer heard, had advanc'd on the third of this month to within Forty Miles of the Miamis Towns, they were there encountered by near Two thousand Indians, who on that day took from them the greatest part of their Horses & Cattle – On the 4th, at Sun rise they attack'd their Camp, but were twice repuls'd, irratated beyond measure, they retir'd to a little distance, where separating into their different tribes and each conducted by their own Leaders, they returned like Furies to the assault & almost instantly got possession of near half the Camp – they found in it a row of Flour Bags, & bags of Stores, which serv'd them as a Breast work, from behind which they kept up a constant & heavy fire, the Americans charg'd them several times with Fixed Bayonets, but were as often repuls'd – at length General Butler, second in Command, being kill'd, the Americans fell into confusion & were driven from their Cannon, round which a Hundred of their bravest Men fell, the Rout now became universal, & in the utmost disorder, the Indians follow'd for Six Miles, & many fell Victims to their Fury, in the Camp they found 5 pieces Brass Cannon, 3 of 6 & 2 of 4 pounds, 14 Mortar & 2 paturaros, all Brass & mounted for field Service, with these they took all Arms, Ammunition, Provisions, Cloathing, entrenching Tools, and Stores of every kind, the Americans had in their Camp for the purpose of erecting Forts, & remaining the ensuing Winter in the Indian Country, besides the Commanding Officer, the Adjt. Genl. & Surgeon Genl., Twelve hundred are said to have Fallen in the Assaults & pursuits – you however know

the Indians, most probably this Number is exaggerated we do not hear of one prisoner – about 50 of the Indians are said to be killed & wounded, the Numbers at first were American Regulars 1500, Militia 800, in all 2300 – of Indians nearly 2,000. Two Forts they had erected on their Rout nam'd Hamilton & Jefferson, are said to be surrounded by the Indians, they contain 100 Men each with but little provisions; the truth of this information may be depended on, Simon Girty, if not in the action, was within view of it. He had join'd Coll. McGee at the foot of the Rapids brought the American Orderly Books & all their papers – Butler's Scalp was brought in, & is sent they say to Joseph Brant with a severe Sarcasm for his not being there – He is at the grand River with the Six Nations – Cowan in the Felicity was dispatch'd with the interesting intelligence. I saw him yesterday at Fort Erie – He left your Brother well on the 14th who had sometime before hurt his arm and was not yet able to write, an Express is now getting ready for Quebec, finding an opportunity I send this by New York. Humanity shudders at the number of poor wretches who have fallen in this Business, but as they were clearly the aggressors, they merit less pity, the horrible Cruelties that may probably now fall on the defenceless Frontiers of the Western American Settlements, is infinitely more dreadful & claims from every person who can feel as a man, every preventative that can be devis'd; I have this morning wrote to our Friend Mr. Askin strongly pressing him to join the Trade in inspiring the Indians with moderation. The Americans must be serevely hurt at this Blow, however willing to resent it, they will find great difficulty in raising another Army for this Service. They would probably listen to any Reasonable Terms of accommodation, if they saw a prospect of its being establish'd on solid Grounds, perhaps this can only be affected by the influence of the British Government & Trade with the Indians – The Terms the Indians ask'd were, that the Ohio shou'd be establish'd as the Boundary to the American Settlements, & that they shou'd enjoy unmolested their hunting Grounds, to the West & North of that River, some of the Branches of the Ohio to the Southward of this come within a few Miles of the Genesea River, which runs into Lake Ontario Sixty Miles East from the Fort of Niagara – If these two Rivers by the interposition of Government cou'd be fix'd as the Boundaries between the Americans and Indians, & between them & us, we shou'd secure our Posts, the Trade, & the Tranquility of the Country; you will know that the present lines must furnish a source of constant Contention & dispute – The others now propos'd being on Streams not navigable, will be free from this, the Indians not having as yet sold their Country between this & the Genesea nor does any of the American Settlements extend to the West of that River, but they very soon will – I wish our Peacemakers of 83 had but known a little more of this Country. I wish our present Ministry were informed of the actual situation – perhaps this is the important moment in which the unfortunate terms of the Peace may be alter'd – Perhaps this moment may never return.[43]

The Indians, exuberant over this second successive and decisive victory, ravaged the defenceless Ohio frontier in the winter and spring of 1792. In fact, after the St. Clair battle the warriors could have swept almost unopposed as far as Pittsburgh. But dedicated solely to the defence and preservation of their traditional lands and cultural values in the Ohio Valley, they showed restraint in pushing no farther than the treaty line agreed upon in 1768. Yet all was not complete harmony in British relations with the tribes. Although the warriors and their families continued to receive food, clothing, supplies and ammunition from the king's stores at Detroit, the Indians began to suggest that the British might wish to assume a more active and military role in the war. With growing frustration, the Algonkian chiefs and warriors pointed out that "you [British] and our Brethren the Six Nations have told us long ago to be of one [mind] … We are so, and hope that You will be the same." Therefore, they demanded, "you will now give some proof of it."[44] The British, of course, were quite willing to support and assist the Indian cause, especially by offering an abundance of advice and encouragement, but it was "neither the Interest, nor the Inclination of His Majesty's Government, to commence *Offensive* Hostilities, against the United States."[45]

The twin Indian victories in 1790 and 1791, however, did provide Whitehall with the opportunity to revive a plan, first proposed by Haldimand in November 1783, for the establishment of an Indian barrier state. To this end, George Hammond, the first minister to the United States, was instructed to offer British mediation between the Americans and Indians to create a separate country for the tribes, independent of Great Britain and the United States.[46] The boundary, not surprisingly, would be formed by the Ohio and Mississippi rivers and the Great Lakes. Lord Dorchester was fully supportive of the scheme, for "if the area northwest of the Ohio between the Mississippi and the Lakes shall be secured exclusively to the Indians, and remain neutral ground in respect to Great Britain and the United States, peace between them and the Indians will be restored immediately, and established upon a solid foundation."[47]

The governor quite legitimately and accurately could have added that the scheme for an Indian buffer was designed to protect Canada from the advance north and west of the aggressive, numerous, and assiduously land-grasping American frontier settlers. The price Britain would have to pay in assisting the Indians to this degree was the surrender of the western posts. But nothing transpired. Hammond, as instructed, approached American officials and put forward the feasibility of establishing, through British mediation, a national home for the Indians in the Ohio Valley. The Americans, after minimal debate and reflection, firmly rejected the idea and the offer, subtly suggesting that Britain was not mediating but meddling.

In the midst of this diplomacy, John Graves Simcoe, first lieutenant-governor of the newly created province of Upper Canada, reached his official residence at Navy Hall (Newark) on the Canadian side of the Niagara River. Simcoe had absorbed a deep antipathy for Americans and republicanism in the course of his active military career as commander of the Loyalist provincial corps of Queen's Rangers during the Revolution. He proudly confessed that there was "no person, perhaps, who thinks less of the talents or integrity of Mr. [George] Washington than I do."[48] He had accepted, in consequence, the Canadian appointment in the hope of being instrumental in the reunion of the empire. Among his policy initiatives, therefore, was not only the desire to ensure the security and defence of Upper Canada, for which he developed a rather exalted opinion regarding its military importance in relation to the rest of British North America, but also to strengthen and extend the king's influence in the interior of the continent.[49] To this end, the lieutenant-governor fully supported the proposal of British mediation for the establishment of an Indian barrier state in the Ohio Valley. Yet his enthusiasms for the welfare of the province, which at times did not take into account the wider implications, were not always shared by Dorchester or by the ministers at Whitehall.

Nonetheless, true to his confident and independent nature, Simcoe attempted to facilitate the project for British mediation in the barrier state discussions by instructing Alexander McKee, the most influential officer of the Indian Department among the tribes, to endeavour

> to impress the Indians now meeting from the "farthest parts of Canada" of themselves to solicit the King's good Offices. It is to be extremely desired that this solicitation should be the result of their own spontaneous Reflections; In all cases it will be advisable, after the repeated Assurances of our Neutrality which we have given to Congress, that there should appear on our part nothing like Collusion or any active Interference to inspire them with such a sentiment; a suspicion of that tendency would infallibly tend to defeat the accomplishment of our object; It will also be essential that all the Indian Tribes bordering on the British Possessions, should concur in the solicitation; not only as so numerous a Confederacy would present to the American an encreased accumulation of Hostile Force; but also as a consolation of the Indian Territorial Claims and Rights is requisite to the formation of so extensive a Barrier, as we have in contemplation.[50]

The large gathering of tribes to which Simcoe referred had assembled at the Glaize, "an old buffalo wallow" at the mouth of the Auglaize River, a tributary of the Maumee. At this composite Indian community, a grand council was held in the autumn of 1792 to discuss military and political strategy.[51] The task for McKee was particularly sensitive, since a "general discontent" prevailed among the tribes that they were being "deceived by the british Government."[52] But for the moment, his influence with the chiefs, and denials to the contrary, arrested this growing suspicion. But friction between some of the Algonkian tribes and the Six Nations Iroquois over the Ohio River boundary line continued to fester. Painted Pole, for instance, a Delaware and delegated speaker for the Algonkian tribes, accused the Six Nations of scheming with the Americans. The Iroquois contingent was shocked at this accusation, and Cowkiller, a noted Seneca orator, remarked that "you have talked to us a little too roughly, you have thrown us on our backs."[53] Yet after leaving the council for a private meeting, the chiefs of the Six Nations soon returned and reconciled their differences with the Algonkian tribes by agreeing to the Ohio line. This gesture was followed by a full council resolution to meet with the Americans at Sandusky the following year for the purpose of engaging in a peaceful, honourable and negotiated settlement.

Although the United States accepted the Sandusky peace proposal, a deadly triangle had been formed. The Algonkian tribes, led by the Shawnee, Miami, and Delaware, were adamant about preserving and defending the Ohio River boundary line. The Six Nations Iroquois, in spite of their adherence to the Ohio line in council, were quite prepared to accept the compromise Muskingum-Venango boundary if it meant the difference between peace and war. For the Americans, the proposed Sandusky peace conference provided another opportunity, through a combination of presents, verbal persuasion, or other inducements, to convince the tribes of the merits of accepting a less rigid position. The only alternative for the tribal confederacy would be the renewal of war.

With all parties seemingly carrying hidden agendas, the Algonkian chiefs invited the Six Nations to attend another general council at the Glaize in the spring of 1793, before they went to meet the commissioners of the United States at Sandusky, so that the confederacy would be well prepared and all speak with one mind. At Niagara, Simcoe was optimistic about the outcome of this gathering and offered hopes that

> the proceedings of the Confederacy will be so managed as to assure to the Indians the greatest part of that Territory which His Majesty's Ministers seemed desirous should intervene between Canada and the United States. Brant considers it absolutely necessary for the Indian security.[54]

In addition, and to support the legitimacy of the Indian land claims, Simcoe forwarded to the Glaize a number of valuable documents, maps, charts and treaties which had been used by Sir William Johnson in 1768. The accumulated material showed the Ohio River as the permanent boundary line between Indians and whites in the Ohio Valley.

This information was a source of joy for the tribes, and in early July the confederacy came to a general resolution "not to make peace on any other terms" except on the basis of holding firmly to the Ohio line.[55] With the Indians apparently in agreement with one another, a deputation of about fifty chiefs from several tribes, and including Joseph Brant, carried the message from the confederacy to the American commissioners. A meeting was finally arranged at the Free Mason's Hall in Newark (Niagara), but during the course of the discussions Simcoe noted that Brant, who was interpreting, "seems inclined to give up some cultivated [American] settlements on the North of the Ohio and intimates the Shawanese to be of that opinion."[56] Although the Iroquois had agreed with all the Algonkians at the Glaize to preserve the Ohio line, Brant led the Americans to believe that the confederacy would compromise on this point. Indian unity was fundamental for a successful and peaceful boundary agreement, and this Iroquois betrayal would prove to be a crushing blow for the Algonkian tribes in their struggle for the Ohio Valley.

The Indian deputation returned to the Glaize, where Brant tried to persuade the confederacy to compromise on the Ohio line. His efforts, however, were useless in the face of the shocked and disgusted Algonkians leaders such as Little Turtle, and the Shawnee chiefs Blue Jacket and Captain Johnny. Brant faced further abuse from Creek and Cherokee delegates, recently arrived from the south, who also urged no compromise. Factionalized and frustrated, the confederacy sent a message to the American commissioners demanding that the Ohio River boundary must be the prerequisite for meeting at Sandusky. The commissioners politely refused, suggesting that both sides must make concessions. They did, however, offer money or goods in exchange for any Indian lands ceded.

But, most significant and revealing, and as a strong inducement for peace, the commissioners admitted that the Indian possessed the "right of soil" and that the United States had not acquired full sovereignty over all their lands by the 1783 treaty with Britain:

> We now concede this great point; We by the express authority of the President of the United States, acknowledge the property or right of soil of the great Country above described, to be in the Indian Nations so long as they desire, to occupy the same. We only claim ... the right to pre-emption, or the right of purchasing of the Indian Nations disposed to sell their lands, to the exclusion of all other White People whatever.[57]

Finally, after ten years of hardship, bitterness, and war, the United States had dropped that long-held assumption of exclusive American sovereignty to the land and reverted to the British position that what had been transferred was not the title to Indian territory, but the right to acquire land from the tribes through formal negotiation and purchase. Unfortunately, the admission came ten years too late.

The American reply was unsatisfactory to the chiefs and warriors who remained consistent in the desire to preserve their ancient hunting grounds, agreed upon by solemn agreement in 1768 as beginning at the Ohio River. In addition, the idea of a cash payment for their land was by this point insulting. As the chiefs explained to the commissioners, "Money, to us, is of no value, & to most of us unknown, and as no consideration whatever can induce us to sell the lands on which we get sustenance for our women and children; we hope we may be allowed to point out a mode by which your settlers may be easily removed, and peace thereby obtained. We want Peace; Restore to us our Country and we shall be Enemies no longer."[58] Although impressed with the dignity of the Indian plea, the commissioners realized that further negotiations would be futile. With regrets that no accommodation could be reached, the American peace party returned east. The failure of the proposed Sandusky conference signalled the death knell of the Indian struggle for the Ohio Valley.

For Simcoe at Niagara, the collapse of the peace initiatives, the schism between the Algonkian and Iroquois which was almost certainly irretrievable, and the angry, defiant, yet unpredictable mood of the tribes along the Glaize, were causes for grave concern. If the British now decided to quit the western posts in the face of a third American military offensive into the Ohio country and beyond, he reckoned that the frustrated warriors would "in an instant destroy the settlement and massacre the unfortunate Inhabitants of Upper Canada."[59] His alarm turned to despair when Dorchester informed him that in case of a war with the United States, Upper Canada, which Simcoe considered the "Bulwark of the British Empire in America," would have to be abandoned.[60]

But the dramatic events in the summer of 1793 did not deter Whitehall from attempting to maintain a friendly and conciliatory disposition towards America consistent with the preservation of the western posts. This disposition, however, did not mean to suggest that the Home Department was ready to sacrifice the British-Indian alliance or the idea of some sort of a barrier state. In a reassuring letter to Simcoe, the secretary of state wrote: "Should the event of the present Campaign prove unsuccessful to the American Army under General Wayne I cannot but still hope that the States will open their eyes to the Advantages of a Final Treaty upon the principles you are already acquainted with. – The Muskingum Boundary, – or any other which will leave a sufficient Interval between His Majesty' Provinces and the American States, is the greatest object to aim at."[61]

In an effort to bolster the confidence of the sullen Indian confederacy along the Glaize, Dorchester informed a tribal delegation
at Quebec in the early part of 1794 that "I shall not be surprised if
we are at war with them [the United States] in the course of the
present year; ... I believe our Patience is almost exhausted," in
regard to obtaining a buffer line.[62] To support his prediction,
Dorchester ordered Simcoe to establish a post on the Maumee
with a garrison from Detroit. In the spring, a new post, Fort
Miami, situated near the Indian communities along the Auglaize,
was duly built. For the confederacy, the Dorchester speech, the
building of Fort Miami, the generous distribution of supplies, and
the encouraging speeches of McKee, Elliott, Simon Girty, and
other members of the Indian Department produced an intoxicat-
ing effect. By mid-summer 1794, the British-Indian alliance
appeared strong and secure.

But whilst these events were proceeding, an enemy army was
inching toward the Glaize. The third American military expedition had left Fort Washington in October 1793, after the failure of
the proposed Sandusky peace conference. The commander of the
force was Major-General "Mad Anthony" Wayne, the nickname
stemming from his great personal courage and tactical boldness
during the revolutionary war.[63] Before proceeding too far, the
army was put into winter quarters where the troops were trained
and molded into a disciplined and efficient fighting force, now
called "the Legion." The following spring, Wayne conducted a
careful and methodical advance towards the towns and villages of
the Indian confederacy.

By June 1794 the Americans had reached the site of St. Clair's
old battlefield and constructed a defensive work called Fort
Recovery. Near this fort, Little Turtle struck at Wayne's supply
columns and routed the escort. Elated by their success, which took
place on the hallowed ground of their massive victory of nearly
three years before, the warriors recklessly charged the well-pro-
tected fort and suffered several casualties. This setback so discouraged and alarmed some of the upper lakes tribes that they decided
to return to the safety and relative isolation of their distant villages north and west of Lakes Huron and Superior. Tribal unity,
fragile at best, began to crumble.

The reverse at Fort Recovery, the defection of the lake Indians,
and the absence of the Six Nations left the confederacy depressed
and uncertain. But officers of the British military and Indian
Department tried to sooth and arrest the Indian discontent by
holding councils, receiving tribal delegations, and pointing to the
increased shipments of provisions and gunpowder recently sent to

the reinforced garrison at Fort Miami. Little Turtle and the chief and warriors naturally assumed that this build-up of war supplies was for the use and benefit of the British-Indian alliance. Thus, with the Americans and Indians now both confident and ready to fight each other again, the two sides finally clashed at a place barely five miles from Fort Miami, in an area distinguished by a thick wood, rendered almost inaccessible by a dense growth of underbrush and fallen timber.

The battle of Fallen Timbers commenced on 20 August 1794. The undisciplined militia, conforming to tradition, soon fled in confusion and a rapid pursuit took place for about a mile, until the Indians discovered a strong double line of American regulars advancing steadily towards them with arms trailed. At this same critical moment, Wayne's Kentucky cavalry charged the warriors, who disengaged themselves after about one hour and withdrew behind the fallen timbers. But the Legion infantry, using the bayonet effectively, prodded their adversaries from the underbrush and forced the whole Indian line to retire at an increasingly rapid rate towards the British fort.[64]

As the warriors began to appear and mill about the post, the British commander, deciding that the situation was becoming serious, reported that "I thought it high time to stand to our Arms, fill up all gaps in our Abatis and shut out all communications from the Fort, by fixing our chevaux de Frise."[65] The Indians instantly understood the full meaning of this symbolic act of British isolation. In spite of a decade of promises and encouragement, the inflammatory Dorchester speech, the building and reinforcing of Fort Miami, the tons of supplies and powder sent from Detroit, and the continual assurances of assistance, the British in the moment of crisis were abandoning the tribes. The events at Fallen Timbers and Fort Miami in August of 1794 destroyed the British-Indian alliance and ended the struggle for the Ohio Valley.

For the Indian tribes of the shattered confederacy, the news from Europe only compounded the despair. The French Revolution and outbreak of war with republican France had forced Britain to subordinate colonial affairs to the interest of national defence. Therefore, the American peace mission to London of John Jay, chief justice of the United States, was both timely and welcome. For the United States, the British surrender of the western posts was the cornerstone of the negotiations. But both countries were sincere in wishing to establish a cordial peace and lasting friendship, and the proceedings were thus conducted in a spirit of mutual amicability.[66] Nonetheless, the British, perhaps feeling the pangs of conscience, attempted to reserve a right to mediate on behalf of the Indians in order to obtain an independent territory for the tribes which could also serve the British interest by providing a convenient barrier between America and Canada.

Whitehall therefore considered some terms or conditions in support of the tribes both necessary and appropriate, for "we certainly had no right to cede to America what never belonged to us." In addition, the British ministers quite rightly appreciated that "the Indians had behaved faithfully" as military allies on behalf of the crown, and that in consequence they "have a strong claim upon us."[67] As a result of these rather latent British efforts on behalf of their traditional allies, a compromise solution (article III) was devised whereby the British agreed to evacuate the western posts by 1 June 1796 on the condition that British subjects, American citizens, and Indians could pass freely back and forth at border crossings.[68] The final result was the Jay Treaty (a Treaty of Amity, Commerce and Navigation) signed by Great Britain and the United States in November 1794. The treaty was no doubt a source of great relief for Whitehall, as it avoided a possible Anglo-American war over the Ohio Valley, showed some minimal consideration for the Indian tribes, allowed the British to leave the western posts honourably, and reduced the cost and responsibility of maintaining order in the volatile frontier wilderness.

The subsequent transfer of the western posts was conducted efficiently and without incident. In January 1796 Dorchester instructed Simcoe to perform a survey of the king's stores and posts, destroy everything that could not be removed, and be prepared to evacuate at short notice. On 1 June 1796 George Beckwith, adjutant-general of Upper and Lower Canada, issued a general order to the commanders at Forts Ontario, Niagara, Miami, Detroit, and Michilimackinac to evacuate the posts "with all convenient speed," taking care to prevent any disorders.[69] By 11 August 1796 the last fort was presented to American forces. Formal British imperial involvement in the Ohio Valley had ended.

These events, however, meant little to the tribes of the Ohio Valley who had no alternative after the sad events of 1794 but to accept the offer of Anthony Wayne and negotiate "a General Treaty for the Purpose of removing all causes of Controversy and establishing a permanent Peace between the United States of America and the Indians North West of the Ohio."[70] The final outcome was too obvious: "... the poor Indians must lose their country." Indeed, by the Treaty of Greenville, signed by all the principal tribes of the northwest on 3 August 1795, the Indians ceded to the United States the greater portion of the Ohio Valley.[71] What followed was a large influx of migrants, rapid settlement, and the beginnings of industry, all of which soon destroyed the wilderness, wildlife, and last vestige of the traditional and nomadic life of the indigenous people of the Ohio Valley.

But was the idea of an independent Indian state between the Ohio River and the Great Lakes, which could act as a buffer between Canada and the United States, really a feasible concept, or was it merely a chimera? The Algonkian tribes and Six Nations Iroquois had a long and rancorous history of mutual acrimony, and the common threat to their survival was not sufficient to preserve the confederacy and prevent the advance of the American frontier. The British-Indian alliance also proved to be as fragile and fleeting as that of the United Indian confederacy. British imperial interests certainly did not include provoking a war with America by actively supporting Indian land claims. The reality was that the tribes were caught in the grip of two forces, an empire and a frontier. Neither side was particularly distinguished for mercy, and both were destined to resolve their differences by less costly methods than Indian wars. With the Anglo-American cordiality of 1794, the warriors were no longer useful or a threat. If the Indians had a flicker of a hope in preserving the Ohio Valley, they had to remain strong and united. The constant bickering, factionalism, and final disintegration over the Sandusky peace conference therefore made the pretence of the existence of such a pan-Indian state the merest of fictions.

Yet the decision of the tribes to fight for their lands in the Ohio Valley halted the steady flow north and west of the American frontier for a decade. As a consequence, during these critical years, the new and nearly defenceless Loyalist and Six Nations settlements in Canada were allowed to grow, strengthen, and prosper unhindered by American and republican intrusions. The Constitutional or Canada Act, for instance, which received royal assent in June 1791, provided the basis of government for both the new provinces of Upper Canada and Lower Canada for the next half-century. The act not only introduced the wisdom of parliamentary democracy, which progressed from representative government to responsible government and finally to dominion status within the British empire, but also secured the foundation of an English-speaking upper province.

But in these first desperate years, the survival and security of the province was almost totally dependent on the resolve and fighting skills of the warriors to the south. Therefore, to maintain the British-Indian alliance, Whitehall denied that the crown had forfeited Indian lands in 1783 and deceived the tribes into believing that their struggle for the Ohio Valley would be supported, if necessary, by military assistance. In the final analysis, British Indian policy in the defence of Canada in the years immediately following the American Revolution was based fundamentally on denial and deception, Machiavellian in style – manipulative, cruel, and successful.

PART THREE

In the Defence of Canada,
1796–1815

CHAPTER 5

RENEWING THE CHAIN OF FRIENDSHIP

T he withdrawal of His Majesty's forces from the western posts in the summer of 1796 marked the end of a critical phase in British-Indian relations. But it did not destroy or sever numerous personal and family associations between officers and agents of the crown responsible for the conduct of Indian affairs and those native people and tribes still residing within the territorial boundaries of the United States. In particular, the intimate relationships established between king's men and Indian women on the Ohio and Great Lakes frontiers produced a host of métis or mixed-blood offsprings whose biological, cultural, and linguistic identity created a distinct society which allowed its members to live and participate in two worlds.[1] However, this flexibility and potential additional source of warriors and allies for the crown caused conflicts of interest for men such as Alexander McKee, Matthew Elliott, Simon Girty, William Caldwell, and many others who had close connections within the native communities. As a consequence, policy directives emanating from Whitehall which threatened the Indian cause were sometimes received at field level with such a mixture of chagrin and disdain that the instructions were questioned, compromised, and not always carried out in the expected prompt and efficient manner. Although the officers of the Indian Department were loyal to the king, they struggled and schemed as much to protect their families and Indian way of life as to defend British imperial and vested interests in Canada.

During the St. Clair campaign in the autumn of 1791, for instance, "a great many young Canadians, and in particular many that were born of Indian women, fought on the side of the Indians." Yet it was with the "utmost secrecy" that they left their homes to participate in the actions, "fearful lest the government should censure their conduct."[2] At the Battle of Fallen Timbers in August 1794, both Canadians and Loyalists, dressed as warriors, actively supported the Indians in the field and suffered casualties. Charles Smith, a man of accomplished abilities who was adopted by the Shawnee, "received a shot through the knees, was then quartered alive, th' shocking to relate, nevertheless true."[3] For Alexander McKee, who was married to a Shawnee woman and who had devoted over fifteen years of his life on the frontier to the cause of the tribes of the Ohio Valley, the events at Fallen Timbers and Fort Miami were personally devastating. In his final report on these affairs, so calamitous for the Indian people, he seethed with despair and bitterness, noting that "the American Army have left Evident marks of their boasted Humanity behind them, besides scalping and mutilating the Indians who were killed in Action, they have opened the Peaceful Graves in different parts of the Country, Exposed the Bones of the consumed & consuming Bodies, and horrid to relate have with unparalleled barbarity driven stakes through them and left them objects calling for more than human Vengeance."[4]

For those officers of the Indian Department and all others who had personal and family connections among the tribes, the struggle to preserve Indian lands and cultural values would never end. In the years after 1796 this determination and genuine concern for the welfare of the native people kept alive the bonds of friendship and maintained at least the threads of a British-Indian association. This continued contact was to prove vital for the future success of British Indian policy in the defence of Canada. For although the relationship was badly weakened and tarnished as a result of the abandonment at Fort Miami, what remained unbroken was the traditional symbol and strength of the British-Indian military alliance – the Silver Covenant Chain of Friendship.

In the late summer of 1796 the British formally began the construction of replacement forts on Canadian soil: Fort George at Newark on the west bank of the Niagara River, Fort Amherstburg (Malden) on the Detroit River, and Fort St. Joseph on the island of the same name at the mouth of the St. Mary's River in Lake

Huron.[5] These posts, along with some scattered blockhouses, the naval base at Kingston and Fort York on the north shore of Lake Ontario provided a thin line of fortifications to counter any potential American military threat. The new and less vulnerable capital at York (Toronto) had been established three years earlier by Simcoe as part of his strategic plan for the defence of Upper Canada.

With the relocation of the British garrisons and the advent of peace on the frontier after many years of violent confrontation, the traditional military role and function of the Indian Department would have to be dramatically altered. Pursuant to this change, and at the request of Lord Dorchester, a proposed "Plan for the Future Government of the Indian Department" was prepared in June 1796 by Alexander McKee, since promoted to deputy superintendent general and inspector general of Indian affairs. McKee recommended the appointment of three superintendents and three storekeepers to manage and administer the three new posts, along with interpreters and clerks to assist with related duties.[6]

The work to be assigned to the superintendents was particularly onerous. They would be expected to provide a corporate memory for the department by keeping regular journals of all transactions with the Indians, detailing "the temper, disposition, and apparent views or designs of all the Tribes in their districts" along with a careful audit of available stores and provisions and recording "all the public speeches that have been made on wampum." This accumulative information was to be forwarded either to McKee or the office of the superintendent general for review and deposit. Yet significantly, McKee's report concluded by emphasizing the importance for the officers commanding the posts to continue to use "their utmost diligence to preserve and promote friendship between the Troops and Indians" in order to maintain "that harmony so necessary for the tranquillity of both and the safety of the King's Posts."[7] Indeed, the veteran McKee, fully expecting another eventual conflict with the United States, stressed the absolute necessity of renewing and strengthening the bonds of the alliance against the common enemy, if there was to be even a tenuous hope for the future survival of the Indian people and Canada.

Dorchester, who left Canada permanently in July 1796, fully supported and approved the plan, which contained decided elements of favouritism and nepotism in the recommendation for appointments. In the event, McKee duly appointed William Claus, son of Daniel Claus and a grandson of Sir William Johnson, as superintendent for Fort George; Matthew Elliott, his long-time friend and colleague from the frontier wars, as superintendent for Fort Amherstburg; and Thomas McKee, his own son, who possessed a "general knowledge of the person, Characters, and Languages of most of the Indian Nations," as superintendent for Fort St. Joseph.[8] Thus restructured to reflect the new peacetime initiatives of British Indian policy, the department, now transplanted in Canada, continued in the performance of its duties.

But the prestige, influence, and effectiveness of the reorganized department with the tribes had waned significantly since Fallen Timbers. In the autumn of 1794 the starving and disgruntled Indian allies, encamped at Swan Creek on the north side of the Maumee, were amply provisioned with commodities of flour, pork, beef, "pease," butter, rice, and corn from the king's stores at Detroit.[9] Yet they remained sullen and aloof to the entreaties of the officers of the department to relocate in Canada. Most of the tribes, following the Treaty of Greenville, spent a second harsh winter at Swan Creek, stubbornly refusing to move north, receive gifts and provisions, or settle at the proposed site of Chenail Ecarté (now Walpole Island Indian Reserve), just a few miles north of Lake St. Clair.[10]

In spite of the repeated efforts of the Indian Department, only a few hundred, not the expected thousands, eventually trekked north. Quite clearly, most of the Indians were reluctant to leave their ancient homelands in the Ohio Valley in spite of the fact that their future welfare and even survival was now to be determined by their recent and hated enemies, the Americans. By 1797-98, therefore, the British Indian Department, accustomed to wartime flexibility and relatively free and liberal spending, was returned to a rigid routine which accentuated the strict accounting of gifts and supplies to the Indians. This reduced role produced frustration, bickering, and jealousies within the department. Added to these unfortunate circumstances, and compounded by the fact that the expenses of the department were defrayed from the army budget, was a series of nasty conflicts between the superintendents and post commanders over military and jurisdictional authority and areas of responsibility in the management and administration of Indian affairs.

Apart from this domestic feuding at the new posts, crown officials reckoned that Indian affairs in Canada in the post–1796 years could now be conducted in an atmosphere of comparative peace and tranquillity. As most of the tribal allies preferred to remain on their traditional hunting grounds within the territorial boundaries of the United States, they were happily beyond the jurisdiction of the British officers and Indian agents. Nonetheless, the potentially volatile relationship which continued to exist between the tribes and the Americans over land acquisition kept the British wary of any events to the south which could endanger the security of Upper Canada. Yet, surprisingly, the crisis which soon erupted came not from the United States but from within Canada and originated among the indigenous Mississauga Ojibwa and recently arrived Mohawk and other Iroquois of Grand River.

For years the Mississauga had been surrendering, through formal agreements, vast tracts of their traditional hunting grounds throughout the southern portions of the province.[11] These land cessions were to allow for the peaceful and orderly settlement of the United Empire Loyalists and other settlers. By the mid-1790s, the Mississauga had come to the painful realization that the loss of their lands, combined with the rapid growth of settlement, was destroying the basic economic and cultural fabric of their lives. As a result of these mounting concerns, they began to complain to the provincial authorities about the extensive amount of surveying being undertaken without permission on unceded lands. These complaints were followed by confrontations with surveying parties. The Mississauga accused the British of being "as bad as the Americans in taking away their lands," and in consequence they would take the cattle of the settlers instead of trying to hunt the rapidly depleting deer.[12]

But the festering problem of unresolved land issues was overshadowed in August 1796 by the brutal beating death of Wabukanyn, the experienced and "greatly beloved" chief of the Credit River band of Mississauga.[13] The details are rather gruesome. The chief and his family had come to York to barter salmon for rum. About midnight, a soldier of the Queen's Rangers, a provincial corps in garrison at Fort York and throughout the province, and two settlers attempted to rape Wabukanyn's sister.[14] Half-asleep and somewhat drunk, the old chief in trying to protect her was knocked senseless by a rock and pummelled with fists and boots. He died within hours. The soldier was subsequently acquitted "for want of evidence," as no Indians attended the trial. There were no other convictions.[15]

Not surprisingly, the Wabukanyn incident only heightened racial tensions in the province, especially around York and north to Lake Simcoe. Yet the Mississauga were equally angry at what they perceived to be a growing British contempt for them. Following the surrender of much of their lands, the government had ceased the ancient ceremony of gift-giving, which to the Mississauga signified friendship and their importance as allies. They observed with a mixture of envy and jealousy the lavish amounts of presents and provisions apparently being bestowed upon tribes in the United States. Further, they were insulted that no officer of the Indian Department was assigned at York to deal with their specific concerns. The Mississauga reasoned, therefore, and with some accuracy, that, with the surrender of much of their lands, the British must regard them as weak, ineffectual, and of little use.

At a council at York in November 1796, band chiefs from Lake Simcoe complained that their people had been "thrown away" by the government.[16] Their talk of violence and threats of revenge against the inhabitants of the province for the death of Wabukanyn worried Peter Russell, the administrator of Upper Canada. In a letter to Simcoe, now in England and just appointed to a new assignment as commander-in-chief at San Domingo in the British West Indies, Russell suggested that "something should be done to conciliate the affections of the tribes in the rear of York, who, for want of some attention, may become unfriendly to the British name and harass the back settlements by their depredations."[17]

Yet at the same time as Russell was pondering a resolution to Mississauga grievances, a controversy erupted with Joseph Brant over the sale and distribution of the Mohawk lands on the Grand River. For Brant, the failure in 1793 of his dream for a united Indian confederation, followed by the British abandonment of their tribal allies between 1794 and 1796, had shattered any illusions he may have continued to harbour on the possibility of defending the traditions, interests, and rights of native people. Like the Mississauga, the Mohawk leader admitted that his vanity and "feelings are much hurt" because the apparently disrespectful British had not shown or placed confidence in him during those critical times. In a letter to his friend Joseph Chew, secretary of the Indian Department, Brant bitterly denounced the move to evacuate the western posts, noting that "this is the second time the poor Indians have been left in the lurch." Although he was "formally in full courage to use my utmost endeavour to promote the welfare of the Indians and English Inhabitants," those thoughts were now "entirely at an end, and I am entirely discouraged from attempting to say any thing further on Public matter."[18] In fact, by the autumn of 1796 Brant had turned from high idealism to the more practical concerns of financial self-interest and land sale profits.

In early November, Brant acquired the power of attorney to sell Indian lands along the Grand River; and this authority was acknowledged and signed by thirty-five chiefs of the Six Nations Confederacy.[19] His intention was to allow non-natives the opportunity to purchase "blocks" of the approximately 570,000 acres of land, which constituted the Haldimand Grant of 1784, in order to create a trust fund for the future welfare and benefit of the Grand River people. Later in the month, Brant met with William Claus at the Indian Department Council House near Fort George to obtain a legal deed of transfer to the Grand River lands. At the meeting, the Mohawk entrepreneur argued that the Haldimand Grant constituted the creation of an estate in fee simple and recognized the Six Nations as a sovereign nation competent to arrange and manage its own affairs.[20]

Superintendent Claus responded by first reminding Brant that the dispossessed Mohawk and others of the Six Nations Confederacy of Iroquois, as a non-indigenous people, had no aboriginal "right of soil" in the province. Secondly, by accepting "a Safe and Comfortable Retreat" along the Grand River, they had put themselves under the protection of the crown. Not only did they have no status as a sovereign nation in Canada, but, by accepting the protection of the crown, their status had changed from faithful allies to loyal subjects who owed allegiance to the crown.[21] Furthermore, concluded Claus, as for the nature and authority for disposing Indian lands, that question had been addressed and settled by the Royal Proclamation of 7 October 1763, which stated in part:

> And whereas great Frauds and Abuses have been committed in purchasing Lands of the Indians to the great Prejudice of our Interests and to the great Dissatisfaction of the said Indians, ... to prevent such Irregularities for the future, and to the end that the Indians may be convinced of our Justice and determined Resolution to remove all reasonable Cause of Discontent, We do ... require, that no private Person do presume to make any Purchase from the said Indians of any Lands reserved to the said Indians, within those parts of our Colonies where, We have thought proper to allow Settlement; but that, if at any Time any of the said Indians should be inclined to dispose of the said Lands, the same shall be Purchased only for Us in our Name.[22]

Brant, furious at the rejoinder put forward by Claus, tried to explain that the Iroquois, conditioned as warriors, made indifferent farmers, that his people could no longer survive on hunting, and that therefore their only recourse was to sell parts of the grant in order to obtain some form of financial relief. The efforts to convince Claus, however, were in vain, and Brant's mission ended in failure. Undeterred, he travelled to Philadelphia early in 1797 to lay his grievances before Robert Liston, the resident British minister in the United States. Liston was impressed by Brant, calling him "so determined, so able, and so artful."[23] But the minister also expressed "a degree of uneasiness for the possible consequences" if the Grand River land controversy was not soon resolved. He therefore suggested that it might be prudent and "proper to soothe him as much as possible by giving him hopes that matters would ultimately be settled to his satisfaction."[24]

By the summer of 1797 the tensions created between government authorities and both the Mississauga and Joseph Brant occasioned wild rumours in Upper Canada that an Indian war was soon to erupt. Added to this speculation were vague reports of a threatened invasion of the province "by French and Spaniards from the Mississippi" in support of the Indians.[25] These alarms pushed senior crown officials in Britain and Canada quickly to formulate and implement an Indian policy based on conciliation and divide and rule. In September, Russell received the approved strategy, marked secret and confidential, from the Duke of Portland, secretary of state at the Home Department. First among his instructions, and in accordance with the request of the Mississauga, was to appoint an Indian agent at York. But

> the primary duty of the new appointee is fomenting the jealousy which subsists between them and the Six Nations, and of preventing, as far as possible, any junction or good understanding taking place between those two tribes. It appears to me that the best and safest line of Policy to be pursued in the Indian Department is to keep the Indians separate and unconnected with one another, as by this means they will be in proportion more dependent on the King's Government.[26]

These instructions were re-emphasized two months later by Portland, who stressed the "strict attention to every possible means of preventing connections or confederations from taking place between the several Nations, and that the rendering of them dependent upon Your Government, and keeping them as separate and distinct as possible from each other," must be the system applied of which "on no account, you should ever depart."[27] Russell duly complied, and James Givins was appointed Indian agent at York.[28] The Mississauga would no longer be required to go to Fort George, thus negating their chances of meeting and exchanging views with the Mohawk at nearby Grand River.

The second act of conciliation was to satisfy the demands of Joseph Brant. To this end, Russell convened a meeting of his executive council at York in early February 1798 where Brant appeared "and declared that he came at the Desire of the five Nations settled on the Grand River, to surrender to the King in their Name a Certain Portion of the lands they held there under a Grant from the late Sir Frederick Haldimand." Council readily and unanimously agreed to this proviso, which formally transferred to the crown the Indian "interest" in those specified tracts of Grand River land that they wished to sell.[29] In conformity, therefore, with the mechanism as stipulated in the Royal Proclamation of 1763, the crown then sold on behalf of the Iroquois the designated tracts, approximately 352,000 acres, to various non-native purchasers with whom Brant, as attorney, was negotiating.

In the following few months there remained some concerns over a potential alliance of tribes in the province, especially when the Mississauga formally appointed Brant as their guardian and agent for all future land sales. But a confederation of Mississauga and Mohawk, who were traditional enemies, was dubious at best, and expressions at this time of mutual friendship were in reality superficial. Furthermore, and as expected, the reports of a French and Spanish invasion and intrigue among the tribes proved to be nonsense. By the end of 1799, therefore, with the Mississauga pacified and Joseph Brant soothed, to all intents and purposes the crisis in Upper Canada was over. The scare, however, had produced an intriguing anomaly which has not previously been considered in scholarly assesments of the period. The inconsistency of 1797–99 was that as a result of the province being threatened by internal rather than the usual external forces, this was the first and only occasion in which British Indian policy in the defence of Canada was actually and deliberately designed to prevent, rather than encourage, the formation of a strong and effective confederation of Indian tribes.

In the years that followed, the Mississauga continued to cede their lands for scant remuneration, of which the 1805 surrender was the most notable. They began increasingly to suffer the evils of disease and an absolute devotion to rum. Being a wandering society based on hunting and gathering, the steady and rapid development of settlement in the province, which soon depleted the forest game, destroyed the basic traditional structures of Mississauga economic and social life. In the late 1790s an astute Irish traveller who was passing through Upper Canada perhaps

Sir William Johnson, 1715–74.
National Archives of Canada, C5197

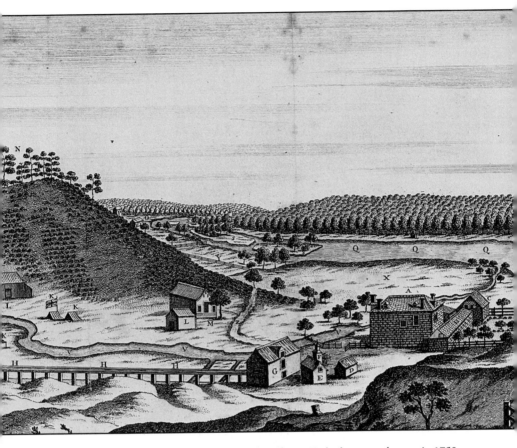

A View of Fort Johnson, Mohawk Valley of New York, drawn on the spot in 1759
by Guy Johnson.
National Archives of Canada, C3442

Council beween Indians assembled and Colonel Henry Bouquet, 1764, by Benjamin West.

National Archives of Canada, C299

Joseph Brant (Thayendanegea), c. 1742–1807, painted by George Romney.
National Archives of Canada, C11092

Lieutenant-General John Burgoyne addressing the Indian allies, summer 1777,
drawn by H. Warren, engraved by J.C. Armytage.
National Archives of Canada, C17514

Sir Frederick Haldimand, 1718–91.
National Archives of Canada, C18298

The Council House.

The Mohawk Church

THE MOHAWK VILLAGE, GRAND RIVER, 1793
(From a Drawing by Lieutenant Pilkington copied by Mrs Simcoe)

The Mohawk Village, Grand River, 1793, with the "neat little church" situated prominently on the right, from a drawing by Lieutenant Pilkington, copied by Mrs. John Graves Simcoe.
National Archives of Canada, C84448

A view of Cataraqui (Kingston), July 1784, by James Peachey. Molly Brant settled here after the American Revolution. A devout adherent to the Church of England and a staunch Mohawk Loyalist, she regularly attended service at St. George's, where she "sat in an honourable place among the English." She died in April 1796 and was placed in the lower burial ground of St. George's (now the site of St. Paul's Anglican Church).

National Archives of Canada, C1512.

The Great Indian Council, 1793, by Lewis Foy. The artist provides no hint as to where this conference took place. However, the struggle for the Ohio Valley and the proposed Sandusky Conference in 1792–93 were popular topics during this period.

Montreal Museum of Fine Arts, MBAM1027

unwittingly explained the fundamental and entrenched philosophy of the Mississauga and Ojibwa people. He observed that "they have no idea of amassing wealth for themselves individually; and they wonder that persons can be found in any society so destitute of every generous sentiment, as to enrich themselves at the expense of others, and to live in ease and affluence regardless of the misery and wretchedness of members of the same community to which they themselves belong."[30] The integrity of these native people, with their refusal to emulate the values so prized by the aggressive and dominant newcomers (who descended in droves to settle on Indian lands) must in retrospect at least be acknowledged, if not respected.

For Joseph Brant, the subsequent sale of blocks of Grand River land, ostensibly to alleviate the economic condition of his people, appeared only to have augmented his personal wealth. Nonetheless, he continued to push his vision for improving the welfare and prosperity of the Iroquois through a policy of Indian integration and acculturation with the surrounding non-native communities. The programs included intermarriage with whites and the promotion of education, agriculture, and the Anglican religion.[31] He was assisted in these efforts by his deputy and eventual successor, John Norton (Teyoninhokarawen), an individual of mixed Scotch-Cherokee ancestry whom Brant had adopted as "a nephew."[32] The policy, however, disturbed the traditional Longhouse people of the Grand, and this alienation may have influenced Brant to move to Burlington Heights at the head of Lake Ontario, where he built a grand home and lived in the style of Sir William Johnson.

Although impressed with the power, wealth, and technology of the British and Americans, Brant's ethnic identity sometimes clashed with his cultural policy. Whilst in England, for instance, he "chiefly admired the ladies and the horses," but thought "the palaces and prisons among you form a most dreadful contrast."[33] Like the Mississauga and other Indian tribes, he was shocked at the harshness and cruelty exhibited in some elements of British society, especially in the deep-seated division between rich and poor which was so anathema to the traditional shared values and communal life of the Mohawk people.

Brant spent his last years engaged in further gnawing land disputes with government officials and especially with William Claus, who with the death of Alexander McKee in 1799, had become deputy superintendent general and inspector general of Indian affairs, second only to Sir John Johnson in Montreal. Joseph Brant – Mohawk warrior, chief, Loyalist, Anglican, statesman, and entrepreneur – died on 24 November 1807 at his Burlington Heights estate, removed from his people on the Grand River and far away from his beloved homeland in the Mohawk Valley. He ended his days unfulfilled in his dreams and ambitions, and in some anguish over the still unresolved question of Indian lands. To John Norton at his bedside, his last words were "have pity on the poor Indians: if you can get any influence with the great, endeavour to do them all the good you can."[34] It was both a plea and a prophetic warning for the future conduct of Mohawk-government relations in Canada.

During the years between 1796 and 1807 the Mississauga and Joseph Brant had been almost constantly engaged in matters of land surrenders and disputes with British officials in Canada. At the same time, the recent and ex-Indian allies of the crown just south of the international boundary were equally involved in land questions, but with the frontier people and government of the United States. After the battle of Fallen Timbers, Anthony Wayne had been instructed to obtain a firm cession of Indian lands to the greater part of the Ohio Valley. In anticipation of this result, a confident Timothy Pickering, secretary of war, wrote to the general in April 1795, four months before the signing of the Treaty of Greenville, reassuring him that "when a peace shall once be established, and we also take possession of the posts now held by the British, we can obtain every thing we shall want with a tenth part of the trouble and difficulty which you would now have to encounter."[35] What the United States consistently wanted, of course, was all the Indian land from the Ohio to the Mississippi.

But after years of tough, bitter, and expensive Indian wars on the frontier, and against particularly tenacious tribes, the Congress was anxious for westward expansion to proceed peacefully. Therefore, in April 1796 it created a system of government-operated trading houses which offered a liberal, friendly, and non-profit trade with the Indian tribes. In addition, a series of acts "to regulate trade and intercourse" with the tribes was passed which forbade settlement on unceded Indian lands and applied severe licensing restrictions on traders. The establishment of this so-called factory system, which was intended to promote peace and friendship and introduce "civilization" to the tribes, formed the basis of American Indian policy until the Indian Removal Act of May 1830.[36]

Like the Society of Friends, the British and Foreign Bible Society (Clapham sect), and various evangelical groups, missionary societies, and philanthropic organizations in Britain and Canada who were devoted to improving the spiritual and economic life of aboriginal peoples throughout the world, a "moral"

Indian policy was also popular within certain influential segments of American society.[37] One of the staunchest adherents of this new morality and civilization for the betterment of Indians was Thomas Jefferson, president of the United States from 1801 to 1809. In a special message to Congress in January 1803, he urged the continuation of the government trading houses in order to encourage the tribes "to abandon hunting, to apply to the raising stock, to agriculture, and domestic manufacture, and thereby prove to themselves that less land and labor will maintain them in this better than in their former mode of living." To Jefferson, the necessity of bringing civilization to the Indians was a duty, for "humanity enjoins us to teach them agriculture and the domestic arts to encourage them to the industry which alone can enable them to maintain their place in existence and to prepare them in time for that state of society which to bodily comforts adds the improvement of the mind and morals."

Yet this Jeffersonian philanthropy and idealism towards the American Indian contained a brutal and practical side when placed beside the driving United States impetus for westward expansion and the rapid acquisition of land. This fundamental conflict in policy was starkly expressed by the president in a private letter to William Henry Harrison, governor of Indiana Territory, only one month after his special message to the Congress. Although alluding to humanitarian concerns for Indian welfare, with hopes that they would in time incorporate into American society, Jefferson stressed that he would tolerate no opposition to the expansionist ambitions of the United States and "should any tribe be foolhardy enough to take up the hatchet at any time, the seizing the whole country of that tribe, and driving them across the Mississippi, as the only condition of peace, would be an example to others and a furtherance of our final consolidation."[38]

In both Canada and the United States during these years, in similar fashion, individuals like Joseph Brant and Thomas Jefferson promoted and encouraged Indian civilization and Christianization through integration (including intermarriage), assimilation, and acculturation. Brant attained modest success among his own people, who were already surrounded by non-native communities, but faced opposition from Mohawk elders and the traditionals of the Longhouse. The wandering Mississauga and other Ojibwa, however, refused to comply, and many simply drifted north to areas of the province still well within the limits of their traditional territory, where no settlement would reach them for years. Thomas Jefferson, whilst never acknowledging as much, failed in his efforts to convert Indians into white Americans.

Although the priority in Canada and the United States was the acquisition of Indian land, with both governments forcing treaties and surrenders on their respective resident tribes, serious Indian resistance took place only in the United States. The reasons were straightforward: Canada, a British province, served as a convenient sanctuary from the Americans for many of the tribes; and the lack of numbers and military strength of the Ojibwa people, combined with the option of preserving their traditional lifestyle of hunting and fishing by migrating north and away from "civilization," resulted in nothing more than occasional alarms and a war scare in Upper Canada.

In the United States, however, the Indian tribes on the frontier were more warlike and conditioned to fighting the American backwoodsmen and settlers. Furthermore, the tribes there did not possess the luxury of moving to remote and uninhabited regions. The Ohio Valley tribes, for instance, had lost their ancient homelands by 1796 and, not wishing to go to Canada, could only retreat west towards the Mississippi, in the same direction as the advancing Americans. But by so doing, these tribes would soon intrude onto the traditional lands of other Indian people, some of whom were old enemies. In the event, the dispossessed Ohio Valley tribes, joined by a few others, had become increasingly frustrated and resentful at the loss of their lands and their ever worsening conditions. Sullen, but desperate, they sat along the Wabash in Indiana Territory, at the very western limits of their traditional territory, and miles from the Maumee in Ohio where they had lived only a few years before. With virtually no place left to turn, the tribes were perplexed and disorganized. All they needed was a sign, a Messiah.

In 1805 a saviour miraculously did appear in the dubious form of a one-eyed, epileptic Shawnee with a drinking problem, named Lalawethika. Born about 1775 in the Shawnee village of Old Piqua in the Ohio Valley, his mission began following his awakening either from a trance or from a particularly severe bout of "sickness" in which he had apparently met the Indian Master of Life. The experience was inspirational and resulted in his proclaiming himself to be a prophet and changing his name to Tenskwatawa (from the saying of Jesus, "I am the door"). The Shawnee prophet was soon preaching a doctrine espousing a pure life "beautiful and sweet" which embodied a return to traditional Indian religious and communal values.[39] This emotional appeal to the native people broadened into an anti-American doctrine which suggested that they might be defeated by supernatural means. In part the revelation read:

I am the Father of the English of the French, of the Spaniards and of the Indians ... But the Americans I did not make. They are not my children but the children of the Evil Spirit. They grew from the scum of the great water when it was troubled by the Evil Spirit and the froth was driven into the woods by a strong east wind. They are very numerous but I hate them. They are unjust – they have taken away your lands which were not made for them.[40]

The teachings of the Prophet found a receptive audience among the despairing tribes of Ohio and Indiana. Other tribes from the upper lakes and the Mississippi Valley soon flocked to hear the rhetoric and embrace the faith. After first establishing a village at Greenville in western Ohio, the Prophet moved to a new settlement, Prophetstown, at the mouth of the Tippecanoe River in Indiana, a location farther to the west where the hunting was better and at a greater distance from the American frontier. In time, the charismatic Prophet rallied and united the tribes into a new confederacy in which the chiefs and warriors exhibited a renewed and confident resolve to fight.

The chances of the Indian Confederacy successfully defending their land was improved in June 1807 as a result of an international incident at sea. In what became known as the Chesapeake affair, the HMS *Leopard* fired three broadsides into the USS *Chesapeake*, killing and wounding some Americans, then boarded the crippled American frigate and removed suspected deserters. Since 1803, with the renewal of war in Europe, Anglo-American relations had been steadily deteriorating and this incident produced a wave of anti-British sentiment in the United States. During these years, both Britain and Napoleonic France had adopted maritime policies that severely damaged the commercial shipping and profits of neutral nations such as the new United States. But with Britain supreme at sea, the Royal Navy was by far the worst offender in disrupting the flow of neutral shipping. For the Americans, the confiscation of cargoes and impressment of men had become particularly sensitive and irritating issues. In an effort to defend national honour and the principle of "Free Trade and Sailors' Rights," Jefferson imposed the Non-Importation Act, followed by the Embargo Act which closed United States ports to all foreign shipping. The effect of these retaliatory measures, however, only caused worsening economic conditions along the Atlantic seaboard and encouraged smuggling with Canada.[41]

The economic hardships were not confined solely to the east; in the south and along the western frontier, Americans were also suffering as a result of the war in Europe and Jefferson's embargoes. Much of the frustration and anger was directed at Britain, and the Chesapeake affair only intensified the mood. In the west particularly, the talk was of striking a blow at Britain by taking Canada, since there appeared to be no method of delivering an effective maritime response. The annexation of Canada, a long-held ambition, would also destroy any further British political and economic influence in North America, whilst at the same time removing any possible future threats of another British-Indian alliance.[42] Along the northern frontier, especially with the rise of the Prophet, the conviction was widespread that once again British intrigue was behind the tribal unrest. Harrison, for instance, viewed the Chesapeake crisis as a signal from the British to the Prophet and the Indian Confederacy to attack the American back settlements, "for who does not know that the tomahawk and the scalping knife of the savages are always employed as the instruments of British vengeance. At this moment ... their agents are organizing a combination amongst the Indians within our limits for the purpose of assassination and murder."[43]

In the summer of 1807 this type of speculation was mere paranoia. Yet most Americans living in the western regions clung to a perception that the British in Canada were behind every instance of Indian opposition to the advance of the frontier. Therefore, a general and popular feeling prevailed, and with considerable reason, that "the Indian problem" on the American frontier could be permanently resolved, or at least significantly reduced, if the imperial presence was removed from Canada. Impetus for accomplishing this objective was soon provided by the influential "War Hawks," a coterie of aggressive, determined, impatient and anti-British congressmen, mainly from the west, who urged war: "The power of Britain must be extinguished in America. She must no longer be permitted to corrupt the principles and disturb the peace and tranquillity of our citizens. Our frontier inhabitants must not be kept in dread and danger from her Indian allies. And never shall we be secure among ourselves, and exempt from the mischievous intrigues of Europeans, until European power is expelled across the Atlantic."[44]

For the chiefs and warriors of the Prophet's confederacy, who were preparing to engage the Americans alone, the subsequent events surrounding the Chesapeake affair had created an unexpected opportunity for cooperation with their old British friends and allies in Canada. The incident had provoked angry Americans into demanding once again that Canada must and should become a part of the United States. For Americans, this annexation was a divine right in that "the Author of Nature has marked our limits in the south, by the Gulf of Mexico; and on the north, by the regions of eternal frost."[45] For the ambitious "War Hawks," of course, who had seized control of the Congress, this prospect was exciting, for they recognized that in the process of satisfying national honour, the expansion of the American frontier could proceed not just west, but north, into the fertile and sparsely populated lands of Canada. The threat to Canada after 1807 was starkly real. Therefore, the Indians of the confederacy had every hope that in the interest of mutual protection and survival against the common enemy, an offer might be made to them from Canada to renew the covenant chain of friendship.

Such an offer was indeed forthcoming, and especially from the vulnerable and weakly defended frontier province of Upper Canada, where the Chesapeake affair and the bellicose American reaction produced a much more severe war panic than the local Indian scare of ten years before. In the summer of 1807 only a few detachments of British regulars were in garrison at the various posts scattered throughout the province, and the militia were so ill-armed that Lieutenant-Governor Francis Gore decided against calling a general muster so that the Americans would not be aware of the general weakness. The precarious position of the province was further jeopardized by the strategy devised at Whitehall for the defence of Canada.

These "secret instructions" were provided to Sir James Craig, the new captain-general and governor-in-chief of British North America. The first and clear objective of the plan was "to preserve [the fortress of] Quebec, to which all other Considerations must be subordinate." As for Upper Canada, Craig could use his own discretion in deciding "the extent of the resistance you may think it prudent then to make in case the American States shall attack it in force."[46] In early December 1807 Craig informed Gore of the defence plans, and commented that as a result of the strategic priorities, "it would be vain for us to flatter ourselves with the hopes of making any effectual defence of the open country, unless powerfully assisted from home." Yet in the same despatch he mused that in the event of a war the Indians would not be idle, and if the British did not use them, they would undoubtedly be "employed against us." Therefore, Craig reasoned, why not summon the chiefs and warriors, hold meetings and conciliate them, but without making any commitments, at least in "public."[47]

During the winter of 1807–8, Craig developed these ideas into a policy for the frontier which was to guide the conduct of the Indian Department for the next three years. He was aware of the of friendship that traditionally existed between the king and the Indians, and that the tribes of the Prophet's confederacy were trying to protect themselves against the Americans, "who obviously desired to take their country." For Craig, there was a linkage between these two themes which could be used to advantage in promoting a renewal of the British-Indian alliance. He therefore informed Gore that "the officers of the Indian Department must be diligent and active, the communication must be constant, these Topicks must be held up to them not merely in Great Councils and public Assemblies, they should be privately urged to some of their leading men, with whom endeavours should be used to lead them to a confidence in us."[48]

The dual Indian policy formulated by Craig, one public and one private, was reminiscent of Haldimand's successful strategy of 1783. The salient features of both policies were to win the allegiance of the tribes by impressing upon them the wisdom of preserving a friendship with the British in the face of American westward expansion. In late January 1808 Gore, who had received several despatches from Craig, sent secret instructions to William Claus at Fort George, directing him to proceed forthwith to Amherstburg, the key Indian centre in the province, where he was to summon the chiefs, "consult privately" with them, and remind the tribes of the "Artful and Clandestine manner in which the Americans have obtained possession of their lands, and of their obvious intention of ultimately possessing themselves of the whole and driving the Indians out of the Country."[49] However, cautioned Gore, the officers of the Indian Department were to dissuade the chiefs from undertaking any warlike action, until or unless the British were actually at war with the United States.

Yet in order to implement this policy successfully, which required delicate and intricate negotiations, Craig needed officers of experience and high quality in the Indian Department. These considerations were particularly important in 1808, since "the Indian Nations owing the long continuance of Peace have been neglected by us, and from the considerable curtailments made in the Presents to those People it appears, that the retaining their attachment to the King's Interests has not of late years been thought an object worthy of serious consideration."[50] In response to the legitimate concerns expressed by Craig, a number of administrative changes were made in the department, of which the most significant was the reinstatement of Matthew Elliott, "the only man capable of calling forth the energies of the Indians," as superintendent at Amherstburg.[51]

Following the completion of these necessary and appropriate internal arrangements, William Claus, Matthew Elliott, and other officers of the Indian Department initiated their crucial assignment of regaining the affections of the Indians by inviting them to meet in general councils at the king's posts in Canada. The invitation was extended broadly, but the chiefs and warriors of the Prophet's confederacy were, of course, particularly pleased to receive such an offer. In consequence, and throughout the spring and summer of 1808, various tribal delegations from Prophetstown travelled to Amherstburg to listen to the British rhetoric. In late March, for instance, a Shawnee contingent arrived, led by Captain Johnny, Blackbeard, and the Buffalo. William Claus, not unaccustomed to the diplomatic rituals, conducted this meeting and all subsequent gatherings with due respect for the ancient ceremonies, including the giving of gifts. His message, repeated again and again over the next several months, was direct and simple. The king, he stated, desired peace with the United States, but if these hopes were dashed, the Indians could expect to hear from the British, and together they would regain the country taken from them by the Americans.

Heartened by the prospects of a renewed British-Indian alliance, delegations gathered in increasing numbers at Amherstburg to meet and plan strategy with the British. Although a number of Indian dignitaries had come to Amherstburg, the Prophet had followed the instructions of the Great Spirit and remained among his followers at Tippecanoe. This decision was a disappointment for officials such as Gore, Claus, and Elliott, who fully understood that winning the public support of the acknowledged leader of the Indian Confederacy would be a significant step in achieving the goals of Craig's frontier and Indian policy. But in July 1808, Gore reported that "the Prophet's brother, who is stated to me to be his principle support and who appears to be a very shrewd intelligent man, was at Amherstburg while I was there."[52]

This man, of course, was Tecumseh (Tech-kum-thai), since immortalized in Canada and the United States as one of the greatest Indian leaders of all time. He was born about 1768 in the Ohio Valley, possibly at the Shawnee village of Piqua on the Mad River (near present-day Springfield, Ohio). Although his father was Shawnee, his mother may have had a Creek connection, which was not uncommon in his tribe, as there was a strong historical link between Creek and Shawnee. This connection accounts for Tecumseh's desire to visit among the southern tribes in 1811–12, where he promoted the idea of a united Indian confederation.

During the long years of warfare between the Shawnee and the American backwoodsmen, mainly Kentuckians, his father and a brother were killed. As a warrior, Tecumseh fought for the confederacy organized by Little Turtle, and was particularly active at the battle of Fallen Timbers. In the years after the Treaty of Greenville he was a band chief and lived at several locations. But with the rise of the Prophet and the formation of a new Indian confederacy, Tecumseh joined his brother at Tippecanoe and worked in support of the tribal alliance.[53]

In July 1808, Tecumseh and about one hundred chiefs and warriors sat through the hours of innocuous public councils at Amherstburg, listening to the standard British appeal for friendship. But the real alliances and formulation of strategy took place following the formal pomp and ceremony in "private communications with confidential chiefs" like Tecumseh, where the British entertained hopes of a "cordial assistance if we show ourselves in any force to join them." At one of these private follow-up sessions, Tecumseh informed Claus and Elliott that the different Indian nations were collecting on the Wabash at Prophetstown in order to preserve their country from all encroachments: "Their intention at present is not to take part in the quarrels of the white people: that if the Americans encroach upon them they are resolved to strike – but he added that if their father the King should be in earnest and appear in sufficient force they would hold fast by him."[54] Tecumseh, his manner both frank and honest, was impressive. Where the Prophet was charismatic, Tecumseh was dedicated and disciplined. His absolute priority was to preserve and defend the lands and cultural values of his people, yet in the years ahead he also became one of the most important and valuable Indian allies of the British crown in their defence of Canada.

Although the tribes in the United States, hoping for a renewal of the British-Indian alliance against the Americans, responded with eager enthusiasm at the request for meetings, the Mississauga and Mohawk in Canada showed little inclination to entertain, cooperate with, or even listen to the king's officials. At York the lack of any correspondence or reports by James Givins on the subject strongly suggests that the local Mississauga were not interested in making any military commitments with the British in the event of an American war. In 1808 there were still racial tensions and incidents of abuse against them by soldiers and settlers. By this time, many of the Mississauga had already drifted north to Lake Simcoe, the Saugeen peninsula, and to other Ojibwa lands in the more remote areas of the province. Yet during the War of 1812 the Ojibwa people in general were loyal and active participants in support of the British crown. In April 1813, for instance, Mississauga warriors under James Givins assisted in providing a futile, but "spirited opposition" to the invading Americans at the battle of York during the War of 1812.[55]

The Mohawk and other Six Nations Iroquois along the Grand River also demonstrated little enthusiasm for supporting the efforts of the Indian Department. The Iroquois had already suffered cruelly during the American colonial rebellion, and especially in Sullivan's campaign of 1779; and Joseph Brant had taught them to remember the British betrayals in 1783 and 1794. Therefore, when a few Iroquois chiefs reluctantly agreed to meet Claus at the Fort George Indian Council House in August 1808, they assembled for the purpose of informing him "of the great distress they are in for Bread" – an indication that Brant's trust fund was not successful – but "that they had come to a Determination to sit quiet in case of any quarrel between the King and America and not to spill the Blood of the white men, and that their Friendship for the King was firm."

At two further meetings with Claus, the Iroquois remained aloof from his overtures of securing a military alliance. In fact, they used the opportunity of these meetings to complain that, like the Mississauga at York and Kingston, they were experiencing difficulties with the settlers around Newark, who were settling on Grand River lands, stealing their hogs, working their horses, and offering them no redress.[56]

In spite of the failures among the Mississaga and Mohawk in Canada, the policy initiated by Craig was an extraordinary success. He had applied carefully and prudently the discretionary authority allowed him in the secret instructions from Whitehall as they related to the defence of Upper Canada, and had restored the prestige and respect of the Indian Department with the tribes. The visit of more than five thousand chiefs and warriors to Amherstburg in the autumn of 1808 was the culmination of twelve months of preparation and work, and indicated the extent of the achievement. Yet the vulnerable part of Craig's frontier policy was its main reliance on the continued allegiance and fighting skills of the Indian tribes in the United States to provide for the future security and defence of Canada.

Tribal delegates constantly visited the British at Amherstburg for the next two years, to pledge their support to the king and to receive gifts and provisions in return. The department, receiving no instructions to the contrary, continued to win and maintain the allegiance of the various tribes. By the summer of 1810 Indian frustration and anger at American encroachments on their lands, along with British Indian Department inspiration, combined to make the Indian appetite for war increasingly difficult to control. In July a Sauk and Fox delegation arrived at Amherstburg and requested clothing, kettles, muskets, shot and powder. Elliott urged the Indians to "keep your eyes fixed on me; my tomahawk is now up; be you ready, but do not strike until I give the signal." This speech exhilarated the tribes, who were now most enthusiastic and confident about formalizing a new British-Indian alliance against the common enemy. Two thousand Shawnee, Sauk, Winnebago, Ottawa, and Potawatomi gathered at Amherstburg in November for a grand council. Tecumseh spoke for the tribes and informed the British that "we are now determined to defend it [our Country] ourselves, and after raising you on your feet leave you behind but expecting you will push forwards towards us what may be necessary to supply our wants."

The officers of the British Indian Department were astounded by these words. Elliott quickly sent a despatch to Claus stating that "our Neighbours are on the eve of an Indian War, and I have no doubt that the Confederacy is almost general."[57] The November council had placed the British in a difficult and embarrassing position. The policy of 1808 had been too successful. Now the problem was to prevent the over-zealous Indians from attacking the Americans before an actual declaration of war between Great Britain and the United States. In a desperate attempt to reverse policy, the department was instructed to dissuade the tribes from their projected plan of hostility. The chiefs were to understand clearly that they must not expect any assistance from the British. Further instructions were issued to Claus that the department must withhold shot and powder from those tribes advocating war. By the summer of 1811, therefore, the officers of the Indian Department were striving frantically to stall the Indian war by attempting to convince various influential chiefs that the time was not ripe. But the Indian desire for war was unshakeable, and sporadic raids commenced against the American back settlements along the Wabash River.[58] The Americans deduced that British intrigue and instigation was behind the revival of Indian resistance, and Indian-American and Anglo-American relations only worsened.

Following the November council of 1810, Tecumseh continued to organize and prepare the confederacy for the expected war with the Americans. In the hopes of broadening and strengthening Indian unity, he departed for the south in the summer of 1811 in an effort to win the support of the Creek, Cherokee, Choctaw, Chickasaw, and Seminole. In his absence, William Henry Harrison took advantage of the temporary loss of leadership within the confederary and advanced with an army against Prophetstown. After various manoeuvring, provocations, and delays on both sides, the Indians attacked the American camp in the early morning of 7 November. The resultant battle of Tippecanoe was a rather confused affair, with Harrison proclaiming a victory, whilst the Indians simply reoccupied their former ground. The Americans suffered considerably more casualties, inflicted upon them mainly by Kickapoo and Winnebago warriors.[59]

The battle of Tippecanoe, like the Chesapeake affair, once again aroused the anger and passions of the American people against Great Britain, especially with the reports that "British muskets were found on the battlefield."[60] This time, however, the vehemence was much more localized in the west, where Harrison in an open letter charged that "within the last three months, the whole of the Indians on this frontier, have been completely armed and equipped" out of the king's stores at Amherstburg.[61] These reports convinced the western states and territories that the British must be eliminated from Canada once and for all in order that they could no longer violate the American frontier by "setting on the ruthless savage to tomahawk our women and children."[62]

The frontier state of Kentucky was particularly determined to destroy British Canada. Since the time some forty years earlier when Daniel Boone had passed through the Cumberland Gap and entered Shawnee territory, Kentuckians and Indians had been fighting and killing each other almost constantly. In the opinion of many Kentuckians, the British and Indian connection had only plagued and perpetuated the long and bloody struggle. Therefore there was little surprise in hearing Richard M. Johnson, a Kentucky congressman, a "War Hawk" and a future hero of the "Battle of the Thames," proclaim vociferously his desire to see the British "expulsion from North America, and her territories incorporated with the United States." Johnson believed in the idea of a divine plan which held that "the waters of the St. Lawrence and the Mississippi interlock in a number of places, and the great disposer of Human Events intended those two rivers should belong to the same people."[63] His belief, of course, was a precursor of the later American concept of "Manifest Destiny."

The heightened desire to take Canada extended to Thomas Jefferson, the ex-president and old land-grabber, now in retirement at his Monticello estate in Virginia, who fired verbal volleys in support of the objective. He reckoned that "the acquisition of Canada, this year, as far as the neighbourhood of Quebec, will be a mere matter of marching."[64] Henry Clay of Kentucky, the leader of the "War Hawks," thought the task would be even easier, and verily believed "that the militia of Kentucky are alone competent to place Montreal and Upper Canada at your feet."[65] Hyperbole aside, most Americans, at least in the west and the south, agreed by the spring of 1812 that as a result of the years of maritime abuse and insults inflicted upon the nation by the Royal Navy, the most effective method of retaliation would be to strip imperial Britain of her land possessions in North America. If successful, the result would assure not only a redemption of national honour, but a deliverance from the evils of the Indian attacks on the frontier people. With these hopes planted firmly in the American national conscience, the moment had arrived to push "on to Canada."[66]

In the frontier province of Upper Canada, where so much of the American attention and hostility was focused, the officers of the Indian Department had made genuine attempts to prevent an Indian war in the months prior to Tippecanoe. But the subsequent outburst of American anger over the reports and accusations of British involvement in the battle allowed for no reasonable alternative but to return to Craig's policy of nearly four years before, and renew the traditional friendship and military alliance with the Indian tribes. This decision was fully supported by Major-General Isaac Brock, administrator of Upper Canada and commander of the forces, who was annoyed that among senior government officials in both Britain and Canada, "a general opinion prevailed that, in the event of hostilities, no opposition was intended" for the defence of the upper province.[67]

Like Tecumseh – with whom he was to share an exalted position in the annals of Canadian history – Brock was bold, innovative, and offensive-minded. Born in October 1769 at Guernsey in the Channel Islands, he had served in the British army from the age of fifteen. His career included enduring the monotony of garrison duty in Barbados and Jamaica and participating in the battle of Egmont-op-Zee in Holland. In 1802, now the commanding officer of the 49th Regiment of Foot (the Hertfordshire Regiment), Brock arrived in Canada. Apart from an eight-month leave in England, he was to spend the rest of his life in the colonies.[68]

In early December 1811, less than a month after the battle of Tippecanoe, Brock argued in a long letter to Sir George Prevost, captain-general and governor-in-chief of British North America, that a successful defence of Upper Canada, contrary to the prevailing opinion, was possible in the face of an American invasion. He reasoned that if the Indian tribes in the United States were liberally supplied from the king's stores at Amherstburg and encouraged to make war, the American frontier would be thrown into such a state of disruption as to reduce significantly the chances of a major enemy thrust against the British province. But, emphasized Brock, "before we can expect an active cooperation on the part of the Indians, the reduction of Detroit and Michilimackinac must convince that people, who conceive themselves to have been sacrificed in 1794, to our policy, that we are earnestly engaged in the war."

The general strategy for the defence of Upper Canada outlined by Brock had some appeal to Prevost, who agreed as "to the advantages which may result from giving, rather than receiving, the first blow."[69] But his instructions from Whitehall were not to commence offensive operations "except it be for the purpose of preventing or repelling Hostilities or unavoidable Emergencies."[70] Therefore, in regard to employing the Indians, Prevost stressed that "the utmost caution should be used in our language to them, and direct explanations should be delayed, if possible, until hostilities are more certain; though, whenever the subject is adverted to, I think it would be advisable always to intimate that, as a matter of course, we shall, in the event of war, expect the aid of our brothers."[71] Although recognizing that this balance required extreme delicacy on the part of the officers of the Indian Department, Prevost enjoined strict adherence to these directives so that there would be no misunderstanding with the tribes.

In mid-February of 1812 Prevost was requested to prepare a detailed report for the secretary of state for war and the colonies "upon the Military position of His Majesty's North American Provinces, and the means of defending them." The report was duly sent on 18 May to the Earl of Liverpool, who was soon to become prime minister. Prevost began by noting that Upper Canada was vulnerable to an immediate attack in the event of war, as it was "the most contiguous to the Territory of the United States and frontier to it along its whole extent." Further, the several frontier posts in the province were either too isolated or too weak to offer resistance. St. Joseph was described merely as "a Post of Assembly for friendly Indians," Fort George as "a temporary work at the Head of Lake Ontario, now repairing to render it tenable," and Fort Amherstburg as "a temporary Field Work in a ruinous State," although "a place of reunion for the Indians inhabiting that part of the Country, who assemble there in a considerable numbers to receive Presents."[72]

Prevost also reported that in the spring of 1812 the total number of British regulars and Canadian fencibles in Canada was only about 5,600 all ranks, of which perhaps 1,200 were stationed at the various and scattered posts in Upper Canada.[73] With Britain engaged at this time in a desperate struggle against Napoleonic France, there was little additional military or other resources available for any of her far-flung territories and colonies in the empire, whether in India, at the Cape Colony or in the remote and isolated frontier province of Upper Canada. With these several considerations placed before him, Prevost realistically assessed that Quebec was "the only permanent Fortress in the Canada: – It is the Key to the whole and must be maintained." Therefore, he concluded, borrowing extensively from Craig's 1808 report, "in framing a general outline of Co-operation for defence with the Forces in Upper Canada, commensurate with our deficiency in strength; I have considered the preservation of Quebec as the first objective, and to which all others must be subordinate."[74]

Although Prevost believed that there was little hope "of making an effectual defence of the open Country" if the Americans attacked, he had not completely snuffed Brock's bold plan for defending the upper province. At about the same time as Prevost was preparing his lengthy report for Whitehall, which avoided a discussion of Indian relations, he instructed Sir John Johnson to soothe native feelings. In part, he desired that "all purchases of lands are to be made in Public Council with great solemnity and ceremony according to the ancient usages and customs of the Indians, the principle chiefs and leading men of the Nation or Nations, to whom the lands belong being first assembled," and that all transactions were to be in accordance with the Royal Proclamation of 1763. Without being too questioning or specific, Johnson relayed Prevost's instructions through the chain of command by issuing directives for "the Good Government of the Indian Department," which included a deliberately vague order urging the officers to continue "your utmost endeavours to promote His Majesty's Indian Interest in general."[75] At Amherstburg the officers of the department, with one hand extended towards the crown and the other clinging to their Indian families, interpreted this phrase in a manner quite satisfying to Brock: they secretly prepared the tribes for war.

The employment of Indian allies by the British crown during the War of 1812 was the single most important factor in the successful defence of Upper Canada.[76] In his May 1812 report, Prevost had stated that the 1,200 regular troops stationed in the upper province consisted mainly of the 41st Regiment of Foot (the Welch Regiment), a few companies of the 10th Royal Veteran Battalion, and some detachments from the Royal Artillery. In addition, there were calculated to be 11,000 men of the Candian militia in the province, of which "it might not be prudent to Arm more than 4,000."[77] Although the ageing original Loyalists and their sons, the mixed-blood people around Amherstburg, and recent British emigrants were considered generally supportive of the crown, the majority of the population in the province by 1812 consisted of "late" Loyalists and American migrants whose loyalty was suspect at best.

These numbers seemed barely adequate to defend a province which shared with the United States a border hundreds of miles long, from the Ottawa River and west to the Detroit. But, surprisingly, there was not a significant difference in military strength in 1812 between the British and American regular establishment in North America. In January and April, Congress passed legislation authorizing increases in both the regular army, which at that time consisted of only 6,700 officers and enlisted men, and the militia. Although the increases on paper were quite high, the quotas assigned were not filled.[78] Yet the United States, with a population in excess of seven million, could count on an enthusiastic and fairly large response from the Ohio, Kentucky, and Tennessee volunteers, along with the militia of other western states and territories who were anxious to begin what was for them the glory, the toil, and the danger of this second struggle for their liberty. In the contest for Upper Canada the Americans were numerically superior, but on balance the advantage was not on all occasions significantly weighted towards them. The North Western Army under Brigadier-General William Hull, for instance, which had the key role of striking at Amherstburg and the western portion of Upper Canada, was composed of about 2,200 mostly untrained and ill-equipped officers and men, drawn from both the regular service and the militia.[79]

Eminently significant to both the British and Canadian defenders and the American invaders of Upper Canada was the active assistance of Indian allies on behalf of the crown. There were an estimated ten thousand warriors scattered throughout the Great Lakes region, and this additional force produced a decided tilt in favour of the king's interest. In a remarkable document, dated Montreal 1814, and previously overlooked by historians of the War of 1812, a "List of Indian Warriors as they stood in 1812 at the time war was declared" provides a thorough breakdown of the various tribes and numbers in relation to their military contribution to the defence of Canada.[80] The figures are quite revealing in showing that of the estimated ten thousand Indian allies, more than eight thousand were so-called Western Indians mostly residing in the United States. Included, for instance, were 450 Wyandot in the neighbourhood of Detroit; 350 Ottawa and Potawatomi from the River St. Clair; 180 Miami (who would remain neutral); 850 Shawnee along the Wabash – "Tecumsehs tribe" and on the west side of the Mississippi (only a few of these joined); nearly 3,000 Ottawa, Potawatomi, and Ojibwa scattered throughout the Great Lakes from Chicago to

Michilimackinac; 450 Kickapoo, 500 Folsavoins (Menominee) from the Green Bay area, 700 Winnebago at the Fox and Rock Rivers, 1,200 Sauk and Fox on the east side of the Mississippi; and 600 Chipaways (Ojibwa) and Ottawa of Saginaw Bay on Lake Huron. These numbers and tribal compositions, according to the unsigned document, "forms a tolerably correct list of the Indian warriors on the frontier of the United States, extending from Sandusky on Lake Erie to the River Mississippi, as they stood the first year of the late War. - They were all in Arms for the British Govt."

The Indians of Upper Canada were estimated as numbering about 1,590, and included 400 Mohawk from the Grand River and another 50 from the Bay of Quinte (Tyendinaga); 220 Mississauga from the area of York, and 70 Ojibwa from Matchedash (Georgian Bay) and Lake Simcoe; 670 "Iroquois" from St. Régis (Akwesasne), Caughnawaga (Kahnawake); and Lake of Two Mountains at Oka (Kanehsatake); 130 Nipissing or Algonkin (Algonquin) in the same area; and 100 Abenaki from the St. Francis River (Odanak). These figures provide ample evidence of the extent of the military contribution of native people in the defence of Canada during the War of 1812. Once again the allegiance and fighting prowess of Indian warriors were to be vital for its survival. Perhaps most revealing, or troubling, is that the vast majority of these Indian "allies" of the crown were from the republic of the United States.

By June of 1812 all sides recognized and understood that a war was imminent. Tecumseh delivered a passionate speech to Elliott on behalf of the Indians assembled along the Wabash, assuring the British that the confederacy would defend itself like men against the Americans, and make it impossible for the British to restore peace between the Indians and the Americans. Following this address, the Shawnee leader visited Fort Wayne on 17 June and mockingly told the Americans that he was going to Amherstburg for powder and lead.[81] The officers of the Indian Department at Amherstburg continued to collect, organize, and prepare the tribes for war, and there was a hopeful mood that the strategies developed in the defence of Upper Canada offered a reasonable chance of success. For the Indian tribes in the United States, the anticipation of an Anglo-American conflict gave them similar hopes that, in conjunction with the British, their lands and other interests could be protected. Together, they had managed to polish, brighten, strengthen, and renew the chain of friendship. With the British-Indian military alliance against the common enemy thus revived, all that remained for them was to wait impatiently for the commencement of a war whose origins were at sea and in Europe, but which for the most part would be fought on land and in Canada.

CHAPTER 6

THE WAR OF 1812: MICHILIMACKINAC AND UPPER CANADA

The United States of America formally declared war against Great Britain on 18 June 1812 and promptly proceeded with their plan for the invasion of Canada.[1] At Fort George, Upper Canada, Brock reacted to the news by assembling and organizing the Canadian militia in the Niagara area (Lincoln County) and issuing a proclamation which required "all his majesty's liege subjects to be obedient to the lawful authorities, to forbear all communication with the enemy or person residing within the territory of the United States, and to manifest their loyalty by a zealous co-operation with his majesty's armed force in defence of the province, and repulse of the enemy."[2] Yet he chafed at the repeated instructions of Sir George Prevost to assume and maintain a defensive posture. Brock steadfastly believed that the weak state of the garrisons at Michilimackinac and Detroit justified "offensive operations."[3] The capture of these two key enemy posts, he reasoned, would enhance the morale and confidence of his few British regulars, Canadian militia, and Indian allies, confuse and stall the expected attacks of the invaders, and thus improve the chances for the defence of the vulnerable frontier province.

Prevost, as governor-in-chief of British North America and commander of the forces, could not afford the luxury of sharing the bold military enthusiasms of Brock. The defence of Canada depended on the preservation of the fortress of Quebec City. If that place fell, the vital lifeline of supplies and reinforcements via the Royal Navy and Great Britain would be severed and the whole country surely lost. The governor therefore devised a military strategy which was defensive in nature and based on caution and appeasement.[4] As for Upper Canada, he patiently continued to remind Brock that "our numbers would not justify offensive operations being undertaken, unless they were solely calculated to strengthen a defensive attitude." Further, Prevost considered it "prudent and politic to avoid any measure which can in its effect have a tendency to unite the people in the American States." He developed this thought by reasoning that "whilst disunion prevails among them, their attempts on these provinces will be feeble; it is, therefore, our duty carefully to avoid committing any act which may, even by construction, tend to unite the eastern and southern states, unless, by its perpetration, we are to derive a considerable and important advantage."[5] This line of argument suggests that in addition to espousing a defensive policy, Prevost also possessed a strong desire to do nothing that might upset the Americans, such as scoring a British victory. This attitude was too reminiscent of that of a previous governor, Sir Guy Carleton, who in the summer of 1776 showed little enthusiasm or diligence in pursuing what he considered to be deluded colonial rebels retreating from Quebec. Carleton had wrongly reckoned that if these Americans were treated with compassion and leniency, they would soon come to their senses and happily renew their oath of allegiance to the king. Prevost inherited some of this conciliatory attitude during the War of 1812 and may have rationalized that if the war was conducted at a slow and gentle pace, the Americans would perhaps not pursue the campaign against Canada with their usual vigour and intensity.

The steady flow of instructions from Prevost to Brock pertaining to this defensive strategy was unequivocal. As a result, at least in the first few opening weeks of the war, Brock complied with these directives and contented himself with improving the general defences of Upper Canada. These preparations included deploying the British regulars to key sectors throughout the province, corresponding with his senior officers along the Detroit, and constantly monitoring the activities of the Indian Confederacy to the south of the lakes. Brock also strengthened Fort George, built additional field works, and established gun batteries at strategic locations along the Niagara to thwart the expected enemy attack from across the river. But most significantly, Brock reached beyond the borders of the province in seeking military assistance. Towards the end of February he had dispatched a confidential communication to Robert Dickson, the most influential British fur trader in 1812 amongst the western Indians of the upper Mississippi. The letter informed Dickson that "as it is probable that war may result from the present state of affairs, it is very desirable to ascertain the degree of cooperation that you and *your friends*, might be able to furnish, in case of such an Emergency taking place." As well, Dickson was instructed to respond "with all practicable expedition" to a series of questions relating to the number of loyal friends he could muster and the amount of supplies required. In particular, Dickson was asked if he could "individually approach the Detroit frontier next spring" and if so, to "state the time and place, where *we* may meet."[6]

Dickson received this secret despatch on 18 June, the day war was officially declared, whilst encamped at the Fox-Wisconsin portage, near Green Bay. He responded immediately by stating that "the number of my friends would have been more, but the unparalleled scarcity of provisions of all sorts, had reduced them to 250 or 300 of all sorts of different languages." The group was ready to march, he promised, but "provisions and all sorts of proper goods [were] required." His friends, he noted, had

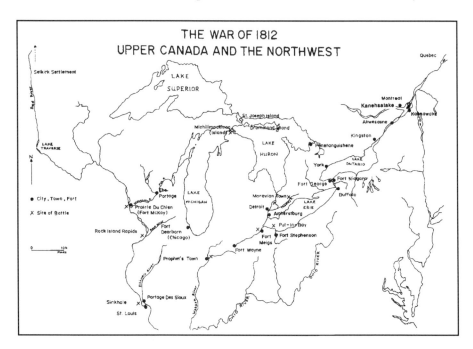

THE WAR OF 1812
UPPER CANADA AND THE NORTHWEST

expressed a particular interest in receiving flags and large medals of King George III, with gorgets. As for coming to Detroit, ostensibly to assist in the defence of Upper Canada, Dickson showed a decided preference for protecting his regional interests west of the lakes by firmly informing the writer that "St: Josephs will be the General Rendezvous and all our friends shall be there about the 30th inst. [June]." In fact, Dickson pushed this view further by suggesting that "an Expedition across to the Mississipi would be of great service and could be accomplished without much risk or difficulty."[7]

There is no doubt that Dickson was a sincere and zealous friend to His Majesty's government. But by 1812 he had been living and trading among the Indians of the Mississippi and upper lakes for twenty-five years. His desire, therefore, to contribute actively in the defence of Canada was motivated by a combination of loyalty, altruism, and economic self-interest. Born about 1765 in Dumfries, Scotland, the son of a local merchant, Dickson was forced to emigrate to Canada sometime towards the end of the American rebellion, probably as the result of financial difficulties in the family business. He was apparently first employed at Oswego on the southern side of Lake Ontario by Robert Hamilton, who may have been a relative, and Richard Cartwright, both prominent Loyalist merchants in the upper province. It was here that Dickson began his apprenticeship, which persuaded him to adopt the fur trade as a life-long occupation. After a few months, the young immigrant was removed to the Niagara area, where he was involved in selling and shipping goods to the upper fur-trade posts and in managing accounts, especially those of ex-officers of the recently disbanded Loyalist provincial corps of Butler's Rangers. Dickson soon tired of this drab routine and in July 1786 was pleased to be transferred to the post of Michilimackinac, which had been relocated to nearby Mackinac Island six years earlier, "to learn the art and mystery of commerce."[8]

Until the War of 1812, Dickson resided in the region west of the upper lakes in the character of a mercantile trader. During these years, he acquired an extensive knowledge of the "Country and its Inhabitants," and especially of the distribution, customs, and languages of the numerous Indian tribes.[9] He appeared to have no particular desire, for instance, to return and settle in Upper Canada, which would have been a sound option for him since he was closely connected with the most respectable families in the province. Apart from his trading association with such Loyalist élites as Robert Hamilton and Richard Cartwright, Dickson had a brother, William, who was a prominent lawyer at Newark

(Niagara-on-the-Lake) and a member of the Legislative Assembly; another brother, Thomas, was a successful merchant at the village of Queenston on the Niagara River and served subsequently as lieutenant-colonel of the Second Regiment of Lincoln militia during the War of 1812.

Yet, in spite of good prospects for commercial success and the obvious domestic comforts he may have attained in the settled parts of Upper Canada, Dickson seemed to prefer the fur trade and the Indians of the upper Mississippi. Evidence of this preference was demonstrated in the spring of 1797 when he married To-to-win, a young woman of the Wahpeton branch of the Santee Sioux (Dakota). She was the sister of a prominent chief, and the union strengthened Dickson's influence with the Sioux and other tribes. Soon afterwards he established a small trading post at Lake Traverse in the upper Minnesota Sioux country.[10] For the next several years Dickson engaged in the fur trade, but commercial profits slumped. The Jay Treaty had forced British and Canadian fur traders to pay severe customs duties on their British goods entering the United States, usually through Michilimackinac, for the upper Mississippi and western fur country.

With the increasing threat of war with the United States, the British and Canadian fur traders in the western country were more than anxious to cooperate with any military plan which might produce British paramountcy in the region. In August 1811, notwithstanding the impediments thrown in his way by the American government at Michilimackinac, Dickson managed once again to return to the Mississippi fur country where he annually conducted his trade. The winter of 1811–12 was particularly cold and harsh and, prompted by humanitarian as well as political motives, Dickson distributed gratis his entire stock of supplies and trade goods to starving Indians. Angry, frustrated, and nearly destitute, he began at the same time to encourage and solicit Indian support for the British by offering every inducement to them to take up the hatchet against the United States. He made no secret of his intentions and sentiments, for Ninian Edwards, governor of Illinois Territory, warned the secretary of state that "Dickson hopes to engage all the Indians in opposition to the United States by making peace between the Chippewa [Ojibwa] and Sioux and having them declare war against us."[11]

At the same time as Dickson was attempting to rally the Indians to the cause of the king, American agents were offering various tribes "unusual presents of goods and inciting them in the most pressing manner to visit the President of the United States at Washington where it was held out to them, they would hear something of the utmost importance."[12] Some of the chiefs accepted the invitation in early 1812, but even while these select dignitaries were en route, eight hundred Winnebago, Sauk, and Fox warriors were gathering at the Rock Island rapids on the upper Mississippi, in preparation for attacking American frontier settlements. The raids duly commenced in the first days of spring, and by May "all the Americans except two had fled from Prairie du Chien, in consequence of the avowed hostility of the Savages toward them."[13]

By June, Dickson had succeeded beyond expectations in winning the loyalty of the tribes of the Mississippi and upper lakes to the British interest. The questions posed in the confidential communication which he finally received at the portage had been anticipated, and the answers took the form of ever-increasing assemblages of Indian allies. From Green Bay, Dickson directed a small band of specially chosen Menominee warriors under Weenusate to proceed to the Detroit front "where they remain'd during the summer and were in every engagement with the Enemy."[14] With a second and larger body of upwards of 130 Menominee, Winnebago, and Sioux, Dickson pushed towards the British post of St. Joseph, and reached the island, as promised, on the last day of June. But the focus and real target was Michilimackinac, the gateway to the western fur trade and Indian country, and long a thorn in the sides of the British and Canadian fur traders.

At St. Joseph, Captain Charles Roberts, who received news of the declaration of war on 3 July, commanded a garrison which consisted of three men of the Royal Regiment of Artillery and forty-five aged rankers of the 10th Royal Veteran Battalion. These men were adequate to guard a peaceful frontier post, but Roberts showed a decided lack of confidence in their ability to conduct an active campaign, commenting that although his veterans were always ready to obey orders, they were "so debilitated, and worn down by unconquerable drunkenness, that neither the fear of punishment, the love of fame or the honour of their Country can animate them to extraordinary exertions."[15] In addition to the concerns about the state of his troops, Roberts was confused and frustrated by a series of contradictory orders from both Major-General Brock and Governor Prevost which he received in late June and early July. Initially, Brock informed Roberts that war was declared and he was "to make an immediate attack upon Michilimackinac." A second letter suspended the orders owing to the arrangement of a temporary general armistice. A third letter directed Roberts "to adopt the most prompt and effectual measures" to take Michilimackinac. Yet at the same time as the arrival of this last letter, Prevost, writing from Quebec, ordered Roberts "to take every precaution to secure his post against any attempt by the enemy, and in case of necessity to effect his retreat."[16] A perplexed Roberts could only wait.

By mid-July the island of St. Joseph had indeed become the general rendezvous in the upper lakes for those forces loyal to the king. Although his garrison was feeble, Roberts now had under his command Dickson and his 130 warriors, about 180 engagés and voyageurs drawn from the North West Company and even a few from the South West Company – a multinational corporation with commercial interests on both sides of the border – and about 300 Ottawa and Ojibwa who had been gathered by John Askin, Jr., the Indian Department storekeeper and interpreter at St. Joseph. Although many of the Ottawa were suspect, merely exhibiting a lukewarm behaviour, the other Indians were eager and impatient for action. The loyalty of the tribes to the king, explained the Sioux chief Wabasha (also known as La Feuille) was in large measure owing to the fact that "we live by our English Traders who have always assisted us, [and] have always found our English Father the protector of our women and children."[17]

To the great relief of Roberts, a dispatch from Brock was received on 15 July with instructions "to adopt either offensive or defensive measures, as circumstances might dictate." Roberts wasted no time in making the decision to attack the enemy, barely fifty miles away. He was probably correct in assessing that "the Indians whose minds had been prepared for hostilities ... would soon have abandoned me if I had not made the attempt." As a result, and believing that his "situation at St. Josephs was totally indefensible," Roberts embarked the next morning with his entire force, including two 6-pounders, for Michilmackinac. By 10 o'clock on the morning of 17 July, the expedition had not only reached its destination, but had managed, with great difficulty, to drag two of the guns across the island "to the Heights above the Fort."[18]

Lieutenant Porter Hanks, in command of the fifty-seven officers and men of the American garrison, was still unsure if an official state of war existed between the United States and Great Britain. But the discovery of the British "in possession of the heights that commanded the fort, and one piece of their artillery directed to the most defenceless part of the garrison," combined with the sight of Indians "in great numbers in the edge of the woods," convinced him. At mid-morning Roberts delivered to the American fort a summons to surrender. Hanks, who was surrounded, outnumbered, ill-prepared to withstand a lengthy siege, and unwilling to chance a possible Indian massacre, fully recognized that his position was untenable. He therefore, after a brief deliberation, agreed to the articles of capitulation which in part granted his men the honours of war.[19]

Immediately after the tiny American garrison had marched out of the north sally port and laid down their arms, Roberts took possession of the fort and displayed the British colours. He expressed "the greatest praise for all those who conducted the Indians, that although these peoples minds were much heated. Yet as soon as they heard the Capitulation signed they all returned to their Canoes, and not one drop either of Man's or Animal's Blood was Spilt."[20] John Askin, Jr. firmly believed that "it was a fortunate circumstance that the Fort Capitulated without firing a Single Gun, for had they done so ... not a Soul of them would have been Saved." He had never seen "so determined a Set of people as the Chippewas [Ojibwa] and Ottawas ... since the Capitulation they have not drunk a single drop of Liquor, nor even killed a fowl belonging to any person (a thing never known before) for they generally destroy every thing they meet with."[21] The Indian restraint was rewarded by Roberts, who distributed amongst them generous amounts of pork, flour, candles, vinegar, blankets, and gallons of wines and whiskey from the captured American stores. He reported that as a result of the capture of Michilimackinac "the Indians are flocking in from all Quarters."[22] Much to the annoyance of Roberts, a host of Ottawa arrived several days after the surrender, which convinced the British commander that these people had been encamped nearby during the action, waiting to hear the result of the attack. Yet by the end of July, with the victory celebrations curtailed and the supplies reduced, most of the Indians and fur traders had left the island to pursue and renew their hunting, trapping, and commercial endeavours. But the prize had been won. The painful thorn – the restrictions – of Michilimackinac had been removed, and with the British now dominant in the upper lakes, for the moment British and Canadian fur traders could look with some optimism towards a viable economic future in partnership with their Indian friends and allies.

News of the fall of Michilimackinac soon reverberated throughout the American frontier and into Canada. Along the Detroit, for instance, Brigadier-General Hull and his North Western Army, with instructions "to commence offensive operations ... take Malden, and extend your conquests as circumstances may justify," had initiated the American invasion of Canada on 12 July, by crossing the river and occupying Sandwich.[23] The following day Hull posted a proclamation to the "Inhabitants of Canada." It read, in part, that the American action was in response to "the injuries and aggressions, the insults and indignities of Great Britain" against citizens of the United States. Further, if the inhabitants remained passive, they would be protected and "emancipated from Tyranny and oppression and restored to the dignified station of freemen." The Canadians were therefore offered a choice between "Peace, Liberty, and Security" under the benevolence of the United States or, if they took up arms in support of the king, to suffer "War, Slavery and destruction."[24]

The proclamation appeared to have the desired effect, as Hull reported that "the Canadian militia are deserting from Malden in large parties; ... I send them to their homes and give them protection," he added. In fact, Hull reckoned that "the probability is that the greatest part of them will desert in a few days."[25] This buoyant optimism masked a growing concern: Hull feared the Indians. Since May, and with some frequency and effect, they had been raiding American back settlements. Hull was afraid that the British had been too successful, especially at Amherstburg, in recruiting Indian allies for the war against the United States and in the defence of Canada. He therefore issued a firm warning in the second part of the proclamation which stated:

> If the barbarous and Savage policy of Great Britain be pursued, and the savages are let loose to murder our Citizens and butcher our women and children, this war, will be a war of extermination.
>
> The first stroke with the Tomahawk the first attempt with the Scalping Knife will be the Signal for one indiscriminate scene of desolation, No white man found fighting by the Side of an Indian will be taken prisoner. Instant destruction will be his Lot. If the dictates of reason, duty, justice, and humanity, cannot prevent the employment of a force, which respects no rights and knows no wrong, it will be prevented by a severe and relentless system of retaliation.[26]

Since the cornerstone of British policy at Amherstburg for the defence of the province was the active use and assistance of Indian allies – a policy endorsed and fully supported by Brock – the threats of Hull went unheeded. As a consequence, for the next fifteen months on the Detroit and Ohio frontiers, the War of 1812 became marked by a mutual and bitter exchange of atrocities in which no quarter was asked nor given.

Although there had been a series of British-Indian military alliances against the Americans for nearly the last forty years, Hull deluded himself into believing that the tribes would adopt a position of neutrality in the war. He knew that "the greatest possible exertions have been made to induce the Indians to join the British standard – The Tomahawk stained with blood has been presented" to them. But by mid-July, Hull reported from Sandwich that "the force under my command and the movement into this province has had a great effect on the Indians. They are daily returning to their villages." He continued by noting that the influential Wyandot were conducting "a very large council" of several tribes with the object "to induce all the nations to be neutral." Several Indian leaders, contended Hull, including the Crane, Walk-in-the-Water, Blackhoof, and Blue Jacket "are zealous friends of neutrality." Seemingly, according to Hull, "Tecumseh and Marpot (Main Poc) are the only chiefs of consequence remaining with the British."[27]

Yet Indian neutrality provided Hull with no inducement to follow instructions and strike in force at the key objective of Malden (Fort Amherstburg). Instead, following the invasion of Canada, both the cautious commander and his army, as if in a semi-catatonic state, barely moved from Sandwich. Tentative probes towards Amherstburg were met on each occasion by stiff resistance at the Rivière-aux-Canard. In one instance, two determined soldiers of the 41st Regiment of Foot (the Welch Regiment), whilst guarding a bridge, contributed significantly to stalling the advance; on another occasion, the tough little band of Menominee sent down by Dickson in June attacked a detachment of the advancing enemy.[28] These set-backs at the Canard, however, paled when compared to the news from Michilimackinac.

With the fall of that strategic post, so symbolically important to the Indians, the worst fears of Hull were realized. In a letter to the secretary of war on 4 August the commanding general discussed the implications of the loss of American influence on the upper lakes by observing that "at the time when the army under my command took possession of this part of the province of Upper Canada every thing appeared favourable." But, he continued, "the unexpected surrender of Michilimackinac and the tardy operations of the army at Niagara" put him in an increasingly dangerous and delicate position. He reasoned that since the pro-British North West Company and South West Company enjoyed a considerable influence over the tribes, and that the companies largely relied on supplying their traders and posts in the upper lakes Indian country via the Detroit River, the necessity for them of maintaining and securing that water route was vital. He therefore had "every reason to expect in a very short time a large body of Indians from the north,

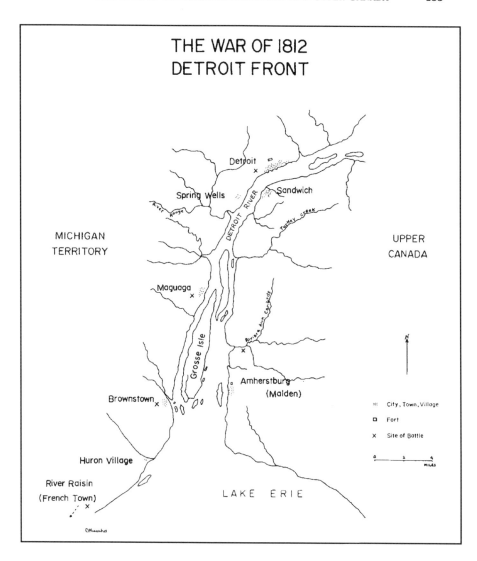

whose operations will be directed against this army."[29]

In a second letter four days later, Hull informed the secretary of war that the Wyandot, who were considered to be "the bravest and eldest" of the tribes, had become hostile "contrary to my expectations" and that "the other nations connected with them are following their example."[30] Faced with these existing circumstances, Hull recrossed the Detroit River with the main body of the army without making an attempt on the British fort at Malden. His invasion of Canada had lasted less than one month.

Throughout the brief period of the occupation of Sandwich by American forces, the British at Amherstburg continued to prepare defences, plan strategy, and hold councils with various tribal delegates. Although the number of Indian allies was difficult to gauge, as they were always "going and coming," the presence and exertions of Tecumseh "has kept them faithful – he has shewn himself to be a determined character and a great friend of our Government."[31] Yet the warriors were anxious for action, and the delays were becoming increasingly detrimental to British and Canadian interests. Keen to ascertain accurately the state of things in Amherstburg, Brock requested Colonel Henry Procter, in whom he placed great reliance, to proceed to the fort and take command. On his arrival at the post on 26 July Procter provided his superior with a detailed report on conditions along the Detroit.

Procter, a good disciplinarian and competent administrator, was born in Ireland, although there is a suggestion of a Welsh background; he was nearly fifty years old in 1812. As colonel of the 41st Regiment of Foot, he had served with his regiment in Canada for ten years. Whilst in garrison at Quebec and Montreal "the zeal of the commanding officer and good discipline of the 41st Regiment" was praised by the local magistrates and citizenry.[32] The regiment was less impressive, however, during a lengthy tour of duty at Fort Amherstburg between 1805 and 1809, when the men showed a decided tendency to desert. But by 1811, the 41st, much improved according to Brock owing to the "indefatigable industry" of Colonel Procter, departed once again for service at the king's frontier posts in Upper Canada. By the early summer of 1812, the 41st, numbering about nine hundred officers and men, and the only regular British line regiment in the province, was stationed principally at Fort George and Fort Amherstburg. For Procter, who had almost no field experience, the pressures over the next fifteen months of directing an active military command in an isolated, vulnerable but strategically important theatre of operations, combined with the frustrations of dealing with the constant fluctuations in numbers and temperament of the Indian allies, presented a challenge of character and personality which was beyond measure.

Within a few days of Procter's arrival at Amherstburg, British, Indians, and a few Canadian "gentlemen volunteers" were crossing the river and attacking American columns south of Detroit. Near the Wyandot village at Brownstown on 5 August, Tecumseh and a small number of Shawnee and Ottawa ambushed and killed about twenty of the enemy.[33] There was only one Indian casualty, a purportedly "very agile and courageous" Shawnee chief named Blue Jacket. Indian women from the nearby village with butcher knives, and a Potawatomi chief with a tomahawk, quickly avenged the death by murdering an American prisoner of war. The incident, which upset two young Canadian witnesses, merely emphasized the growing brutality of the War of 1812 on the frontier.[34] A few days later at Maguaga (referred to as Monguagon in American sources), a "warm Action" took place between American troops and a mixed force of British regulars, Canadian militia, and Indians under the command of Captain Adam Muir of the 41st Regiment of Foot, Tecumseh, and other chiefs.

At Detroit on 9 August, the same day as the confused affair at Maguaga, Hull sent orders to Captain Nathan Heald at Fort Dearborn (Chicago) on the southwest tip of Lake Michigan, directing him to evacuate the post. The fall of Michilimackinac, which boosted Indian confidence throughout the frontier, along with the fairly heavy fighting around Detroit, left Heald in an isolated and dangerous position, with the closest help being Fort Wayne on the Maumee, about 125 miles to the east. In fact, reported Heald in mid-July, the garrison had been somewhat confined to the fort on account of the hostile disposition of the local Potawatomi and Winnebago.

Upon receiving his instructions, Heald evacuated the post on the morning of 15 August, taking with him about two hundred military and civilian personnel, including women and children, with wagons, supplies, and animals. The column was led by about thirty Miami Indians who had been sent by Hull as a security escort. This tribe, a dominant force under Little Turtle during the long struggle for the Ohio Valley in the 1790s, had suffered greatly in that conflict, and as a result, firmly declared their neutrality in the War of 1812. As the group trudged east along the beach, with the lake on the left and a high sand bank on the right, a large band of Potawatomi under Black Bird attacked them from behind their sand bank hiding place, and in a fiercely contested fifteen minutes, during which the Miami stood back, killed twenty-six regulars, twelve militia, and slaughtered a number of women and children.[35] Heald and the rest of the Americans were made prisoners.

The commanding officer was soon paroled to Detroit, others were subsequently ransomed by Robert Dickson, but most were carried off to distant and scattered Indian villages. For Hull, the fall of Michilimackinac, his failed invasion of Canada, the reverses along the Detroit, and his apprehensions for the yet unknown fate of Fort Dearborn, had made him a rattled and desperate man. By mid-August, with the added pressure of his officers demanding that he resign on the grounds of incompetence, the aged veteran of the Revolutionary War had lost completely the vigorous "Spirit of 1776."

By contrast, along the Niagara during the months of July and first part of August, Brock was more frustrated and angry than desperate. His plans and hopes for the successful defence of the province included the loyal and active support of the Canadian militia and the use of the Indian allies. But he could motivate neither group to the cause of the king. As both civil and military administrator of Upper Canada, and therefore president of the Executive Council, Brock was dismayed at the strength and influence of the numerous settlers from the United States over the decisions of the lower house. His speeches to both the Legislative Council and Legislative Assembly and his counter-proclamation to that of Hull on 22 July, which emphasized loyalty and resistance in defence of invaded rights, won few converts. He could only lament that his "situation is most critical, not from any thing the enemy can do, but from the disposition of the people – the population, believe me is essentially bad – a full belief possesses them all that this Province must inevitably succumb ... Most of the people have lost all confidence. I however speak loud and look big."[36]

Equally despairing for Brock was the neutral stance of the Six Nations Confederacy of Iroquois along the Grand River. These people were traditional allies of the king. The "faithful Mohawks," who dominated the settlement, had zealously supported Sir William Johnson in the old French war and served with distinction on behalf of the crown throughout the American Revolution. Many of their chiefs and warriors, notably Joseph Brant, had been proud of their designation and status as United Empire Loyalists. But the chiefs in council had reflected on this matter, and their reluctance to declare themselves for the king in the summer of 1812 was consistent with their position following the Chesapeake affair of 1807.

Thus, following a council on neutrality with American Tuscarora and Red Jacket, the Seneca chief and orator, and gaining assurances from Hull that their lands and rights would be guaranteed, few warriors from the Grand responded to requests for military assistance from Brock. This decision alarmed loyal elements of the Canadian militia, who became hesitant about leaving "their families to the mercy of 400 Indians" who lived in the heart of the country and amongst them. Brock mockingly wrote that the conduct of the Grand River Iroquois "affords wide room for suspicion; and really to expect that this fickle race will remain in a state of neutrality in the midst of a war, would be truly absurd."[37]

The heartening news from Michilmackinac, however, removed some of his annoyance and anxiety. For Brock, convinced that the capture of both Michilimackinac and Detroit were absolute necessities if there was to be any hope of providing for the successful defence of Upper Canada, the fall of that key American post on the upper lakes achieved the first of his two strategic objectives. Yet he considered that his situation remained critical, for with only a few British regulars and a sullen Canadian population, along with the passive stance of the Grand River Iroquois, Brock held that unless the enemy was driven from Sandwich and Detroit taken, it would be impossible to avert much longer the impending ruin of the country. Therefore, with time critical, Brock devised desperate remedies and made a dash to reinforce Procter. This decision was a calculated but prudent risk. The tardy operations of the enemy along the Niagara, the information recently received that the American army had lost all confidence in Hull and that despondency prevailed through their ranks, afforded good opportunities for success. Determined on his course, and with a force of British regulars and Canadian militia, Brock set forth from Fort George, travelling via Long Point and along the north shore of Lake Erie, reached Amherstburg just before midnight on 13 August.

Within hours of his arrival, Brock was introduced to Tecumseh, whom the general had described only a few months earlier as "a Shawnee of no particular note."[38] The two men gained an instant respect for one other. After exchanging greetings, Tecumseh supposedly exclaimed, "Ho-o-o-e: This is a man!" This declaration may well be apocryphal, but has been so recorded and enshrined in the annals of Canadian historical folklore. For his part, Brock was of the opinion that in regard to the Shawnee leader, "a more sagacious or gallant Warrior does not I believe exist."[39] A scant forty-eight hours after their meeting, the combined forces of Brock and Tecumseh, consisting of three hundred British regulars of the 41st Regiment, the Royal Newfoundland Regiment of Fencible Infantry and Royal Artillery, four hundred Canadian militia, drawn from the counties of Essex, Kent, Norfolk, Middlesex, Oxford, Lincoln, and York, and about six hundred Indian allies, had crossed the river unopposed and invested Detroit.

With the British shore batteries from Sandwich punishing the fort and town, the badly shaken Hull proposed a cessation of hostilities on the morning of 16 August. As governor of Michigan as well as commander of the army, he was responsible for the welfare of the civilian inhabitants. The potential for an Indian massacre had become an obsession and he feared for the safety of the women and children. After a short delay, therefore, the governor agreed to terms of capitulation and surrendered Detroit, Michigan Territory, vast amounts of ordnance, supplies, provisions and 2,500 American troops, all "without the sacrifice of a drop of British blood."[40] In a lengthy review of his campaign, Hull explained in part that the fall of Michilimackinac "opened the northern hive of Indians, and they were swarming down in every direction," and that they then "joined in open hostility under the British standard ... contrary to the most solemn assurances of a large portion of them to remain neutral."[41] Tecumseh, Marpot, Logan, Walk-in-the-Water, and Split Log were identified as the principal chiefs. For Hull, there was little doubt that his surrender of Detroit, and probably the fall of Michilimackinac, was occasioned and prompted by the use and assistance of Britain's Indian allies.

Michilimackinac, Detroit, and the horror of Fort Dearborn produced instant and untold havoc throughout the nearly defenceless American frontier, and emboldened and intensified Indian raids against such places as Pigeon Roost Creek, Fort Harrison, and Fort Madison. Even when cooperating with British regular forces, the Indian allies proved difficult, and sometimes impossible, to control. Along the River Raisin, for instance, just south of Detroit, the Wyandot, much to the mortification of Major Peter Chambers of the 41st, were strongly disposed to "Pillage, Ravage, and destroy," and the area soon became "one Universal scene of desolation." Only Tecumseh and the Wyandot chief Roundhead prevented further "Scenes so disgraceful to Humanity."[42] Yet under Major Adam Muir of the same 41st, a British-Indian expedition in the direction of Fort Wayne in September was conducted with skill, competence, and a uniform display of good discipline. By the early autumn, military activities along the Detroit had subsided and would remain quiet until after Christmas.

This condition, however, did not relax the vigilance of Procter, for William Henry Harrison, governor of Indiana Territory and the new and more able commander of the North Western Army, was organizing along the Maumee a formidable array of Ohio, Kentucky and other troops to strike at what was now called the British Right Division, retake Detroit, and push into Canada. Brock was fully sensible to the future dangers facing Procter and urged him to remain on the defensive, commenting that "an active interesting scene is going to commence with you." But a key element of his policy for the defence of Upper Canada, the use and assistance of Indian allies, had been dramatically assured, at least for the time being, with the fall of both Michilimackinac and Detroit. Brock therefore expressed confidence in what was probably his last letter to Procter, speculating that the province, especially the western part, could be preserved "provided we can manage the Indians and keep them attached to your cause, which is in fact theirs."[43]

Following the surrender of Detroit, Brock hurriedly returned to Fort George. American forces had been massing along the Niagara for some time, and a second invasion of Canada appeared imminent. The attack finally came in the early morning of a grey and chilly day on 13 October. After crossing at a very narrow point in the river opposite Queenston, the enemy, numbering about 1,600, positioned themselves on the densely wooded heights above the village. Upon hearing the guns and rattle of musketry, Brock raced to Queenston and boldly, but rashly, attempted to dislodge the invaders by leading a frontal assault with just two companies of the 49th Regiment of Foot (the Hertfordshire Regiment) and a few of the York militia. The impetuous charge failed and Brock, a distinguished figure and easy target, was killed.[44]

Later in the day, reinforcements arrived from Fort George, as well as some Iroquois from Grand River who, after the news of Detroit, had promised to erase the disgrace into which they have fallen by their late conduct. At that time, Brock was still petulant over their brief neutrality stand, and was neither impressed with their sincerity nor usefulness, suggesting that "they may serve to intimidate otherwise expect no essential service from this degenerate race."[45] In fact, however, the British, Canadians and Indian allies coordinated their counterattack smartly and won a stunning victory at the battle of Queenston Heights. The Grand River Iroquois "particularly distinguished themselves" in the operation as a result of "the judicious position which Norton and the Indians with him had taken on the woody brow of the high ground."[46]

Following the battle of Queenston Heights, apart from some minor skirmishing and deployment of troops by both sides, the first year of the War of 1812 ended in Upper Canada with His Majesty's forces and Indian allies victorious on all fronts. At Fort George, William Claus concluded the year by assembling the Grand River Iroquois at the nearby Indian council house and encouraging them to maintain their allegiance to the king. Along the Detroit, Matthew Elliott and other officers of the British

Indian Department were engaged in similar duties, meeting with Indian delegates at Amherstburg and working in close alliance with Tecumseh.

The successful defence of the province in 1812 was the result of the bold offensive strategy of Isaac Brock, "the hero and saviour of Upper Canada" in traditional Canadian historical accounts of the War of 1812.[47] Yet the victories at Michilimackinac, Detroit, and Queenston Heights were all determined in large measure by the physical presence or active military use of significant numbers of Indian allies. The warriors, either by inducing a terrible psychological fear on the enemy, as at Michilimackinac and Detroit, or by fighting with a passionate intensity, as at Queenston Heights and other places, appreciably affected the final outcome. There is little doubt that Tecumseh, a dedicated and influential leader among the tribes, was important to the British war effort. But, with the fall of Michilimackinac, Indians from the upper lakes and Mississippi fur country began to arrive along the Detroit in increasing numbers. Behind this steady influx of western warriors which contributed so significantly in the defence of Canada, especially during the first few critical summer months of 1812, loomed the dominant figure of Robert Dickson.

The contribution of Dickson in collecting, organizing, feeding, and despatching Indian warriors to Amherstburg was acknowledged and rewarded on 1 January 1813 when he was appointed agent and superintendent "for the Indians of the Nations to the Westward of Lake Huron." His salary was £200 per year, payable through the accounts of the Indian Department, and £300 for travel and expenses, to be paid out of the secret service fund. In addition, a claim for £1,875, which Dickson had submitted personally at Quebec for distributing his trade goods and supplies to starving Indians during the previous winter, was accepted in full by Prevost "as compensation for the eminent services which he had rendered to His Majesty's government by his loyalty, zeal, and exertions in bringing forward the Indians to aid in the capture of the post of Michilimackinac and that of Brigadier-General Hull and his army at Detroit."[48]

The powers granted under this appointment were extensive. Dickson was given the authority to employ five officers and fifteen interpreters, and "to make requisitions as may be necessary upon His Majesty's Indian Storekeepers or other proper officers for such Goods and Provisions as from Time to Time shall be considered necessary to successfully carry out the Object." The object, the fundamental tenet of British Indian policy in the War of 1812, was to court and maintain the affections of the Indians, so that they

could provide continued military assistance "where Circumstances may require their Aid in the Province of Upper Canada."
Finally, his instructions stressed that "in the policy to be strictly
observed in your conduct towards the different tribes, it is desirable that you should endeavour to conciliate them to act together
harmoniously, that you should restrain them by all the means in
your power from acts of cruelty and inhumanity" and that
Dickson must encourage the preservation of the British-Indian
alliance against the common enemy. [49]

Armed with this new authority and a policy speech which he
was instructed to deliver repeatedly to various tribes, Dickson
departed Lower Canada for the upper lakes and Mississippi country. The extent of his mandate initially caused some jealousy and
factionalism within the Indian Department. Therefore, he was
given additional autonomy and instructed to report only to senior
officers of the British army, a requirement which was to embroil
him in controversy later. By mid-March, Dickson was at St. Joseph,
where he wrote Procter announcing that he was preparing to
carry His Excellency's message to various tribes throughout the
region.

Dickson was "a large man, of full face, tall and commanding."
He also possessed flaming red hair, a physical characteristic quite
rare to the Indians, who consequently and affectionately referred
to him as "the Red Head," Mascotopah in the Dakota language.
The speech he was to deliver exuded warmth and affection,
emphasizing the strong historical bonds of trust and friendship
between the Indian people and the British crown. References were
made to Sir William Johnson who had promised the Indians that
the king "never would forsake or abandon" them, but that on the
contrary, British and Canadian traders had been sent amongst
them with "cloathing and Ammunition, and even a little Milk
[spirits] to gladden your Hearts." As to the present war, which "the
Big Knives [Americans] have most unjustly began and carry on
against the Indians" and the British, the speech explained that the
king knew that the western tribes "have long felt the effects of
their wicked Policy." The chiefs assembled were then encouraged
"to rouse up your young Warriors, and to Join my Troops with the
Red coats and your ancient Bretherin the Canadians, who are also
my Children, in order to defend your and our Country, your and
our Wives and Children from becoming Cariers of Water to those
faithless people ... our common enemy." The speech warned again
that the Americans wanted "to possess themselves of all the
Indian lands and to destroy one Nation after an other until they
got the whole Country within the Rocky Mountains." The king's

message concluded with the news that because of his great regard for the Indians, he had made "your old friend the Red Head a chief in order to carry to you my Speech."[50] At this point, flags and medals of King George were distributed amongst the tribal delegates.

The text, which echoed Dickson's instructions, appeared to achieve the desired effect, as evidenced by the comment of John Askin, Jr. at Michilimackinac that every Indian that can bear arms on Lakes Michigan and Huron will exert himself to drive away the Americans. The Sioux or Dakota bands, whom Dickson knew so well from his fur trading years and marriage to To-to-win, responded to their friend's plea with particular enthusiasm. Most revealing, however, is the subsequent version of these events by the Dakota people who ever after referred to the War of 1812 as "Pahinshashawacikiya," meaning "when the Redhead Begged for Our Help."[51] Other Indian delegates told Dickson that they would lose no time in "joining their Father at Detroit." During the next several weeks Dickson travelled and held councils with various tribes of the western Indians. In April he was at Prairie du Chien on the upper Mississippi, and by the end of May he was at Green Bay, assembling Indians. After pausing for a time at Michilimackinac, Dickson, with a force of "one thousand picked Warriors," including one hundred Sioux from Lake Traverse and two hundred Sauk and Fox from the Mississippi under their leader Black Hawk (Ma-ka-tai-me-she-kia-kiak), departed for Detroit.[52]

Whilst Dickson was collecting and organizing the western Indians, Procter with his British Right Division was maintaining a defensive position, as instructed, along the Detroit. The commander, however, dreaded the thought of the Indian reaction to any withdrawal of British forces from Michigan Territory, commenting that "if it should be ceded we sacrifice their Interest and nothing will satisfy them nothing appease them."[53] In the cold of January, his strength of commitment was first tested when an American force of about one thousand regulars and Kentucky militia under Brigadier-General James Winchester marched to the River Raisin Settlement (Frenchtown), southwest of Amherstburg, in search of badly needed supplies.

Procter, concerned that Harrison and the rest of the North Western Army might also be arriving soon, attacked Winchester without delay. In a bloody fight, in which "the Indian Warriors displayed their usual courage," the American troops were nearly annihilated, Procter reporting that "upwards of 400 men are prisoners, the remainder being killed by the Indians in their flight."

In fact, Winchester himself was "taken in the pursuit by the Wyandot Chief Roundhead." Procter also reported that he "had much Difficulty in bringing the Indians to consent to the Sparing of their Lives." This statement proved all too true, for the next day, 23 January, some Potawatomi and Wyandot slaughtered a number of American wounded prisoners.[54] This "Frenchtown massacre" naturally provoked bitter feelings and cries for reprisal in the United States, but the killings merely reflected a standard of conduct which was longstanding and mutual in American frontier warfare.

In the weeks following the events at the River Raisin, Procter, promoted to brigadier-general, continued to monitor the movements of the enemy by detailing Tecumseh, who was not present at Frenchtown, to harass Harrison's army and intercept any communications. The American general had reorganized his command after the January debâcle and fortified a position on the Maumee River known as Fort Meigs. In the spring Procter decided to attack the American fort before Harrison, waiting for additional reinforcements and supplies, could commence active operations to retake Detroit. At Fort Meigs, a siege and battle, "a severe Contest tho' not of long Continuance" ensued on 5 May in which an American relief column of Kentucky militia was caught in the woods by Tecumseh and the Indian allies and suffered two hundred killed and 547 prisoners, not counting a great number who were taken by the Indians to their villages. Procter's looses in regulars, militia, and Indian numbered only sixty.[55]

The British commander praised the Right Division, and especially "the Courage and Activity displayed throughout the whole Scene of Action by the Indian Chiefs and Warriors [who] contributed largely to our Success." Yet after the battle the Indian allies, representing several tribes, dispersed with their booty and prisoners, leaving Procter with only "Tecumseh and Less than twenty Chiefs and Warriors." As an immediate consequence, the British force withdrew to Detroit. Although pleased with the victory, Procter was deeply concerned with the subsequent conduct of the warriors. As the unreliability of the Indian allies had became glaringly apparent, Procter declared that "under present Circumstances at least, our Indian Force is not a disposable one, or permanent, tho' occasionally a most powerful Aid."[56]

Dickson, who had succeeded to the full extent of his hopes among the Indian tribes, finally reached Detroit in July with a host of Ottawa, Ojibwa, Potawatomi, Sauk, Fox, Sioux, Menominee, and Winnebago warriors. But the influx of these western Indian allies soon caused severe provisioning problems for the Indian Department. As well, the warriors were becoming bored and impatient with the lack of action. These conditions prompted a reluctant Procter to undertake another expedition into the Ohio, "where we might be fed at the Expense of the Enemy," and where the warriors could again demonstrate their military prowess. Yet at Fort Stephenson on the Sandusky River on 1 August, the 41st Regiment of Foot lost about one hundred officers and men attempting to storm the place, whilst the Indian allies "scarce came into Fire, before they ran off out of it's Reach." An angry Procter could only conclude that "the Indian Force is seldom a disposable one, never to be relied on in the Hour of Need."[57]

By September, Procter's frustration with the Indian allies, now lounging around Amherstburg with their wives and children, was compounded by the fact that they were consuming vast quantities of beef and flour. With the Indian Department stores already low, Procter demanded "a timely, and adequate Supply of Indian Goods and Ammunition," in order to avoid "frightfull Consequences." The commander realized that the Indians, "suffering from Cold, will no longer be amused with Promises," and he feared not only mass defections, but a violent backlash against the British. [58] The situation for Procter, however, became crippling on 10 September with the loss of the British fleet on Lake Erie at Put-in-Bay. With the Americans in control of the lake, the logistical lifelines of the British Right Division to the British Centre Division in the Niagara peninsula and beyond to Quebec were virtually severed. Procter was thus isolated and trapped.

Procter was fully aware that if Detroit was retaken, it would alarm and annoy the Indian allies. Nevertheless he was a realist, and with Harrison and a large and confident American North Western Army rapidly advancing, he ordered the troops under his command to withdraw. This decision aroused vehement Indian opposition. In a passionate speech at Fort Amherstburg, Tecumseh reminded the general of his pledge never to draw a foot off British ground: "but now, Father, we see you are drawing back, and we are sorry to see our Father doing so without seeing the enemy. We must compare our father's conduct to a fat animal, that carries its tail upon its back, but when affrightened, it drops it between its legs and runs off."[59] The anger and bitterness expressed by the Shawnee leader was shared by the other chiefs and warriors who remembered 1783 and 1794. To the Indian allies, the British abandonment of Detroit and Amherstburg in September 1813 was a third betrayal.

Despite the protestations of the Indian allies, Procter conducted a slow and agonizing retreat along the Thames River, with the intention of linking at Burlington Heights at the head of Lake Ontario with the British Centre Division. But at the Moravian Town on 5 October, the British and Indian allies were forced to turn and engage the fast-moving Americans. The 41st Regiment of Foot, discouraged, depleted, and physically exhausted after fourteen months of almost continuous and arduous campaigning against superior forces, uncharacteristically broke ranks after firing two ragged volleys, and surrendered or dispersed. At this juncture, Procter, promoted again four months earlier to major-general, quitted the ground and narrowly escaped capture.[60]

The Indian allies under Tecumseh, however, concealed in the woods and swamps to the right of the British position, had managed initially to turn the left flank of Harrison's army. But the collapse of the 41st exposed the warriors to the full fury of the enemy. Bloodied but rampant, and perhaps feeling that courage and defiance were their only remaining true allies, the Confederacy of Shawnee, Ottawa, Ojibwa, Potawatomi, Winnebago, Sauk, and other tribes stood grimly with Tecumseh, and faced for a final time the American advance. After fighting for about on hour, especially against the mounted Kentuckians – their traditional and vociferous foes from Blue Licks, Fallen Timbers, Frenchtown and countless other frontier engagements – and witnessing the death of Tecumseh, the warriors finally and stubbornly retired, in good order, through the woods. During the final phase of the battle, "the Conduct of the Enemy's Cavalry was marked by peculiar Cruelty to the Families of the Indians who had not Time to escape, or conceal Themselves."[61]

The battle at the Moravian Town, also known as the battle of the Thames, virtually terminated the War of 1812 along the Detroit.[62] For Procter, the disaster ruined his military career. In December of 1814 he faced a court martial in Montreal, and was sentenced to a public reprimand and suspended from rank and pay for six months, although acquitted in regard to his personal conduct during the action.[63] Feeling the scapegoat, Procter retired to England and died at Bath in 1822. Indeed, until recently, the commander of the British Right Division has been treated harshly by Canadian historians because he lost, and by American historians because he won too many times and with Indian allies. In fact, Procter had waged a remarkable fourteen-month campaign in the defence of Canada, with a relatively isolated command which was often starved for supplies and provisions. His efforts and that of the British Right Division absorbed the collective military energies of the aggressive "war hawk" states and adjacent territories, and thus lessened significantly the potential American pressure from the west which could have been applied with telling effect on the Centre Division and throughout the province. The final irony for Procter was that a battle on water had already decided his fate on land.

For Tecumseh, by comparison, the battle at the Moravian Town elevated him to the status of a folk hero in both Canada and the United States. His death on 5 October 1813 destroyed the confederacy and ended forever the dream of a united Indian resistance against the territorial ambitions of the United States in the lower Great Lakes region. But, like Brock, the Shawnee leader had died gallantly on the field of battle in defence of his country, his people, and his cultural values. For Canadians, therefore, he has been honoured as a competent and respected ally during the War of 1812, who helped save Canada from American frontier imperialism. For their part, Americans came to regard Tecumseh as an effective, yet compassionate, foe who epitomized the "beau ideal" of the proud and noble Indian, fighting desperately and passionately to preserve an ancient way of life in the face of the inexorable advance of "civilization."[64]

With the defeat of Procter and the death of Tecumseh, the shattered remnants of the British Right Division, along with some of the Indian allies, eventually joined the British Centre Division at Burlington Heights in the Niagara peninsula, where military events, especially in the spring and summer, had been equally dramatic. In late May the Americans captured Fort George and other defences, and forced the British to retire towards the head of Lake Ontario. But in June the enemy advance was checked at the Forty, Stoney Creek, and Beaver Dams. The latter engagement was fought on 24 June solely by Indian allies from Caughnawaga (Kahnawake), St. Régis (Akwesasne) and Oka at Lake of Two Mountains (Kanehsatake) in Lower Canada, along with some Mohawk from Grand River. Lieutenant James FitzGibbon of the 49th Regiment of Foot subsequently took the surrender of over five hundred American officers and men who feared a massacre. The British reports were initially confusing, which provoked John Norton to exclaim that the "Cognauaga [sic] Indians fought the battle, the Mohawks got the plunder, and Fitzgibbon got the credit."[65]

Throughout the rest of the summer of 1813, the American invaders assumed a laager mentality and remained huddled behind the safety of the breastworks at Fort George, refusing to venture into the surrounding woods to face the lurking warriors. One senior American officer, disgusted with this stalemate, reported that "this army lies panic-struck, shut up and whipped in by a few hundred miserable savages, leaving the whole of this frontier, except the mile in extent which they occupy, exposed to the inroads and depredations of the enemy."[66] By December the American force at Fort George was severely reduced owing to desertion, expiration of terms of enlistment, boredom, and the cold weather. Under these circumstances, the British easily recaptured the place, and continued their advance by crossing the river, seizing Fort Niagara and burning everything on the American side from Lewiston through Black Rock to Buffalo. Throughout these manoeuvres the Indian allies ravaged homes and killed anyone they found. This cruel thoroughness in despatching the enemy allowed the senior British officer present to compliment the warriors in his report for committing "no Act of Cruelty ... towards any of their Prisoners!"[67]

The war on the Niagara went into a winter slumber following the British and Indian counterattacks of December 1813. In the summer campaigns of 1814, the predominant use of British regulars and Canadian fencibles in the tough and stand-up slugging of the European-style battles of Chippewa, Lundy's Lane, and around Fort Erie reduced the role of the Indian allies mainly to scouting expeditions and harassing forays. In fact, the only fighting of any consequence in 1814 involving the Indian allies of Upper Canada took the form of squabbling between the Indian Department, British officers, and various "Chiefs of Renown," such as John Norton, over the authority to distribute "Awards of Presents to the Indian Warriors."[68] This jurisdictional feud, which became centred around Claus and Norton, ended only with the termination of the war.

To a considerable degree, the defence of Upper Canada in the War of 1812 was the result of a planned strategy under the direction of Major-General Isaac Brock, which combined the active use of Indian allies with lightning offensive moves early in the conflict, aimed at forcing the surrender of the key enemy targets of Michilimackinac and Detroit. The initiatives for achieving these goals were begun in 1808 through the efforts of the officers of the Indian Department who nourished a careful renewal of the old British-Indian friendship and military alliance which had lapsed after 1794. With the formal declaration of war in June of 1812, the plan was immediately put into operation with overwhelming success.

These victories in the first few critical weeks of the war bolstered the confidence and determination of the British, Canadians, and Indians to resist the ambitions of the invaders. The death of Brock in October 1812 only provided an added impetus to fight. For the Indian allies under Tecumseh, the war was fought to preserve and protect lands other than those of Upper Canada. But the warriors nonetheless contributed significantly to the defence of the province, until the death of their leader at the Moravian Town. Yet the impact of Tecumseh on Canada and the War of 1812 survived his death. In 1811–12 he had toured the southern United States, visiting among the several tribes and encouraging them to join the pan-Indian movement. The outbreak of the Creek War in August 1813 thus drained American military energies away from the north, and consequently, if indirectly, materially assisted in the defence of Canada.[69]

But by mid-1814 the usefulness of the Indian allies in Upper Canada had so diminished that they were regarded as more of a liability. A veteran sergeant of the 8th Regiment of Foot (the King's Liverpool), for instance, viewed the warriors as nothing more than "a Cowardly, Pusillanimous Filthy Crew" whose excessive cruelty shocked him.[70] Another writer considered the Indians as feeble and useless allies, but dangerous enemies. This last observation may be slightly closer to the mark, but it overlooks Michilimackinac, Detroit, the River Raisin, Fort Meigs, and Beaver Dams – all victories which helped in the defence of Upper Canada, and all won principally by the Indian allies. In addition, warriors fought for the king to the west and north of the province, and in this vast region loyal subjects had visions of expanding and entrenching a British military and economic influence, and by so doing, providing for the possible political creation of a wider Canada.

CHAPTER 7

THE WAR OF 1812: THE NORTHWEST

The Northwest, sometimes known as the "old" Northwest, was a vast region stretching west from the Detroit River to the Mississippi, north to the upper reaches of that river, and south to St. Louis on the Missouri. It included the present American states of Ohio, Michigan, Indiana, Illinois, Iowa, Wisconsin, Minnesota, and parts of Missouri and the Dakotas. The area was inhabited by several Indian tribes, but by the end of the seventeenth century French explorers and voyageurs had also traversed and frequented these lands. The Quebec Act of 1774 appended this huge expanse of territory to the "old" province of Quebec (from 1791, Lower Canada and Upper Canada).[1] By June 1812 the Northwest had become a fairly active fur trade region in which the native people combined with Montreal-based British fur traders (mostly Scotch) and Canadian fur traders (mostly French-speaking) to become partners in fur.

The evolving relationship between the tribes and the fur traders was not solely confined to economic profits. Over the years, "many tender ties" developed through numerous marriages, "à la façon du pays."[2] For the British and Canadian fur traders of the Northwest, their blood was in the soil. The attachments to their Indian families, personal friendships among the tribes, and the commercial profits of the fur trade, steeled them to resist any intrusion which might threaten their way of life. They persisted in their determination in spite of the fact that the Northwest by the terms of the Treaty of Paris (1783) was placed within the political boundaries of the new republic of the United States of America. Seemingly undaunted, and ignoring also the Jay Treaty, the withdrawal of British troops from the western posts in 1796, and the lapsed Quebec Act, the fur traders continued to regard the Northwest as a natural geographic and economic extension of the Canadas and as such, an integral part of British North America.

For the British and Canadian fur traders and the Indian tribes of the Northwest, therefore, the War of 1812, and more particularly the American invasion of Upper Canada in that first summer of conflict, was viewed as the ultimate threat to the continuation of their very existence. An American victory would surely result in the advance north and west of the American frontier and settlement which would mean the dispossession of the Indians from their traditional lands and the end of the fur trade. With no British Canada, there would be no British Northwest. Thus, from the opening days of the War of 1812, the fur traders and warriors of the Northwest threw their collective energies against the common enemy and into supporting the British war effort.[3] Yet, although British Indian policy in the War of 1812 was primarily geared to protect Canada, the fur traders recognized that by defending Canada they could also not only preserve, but entrench and expand a British paramountcy in the Northwest. This prospect, if achieved, could have dramatically altered the international boundary between the United States and the future Dominion of Canada. Thus, economic self-interest, a stubborn determination to preserve the traditional lands and cultural values of the local tribes, along with a natural desire to protect their Indian families, motivated the British and Canadian fur traders of the Northwest. Some of them also possessed, with varying degrees of enthusiasm, a loyalty to the crown. These several considerations were more than sufficient inducements to attempt a renewal and enhancement of British military and political ascendancy in the region. During the War of 1812 in the Northwest, this goal was for the fur traders their hidden agenda.

The British and Canadian fur traders of the Northwest were fully supported and financed by the fur merchants, barons, and entrepreneurs of the North West Company in Montreal; and during the War of 1812 these gentlemen of power and influence made no secret of their desire to promote British domination in the Northwest. Whether through formal correspondence, or at social functions, general meetings, or in the comforts of the prestigious

Beaver Club, the fur barons articulated their point of view to British government officials and military officers. In a letter to Sir George Prevost, for instance, the Glasgow-born James McGill, an early stalwart in the North West Company and a man who established strong partnerships in the fur trade business with relatives and close friends, was particularly vociferous. He wrote to Prevost that "the nations of Indians near the Mississippi have hitherto had little or no connection with Government except through British traders who have individually contributed very materially to preserve alive their attachment to Great Britain." In the same letter, McGill reminded the governor of the symbiotic relationship between the preservation of Canada and the survival of the Montreal-based fur trade. He concluded by stressing the military importance of His Majesty's Indian allies, "the only Allies who can aught avail in the defence of the Canadas. They Have the same interest as us, and alike are objects of American subjugation, if not extermination."[4]

The views of McGill were echoed by fur barons and traders from Montreal to the Northwest; and they became louder following the collapse of the British Right Division at the Moravian Town in October 1813. William McGillivray, from Dunlichty in Scotland and the head of the North West Company, began increasingly to use his considerable influence and friendships with the British political and military élite to obtain a commitment that Michilimackinac and the Northwest would be reinforced in the spring of 1814. With the approaching spring, the British and Canadian fur traders in the Northwest recognized the urgency and need for a revised British military strategy which would in part focus on the Indian and fur trade country west and north of the Detroit. At Lake Winnebago on the upper Mississippi, Robert Dickson, in a letter written in early February 1814, epitomized the feelings of those fur traders who were becoming increasingly anxious about defending local interests. He offered that in the Northwest "we should find something worth fighting for ...;" and reckoned that "St. Louis might be taken this spring with 5 or 600 men it is unfortunate that we are required in another Quarter [meaning Upper Canada]."[5]

The arguments put forward by the Montreal-based fur trade interests eventually stirred the British government and military into adopting measures which they hoped would preserve the Northwest for the king. This is not to say that the British authorities were not already fully aware of the strategic and economic importance of that vast region to Canada. From the earliest days of the War of 1812, and even before, a number of local British commanders had prepared information and detailed reports relating to this theme. One of the more astute analyses was provided by Brigadier-General Henry Procter. Stationed along the Detroit for several years and actively involved as commander of the British Right Division until October 1813, he had both the time and interest to reflect carefully on this matter. Although there is some debate as to his ability as a field commander, he was certainly competent, even insightful, in grasping the vital importance of the Northwest to Canada and the British empire.

In a lengthy and undated report, but probably written during the winter of 1812-13, Procter addressed the major strategic and economic concerns relating to the Northwest and Canada. He began by speculating that "the Province of Upper Canada (it appears to me) will be of little value to Britain unless accompanied" by the lands of the Northwest.[6] The province, he noted, was almost surrounded by the Americans; and if they possessed the Northwest, communications would surely be severed between "Canada and the Western Indians the most powerful and the most warlike of the Indians." With the United States in control of the region, Procter predicted that the British and Canadian fur trade would soon disappear.

Procter continued his report by noting the defeat of the Americans at Detroit (16 August 1812) and "the very effectual assistance given by the Indians." But again, he expressed concern that if the Americans gained and settled the Northwest, the Indians would be forthwith expelled and therefore be unable to assist His Majesty's forces in Canada in any possible future conflict with the United States. The general problem could be solved, according to Procter, "if the boundary between the British provinces and Upper Canada were a line drawn from Lake Erie westward to the Mississippi; that is nearly the territory that we actually at present have in possession." This political boundary would, of course, provide some obvious strategic and economic advantages for the British government. First, Procter regarded the Northwest as "the most beautiful and the most valuable portion of North America ... an extensive tract of the most temperate and healthy climate, of fertile soil and picturesque surface ..." Secondly, Britain, as a commercial and manufacturing nation, was being excluded in her trade and manufactures from the whole of Napoleonic Europe and from the United States. Therefore, reasoned Procter, a British Northwest could supply the mother country "with all those commodities of which she stands in want: timber, tar, wheat when necessary, copper, lead, iron, hemp, hides, furs" and, he continued, reciting the classic principles of eighteenth-century mercantilism, the carrying of these raw materials in British bottoms would "be a nursery of seamen and ships and the surest means of perpetuating the naval power of Britain." In all of this, Canada and a British Northwest would receive "the greatest share of benefit by their connection with Britain."

Procter next turned his attention more specifically to the fur trade and Indians of the Northwest. The extension of Canada to include the lands north and west of the Detroit would also be greatly to the advantage of the British and Canadian fur trade interest, he noted, as there would then be a direct, safe, and relatively easy connection via a water route through rivers and lakes between Canada, the Mississippi, Hudson Bay, and beyond. As for the Indian tribes of the Northwest, if the United States controlled this valuable and fertile tract, the Indians would be "rendered incapable of giving us assistance by being left to the vengeance ... of an unwieldy and Discordant republic; subject to all the troubles and vicissitudes which may take place." Thus, "the Indians will lose confidence in Britain" and, worse, Britain would lose the "Balance of Power" in North America. The final and only result, lamented Procter, was that the United States at any future period could easily take a near defenceless Canada. He concluded his analysis by observing that the Indians already distrusted the king's men for luring them into the war. In a final, thoughtful comment, Procter expressed his deep concern for the Indian allies who feared that the British would "leave them as soon as it suits our convenience to the vengeance of their inveterate enemy [and that the native people] will ever after regard Britain as a deceitful ally whose friendship is harmful and whose alliance is destruction."

The prospects of a wider Canada, meaning the inclusion of the Northwest, as envisioned by men such as Procter, McGillivray, Dickson, and others, suffered at least a temporary setback with the total collapse of the British Right Division in October 1813. Thereafter, until the end of the War of 1812, the Americans retained control of both Lake Erie and the Detroit sector, and thus effectively drove a firm wedge between Canada and the lands to the west and north. Undeterred, the British developed an alternate route to Michilimackinac and the upper Mississippi region of the Northwest via land and water by way of York (Toronto), Yonge Street, Holland Landing, Lake Simcoe and Kempenfelt Bay, the Nottawasaga river and bay, and finally across Lake Huron to the island fortress, the gateway to all the lands beyond.

Departing York on 2 October, Robert Dickson, laden with provisions and supplies "fully adequate to support the Indians for this winter," followed this new route.[7] Although delayed twenty days "by tempestuous weather," he finally reached Michilimackinac and then pushed on to the upper Mississippi where he spent the winter of 1813–14 at Lake Winnebago. Dickson was worried. How could he maintain the allegiance of the Indians to the British crown? With the defeat of the British along the Detroit and with the Tecumseh confederacy in tatters, would there be a useful role in the campaigns of 1814 for the Indian allies in the Northwest? Where would they fight? How would they react to being sent possibly to the Niagara front of Upper Canada, a great distance from their traditional lands? These questions gnawed at Dickson, but he nonetheless tirelessly attempted to encourage and win the confidence of the tribes through the distribution of foodstuffs and presents and by holding frequent councils with chiefs and warriors. By mid-December he had "seen all the Indians of the Rock River and a good number from the Ouisconsin [Wisconsin]."[8]

A second and mounting problem for Dickson was insufficient provisions and supplies. In a particularly despairing letter, written on Christmas Day, he discussed ice fishing and the making of spruce beer as diet supplements, but confessed that "I am most heartily tired of this distributing of Goods and wish for the Spring. I hear nothing but the cry of hunger from all Quarters."[9] Conditions only worsened in what became a particularly cold and starving winter. The Indians have "eaten me even to the nails," he wrote in March 1814. "There is no situation more miserable than to see objects around you dying with hunger, and unable to give them but little assistance. I have done what I could for them, and will in consequence starve myself."[10]

Although suffering severe physical hardships and famine, Dickson managed to survive the winter by eating black bread and roots. He had retained, to a surprising degree, the affections of the Indians. This achievement was remarkable, considering the events of October 1813 and the increased pressure applied by the Americans to neutralize and pacify the tribes. Throughout the winter Dickson recorded the inter-tribal rivalries and the various intrigues in which everybody was attempting "to gain allies." He was pleased that the Sauk remained loyal; yet he found that the Potawatomi were "villains" to both the British and Americans. The Menominee and Winnebago were steadfast, but his wife's people, the Sioux, annoyed him for a time when they attacked their ancient enemies to the north, the Saulteaux (Plains Ojibwa), after being provided with shot and powder by Dickson.

In the late spring, after despatching Sauk and Fox warriors to the Rock Island on the Mississippi to guard against a possible attack from the Americans to the south, Dickson, with about three hundred Indian allies, of whom more were to follow, proceeded to Michilimackinac. As promised, and under the final authority of Sir George Prevost, a British plan was approved in which the greatest exertion was "to be made for the preservation of Michilimackinac," in order to "maintain uninterrupted our Intercourse with the Western Indians."[11] The relief force, consisting of two companies of the Royal Newfoundland Regiment of Fencible Infantry, some gunners from the Royal Artillery, and a detachment of Royal Navy personnel, arrived by batteaux from Nottawasaga Bay on 18 May, after battling through floating ice. Although not much of a military force, it carried bountiful supplies, and was a welcome sight to the small garrison, composed of a few aged, tired, and bored rankers of the 10th Royal Veteran Battalion, and fifty Michigan Fencibles, a provincial corps raised in the summer of 1813, "chiefly Canadians inlisted from the service of the Traders."[12]

The new post commander and senior British officer in the Northwest was Lieutenant-Colonel Robert McDouall. Born in March 1774 and from Stranraer, Scotland, McDouall was a competent officer who had previously seen service in Egypt, Copenhagen, and the West Indies. Posted to Canada in 1810 as part of the 8th Regiment of Foot (the King's Liverpool Regiment), he transferred to the Glengarry Light Infantry Fencibles, formed in the first weeks of the War of 1812, where he was promoted to his present rank.[13] Most fortunately for McDouall, he had become socially cosy in Montreal with his Scotch countrymen, namely the "Lords of the North," or the fur barons and partners of the North West Company. In particular, he seemed to have developed a genuine friendship with the head of the company, as evidenced by his frequent letters to "My Dear McGillivray."[14]

This Scotch family compact between the British military and the Montreal fur trade interests was mutually beneficial. Both wanted to preserve the Northwest, one for the empire, the other for commercial profits. As a result, the two components formed a strong and determined team. McDouall continually sought the advice and assistance of McGillivray and others of the fur trade on a host of matters relating to his new command at Michilimackinac. The fur traders' local knowledge of the country was indispensable, as they were able to provide valuable information to McDouall on everything from appropriate water routes and provisioning procedures to personality assessments, both native and non-native. In one letter, McDouall discussed the outfitting of the schooner *Nancy*, and asked McGillivray if the *Mink*, another North West Company vessel, could be sent immediately to the island with additional supplies. In another letter, he thanked his friend for "having the good fortune of safely conveying down your fleet, so richly laden." Yet again, he "was glad to find that you have such a quantity of gunpowder, guns and tobacco at Lake Nippissink [Nipissing], which will be valuable to us" and was cheered by the "potent proof of indefatigable exertion," on the part of McGillivray and the North West Company.[15]

By the early summer of 1814, McDouall, Prevost, even His Majesty's government in London were fully aware that Michilmackinac was "the life and soul" of the Northwest. The geographical position of the island was admirable, as "its influence extends and is felt amongst the Indian tribes at New Orleans and the Pacific Ocean; vast tracts of country look to it for protection and supplies, and it gives security to the great establishments of the Northwest and Hudson's Bay Companies by supporting the Indians on the Mississippi."[16] Indeed, Michilimackinac was for the Northwest what the fortress of Quebec City was for Canada – absolutely vital for the preservation and defence of British interests in North America.

To consolidate and secure his position, McDouall and the recently arrived Robert Dickson held an impressive and formal council with chiefs and warriors of their Indian allies, who renewed their pledge to support the king. Wabasha spoke for the Indians assembled and praised Dickson for his "courage and good heart" in coming to the assistance of the Indian families during the last winter.[17] In fact, Prevost reported to the secretary of state for war and the colonies that "most of the Indians would have been lost to the British cause had it not been for the judicious, resolute and determined conduct of Mr. Dickson and his foresight and promptitude in forwarding supplies after Procter's defeat."[18]

Whilst the British were reinforcing Michilimackinac and meeting with tribal delegates, the Americans were putting into motion their 1814 campaign strategy for the Northwest. Their goals were to oust the British from the island and the important village and trading depôt of Prairie du Chien on the upper Mississippi. As a consequence, in late May of that year an American force from St. Louis under General William Clark, governor of Missouri Territory, ascended the Mississippi and, meeting only token resistance from the Sauk and Fox, took possession of Prairie du Chien. Content with his success, and following the construction of a stockade which he named Fort Shelby, Clark returned to St. Louis. He left a small garrison of about seventy men under Lieutenant Joseph Perkins of the 24th United States Infantry to guard the village and the new post.[19] This action was a godsend to the British and Canadian fur traders of the Northwest: their region was to become a major theatre of military operations in the War of 1812. With the western Indians now happily required to stay at home and fight on their traditional lands, and with British reinforcements at Michilimackinac, the fur traders uncovered the hidden agenda, buried since June 1812, and began overtly to implement their plan for achieving an unchallenged British domination in the Northwest.

The news of the capture of Prairie du Chien reached McDouall on 21 June. He reacted immediately by organizing a force "to dislodge the American General from his new conquest, and make him relinquish the immense tract of country he had seized upon in consequence and which brought him into the very heart of that occupied by our friendly Indians." Both the British military and fur trade interests really had no choice, for, as McDouall explained, if the Americans were allowed to remain in possession of that area,

> there was an end to our connection with the Indians … tribe after tribe would be graned [sic] over or subdued & thus would be destroyed the only barrier which protects the Great trading establishments of the North West & the Hudson's Bay Company. Nothing could then prevent the enemy from gaining the source of the Mississippi, gradually extending themselves by the Red River to Lake Winnipeg from whence the descent of Nelson's River to York Fort would in time be easy. The total subjugation of the Indians on the Mississippi would either lead to their extermination by the enemy or they would be spared on the express condition of assisting them to expel us from Upper Canada. [20]

The ironic twist to the Red River reference was that in 1811 Thomas Douglas, 5th Earl of Selkirk, through a family purchase, established an agricultural colony at the forks of the Red and Assiniboine rivers for evicted Scotch tenant farmers. This colony, located in an area known as Assiniboia (now part of the province of Manitoba), was bitterly opposed by the North West Company, as it blocked their trade route from Fort William on Lake Superior to the Saskatchewan country and beyond; moreover, it interfered with the Métis buffalo hunt and the making of pemmican, the staple foodstuff for the company's interior posts. McDouall was trying to preserve all of the Northwest for the British and the fur traders, including the Red River. Although this dedication was commendable and fortunate for the future geographic boundaries of western Canada, the protection of the Red River was the one area of dispute between the Scotch commander and the Scotch fur traders, who decidedly wanted to have this intruding Scotch colony scotched.

The leader of the expedition to retake Prairie du Chien was William McKay, a most prudent choice. Born in Scotland around 1772, his family had moved to Canada when he was a lad and settled along the upper St. Lawrence, near Cornwall. About 1790 McKay entered the service of the North West Company and over the next several years became well acquainted with the lands, transportation routes, and languages and customs of the various Indian tribes of the Northwest. He retired in 1807, a prominent partner in the company, a member of the Beaver Club, and a popular and respected figure among the social élite of Montreal. He and McDouall were friends.

With the outbreak of the War of 1812, McKay immediately volunteered his services. In late June he journeyed from Montreal to St. Joseph in a mere eight days, carrying secret instructions to attack the unsuspecting Americans at Michilimackinac. Following his return to Montreal, McKay raised a corps of North West Company voyageurs for batteaux service, and subsequently saw action at LaColle along the Richelieu in the autumn of the first year of the war. In the spring of 1813 he was appointed a captain in the 5th Battalion of Select Embodied Militia of Lower Canada, but his interest and experience took him back to the Northwest, this time carrying canoe loads of supplies. He returned again with McDouall and the reinforcements in May 1814. At Michilimackinac, he was awarded with the command of the Michigan Fencibles which pleased the corps, as McKay was "very popular with them and all the Canadians."[21]

In late June, McKay and a determined little force, initially consisting of 136 Indians, a group of Canadians, calling themselves the Mississippi Volunteers, Bombardier James Keating of the Royal Artillery with a 3-pounder and "twelve smart fellows of the Michigan Fencibles," left Michilimackinac and began their trek to Prairie du Chien.[22] The party was joined en route by voyageurs, Green Bay militia, and a horde of Indians. McKay was singularly unimpressed with the tribal allies and commented upon his arrival in front of Fort Shelby that his contingent had swelled to 650 men, of whom 120 were Canadian Volunteers, Michigan Fencibles, and officers of the Indian Department, with the remainder Indians who proved to be "perfectly useless." The small American fort contained two blockhouses and six pieces of cannon and was situated on a hill overlooking the village. A large gunboat, the *Governor Clark*, was anchored in the middle of the Mississippi River. This floating blockhouse, immune from the effects of musket fire, mounted fourteen cannon and had a crew of eighty men. It was constructed so that the men on board could row swiftly in any direction.

The unexpected appearance of McKay and his mixed force on Sunday, 17 July, caught the Americans by surprise. It was a pleasant day and the officers were preparing to take a pleasure ride and enjoy an outing in the country. After a dramatic exchange of notes, Perkins concluded by stating that he preferred to defend to the last man rather than surrender. This produced a three-hour barrage against the fort and gunboat. The Americans returned the fire. The *Governor Clark*, leaking and taking casualties, withdrew downriver. For the next two day McKay conducted siege operations. Two breastworks were constructed, and "a constant but perfectly useless" musket fire was maintained against the fort. During this time some of the Indian allies "behaved in a most villainous manner" and plundered the inhabitants in the village. The Indian action was largely motivated by their outrage at the killing of eight Winnebago who were "butchered like so many dogs" a few weeks before by troops under Clark; and by the murder of four others, of whom one was the wife of Wabasha.

Impatient with the standoff, McKay "resolved to accomplish something more decisive," and on 19 July marched his troops into the recently completed works and prepared red-hot shot for the cannon. The Americans, seeing "that a severe assault of some kind was about to be made, raised the white flag." By the terms of the capitulation, McKay took possession of the fort, several pieces of cannon, military and camp equipment, and a large quantity of ammunition and foodstuffs. The surrendered garrison was permitted to retire unmolested in boats downriver to St. Louis. McKay was pleased with the Michigan Fencibles, who "behaved with great courage, coolness and regularity," and "tho in the midst of a hot fire not a man was even wounded." Indeed, enthused McKay, "all acted with that courage and activity so becoming Canadian Militia or Volunteers."[23]

Two days after the success at Fort Shelby, the Indian allies, whose military prowess had been so recently maligned by McKay, won a crushing victory over the Americans at Rock Island Rapids, a few miles south of Prairie du Chien. This American force of about 120 regulars and rangers under the command of Major John Campbell, unaware of the recent developments, was arriving in six keelboats to reinforce the garrison at Fort Shelby. Near the

Indian villages scattered along the banks of the Rock River, about four hundred Sauk, Fox, and Kickapoo attacked and severely mauled the relief column. The Indians fought with a fierce intensity and, desperate to protect their villages and property, "the women even jumped on board with hoes and some breaking heads, others breaking casks, some trying to cut holes in her bottom to sink her, and others setting fire to her decks." About fifty Americans were killed or wounded in the engagement. Joined by the timely arrival of the *Governor Clark*, Campbell and his remnant made a precipitate retreat to St. Louis. A jubilant McKay offered his opinion that "this is perhaps one of the most brilliant actions fought by Indians only since the commencement of the war."[24] He then crowned his success in a symbolic sense by modestly renaming Fort Shelby, Fort McKay. After this gesture, McKay promptly retired to his quarters, for he had developed "a violent fever." In fact, he was suffering from a severe case of mumps, but soon recovered and departed for Michilimackinac and subsequently for Montreal.

His successor at Fort McKay was an ex-fur trader originally from Upper Canada, Captain Thomas Gummersall (Tige) Anderson, the commander of the Mississippi Volunteers. As post commandant, Anderson strengthened Fort McKay and built a northeast blockhouse. He worried about the poor harvest that year, and because of the want of provisions, he ordered the Mississippi Volunteers to help the local farmers in harvesting the grain. The troops were also kept occupied performing daily garrison duties. There were few diversions, except for excessive rum drinking and watching the occasional spectacle of inter-tribal lacrosse in which several participants usually "got sore wounds from the ball and the hurl stick."[25]

In late summer a second and larger American expedition of 350 men and eight gunboats under the command of Major Zachary Taylor, future president of the United States, was launched against the Indian villages along the Rock River. About 1,200 Sauk, Fox, Kickapoo, Winnebago, and Sioux under the leadership of Black Hawk, a "zealous partisan of the British cause," assembled to meet the American threat. Informed of this new American thrust, Anderson despatched Duncan Graham of the Indian Department and thirty men, and James Keating of the Royal Artillery with two swivel-guns and the 3-pounder to bolster Indian courage. In the early morning of 5 September the Indians and Canadians attacked Taylor's flotilla at Rock Island. The accuracy of the guns under Keating, which was "base enough to knock the Splinters into the men's faces" in the gunboats, combined with the confidence of the

Indians who "raised a yell and commenced firing on us in every direction," convinced Taylor of the futility of attempting to destroy the Indian villages and corn fields, and of pushing north to Prairie du Chien.[26] With the Indians in pursuit for nearly three miles, the Americans retreated downriver. They had suffered about fifteen killed and wounded. At the entrance of the Des Moines River, Taylor built Fort Johnson. In October this vestige of an American presence in the upper Mississippi was burned, and the garrison retired to St. Louis. No further military efforts were made against Rock Island or Prairie du Chien.

The sweeping of the Americans back to St. Louis left the British and Canadian fur traders and the Indian allies supreme in the upper Mississippi, the southern portion of the Northwest. But all would be for nought if Michilimackinac, the gateway to the north, should fall. Whilst Prairie du Chien was exchanging flags, a second and larger American expeditionary force of more than seven hundred had sailed from Detroit for Michilimackinac under the command of Lieutenant-Colonel George Croghan, the hero of Fort Stephenson. The five American naval vessels, delayed by contrary winds, did not reach St. Joseph until 20 July, where they amused themselves by burning the old British post and some public buildings. Over the next few days they managed to capture the *Mink*, destroy the North West Company post at Saint Marys (Sault Ste Marie), and murder a number of Indian families camped about the place. This force reached the island of Michilimackinac on 26 July.[27]

McDouall expected them and was prepared, commenting that "we are here in a very fine state of Defense the Garrison and Indians in the Highest spirits, and all ready for the attack of the Enemy."[28] For several days the Americans remained anchored off Michilimackinac, apparently reluctant to attempt a landing and assault against the Indians in the dense and unfamiliar woods. As well, the high elevation prevented the American guns from engaging the fortifications. Finally, on 4 August, Croghan ordered his troops ashore, after a "tremendous fire" from his naval vessels had raked the beach. McDouall countered quickly and decisively. After leaving a few militia and Royal Artillery to hold the forts, he rushed his entire disposable force consisting of "140 bayonets" drawn from the Royal Newfoundland Fencibles, Michigan Fencibles, and a few of the 10th Royal Veterans, all supported by about 315 Indian allies, to meet the enemy in the woods near the middle of the island. Rather than engage directly, both sides moved about the trees and thick bush in some confusion. The critical point of the battle, however, took place when McDouall began a withdrawal of his "regulars" to combat a supposed second landing by Croghan. The Americans in the woods, sensing a victory, moved forward. At that very moment, they received a deadly volley of musket fire at close range by a hidden band of Menominee under the leadership of the "six foot and handsome" Tomah and two other chiefs named L'Espagnol and Yellow Dog. The warriors then "commenced a spirited attack upon the Enemy, who in a short time lost their second in Command [Major Andrew Hunter Holmes] and several other Officers ... The Enemy retired in the utmost haste and confusion ... till they found shelter under the very Broadside of their Ships anchored within a few yards of the Shore – They re-embarked that Evening and the Vessels immediately hauled off."[29]

Croghan had suffered a humiliating defeat at the cost of about fifteen killed and forty-eight wounded. British and Indian losses were minimal. On their return to Detroit, the Americans located and destroyed the *Nancy*, the last remaining British vessel on the upper lakes, which had been maintaining communications with Michilimackinac. In September the British struck back by capturing the American schooners *Tigress* and *Scorpion*. The vessels had been left by Croghan to patrol Lake Huron and prevent supplies from reaching McDouall. These acquisitions provided the Royal Navy at Matchedash Bay and Penetanguishine with a makeshift force on Lake Huron; and if the war had continued into 1815 there probably would have been some sort of naval contest to decide the supremacy of the upper lakes. Of more immediate and particular significance, however, was that Michilimackinac was ignored by the Americans for the duration of the War of 1812.

The twin victories at Prairie du Chien and the Rock Island Rapids in July, coupled with the successful defence of Michilimackinac in August, reasserted and confirmed British superiority throughout the Northwest. At Michilimackinac, nonetheless, Robert McDouall continued to improve his defences in anticipation of another American attack, possibly next spring. In fact, he reported months later that "we have been indefatigable the whole winter in improving and strengthening our position."[30] He was heartened by the arrival in September 1814 of additional reinforcements in the form of one company of the 81st Regiment of Foot (the Loyal North Lancashire Regiment), and sixteen large canoes laden with rum, gunpowder, and sundry supplies and foodstuffs. By the end of October, William McKay, who had brought the supplies, was ready to depart again for Montreal where he would carry a message concerning "the very great anxiety evinced by Mr. Dickson to have instructions from Government for his Guidance and conduct in respect to the Tribes of Indians under his influence." Dickson was becoming increasingly concerned about the nature and extent of his role in the Indian Department and was "quite at a loss how to act."[31] Apart from this seeming niggling matter, events on the island were uneventful; and Michilimackinac tucked down for the winter.

By the late autumn of 1814 however, rations at Fort McKay were becoming scarce. To alleviate the food shortage, Tige Anderson discharged the Green Bay militia and sent them home. The remaining troops received corn one day, flour and pork the next. Of greater concern was the increasing numbers of Indian families who were camping around Prairie du Chien awaiting the arrival of the annual supplies from the Indian Department. These problems remained unresolved until 30 November when Robert Dickson duly arrived with supplies from Michilimackinac.[32] With him came most of the Michigan Fencibles and the new young post commander, Lieutenant Andrew Bulger, bestowed by McDouall with the local rank of captain and invested with "the exclusive direction of all operations on the Mississippi."[33] Bulger was tough, bold, and intolerant of any challenge to his authority. His military record during the War of 1812 was impressive. Born in Newfoundland, Bulger joined the Royal Newfoundland Fencibles and subsequently fought in Upper Canada at Detroit, Fort George, Stoney Creek, and Chrysler's Farm. Upon arrival at Michilimackinac, he took part in the battle of 4 August, and was prominent in the daring capture of the *Tigress* and *Scorpion* in September, receiving a slight wound in the former episode.

The situation at this new posting was both dangerous and delicate for Bulger, as he had inherited the twin problems of garrison discontent and tribal irritation at the scarcity of provisions. Determined to preserve order, Bulger retained Anderson and placed him in local command of the Michigan Fencibles. The troops were bored and insolent. They were existing mainly on a scanty allowance of bread and a ration of "wild meat" when available. But the two officers began to instil a renewed sense of pride and discipline in the men. This goal was achieved in early January 1815, when a near mutiny among the Michigan Fencibles was quickly suppressed and the three worst offenders summarily flogged. Thereafter, the corps performed their routine duties well.[34]

In addition, Bulger was instructed to cultivate a good understanding with the Indian tribes and maintain their allegiance to the British. Throughout the winter of 1814-15, his duties were "as unceasing as they were arduous," and he succeeded in gaining the continued affection of the Indians by visiting several of their villages. Unfortunately, he also became embroiled in a bitter feud with Robert Dickson, who was already chafing about the confusion in his role and status over the control and feeding of the Indian allies. As the senior officer of the British Indian Department in the Northwest, Dickson was genuinely concerned at the destitute condition of the Indians, apart from their military value. Relations between the two men became increasingly strained over specific areas of responsibility. Dickson insisted that supplies to the Indians must be increased; yet married to a Sioux woman, he showed a bias in feeding the Sioux bands. Bulger endeavoured "to promote a fair, equal and judicious distribution" of provisions and gifts to the Indian families, but he refused to allow the Indian Department to usurp his authority or that of the British army. He reported to McDouall that the conduct of Dickson had placed the garrison and others of His Majesty's Indian allies in danger of further starvation. The feud became petty and degenerated into name-calling. McDouall fully supported Bulger, and in one letter he referred to Dickson as that "insidious, intriguing, dangerous, yet despicable character." This nastiness was terminated only when McDouall formally re-emphasized that "the Indian Department on the Mississippi is subject to and entirely under the orders of Captain Bulger."[35] In April 1815 Dickson was ordered to Michilimackinac.

This whole episode, coupled with the boredom and isolation of Prairie du Chien, so disgusted Duncan Graham that "was there not favourable appearances to the termination of this drudgery," he reckoned that "he would throw up instantly." The disconsolate Graham proved prophetic when he wrote: "Here we are posted since last fall, without news from any quarter, and destitute of provisions, sociability, harmony or good understanding. Not even a glass of grog, nor a pipe of tobacco, to pass away the time, and if a brief period don't bring a change for the better, I much dread the United Irishmen's wish will befall this place which God forbid it should – a bad Winter, a worse Spring, a bloody Summer, and no King."[36] For Graham, apparently, the situation was desperate but not serious.

In fact, official news of peace reached Prairie du Chien in the spring of 1815. Strong war parties to threaten St. Louis and "keep the Americans at home to defend that place" had already been despatched. In these raids the Indians "took more scalps within the last six weeks than they did during the whole of the preceding spring and summer upon this frontier."[37] Bulger immediately recalled his Indian allies. But the ever defiant Sauk struck one more time; in late May, at the battle of Sinkhole, near Fort Howard, just north of St. Louis, the warriors killed eight American soldiers.[38] This was the last military engagement of the War of 1812 in the Northwest. The basis of the peace treaty, however, was *status quo ante bellum,* and the "mutual restoration of all Forts" became mandatory. With no option, Bulger assembled the chiefs at Fort McKay on 23 May for a final grand council and explained the terms of the peace. Black Hawk, that "whole hearted man and unflinching warrior, cried like a child saying our Great Mother [Great Britain] has thus concluded, and further talk is useless." The next day, after firing a nineteen-gun salute, distributing presents to the tribes, and leaving them "above want," His Majesty's troops gathered their possessions, burned the fort and departed the upper Mississippi forever.[39] It is noteworthy that, during this period of the so-called British occupation of Prairie du Chien, all three post commanders and most of the garrison could loosely be defined, even then, as Canadians.

At Michilimackinac the terms of the peace devastated McDouall, who confessed Shakespeare-like to be "penetrated with grief at the restoration of this fine Island, 'a fortress built by Nature for herself.'" He was "equally mortified at giving up Fort McKay to the Americans." His orders were definite, however, and left "not alternative but compliance." The crestfallen McDouall, echoing the cries of the fur traders, could only conclude by observing with some validity that "our negociators, as usual, have been egregiously duped: as usual, they have shewn themselves profoundly ignorant of the concerns of this part of the Empire."[40] The end came quickly and without incident on 18 July 1815 when McDouall "delivered over the island and Fort of Michilimackinac to Colonel [Anthony] Butler of the United States Troops."[41] The transfer took thirty minutes.

The War of 1812 in the Northwest was a very different matter from the one played out in Upper Canada. When the United States went to war against Britain in June 1812 to redress national honour, the capture of Canada, an early territorial ambition which anticipated the American vision of manifest destiny for the continent, was also a key consideration. The concept of manifest destiny, replete with spiritual and religious connotations, was used by the United States to justify that westward sweeping movement in which successive Indian frontiers were conquered and pacified. It was God's will, apparently, that Americans must dominate and control North America. The suggestion that the United States usurped a large part of the continent by purchase, war, and theft, is too harsh. But an argument can be made that the zealous young republic dispossessed tribe after tribe during the long epic years of "Westward Ho" and it did so by taking thousands upon thousands of acres of unceded Indian lands, to which no consideration, recognition, nor acknowledgment was given that these indigenous peoples might have at least the benefit of the right of prior occupancy or aboriginal title, as they had enjoyed the use and occupancy of these lands since time immemorial.

Manifest destiny proved most successful for the expansionist ambitions of the United States, except, of course, in the case of Canada during the War of 1812. The failure to take Canada was a rare exception through these many years in which American destiny did not manifest. Yet Americans were mollified, for they did win the Indian war in the War of 1812, as Tecumseh's confederacy was irretrievably crushed and the Great Lakes Indian frontier secured. But the War of 1812 also provided the prospect for a little "Canadian" manifest destiny. A number of prominent fur traders loyal to the crown and supported by the Indian tribes of the upper Great Lakes and Mississippi Valley also viewed, in their way, the War of 1812 as an opportunity to grasp and consolidate territory in the Northwest. For these two groups, the war became a common struggle to achieve a possible permanent British hegemony in that hinterland and thus preserve the fur trade and the traditional Indian way of life against American expansion and settlement. These fur traders and the Indian allies won their war but lost the peace; and with it, a chance to grab at destiny. For at Ghent, British negotiators sacrificed Indian and Canadian ambitions in the Northwest for a renewed Anglo-American cordiality.

PART FOUR

*Government-Indian Relations in the
Post-1815 Years:
Canada and the United States*

CHAPTER 8

FROM WARRIORS TO WARDS

P rior to the signing of the Treaty of Ghent on 24 December 1814, senior ministers at Whitehall reasoned that "if our success shall enable us to terminate the war by the retention of the Fort of Niagara, and the restoration of Detroit and the whole of the Michigan Country, the British Frontier will be materially improved."[1] In Canada this view was shared and enthusiastically supported over the next several months by Robert McDouall, William McGillivray, and even Sir Gordon Drummond, the Canadian-born commander of His Majesty's forces in the upper province who pleaded for the retention of Niagara and Michilimackinac. But Britain, burdened with financial difficulties and increasingly preoccupied by events in Europe following the defeat and abdication of Napoleon, became anxious to rid itself of the American war.

At Ghent, therefore, the British plenipotentiaries, pressured to conclude a treaty, capitulated on *uti possidetus* and accepted *status quo ante bellum*.[2] This decision was harshly criticized in London by *The Times*, which rightly denounced the British negotiators for yielding the Northwest and abandoning the Indians to the mercy of their enemies.[3] But there had been scant latitude for the British on this point, for 1814 was not 1783, particularly with the Americans in possession of Fort Malden (Amherstburg) and much of the southwestern portion of Upper Canada.

Although the "mutual restoration of all Forts" and territories to the country who had jurisdiction, if not full control, in 1811 was agreed upon, the British peace negotiators, unlike their predecessors in 1783, did manage to provide in article IX of the Treaty of Ghent at least some token evidence that they were concerned for the future welfare and security of their late and recent Indian allies. Article IX stipulated that both the United States and Great Britain would strive

> to put an end, immediately after the ratification of the present treaty, to hostilities with all the tribes or nations of Indians with whom they may be at war at the time of such ratification; and forthwith to restore to such tribes or nations respectively all possessions, rights and privileges which they may have enjoyed or been entitled to in one thousand eight hundred and eleven, previous to such hostilities: Provided always that such tribes or nations shall agree to desist from all hostilities against [the United States and Great Britain], upon the ratification of the present treaty being notified to such tribes or nations, and shall so desist accordingly.[4]

In reality, however, article IX was meaningless, for the Americans had no intention of restoring anything to the tribes of Tecumseh's old confederacy, especially to the roaming warriors of the Northwest. Nonetheless, at Portages des Sioux, a village on the west bank of the Mississippi just north of St. Louis, American commissioners, headed by William Clark, and in accordance with article IX, duly concluded a number of "peace and friendship" treaties between July and September of 1815 with various tribes of Britain's Indian allies.[5] The first treaty was signed with the Potawatomi on 18 July, the very day that the British were vacating Michilimackinac. Other tribes and bands soon followed. The Piankashaw, Kickapoo, Osage, Iowa, several bands of Sioux, and elements of the Sauk and Fox all put their mark on the paper. Likewise, at Spring Wells, near Detroit, tribes and remnants of the Tecumseh confederacy took treaty on 8 September. These signatories were Wyandot, Delaware, Seneca, Shawnee, Miami, Ottawa, Chippewa (Ojibwa), and Potawatomi.[6]

Some Indian groups remained aloof, notably Black Hawk and the Sauk of Rock River. The Americans prodded these and other recalcitrants by invading the upper Mississippi in 1816; and there they built military posts: Fort Armstrong at Rock River, Fort Crawford at Prairie du Chien, and Fort Howard at Green Bay – sites which for the Indian warriors stirred very recent memories

of military glory. Michilimackinac and Detroit were also reoccupied, along with Fort Dearborn. The building program continued
between the years 1819 and 1822 with the establishment of several
other forts by the United States army, most notably Fort Snelling
at the junction of the Minnesota and Mississippi. This new post,
due south of the Red River settlement, by blocking a major
Canadian fur trade water route used since the days of the French
regime, severely limited what little contact remained between the
old partners in fur in the Northwest.

These actions persuaded the Sauk to capitulate for the
moment to the American peace overture; and on 13 May 1816,
Black Hawk and other headmen of the Sauk signed treaty. This
decision induced the remaining Sioux bands, the Winnebago,
more of the Wea and Kickapoo, the Ottawa, Chippewa (Ojibwa),
and Potawatomi – and in March 1817, even the fiercely independent Menominee – to accept the treaty offerings of the commissioners. Although these coerced "peace and friendship" treaties
did not include the negotiation of any new land surrenders, the
United States violated article IX of the Treaty of Ghent by invading
the Indian country and building forts. Yet mere Indian treaties
were not sufficient to ensure American control in the Northwest;
something more formal and internationally binding was needed.
This objective was satisfied by the Convention of 1818, signed on
20 October between the United States of America and Great
Britain. In part, the convention extended the boundary line of
1783 west from the Lake of the Woods along the 49th parallel to
the Rocky Mountains. The Oregon country beyond the mountains
was left under joint Anglo-American occupation.[7]

Although many of Britain's former Indian allies were signing
"peace and friendship" treaties with the United States, those negotiations did not deter a significant number of chiefs and tribal delegations from continuing at the same time to visit their British
"friends" at Fort Malden (Amherstburg) and at the new post of
Drummond Island in the upper lakes.[8] The frequency of these visits, and the friendliness with which the chiefs were received by
officers of the British Indian Department, aroused an angry jealousy and concern on the part of the Americans, especially in the
border region around Detroit. Lewis Cass, governor of Michigan,
was particularly miffed at the enduring loyalty and friendship
between the British and Indians; and he resented the large quantity of presents annually distributed at Fort Malden to tribes who
"largely live under the territorial jurisdiction of the United States."
For Cass, the possibility of a revival of a Tecumseh confederacy,
prompted by tribal restlessness and British encouragement,

became a haunting obsession.

The "visiting Indians" in Canada, he contended, were a nuisance to the Michigan frontier, as they "assault the Inhabitants, steal their horses, kill their cattle and hogs, and forcibly enter their houses." Further, protested the governor, these depredations usually occurred upon their return from receiving gifts and counselling from "British agents."[9] Convinced that the Indians were secretly being kept loyal in case of future hostilities between the United States and Great Britain, and that "their minds are embittered and poisoned towards us," Cass did everything within his power to thwart the British influence with the tribes.[10] He met with the Indians, provided them with generous presents, tried to prevent them from crossing the Detroit River, supported the fort building program, and even strode into an Indian village on the American side of the line and tore down a British flag hanging from a lodge pole.

As a result of the continued and sometimes extensive interaction between the British, the Indians, and the Americans along the Detroit following the War of 1812, a war spirit continued to permeate the area. The suspicions and ill-feelings thus provoked a series of nasty border incidents of which the most serious was the killing by American soldiers of a Kickapoo named Akochis, who had been visiting the British at Fort Malden.[11] Yet, although the determined and tireless efforts of Cass to combat this continued British-Indian friendship were understandable, his concerns were exaggerated, as the visits had little or no political significance for the British, who had neither the funds nor the inclination to foster and promote another alliance. Indeed, relations between Great Britain, the United States, and Canada were in such a state of general harmony in the post-1815 years as to be considered "an era of good feelings." By 1819, for instance, British military forces for the defence of Canada were significantly reduced, and at the frontier posts, including Fort Malden, there was such a sense of calm and security that of 173 officers, eighty were absent for the winter.

For Britain's former Indian allies in the United States, however, these years were not particularly marked by good feelings. Following the War of 1812, the tribes were generally forsaken by the British, and left isolated, politically weak, and disunited. In the succeeding years, the United States introduced an optimistic, even naïve, "humane policy."[12] This policy supposedly was "founded in pure and disinterested motives," and intended ultimately to benefit the Indians by providing "the benign influences of education and instruction in agriculture and the several mechanical arts, whereby social is distinguished from savage life." These benign considerations evolved from serious doubts as to whether "even with the fostering care and assured protection of the United States, the preservation and perpetuity of the Indian race are at all attainable." In order, therefore, to help in the resuscitation of a weak and fading people – the vanishing American theme of later days – a "salutary principle" was introduced in the system of removal, whereby the tribes would be collectively settled far to the west in territories "exclusively their own" and under the paternal care of the United States.[13]

The culmination of the rationalization to justify this humane and salutary principle of American Indian policy was the Removal Act of 28 May 1830.[14] This piece of congressional legislation set the future standard, pattern, and attitude for government-Indian relations in the United States. The act had the net effect of dispossessing and dislocating the tribes of the eastern United States from their traditional lands to distant designated locations west of the Mississippi. The result was a tragic diaspora of human suffering, most remembered by the trek of the "Five Civilized Tribes" on the "Trail of Tears." Many tribes protested against their removal; and in the case of *Cherokee Nation* v. *Georgia* (1831), Chief Justice John Marshall argued that the Indian tribes in the United States were "domestic, dependent nations," and as such were like wards to a guardian, and therefore not to be regarded in the same fashion as foreign nations.[15]

The Marshall decision was momentous and permanent. The United States government and its agent, the Bureau of Indian Affairs, which was established in 1824, assumed a trust responsibility on behalf of the Indian tribes, managed and administered for their general welfare on the basis of a persistent paternalism with an emphasis on Christianizing and civilizing the Indians. This omnipotent control over every facet of Indian life produced among the Indian people (with just a touch of sarcasm) a special if not endearing name for the Bureau – the Great Father.[16]

In the post-1815 years, American Indian policy was a transparent tissue of contradictions, and neither humane nor principled. Removal had managed, however, to clear Indian title and occupancy to most of the lands around the Great Lakes. With the tribes, Britain's ex-Indian allies included, sent "on their way to their western home," there was in consequence no further threat or impediment to the advance of American settlement. But the removal policy could not mask the dominant economic motives of acquiring and settling Indian lands for the general benefit and prosperity of the American people and government. By the late 1830s the process was largely completed, and with this denouement ended forever the capability, need, or desire to maintain a British-Indian military alliance in the defence of "old" Canada. In the final analysis, Lewis Cass was quite correct when predicting years before that the future power and control of the United States would soon present "an iron frontier which [will] laugh to scorn the combined efforts of British and Indians."[17]

In Canada, and concurrent with the events surrounding government-Indian relations in the United States, British Indian policy was also being reshaped to meet the new demands and circumstances of the post-1815 years. The Treaty of Ghent and the Convention of 1818 destroyed the dreams and aspirations of the Montreal-based fur traders, denied to British Canada an easily accessible western frontier, and completed the loss of imperial political and economic hegemony in the "American" Northwest. But the opportunity remained for the people of Canada to reach out towards the beckoning "great lone land" of the western prairies, north and west of Lake Superior – a new empire. It was a chance, therefore, to realize their own form of manifest destiny, denied them in the upper Mississippi during the War of 1812. To this extent, the peace settlement at Ghent and the Convention of 1818 did much to determine and shape the outlines and character of the future dominion of Canada.

The continued settlement and expansion of Canada in the decades following the War of 1812 was largely conditional, however, on pacifying Britain's ex-Indian allies, negotiating treaties and land surrenders, and establishing reserves. Not surprisingly, the whirlwind of events taking place in the post-1815 years left the chiefs and warriors not only reeling, but feeling decidedly isolated, vulnerable, and alarmed. They sought answers from their British friends, if not reassurance. The response from the king's officials was to be a bitter disappointment, for the crown was now opposed to maintaining the expense of preserving a British-Indian military alliance. Although this policy direction was officially approved, there remained once again a nagging reluctance in some quarters in Canada to sever the connection completely in case of future hostilities with the United States.

Nonetheless, barely a year after the Treaty of Ghent, and in conformity with the desire for imperial financial retrenchment, Sir Gordon Drummond was ordered to reduce immediately "the Indian Establishment to the footing upon which it stood in the Year 1811."[18] With no more wars to fight on behalf of Great Britain in North America, the purpose of cultivating the tribes as prospective allies on the battlefield against the United States was considered largely unnecessary and even irrelevant. The need, therefore, for continuing the distribution of supplies and gifts to the tribes through the agency of the Indian Department was seriously questioned by Whitehall. But, although the Indian allies were no longer a priority in the thinking of the imperial strategists and policy-makers, these officials were advised that the tribes depended on the "King's Bounty." Furthermore, their claim to annual presents was based upon custom and necessity. More telling was the reminder that the termination of the presents would amount to an impolitic gesture of ingratitude since "it was at least doubtful whether without the cooperation of the Indians who combatted with us in the defense of their own soil against invaders, this Province [Upper Canada] would have been preserved to the Empire."[19]

The moral suasion of these arguments, combined with the outside possibility of renewed difficulties with the United States, influenced the imperial authorities to maintain some contact with their Indian allies and to continue, at a much reduced level, the issuance of the customary gifts and presents. Following the War of 1812, therefore, a form of the old British-Indian alliance endured for another three or four decades. Yet the immediate task of the post commanders and officers of the Indian Department at the end of the war was to assemble the tribes and explain the new policy initiatives and directions. Foremost among the instructions was to inform their late allies "distinctly and explicitly" that the king would neither assist nor countenance the tribes in any future hostility against the United States. This was no easy task. The dramatic about-face in policy naturally produced a disquieting effect, especially among the tribes of the Northwest. Nonetheless, over the next several years and at many locations, the officers confronted the Indians with the hope of pacifying them through a combination of rhetoric and reason.

At Burlington Bay in April 1815, for instance, William Claus met with the Six Nations of the Grand River, along with other Indian bands from the western part of the province. After providing the delegates with various details and information on the terms of the peace treaty at Ghent, British policy intentions, and border crossing rights for native people under the Jay Treaty which may have been abrogated by the War of 1812, he told them to bury the hatchet. Yet, although the crown was determined to diminish the Indian expenses of the government, Claus concluded the meeting by distributing £2,300 worth of presents to the Indian allies as a gesture of gratitude by the king for the military assistance of the tribes during the late war.[20]

Not surprisingly, the more difficult and dangerous assignment

for the officers was to convince the tribes of the Northwest to cultivate a good and peaceful relationship with the Americans. At the
new British post on Drummond Island, located just east of
Michilimackinac and almost at the confluence of Lake Huron and
Lake Superior, Robert McDouall was still distraught that "the mis-
tress of the world" would make concessions to the United States.
The western Indians, he wrote, were "taught to cherish brighter
hopes, to look forward to happier days, to repose with confidence
in the sacred pledge of British honour." In councils throughout
the summer and autumn of 1815, he nonetheless dutifully shared
the substance of the new policy directives with the shocked chiefs
and warriors. Their trust in him soon vanished. McDouall could
not blame them, for "after what I have told them what a superla-
tive and unequalled —— they must think me."[21]

In June 1816 two more councils heightened even more the personal anguish of McDouall. At the first council a Winnebago chief
pledged the continued loyalty of his tribe to the British and proclaimed: "I detest the Big Knives [Americans] from the bottom of
my heart, and never took from them a glass of whiskey nor a nee-
dle, which is a convincing proof of my dislike to them. Father, I
know of no other Father but you, and never will be considered a
Bastard, which would be so if I acknowledged the Big Knives to be
my Father also."[22] The next day about four hundred Sioux under
Wabasha and Little Crow arrived. They came to the island in anticipation of receiving British support to resist the American
advances and fort-building which, argued the chiefs, were
designed to ruin the Indians and achieve their final extinction.
The request was denied. These meetings were enough for
McDouall; sometime later, this principled and dedicated Scotch
officer left the Northwest and returned to Scotland and "his
retreat" in Stranraer, where he was to spend the rest of his life.

William McKay, appointed deputy superintendent and agent
of the Indian Department on 25 December 1814, assumed the
unpleasant duty at Drummond Island of representing the British
crown in council with the Indians.[23] Towards the end of June he
met with Sioux, Winnebago, Menominee, Ottawa, and Ojibwa, all
staunch allies of the king. They pressed McKay for assurances of
British support in the continuing fight by the tribes with the ever-
advancing Americans. McKay, of course, could not give that assurance. He offered them instead a few gifts. This gesture infuriated
Little Crow, the respected Sioux elder, and he lashed out at
McKay: "After we have fought for you, endured many hardships,
lost some of our people and awakened the vengeance of our
powerful neighbours, you make peace for yourselves, leaving us to

obtain such terms as we can. You no longer need our service; you offer us these goods to pay us for having deserted us. But no, we will not take them; we hold them and yourselves in equal contempt."[24] The Sioux then left the council and few ever returned to Drummond Island.

McKay continued with this tiresome and painful duty for a few more years. In August of 1817 he told a delegation of Winnebago, Sauk, and Fox to "be on good terms with our Neighbours the Big Knives," and suggested that they hunt and plant corn "for the Support of your families." Black Hawk rose and spoke for the tribes. He reminded McKay that the warriors had been successful in the recent war and that his "young men took the Hair Off from a great many Big Knives." Yet, he continued, although the British-Indian military alliance had been completely successful in the Mississippi, the king had made a bad peace with the Americans. The chief confessed that "at this news I many times rubbed my eyes and cleared my ears before I could believe what I saw or what I heard." Black Hawk was angry that the British had made a peace and departed from Michilimackinac "without consulting us." The result, he noted, was that now the Americans "treat us worse than dogs."[25]

Although McKay was becoming increasingly uncomfortable at this long recital of British injustice, Black Hawk pushed on by saying that "a black Cloud [the Americans] is running over our Country taking our lands from us and threatening us with destruction – We have not slept either in peace or tranquillity since we laid down the Hatchet and smoked the pipe with the big Knives as you desired us." The chief concluded by asking "our Great Father" [to] "blow those bad spirits off the Earth"; and he urged that the Indians "should be considered as Englishmen and your brethren." What could McKay say to all this? He provided some food, clothing, tobacco, and powder to his guests, but knew that back in the Sauk and other villages were refugees, widows, orphans, and wounded warriors for whom the crown in Canada was no longer prepared to offer encouragement, protection or material assistance. Embarrassed and piqued, he could only respond that "I have my Great Father's orders to obey and all the Indians in the universe will not make me deviate from them – The Council is Ended and you must withdraw."

Notwithstanding this curt rebuke, another major council with Ottawa, Ojibwa, and Winnebago took place in July of 1818, and even Black Hawk subsequently returned for a visit. In 1820 the number of Indians who visited Drummond Island totalled 4,034; and in 1821, 3,333.[26] McKay was finally recalled to Montreal in

1828, the same year that an international boundary commission awarded Drummond Island to the United States. The few Indian bands from the Northwest who continued to visit the British were told to go to Amherstburg or the new Indian Department post at the Penetanguishine naval depôt. But few Indians from the United States continued to visit the British posts. In 1827 a Winnebago war scare was quickly suppressed by American troops. Following this threat to the general safety and security of the settlers, the freedom of movement among the tribes of the upper Mississippi was severely curtailed.

Black Hawk and his "British" band of Sauk, however, still managed to make an annual pilgrimage to Amherstburg by trekking from the Mississippi along the "Great Sauk Trail" to the Detroit. But these visits abruptly ended with the summer confrontation known as the Black Hawk War of 1832 in which his Sauk people were slaughtered in "that disgraceful affair," dignified by some as the battle at the Bad Axe River. Captured and imprisoned, he was subsequently released into the custody of the pro-American Keokuk and the peace faction of the Sauk who were living west of the Mississippi near the Des Moines River in Iowa. This staunchest of Indian allies to the British died there on 3 October 1838. Before his death, Black Hawk dictated an autobiography which has become a classic statement of Indian resentment and grievances against the white interlopers.[27]

More enduring in terms of a British-Indian connection was the annual compensation paid to some of the Indians "wounded in action with the enemy, and for their Wives, and for the Widows of Indians killed in action, as well as for others having extraordinary claims."[28] These pensions, however, applied only to Indians in Canada. There was to be no such compensation to the 80 percent of the Indian allies residing south of the international border. This unfortunate omission was somewhat understandable, for after 1815 Britain had no influence in the internal affairs of a sovereign United States, no further territorial ambitions or claims to the Northwest, and therefore no need or desire to befriend or financially assist American-based tribes. Finally, although "American" Indians continued to visit the British at the frontier posts, their departure to new "homelands" west of the Mississippi under the removal policy severed the last threads of the military alliance between the British and the Indian tribes in the United States. By the late 1830s, the old days of courting the military allegiance of the tribes against the Americans, of grand and colourful councils full of pomp and ceremony, of fiery speeches, pledges of mutual loyalty, and the distribution of gifts, flags, and medals of King

George III, were becoming a distant memory.

Along with the plan to reduce drastically expenditures in the Indian Department and ease out of the military alliance with the tribes, British Indian policy in Canada following the War of 1812 was equally dedicated to renewing the process for obtaining Indian land surrenders in order to accelerate the unhindered progress of settlement. The first of these postwar cessions took place in the Lake Simcoe region and was intended to complete the extinguishment of aboriginal title from the Toronto Carrying Place at York, north to Lake Simcoe and west to the Penetanguishene naval depôt on Georgian Bay. This route would facilitate settlement and, in the event of a future war with the United States, provide a safer and more convenient avenue to the upper lakes than the more vulnerable Amherstburg.

In accordance with these requirements, William Claus in November of 1815 met in council at "the Point" on Kempenfelt Bay in Lake Simcoe with an Ojibwa delegation, led by Aisance and Yellowhead, both of whom were veterans of the War of 1812.[29] A treaty was soon ratified, and in exchange for £4,000 in goods and provisions, the Ojibwa surrendered a 250,000-acre tract of land between Kempenfelt Bay and Georgian Bay.[30] Three years later, in October of 1817 at "The Landing" on the Holland River, the Ojibwa surrendered a further 1.5 million acres of their land to the west and south of Lake Simcoe.[31] For this huge expanse of territory, which today forms parts of four counties, including the expensive shoreline of Wasaga Beach on Lake Huron, the Indians received gifts, provisions, clothing, medical care, and a "perpetual" annuity of £1,200. Subsequent land surrenders were concluded throughout the province at Rice Lake in 1818, along the Rideau River between 1819 and 1825, and to the west with the Longwoods and Huron Tract purchases during the years from 1819 to 1827.

Integral to these vast cessions was the promotion and development of a plan to settle the Indians on reserve lands. At these designated locations the aboriginal or native people supposedly could make the transition from hunting to farming and a Christian life, all under the paternal care and guidance of missionaries and Indian agents who would provide appropriate religious and educational instruction. Nurtured following the War of 1812, the reserve system in Canada had its origins rooted in the philosophy and beliefs of Wilberforce and the Clapham Sect, the Aborigines Protection Society, the abolition of slavery movement, and in the new form of philanthropic liberalism sweeping across Britain which was calling for the better treatment of native people throughout the empire. In addition, influences from the United

States, namely the practical approach and work of the American Methodists who stressed "First civilize, then Christianize," along with the popularity of American novels such as James Fenimore Cooper's *The Leatherstocking Tales* and Lydia Signourney's *Tracts of the Aborigines of America*, which both emphasized the "noble savage" image, had an appreciable effect.

Much of the early effort to establish these "civilization" programs was the work of Sir Peregrine Maitland, lieutenant-governor of Upper Canada from 1818 to 1828. Maitland was by training a soldier. Promoted major-general in 1814, he commanded the 1st Brigade of the Foot Guards at the battle of Waterloo.[32] In consequence, although he had no former experience in dealing with native people, evidence suggests that there may have been some sympathy or compassion in the man towards the Indian allies as a result of their military contribution in the defence of Canada during the War of 1812. What remains certain was Maitland's interest and energy in promoting Indian improvement. Faced with tribal disintegration and reduced expenditures for the Indian Department, he wisely sought out John Norton and others to advise him on various aspects of Indian policy and administrative structures within the provincial government. The result of these efforts was that after considerable preparation and thought, Maitland devised a strategy which, he contended, would economically benefit native people, instil self-reliance and offer a degree of band autonomy on their settlements, and at the same time save money for the British Treasury.

His program was based on providing each Indian family in a band with a parcel of crown land, and then building for the band community a church, mission house, and "school houses for instruction and industry." These Indian communities would be managed and administered by missionaries and departmental agents modelled on the form of an industrious white settlement. The experiment would be financed by vesting surrendered Indian lands "no longer useful as a hunting ground" in a board of trustees for disposal by lease or sale. The resulting trust fund, invested in provincial bonds and various enterprises, would supposedly produce interest revenue sufficient to cover the costs of running the Indian communities and paying the salaries of the Indian agents, as well as the expense of the annual distribution of presents.[33]

The Indians were provided with details of the proposed plan at several land cession meetings. The council at York in February of 1820 with the Mississauga, for instance, was typical. In concluding the negotiated agreement, the crown assured the Indians that "the

whole proceeds of the surrenders ... shall be applied towards edu-
cating your children and instructing yourselves in the principles
of the Christian religion – and that a certain portion of the said
Tract – will be set apart for your accommodation and that of your
families, on which Huts will be erected as soon as possible."[34] Yet
although Maitland's plan enjoyed reasonable success with the
Mississauga and other Ojibwa groups, it was dependent on the full
and general cooperation of all the Indians in the province.

The powerful Six Nations at the Grand were not particularly
enthusiastic about the plan, and became embroiled with the lieutenant-governor over longstanding land claims and other grievances. To complicate matters further, the Indian fund was not
standardized, but was managed at the community level by each
local agent. Also, the monies raised from the sale and lease of surrendered lands proved insufficient to make the program self-suffi-
cient. As a result, the trust fund become the object of intense suspicion on the part of the Six Nations and the Ojibwa people. In
time, both native groups came to believe that in addition to
administrative irregularities and outright mismanagement, there
was an unfairness and inequality between the bands in making
contributions to the fund.[35] Along with these nagging problems,
the imperial authorities at Whitehall throughout the 1820s
seemed lukewarm to Maitland's creative proposal for Indian self-
reliance and autonomy, preferring instead to focus merely on
methods of reducing the expenses in the Indian Department.

Yet this recalcitrance did not mean that the crown was insensi-
tive to the idea of improving the welfare of the native people.
Although the "civilization" program put forward by Maitland
stalled, and he subsequently departed the province in the autumn
of 1828, the basic premise upon which he had prepared and struc-
tured his plan endured. With Whitehall concentrating on reducing
expenses, senior crown officials in Canada came to the realization
that in order to obtain approval for a new Indian program, what
had to be altered was not the substance, but the form of the submission. Therefore, in early May of 1829, Sir John Colborne, the
new lieutenant-governor of Upper Canada, suggested a Maitland-
like plan, but which emphasized economy and cost-savings to the
imperial government, rather than Indian betterment.

The plan would extend "civilization" to the Indians of the
province through a fund created for their future support by granting leases of their lands, and selling parts of them. As well, the
Indian Department could be employed in "collecting the Indians
in villages (reserves) and inducing them to cultivate their lands."[36]
Religious and educational instruction, along with medical expens-

es, would also be provided. Colborne received strong support and cooperation from Sir James Kempt, administrator of Lower Canada, and on 16 May 1829 a formal submission was put forward which contained four points:

1. To collect the Indians in considerable numbers, and to settle them in villages (reserves), with a due portion of land for their cultivation and support.
2. To make provision for their religious improvement, education and instruction in Husbandry, as circumstances may, from time to time require.
3. To afford them such assistance in building their houses; and in procuring such seed and Agricultural implements, as may be necessary, commuting when practical, a portion of their presents for the latter.
4. To provide active and zealous Missionaries for the Indians at the Bay of Quinté and Guillimburg; and to send Wesleyan Missionaries from England to counteract the antipathy of the established church, and other objectionable principles, which the Methodist Missionaries from the United States are supposed to instil into the minds of their Indian converts.[37]

The financial savings that would result from this proposal heartened the liberal-minded but economically-fixated imperial authorities at Whitehall. They were fully aware that the Indians in the Canadian colonies were becoming increasingly destitute and unable either to sustain their traditional lifestyle or to defend their land and property. The reality was that the tribes could "no longer lead a wild and roving life in the midst of a numerous and rapidly increasing white population. Their hunting grounds are broken up by settlements; the game is exhausted, their resources as hunters and trappers are cut off; want and disease spread rapidly among them, and gradually reduce their numbers. To escape these consequences no choice is left but to remove beyond the pale of civilization or to settle and cultivate the land for a livelihood."[38] Thus, confronted with this dilemma, yet not wanting the Indians to be "entirely maintained and supported by Government" nor to starve in the streets and crowd the gaols, Whitehall struggled to find a solution to the "Indian problem" which would balance conscience with pocket-book.

There was also some concern that if the social and economic conditions of the Indians in the province were not soon ameliorated, they might with vengeance in their hearts accept the repeated

American offers of lands on the Mississippi. The Colborne-Kempt proposal, therefore, which was sent to Sir George Murray, secretary of state for war and the colonies, was both timely and responsive to the policy directions demanded by the British government. Upon receiving the plan, Murray immediately referred the text to the Treasury, with the revealing comment that the subject matter related more to imperial finance that to colonial affairs. After some deliberation, the new program was approved, with an authorized and annual parliamentary grant of £20,000. Murray duly gave formal imperial sanction to the Indian program in a despatch to Kempt on 25 January 1830, observing that "the course which had hitherto been taken in dealing with these people has had reference to the advantages which might be derived from their friendship in times of war, rather than to any settled purpose of gradually reclaiming them from a state of barbarism and of introducing amongst them the industrious and peaceful habits of civilized life."[39]

The program was soon put into effect with the establishment of several new Indian settlements dedicated to farming and providing religious and educational instruction. These settlements experienced varying degrees of success. The Six Nations Iroquois along the Grand River, for instance, were reasonably viable, as they had long possessed an agricultural tradition. But the Ojibwa people were by custom nomadic hunter-gatherers. Nonetheless, at the mouth of the Credit River, just west of York, a Mississauga Ojibwa farming settlement founded in the mid-1820s was already prospering, owing to the leadership of Peter Jones, the Welsh-Mississauga Methodist missionary, gospel preacher, and defender of native rights.[40] In the Lake Simcoe region the experiments at Coldwater and the Narrows (Orillia) were frustrated, in large part because the surrounding white settlers demanded that the government remove the Indians to some distant northern location.

Indeed, British Indian policy in Upper Canada suffered an aberration in the 1830s by actually entertaining for a time the idea of removal. The moving spirit behind this concept was Sir Francis Bond Head, who arrived in the province in 1836 as lieutenant-governor. He reckoned that as far as the Indians were concerned, "we have only to bear patiently with them for a short time, and with a few exceptions, principally half-castes, their unhappy race beyond our power of redemption, will be extinct."[41] Therefore, and in conjunction with the desire to free up lands for white settlement, Bond Head decided that the Indians would be best served by their removal north to the land of the Great Spirit (Manitou), namely Manitoulin Island, where this doomed race could spend their last years in quiet, if not splendid, isolation, sustaining themselves on the traditional economy of hunting and gathering. Although there is no extant documentation to support the opinion, a reasonably confident argument can be made that Bond Head was unduly influenced by the perceived success of the removal policy in the United States.

But the scheme desired by Bond Head, which would destroy the "civilization" program, was vigorously opposed by the Methodists, the Aborigines Protection Society, and even some of the general public in the province. Although the lieutenant-governor managed to obtain a land surrender from the Ojibwa and Ottawa in the Saugeen peninsula on Lake Huron, totalling 1.5 million acres, only a few of these Indians moved to Manitoulin Island.[42] Mercifully, there would be no cruel parallel "Trail of Tears" in Canada. The intense opposition, the general refusal of the Indians to budge from their established settlements, and the outbreak of rebellions in both Lower Canada and Upper Canada blocked Bond Head's narrow vision.

By the late 1830s the Indians were in general settled in their communities throughout the Canadas, and at various stages of becoming Christian farmers. As for their traditional and close connection with the British Indian Department, the focus of the relationship had changed dramatically. In 1830 the administration of Indian affairs had shifted from military to civil jurisdiction. Therefore the war-oriented departmental personnel were forced to assume a quite different, but equally controlling, role over the lives of the native people through a new trust responsibility. For the Indian allies, the formal and entrenched development of the evolving paternal reserve system left them increasingly dependent on government policy, generosity, and good will. With no choice left, the warriors put aside the musket, tomahawk, and scalping knife and replaced them with the Bible, hoe, and plough. Britain's Indian allies in Canada had been thus transformed and reduced from warriors to wards.

In the post-1815 years both the United States and Canada reverted to prewar Indian policies of acquiring land and promoting "civilization" programs. The resurgence of American expansionist ambitions, however, along with a series of testy border incidents along the Detroit, kept crown officials in Canada mindful and wary of the potential for future conflicts with the United States. In the event of a subsequent threat to the security of Canada, imperial strategists considered the emergency employment of Indian allies to be necessary and appropriate. As a result, although the need for utilizing warriors to assist in safeguarding the interests of the crown had been significantly diminished following the War of 1812, there was a reluctance to dissolve completely the military alliance with the tribes, for upon that foundation rested the fundamental tenet of British Indian policy in the defence of Canada.

The wisdom of this decision became evident during the Rebellion of 1837 in Upper Canada. Although an internal insurrection, Indian warriors "turned out with alacrity, and joined their brethren the Militia in the defence of the Country" against the rebels.[43] Ojibwa allies from Lake Huron and Lake Simcoe, for instance, camped at Holland Landing and other places to protect the vital route from York to Penetanguishene. As for the Grand River people, it had now been "nearly Two Centuries since the Chain of friendship was first handed to the Six Nations Indians by Great Britain, during which period, they have not allowed it to rust, but have kept it bright."[44] In 1837, in spite of serious land claims disputes with the government, their attachment to the crown remained steadfast, and about one hundred warriors volunteered to serve under the command of William Johnson Kerr, a grandson of Sir William Johnson.

The contribution of the warriors in 1837 and 1838 was the last occasion in which tribal allies served directly and formally as part of British Indian policy in the defence of Canada. In what amounted to a farewell salute, the crown politely expressed its gratitude for "their faithful and honourable Conduct while engaged in Her Majesty's Military Service."[45] Yet in truth, the imperial strategists and decision-makers at St. James's Court and Whitehall in the new Victorian England had little further interest in reflecting too long on the old frontier and Indian wars in America and Canada. To them, the Indian allies who had fought and died in the defence of the crown's vested interest in Canada, although important for a time, were merely a brief scene on the grand and sweeping stage of British imperial history. Now there were other and more pressing imperial concerns, including racial conflicts with the aboriginal peoples of southern Africa and New Zealand. The efforts of the Indian allies soon began to fade from the minds of the Victorians, and then to vanish forever, a lingering memory for a very few.

For the chiefs and warriors, the long period of British-Indian military alliances in North America was a mixed blessing. Caught between two competing forces – an empire and a frontier – the tribes repeatedly attached themselves to the British crown in the hopes of better salvaging some remnants of their traditional lands and cultural values. The Indians were manipulated, but not duped, and a counter-argument of equal validity could be present-

Amherstburg and the Detroit River, summer 1813, by Margaret Reynolds. Major-General Henry Procter is reputedly the cocked-hat figure in the middle. The HMS *Detroit* is shown on the stocks at the Amherstburg Navy yards.

Fort Malden National Histroic Park, Amherstburg, Ontario

Two Ottawa chiefs, Michilimackinac, 1812, by Joshua Jebb.
National Archives of Canada, C114384

Major-General Isaac Brock, 1769–1812, by J.W.L. Forster.
National Archives of Canada, C7760

Captured colour of the 4th United States Regiment, Detroit, August 1812.
The Welch Regiment Museum, Cardiff, Wales

Tecumseh (Tech - kum -thai), *c.* 1768–1813, by an unknown artist.
National Archives of Canada, C319

The death of Tecumseh, Moravian Town, Thames River, Upper Canada, October 1813, by
Dorival, after the drawing by Clay (a fanciful depiction).
National Archives of Canada, C41031

Deputation of Indian allies from the upper Mississippi Valley to meet with Sir George
Prevost, 1814, by Rudolph von Steiger. One of the women on the left is supposedly
Tecumseh's sister. Although the watercolour is intriguing in detail, the artist's perception of
Indian facial characteristics is unflattering.

National Archives of Canada, C134461

Major John Norton (Teyoninhokarawen), *c.* 1762 - *c.* 1831, painted in 1805
by Mary Ann White.

National Archives of Canada, C123832

Indian salute and farewell to the British at Fort McKay, Prairie du Chien,
upper Mississippi Valley, May 1815, by Peter Rindisbacher.
McCord Museum of Canadian History, Montreal, M1378

Black Hawk (Ma-ka-tai-me-she-kia-kiak), *c.* 1767–1838, by Homer Henderson,
from a copy of the 1837 portrait by Charles Bird King. The identity of the individual
in the miniature is not known.

Chicago Historical Society, 1920.557

ed to demonstrate and evaluate their manipulation of the British. Yet the significant difference was that the British manipulation was successful. The Indians perhaps faced a hopeless task in attempting to halt the advance of the seemingly inexorable American frontier. Nonetheless, the results were conclusive, as the Six Nations Confederacy of Iroquois lost their ancient castles in upper New York, and the tribes of the Ohio Valley and the Northwest were forsaken and defeated. Yet Britain's Indian allies had sacrificed their blood and their land in the defence of Canada. To that extent, their failures became Canada's successes.

But from the moment Europeans first landed on their shores, the native people of the Americas could only delay or retard, but not stem the Tsunami tide of these ever-intruding newcomers. The Indian struggle was made even more difficult by the rampant tribal factionalism which too often, and at critical times, broke the spirit and strength of Indian harmony and unity, and made the pretence of the existence of a pan-Indian and sovereign nation the merest of fictions. In the War of 1812 the Indian allies lashed out in one final and desperate defence of the old order.

Yet even in the post-1815 years, when the Indian tribes were no longer particularly needed nor desired, they retained an affection and loyalty to the British crown and after 1867 to the Canadian government. This continued attachment may have stemmed in part from a conditioned dependence on government. But more relevant was the Indian respect for the periodic bouts of British fairness and justice towards them, as evidenced, for instance, by the Royal Proclamation of 1763, the *magna carta* of native rights in Canada. As well, emotional and family ties remained strong for a long time, owing in large part to the fact that against the common enemy – the Americans – the warriors, British and Canadians had fought side by side over many years as friends and comrades-in-arms. In the years that followed, native people volunteered in unprecedented numbers to serve and fight for Canada in the Great War, the Second World War, and during the Korean conflict.

In spite of this long and impressive military contribution in the defence of Canada, there are few acknowledged Indian heroes today. Among Britain's Indian allies, Joseph Brant and Tecumseh have been commemorated by the Historic Sites and Monuments Board of Canada as persons of national and historic importance. The most popular of the Indian allies, however, is Black Hawk, but only because his name is emblazoned on the jersey of an American professional ice hockey team. It is doubtful, however, if many of the fans have any knowledge or interest in the Sauk chief.

In Canada today, native people, many of whom are descendants of Britain's Indian allies, are frustrated at the slow rate of
progress and their position in society. The reserve system still
exists, social and economic conditions in the Indian communities
are generally well below the national average, efforts to resolve
ancient land claims and treaty and aboriginal rights are frustrated, as are attempts to achieve, either through legislation or a
national referendum, native self-government and sovereignty. Yet
like the old military allies, Indian people, as a trusted symbol of
patience, integrity and all that is noble regarding the land and the
environment, are still being trotted out on an emergency basis by
governments and lobbyists to help sell a program, a cause or a
vision of Canada.

Ocaito, a sage elder and chief of the Ottawa in the early part of
the nineteenth century, would have easily recognized the tactics
and processes of government-Indian relations in contemporary
Canada. At Drummond Island on 7 July 1818 he rose to address
the council. He was fully aware of the significant events transpiring around him, and knew that all was lost for his generation.
After a lengthy and minutely detailed recounting of the British-
Indian military alliance from the days of Sir William Johnson to
the end of the War of 1812, he succinctly summarized that long
association. When the British wanted the Indians to fight for
them, he observed, they were always very kind, but when that military service was completed, "the store door be shut against us."[46]
Little has changed. The only hope, though the heavens may fall, is
that eventually "justice be done" on behalf of the native people,
for only then will there be in the eyes of the international community an honourable defence of Canada.

Chapter 9

EPILOGUE:
RECASTING THE CHAIN
OF FRIENDSHIP

I n the autumn of 1876, following the annihilation of George Armstrong Custer and some 250 men of the Seventh United States cavalry at the battle of the Little Big Horn, Teton Sioux warriors with their families crossed "the Great Medicine line" and sought sanctuary in Canada. Upon first encountering a detachment of North West Mounted Police, resplendent in red coats and wearing the insignia of the crown, a small party of the Sioux moved towards them, and with arms extended, dangled and waved for all to see gorgets and medals of King George III. The symbolism and intent of this gesture was immediately understood. These desperate people, fleeing the wrath of a vengeful enemy, were reminding their old "British" allies that Sioux warriors had fought loyally for the king during the War of 1812 in the defence of Canada.

This Sioux method for refreshing the memories of Canadian officials influenced the new dominion government to grant asylum to these and other arriving refugees. Within five years, however, many of the Sioux, including Sitting Bull, had been coaxed or pressured to return south in order to be settled on reservations in their traditional Dakota homelands. This move was grudgingly accepted by the Sioux. They had believed that, owing to their significant military contribution on behalf of the British during the War of 1812, they possessed legitimate historical and diplomatic rights to enter and use Canada as a place of refuge. Furthermore, their elders recollected that assurances had been made that Dakota culture and freedom would always be respected and honoured wherever the crown had jurisdiction. The dominion government, however, regarded the Sioux as non-indigenous to Canada. They were, according to the official government view, an "American" plains tribe which practised horse nomadism and the buffalo chase. This lifestyle carried them occasionally and seasonally across the international border and onto lands which the Sioux considered to be the northern periphery of their traditional territory. These forays increased in the 1860s and 1870s when their main food supply (the northern bison herd) was being systematically exterminated as part of a United States Indian policy of forcing the nomadic plains tribes onto reservations by starving them into total submission and dependence on government. For those Sioux who remained in Canada, therefore, although denied the right of soil (aboriginal title) to the lands upon which they were now residing and thus unable to participate in treaty negotiations or receive treaty benefits, the dominion government nonetheless provided reserves of land on the basis of grace and benevolence and in recognition of their past service as military allies on behalf of the crown and Canada. The Sioux recipients at that time fully understood and accepted the offer, intent and conditions.

The Teton Sioux in 1876 were hardly unique among "American" Indian tribes who sought sanctuary in Canada. As early as the seventeenth century, New York Mohawk of the Six Nations Confederacy of Iroquois had found a spiritual haven in New France through the guidance and religious teachings of the Jesuit and Sulpician Orders of the Catholic Church. Towards the end of the American Revolution, and as a direct result of the horrific slaughter of Christian Delaware men, women, and children at Gnadenhutten in 1782, the Moravian mission to the Delaware moved north from the Ohio Valley and established a new settlement (Moravian Town), along LaTranché (the Thames River). In 1784 Mohawk Loyalists resettled along the Grand River and at Tyendinaga on the Bay of Quinte. Following the struggle for the Ohio Valley, several Algonkian-speaking tribes were encouraged in the late 1790s to move north and settle at Chenail Ecarté (Walpole Island), near Lake St. Clair. Other American-based tribes also escaped or relocated in Canada. Nearly fifteen years before the dramatic arrival of the Teton Sioux, their fellow warriors to the east, descendants of Robert Dickson's Santee Sioux people from the War of 1812, had fled north to Fort Garry, following the Minnesota Sioux War of 1862. These refugees also remained in Canada, but not before overcoming initial opposition from the local Ojibwa, Saulteaux, and Métis who worried that these "alien" Dakota could become yet another claimant group to compound the difficulties of negotiating and concluding land settlement agreements. With the surrender of Chief Joseph in October of 1877 at the Bear Paw mountains in western Montana following a desperate run which took his warriors within fifty miles of the "British Possessions," even a few Nez Percé managed to reach the safety of Canada.

A final, but rather anomalous example of Britain's Indian allies or their descendants coming to Canada is the Potawatomi people. This tribe has had a long association with Canada. During the French regime, the Potawatomi both traded and allied themselves with the French. After 1763 the Potawatomi, like most of the Algonkian and Iroquoian tribes, developed an enduring and symbiotic relationship with the British crown. As such, and for mutual protection and survival against the Americans, the Potawatomi and other tribal allies fought in the king's interest throughout the American colonial rebellion, and more especially in the defence of Canada during the War of 1812.

Between 1789 and 1846 the Potawatomi were also participants in several treaties and land cessions with the United States of which the Treaty of Chicago in 1833 was particularly significant in its impact on Canada. Following the signing, the Potawatomi people were increasingly pressured by American authorities and settlers to vacate their ancient homelands in Ohio, Michigan, Indiana, Illinois, and Wisconsin and move west. But in spite of the success of the Removal Act in forcing tribes to take an epic journey to distant and unknown lands beyond the Mississippi, many of the Potawatomi refused to walk the cruel "Trail of Tears." The Potawatomi, however, were decidedly less than popular with the government, the military, and the general public. The events of the War of 1812 still burned in the memories of both the native and non-native populations in the area. A notable example was the Fort Dearborn Massacre (Chicago) in August 1812 where Black Bird and Potawatomi warriors slaughtered the garrison and some civilians. These considerations prompted a significant segment of the Potawatomi, recent and stalwart military allies of the British crown, to remove to Canada.

Between 1835 and 1840 about three thousand people, nearly one-third of the tribe, migrated to various sections of what is now the southern and central parts of the province of Ontario. Those Potawatomi who moved to Canada believed that their general welfare would be better assured, if not enhanced, under the protection of the British crown. As well, they could continue to enjoy the Great Lakes environment, and integrate, if necessary, with their Ottawa and Ojibwa brothers.

Once in Canada, these Potawatomi moved from place to place, subsisting on hunting, fishing, and presents from government and private organizations. They were not indigenous to the area and thus, like the Sioux in later years, were not eligible for any treaty or benefits. As such, these "American" Potawatomi wandered about the province, "in a most deplorable state of poverty and degradation."[1] They eventually dispersed and settled at such places as Walpole Island, Manitoulin Island, and on other reserves scattered throughout the province.

In Canada and the United States, government-Indian relations in the post-1815 years were primarily concerned with the pacification and removal of most of the tribes to specific and designated locations, usually away from the mainstream progress of Canadian and American life. This process had been generally completed by the end of the nineteenth century. Yet some brief assessment of what happened to the tribes (many of which were Britain's allies), from the end of the period of alliances and the closing of the military frontier to more recent times, seems both necessary and prudent in order more accurately to gauge and understand the subsequent and shifting Indian policies in both countries. In the United States, for instance, the dynamism and violence in American society has been particularly reflected in the history of Indian policy and relations. Born of a bloody revolution and with the right to bear arms enshrined in its constitution, the United States has developed a different national character and personality to that of Canada. An emotional and overt patriotism, a distrust of big government, and periodic outbursts of bold and creative energy are all traditionally parts of the American persona. This pride and conditioned use of arms, however, combined with an impatience and intolerance for those opposing the American dream, have produced violent and inexcusable historical episodes in the United States, as evidenced by the killing of native peoples at such places as Gnadenhutten (1782), Sand Creek (1864), Washita (1868), and Wounded Knee (1890).

In the United States, therefore, the first one hundred years of government-Indian relations featured the dispossession of tribal lands, broken treaties, war, and the creation of huge western reservations. This century of dishonour ended with the utter defeat, demoralization, and dependency of the Indian tribes on private charities and the paternalism of the Bureau of Indian Affairs. The government response for alleviating the plight of the Indian people on the reservations was the enactment of the Dawes Act of 1887 (or more accurately, the General Allotment Act). The act dealt primarily with land, and was intended to break up the reservation system and dissolve the "tribal mass." Indian heads of families were therefore allotted 160 acres of reservation land and 80-acre allotments were provided to single adults, all allotments to carry patents inalienable for twenty-five years. In other words, these lands were to be held in trust by the Bureau of Indian Affairs. After this time period, the allotted land would become the property of the individual Indian, who would then be subject to all the normal state and federal laws. The intention was clear. Traditional tribal values and the communal sharing of land were to be replaced by individual ownership of land. Further, through an educational process of Christianization, Indians would become assimilated into the dominant society, attain citizenship (granted to all Indians in 1924), rid themselves from economic dependence on the federal government and even become useful taxpaying Americans!

The Dawes Act was motivated by humanitarian good intentions, an act of faith by those private citizens, government officials, and politicians who believed that Indians would be more healthy and happy, cultural deprivation aside, by becoming Americans. But assimilation did not materialize. Instead, the act resulted in a deterioration in the economic conditions of Indian society. Worse, through the sale of surplus reservation lands and subsequently even Indian allotment lands, the Indian land base was reduced from 128 million acres in 1887 to 47 million acres by 1934, when the policy was changed. The only assimilation that took place during this period was "the assimilation of a great deal of Indian land into white ownership."[2]

The dismal failure of both the allotments and the assimilationist assumptions underlying the Dawes Act provoked an independent report, commissioned by the secretary of the interior, entitled *The Problem of Indian Administration* (1928), more commonly known as the *Meriam Report*. The comprehensive report, now regarded as the beginning of the modern era in Indian affairs in the United States, covered the entire spectrum of government-Indian relations, and was highly critical of federal policy and the Bureau of Indian Affairs. It also described in painstaking detail the desperate problems facing Indians in the areas of economics, health, and education. The *Meriam Report*, combined with the increasing activity of reformers who supported Indian aspirations for preserving their own cultural and political autonomy, was the impetus for an Indian New Deal in the form of the Indian Reorganization Act of 1934.

The act contained new provisions in four major areas: Indian self-government; special education for Indians; Indian lands; and a court of Indian Affairs. This reform, based on an appreciation for Indian culture, a concern for Indian self-determination and self-government, and a movement toward tribal economic activity, ended the policy of individual allotment and the general alienation of Indian land. The act also, however, envisaged a more active role for the Bureau of Indian Affairs in planning and monitoring the various new policy initiatives. But at the same time, the act extended Indian preferential hiring at the bureau. The enforcement of the Indian Employment Preference Act (a form of which has existed since 1834) gave some assurance that qualified Indians would have a role in determining the destiny of their own people. The result has been that at the bureau, native representation now stands at about 90 percent (by comparison, the number of native employees at the Department of Indian and Northern Affairs Canada hovers at about 20 percent). Whether the high native employee representation at the bureau causes undue conflict of interest or serious inter-tribal jealousies over hiring is a sensitive and debatable issue.

To improve further the welfare and trust of the tribes, the Indian Claims Commission Act of 1946 was created with a special court to deal with claims against the federal government for broken treaties or agreements, usually about land, with provision for financial recompense (based on value at the time of the treaty or agreement) if the claim proved justified. Hundreds of claims were heard in which the Indians often argued not for money but for the return of land. To accommodate the claimants, the act was extended at intervals until 1978 when it was permitted to lapse. The remaining cases were transferred to the United States Court of Claims. The commission proved to be a major resource in terms of economic development, as approximately two billion dollars were awarded to various tribes in claims. But the formation and operation of the Indian Claims Commission suggested another shift in government policy. Concerns were raised that if all claims could be settled, the federal supervision and control over Indians could be ended. These apprehensions were confirmed in 1953 with the passing of a House resolution aimed at withdrawing all federal services to Indians. This short-lived termination policy, which included the dismantling of the Bureau of Indian Affairs, was seen by most Indians as an unwelcome abdication of the trust responsibility, and an attempt to reintroduce the assimilation process.

The termination policy faded by the 1960s. In July 1970 President Richard Nixon submitted a message to Congress which enunciated an Indian policy of "self-determination without termination." Between 1972 and 1976, Congress passed several acts improving its provisions of educational, health, and financial assistance to Indians, and even returned lands to Indians. The impetus towards emphasizing and securing "Indian sovereignty" and tribal self-government has been entrenched in the Indian Self-Determination and Education Assistance Act of 1975. A series of Supreme Court decisions also reinforced the power of Indian tribes to assert their economic, political, and cultural authority. The Reagan and Bush administrations have made it clear that Indians can become independent of federal control without being cut off from federal support. There is no reason to suggest that the Clinton administration will not maintain this policy.

In Canada, government-Indian relations in the years following the War of 1812 and the end of the British-Indian military alliances have not been characterized by wars and violence. This does not mean to suggest even remotely that the results for the native people of Canada were any different from those in the United States. Indeed, in many respects, Indian conditions in Canada today are no better, and in some cases worse, than those across the border. Rather, the contradictory attitudes towards the treatment of native people reflected the different national characteristics of the two evolving and separate nations.

For instance, and in general terms, Americans, espouse "life, liberty and the pursuit of happiness," whereas Canadians appear content with "peace, order and good government." In Canada, therefore, following the passage of the British North America Act in 1867, the new dominion government assumed responsibility for "Indians and Lands reserved for the Indians." In turn, the establishment of the Indian Act provided the legislative base and mandate for the present Department of Indian and Northern Affairs to manage and administer the affairs of the native people. As a direct result of this dominant and controlling influence, the native people have long been dependent on the federal government, which took a formal, centralized, and paternal approach in its early relations with the Indian tribes. The nature of this relationship thus produced the fairly steady and peaceful settlement of Canada (the Northwest Rebellion of 1885 notwithstanding), highlighted by the continued recognition of the Royal Proclamation, treaty-making, the establishment of reserves, the formation of the North West Mounted Police, the building of the Canadian Pacific Railway, and a federal government plan of controlled colonization for the prairies.

In the years following confederation, the dominion government undertook the major process of extinguishing aboriginal title to allow for the unhindered construction of the railway to the Pacific and the expansion of settlement. Between 1871 and 1923, therefore, eleven numbered treaties and the Williams treaties were concluded in which the Indians surrendered title to lands in exchange for specified reserve lands, and benefits common to many of the western treaties such as annuities, gratuities, clothing, cattle, ammunition, twine, flags, medals, educational instruction, agricultural implements, hunting and fishing rights; and in the case of Treaty Six (1876), a "medicine chest." These "numbered treaties" encompassed most of the present provinces of Ontario, Manitoba, Saskatchewan, Alberta, and the Mackenzie District of the Northwest Territories. Treaty Eight (1899) covered the northeast corner of British Columbia, whilst the two Williams treaties of 1923 extended to the lands south and east of Georgian Bay.

In more recent times a number of complex comprehensive land claim agreements have generally followed the process and pattern established by the earlier treaty-making. These agreements include the James Bay and Northern Quebec Agreement (1975), the Northeastern Quebec Agreement (1978), and the Inuvialuit Final Agreement (1984). As well, negotiations have taken place in Yukon, Nunavut (Eastern Arctic), and among the Dene-Métis of the Mackenzie Valley in the Northwest Territories. Since 1982 existing aboriginal and treaty rights have been recognized and affirmed in the Constitution Act, 1982 (previously the British North America Act of 1867). As a result of the constitutional amendments of June 1984, treaty rights include rights that exist by way of land claim agreements or may be so acquired.

In addition to obtaining the surrender of Indian lands in the post-confederation years, the dominion government pursued a policy of attempting to eliminate Indian status through enfranchisement. The Gradual Enfranchisement Act (1869), for instance, was in part "designed to lead the Indian people by degrees to mingle with the white race in the ordinary avocations of life." Yet it was not until 1960 that registered Indians became eligible to vote in federal elections on terms equal with other Canadians. But as with the failed assimilationist efforts in the United States, the native people of Canada managed, in spite of the impact of residential schools on families, the intrusion of the Indian Act on every facet of daily life, and the proselytizing of the churches, to retain elements of their cultural traditions and customary law, along with the religious and spiritual teachings of their elders.

Government-Indian relations in Canada's first century following confederation emphasized treaty-making and vigorous efforts to integrate and assimilate native people into the dominant non-native Canadian society. Treaty-making and the establishment of Indian reserves was successful; the disappearance of native people as a distinct society possessing a unique cultural and ethnic identity in Canada was decidedly unsuccessful. By the end of the Second World War, therefore, the federal government began to question and review the Indian "civilization" programs and policies which had remained virtually unquestioned since the post-1815 years. The result was a number of royal commissions, parliamentary committees, task forces and government reports, the first two of which were joint Senate and House of Commons committees in 1946–48 and 1959–61 to investigate the problems and concerns inherent in Indian affairs.

In 1966 the *Hawthorn Report*, a survey of the economic, political, and educational needs of the Indians of Canada recommended that the native people be accorded the status of a unique ethnic group as "citizens plus." The report in many instances was a Canadian version of the 1928 *Meriam Report* in the United States. The mood engendered in the *Hawthorn Report* of promoting the general welfare and distinct ethnic identity of the native people was reversed three years later in a federal white paper on Indian affairs. The government proposed the repeal of the Indian Act, the dismantling of the Department of Indian Affairs, the ending of treaty-making, and the transferring to the provinces of all administrative and other services relating to Indian affairs. This 1969 white paper provoked an angry formal response from the Indian communities in the form of three rejoinders: the Red Paper (or Citizens Plus) of Alberta Indians, the Brown Paper of British Columbia Indians, and the Manitoba Indians' Wahbung. These briefs argued against the repeal of the Indian Act, and urged instead a thorough review and amendments to various provisions of the act. The Indian responses also called for the immediate recognition of treaty and aboriginal rights, and regarded anything less as a betrayal of Canada's fiduciary or trust responsibility to native people. Other topics of concern to the Indian people included health, education, and economic development programs to assist Indian advancement. This overwhelming and intense response surprised the federal government and the general public, who assumed that the native people wished to be rid of the dependent nature of the paternal care imposed upon them by the Indian Act, and to become instead equal and full citizens in Canada.

The white paper was quickly shelved, but it had shown the

depth of misunderstanding between the native and non-native communities. Thereafter, the native people began increasingly and effectively to develop an "Indian agenda" separate and apart from that of the government. The new relationship would be based more on a return to the historical relationships, involving assertions of treaty and aboriginal rights, self-determination, and a recognition of the native people as the "First Nations" of Canada. This proactive approach was assisted at the same time by a renaissance of native pride in their spiritual and cultural traditions. The overall results of the white paper, therefore, were a new Indian assertiveness in demanding their rightful place in Canada; the decision of the federal government to negotiate native land claims on some basis of acknowledging "aboriginal title" (the *Calder* case of 1973); the entrenchment of treaty and aboriginal rights in the Constitution Act, 1982; four first ministers' conferences on aboriginal affairs between 1983 and 1987; a 1983 report of the Special Committee on Indian Self-Government (the *Penner Report*); a 1985 task force report to review comprehensive claims policy (the *Coolican Report*); and Bill C-31, "An Act to Amend the Indian Act (June 1985)," which provides the opportunity for a native person who is no longer status (an Indian woman, for instance, who married a non-Indian) to be reinstated and registered as a status Indian under the Indian Act.

Towards the end of the 1980s the government of Canada was reacting to the native agenda by relinquishing some of its historical and traditional control over their everyday lives. The Department of Indian and Northern Affairs, for instance, now supports the goal of native self-government; provides funding and economic development opportunities for native initiatives; and advances the goal for ensuring the future welfare and autonomy of native people through the negotiation and resolution of land claim settlements. The nature, extent, and definition of native sovereignty within a federal Canada, however, remains a complex, muddled, and unresolved question.

Today both Canada and the United States are struggling with the key issues of self-reliance and self-government for native people. There are differences, both historical and contemporary, but many of the challenges currently facing the Bureau of Indian Affairs and the Department of Indian and Northern Affairs are remarkably similar. Some indication of the sameness of the issues can be drawn from the 1989 *Report of the Special Committee on Investigations of the Select Committee on Indian Affairs* of the U.S. Senate. For instance, the special committee is concerned with the overlap of responsibilities between the federal government and

Indian governments which leaves no clear accountability nor responsibility; the impact of federal government bureaucracy and procedures as an impediment to local decision-making – "the micro management of tribal affairs"; the conflict over federal administration of natural resources and allegations of neglect resulting in major revenue losses to Indians; the potential conflicts of interest within Indian governments and the lack of clear standards for holding office; the poor quality of housing on reservations; the quality of management and value for money in programs and services; and the slowness of the federal bureaucracy to identify problems and initiate substantive changes to alleviate Indian conditions.

These issues for the 1990s represent important, tough and similar challenges for both the Bureau of Indian Affairs and the Department of Indian and Northern Affairs. In the United States, tribal sovereignty and self-determination have become entrenched and powerful forces; whilst in Canada, constitutional proposals on native self-government indicate that the federal government is supportive of the Indian desire for fuller political and economic autonomy, as seen in the Sechelt legislation; and in the ongoing self-government negotiation process with a number of Indian communities.

For both the United States and Canada, the old days of the "vanishing American" and the "narrow vision" are over. In the United States there appears an interest in reducing the Indian economic dependency on the public purse, whereas in Canada federal expenditures for native people are increasing. Both federal governments, however, share the goal of achieving a fuller degree of native self-reliance and self-government through economic initiatives under native control. But for the moment, although the yoke of power is loosening, the Bureau of Indian Affairs and the Department of Indian and Northern Affairs remain the chief government agencies in their respective countries for managing and administering the federal trust responsibility to native people. Thus, the Great Father (in Canada more appropriately, the Great Mother) endures, and as long as this bureaucratic paternalism and centralized power exists, the spiritual, political, and economic autonomy of the aboriginal or native people of North America will not truly become a reality.

There is, however, ample recent evidence in Canada and the United States of native people accelerating the rate of progress in demanding fuller economic and political autonomy. The Sioux and Potawatomi of Canada, for instance, seem particularly appropriate choices to illustrate this trend. Although these non-indigenous native peoples originally came to Canada as refugees, both groups today live on various reserve lands and enjoy such rights and benefits associated with being registered Indians on reserve as free medical care, free post-secondary education, housing subsidies, and exemption from personal income tax. Yet in the case of the Sioux (the Dakota Nations in Canada), there are now formal requests from some of their band chiefs and councils that they should be able to sign adhesion to treaty in the areas where they reside. This type of demand is quite contrary, of course, to the mutually agreed terms and conditions upon which the Sioux were first allowed to remain in Canada. The Sioux, however, are fully cognizant of the additional potential benefits to them if they could acquire treaty rights. These potential benefits include treaty annuities (minimal), the right to present the federal government with a formal submission pursuant to a land entitlement claim or any claim relating to the non-fulfilment of lawful treaty obligations, and requests for research funding in support of such claims. As well, the Sioux are pursuing with the Department of Indian and Northern Affairs a discussion paper relating to self-government negotiations; and a Dakota Project Working Group is conducting research in anticipation of submitting a comprehensive land claim based on traditional use and occupancy of lands in Canada.

In regard to the Potawatomi, the anomalous nature of their requests to the government of Canada is in the form of seeking financial assistance and support in their longstanding and unresolved compensation claim against the United States, which dates from the Treaty of Chicago in 1833. Since 1864 the Potawatomi have been attempting to obtain redress to this ancient claim which merits resolution. In fact, an act of Congress in 1908 actually acknowledged that the "Potawatomi Nation in Canada" had not received fair and just compensation for treaties negotiated with the United States. The monetary value at that time was assessed at $1.5 million. Today's claim seeks this amount plus interest and special damages for breach of trust. The American legal position has consistently argued that the Potawatomi in Canada are foreign nationals, and therefore compensation is denied as they are beyond United States jurisdictional authority. This contention is remarkably similar to the British attitude towards their Indian allies in the United States following the War of 1812. In the event, Canada has provided historical research assistance through the Department of Indian and Northern Affairs and diplomatic "good offices" through the Department of External Affairs. For Canada and the Potawatomi, the historical roles have been reversed, with the Canadian government now being used to assist in the defence of the Potawatomi.

As these Sioux and Potawatomi episodes show, there is often a remarkable and direct link between historical events and contemporary native-related issues. It follows that a knowledge of Indian history and cultural traditions, an appreciation for cross-cultural variances, and some sensitivity to native goals and aspirations are fundamentally important for the success of Canadian Indian policy. Yet although these points seem simplistic and self-evident, many senior departmental and other officials, well versed in government policies and programs, all too often engage in high-level meetings and negotiations with "First Nations" ill prepared to deal with cultural differences, and at a disadvantage because of their lack of knowledge of native history and native values. It is therefore hardly surprising that land claims, self-government initiatives, economic development programs, and aboriginal and constitutional rights questions remain largely unresolved after many years and millions of dollars of public money.

The agonizing and frustrating pace of government-Indian relations is unfortunate at this time, because whereas the native people are increasingly well-organized and optimistic about their future, Canada is experiencing a crisis of structure and spirit, accentuated by a loss of national self-confidence. The free trade agreement, economic recession, failures of the Meech Lake constitutional accord and the Charlottetown Accord, along with the threat of Quebec sovereignty, have all pushed Canada farther along the road towards continentalism, Americanization, decentralization, and possibly dissolution.

Native people, however, after waiting patiently for two hundred years, are determined to achieve their goals and ambitions which now finally seem obtainable. But native people are also fully aware that in order to succeed, what is required is the survival of a strong central government in a united Canada. For the non-native community, it is therefore critical to "regain the affections and loyalty" of the First Nations by understanding and appreciating their history and culture, and by showing them genuine respect. More to the point, and in conformity with the historic British-Indian alliance in North America, the assistance of Indian allies is required again. Herein lies the vital importance of bringing the Indian past to the present defence of Canada.

In the summer of 1990 the Indian past was brought dramatically and forcefully to the present. With the three-year time limit rapidly winding down for the ten provinces and federal government to ratify the Meech Lake constitutional accord, a little-known opposition backbencher in the Manitoba legislature, an eagle feather held in his right hand, repeatedly refused the required unani-

mous consent to debate the issue. The decision was a major con-
tributing factor to the "draining of Meech Lake."[3] This symbolic
and courageous action was initiated by Elijah Harper, a Cree-
Ojibwa from the Red Sucker Lake band in northern Manitoba.
Harper opposed the constitutional accord because he could not tolerate the exclusion of native participation or interests in the discussions, or the proviso which recognized the province of Quebec as a
"distinct society" in Canada. Harper's rejection of the accord was
shared by First Nations people across the land. For them, this made-
in-white-Canada constitutional arrangement was the final insensi-
tivity to centuries of European injustices against native people.

The First Nations reminded these non-native constitution-mak-
ers that the aboriginal peoples of Canada were a conscious and
easily identifiable collection of linguistic and cultural entities
which existed as a "distinct society" long before the arrival and
settlement of any Europeans in North America. Therefore the historically enshrined principle that Canada was created by "two
founding peoples" – the French and the English – was fundamentally wrong. Whether the principle was right or wrong mattered
little, for the perception became the reality. As early as 1838 Lord
Durham, in his *Report on the Affairs of British North America*,
strengthened this belief by observing that Canada was composed
of "two nations warring in the bosom of a single state." From this
oft-quoted remark evolved the concept of "two solitudes," in
which French Canada, rooted in Quebec, must be assured of *la
survivance* through some flexible accommodation in the constitutional process to provide it with a special status within the
Canadian federalism.

But the distinct society clause and special status for Quebec
were also opposed by many English-speaking Canadians. Harper's
contribution to the destruction of the Meech Lake accord was
therefore applauded by those Canadians who were becoming
increasingly annoyed and resentful of Quebec's special demands
and its threat of seeking sovereignty-association or outright independence. In the minds of many Canadians, the rejection of
Meech Lake by Harper and the native people, who represented a
"third solitude," had assisted in the preservation and defence of
the "old" united Canada, or at least in a Canada composed of ten
equal provinces and two territories.

Less than a month after Harper's dramatic stand, the Mohawk
of Kanehsatake (Oka) repelled by force the Sûreté du Québec effort
to remove barricades constructed by the Indians to halt the expansion of a municipal golf course onto "the pines," an area which
included a sacred native burial ground. The Mohawk insurrection,

which lasted all summer, pitted "the Warriors" against the Sûreté du Québec, the Royal Canadian Mounted Police, and the Canadian army. Historically, the "faithful Mohawks" had been loyal and active military allies of the British crown since well before the days of Sir William Johnson. At Oka in the summer of 1990, with the Mohawk combatting the forces of the crown, the wheel had come full turn.

The stand-off at Oka became in essence a struggle between two solitudes – the Mohawk Nation and French Quebec – a contemporary version of Durham's observation; only this time it was two "nations" warring in the bosom of a single province. Many Canadians were bemused by this contradictory dilemma of Quebec demanding recognition of its distinctiveness based on history and culture, whilst appearing to deny similar claims to the aboriginal minority in its own province. Although the Oka crisis had hardened the demands of French Quebec to be "maîtres chez nous," the Mohawk resistance unleashed across the country a renewed determination on the part of native people to assert their rights and find a legitimate and fair place in Canadian society. In working towards these objectives, these modern warriors no longer wear the breechclout, or carry the tomahawk and the scalping-knife. Now the costume of battle and the effective weapons are the blue three-piece suit and constitutional briefs, court actions, blockades, and occasionally an AK-47.

Just prior to Oka, a Supreme Court of Canada decision in May 1990 (*Sparrow* v. *The Queen*) had re-emphasized that the relationship between the government and the aboriginal or native people is trust-like rather than adversarial, and that "contemporary recognition and affirmation of aboriginal rights must be defined in light of this historic relationship." This relationship had previously been incorporated, in the Constitution Act, 1982 under section 35. The *Sparrow* decision and the Mohawk stand at Oka helped motivate the federal government to create a Royal Commission on Aboriginal Affairs "to examine the economic, social, and cultural situation of the aboriginal peoples" of Canada.[4]

In 1991, a new round of talks (the "Canada Round") was initiated in the hope of moving constitutional renewal forward from the failure of Meech Lake. The desire of the federal government to achieve working harmony was marked by an agreement that summer between the leader of the Assembly of First Nations and the minister responsible for constitutional affairs which enabled native people to conduct a "parallel process" to define their role in a new federalism. Further advances were made when the leaders of four national native associations joined the federal, provincial, and territorial constitutional affairs ministers as participants in the "Canada Round" negotiations. In the resulting Charlottetown Accord of August 1992, constitutional proposals for native people included the formal recognition of the inherent right of self-government, essentially creating a third order of government in Canada. This proposed new working order – a recasting of the chain of friendship – appeared to mirror the historical Two Row Wampum and later Silver Covenant Chain of Friendship. The relationship had traditionally stipulated peace and friendship between Indian people and the crown. The two parallel rows of coloured beads symbolize a separate, but equal, status in which neither would interfere with the integrity of the other's culture, language, law, or religious and political systems.

A national referendum on the Charlottetown Accord was held on 26 October 1992. A majority of Canadians rejected it. In spite of what appeared to be substantial constitutional gains for the aboriginal peoples, 62 per cent of Indians voting on reserves also rejected the accord. Some band leaders and elders held that the process left insufficient time for discussion, clarification, and due reflection. There was also a concern that government-Indian relations in Canada, which dated back to the old alliances with the British crown, could be jeopardized by any diminishing of the federal role, especially as it related to long-cherished treaty rights and the fiduciary or trust responsibility of the crown.

Yet, in spite of the Indian rejection of the Charlottetown Accord, the First Nations remain fully aware that if they are to succeed in securing a new and modern relationship with government, it is most likely to be accomplished within a political and economic framework of a strong central government in a united Canada. The final irony, therefore, is that with Quebec pushing for decentralization, sovereignty-association or, if necessary, independence, the last cannon shot fired on behalf of Canadian sovereignty would no longer be undertaken by a French Canadian.[5] Now, in the fast-changing order of vested interests and real-politik, that action may well be performed by a native person (perhaps a descendant of one of Britain's Indian allies), who, in some conformity with the historic British-Indian alliance, would remain the last individual ready and willing to "Stand on Guard" in the defence of Canada.

APPENDICES

APPENDICES

A). The Declaration of the Account of Daniel Claus Esquire for Public Expenses as Agent for the Indian Department of the Six Nations in Canada from 1777 to 1782.

B). List of Indian Warriors as they Stood in 1812 at the time war was declared.

C). Speech of Robert Dickson Esquire to Indian tribes, 18 January 1813.

D). Lt.-Gov. Sir John Colborne to R.W. Hay, York, Upper Canada, 3 May 1829.

APPENDIX A

The Declaration of the Account of Daniel Claus Esquire for Public Expenses as Agent for the Indian Department of the Six Nations in Canada from 1777 to 1782

Disbursements for the Refugee Mohawks between 1 November 1777 and 25 June 1778

Sundry Articles of Clothing	£551.14.8 ¹/₄
Fresh Provisions & Necessaries	£169.7.9
Armourers & Blacksmiths Work	£26.6.0
Siversmiths Work	£18.12.0
Spruce Beer, Rum Wine & Tobacco	£66.0.0
Soap, Candles, Tea and Sugar	£50.5.0
Buffalo Blankets and Bear Skins	£19.17.6
Sundry Articles furnished as presents to Mary Brant	£114.16.0
House Rent for Indians in town	£37.10.0
Camp Equipage for use of Ind. Department	£32.6.0
Pay of Officers, Assistants, Mohawk Interpreters and Rangers	£354.11.3
In all between 1 November 1777 and 25 June 1778	£1496.19.8 ¹/₄

Disbursements between 25 June and 24 December 1778

Goods and Various Articles furnished as present to the Mohawks	£185.16.5 ¹/₂
Tea and Sugar furnished Mohawk Women in absence of their Husbands	£25.10.3
Rum for use of Indians	£97.0.9
Ammunition and Arms furnished the Mohawks House rents and repairing	£38.11.7
Necessaries for Fugitive Mohawks in their Village	£49.13.4
Building the Mohawk Village in the Woods near Lachine	£45.16.0
Reconnoitring Parties	£505.10
Calash	£24
Clothing	£32
Silversmiths work for the Mohawk	£38
Armourers work	£17
Blacksmiths work	£28
Pay for Officers Sec, Interps and Rangers	£307.2.6
In all between 25 June and 24 December 1778	£1166.0.1 ¹/₂

Disbursements between 24 December 1778 and 25 June 1779

Hats, Handkerchiefs etc.	£362.10.5[?]
Rum, Indian Corn	£99.9.0
Ammunition	£80.8.10
Reconnoitring Parties	£48.2.6 ¹/₂
Sugar	£18.6.8
House Rent for Indians	£25.0.0
For Clothing etc.	£65.4.5
Expenses going to Quebec	£87.18.10
Calash	£23.2.3.
Boarding and Schooling Mary Brants Children	£45.12.10
Necessaries furnished Mary Brant	£18.5.7
Postage and Stationary	£9.13.0
Silversmiths Work	£35.4.3
Armourers Work	£18.7.8
Blacksmiths Work	£17.14.1
Ferriage	£33.6.8
Pay for Officers, Assistants, Interpts and Rangers	£371.6.3

In all between 24 December 1778 and 25 June 1779   £1365.3.3 ¹/₂

In all between 25 June and 24 December 1779   £1510.6.6

Disbursements between 25 December 1779 and 24 June 1780

Various Articles furnished Indians	£858.12.4
Ammunition	£67.2.4 ¹/₂
Reconnoitring Parties	£75.11.3
Expenses attending the taking of 42 prisoners	£84.0.0
Canoes bought for Mohawks	£58.5.0
Clothing	£96.15.4
Board and Schooling Mary Brants Children	£118.12.6
Pay of Officers, Asst. Interpreters and Rangers, and Men under Joseph Brant	£307.2.6

In all between 25 December 1779 and 24 June 1780   £1786.11.11 ¹/₂

Disbursements between 25 June and 24 December 1780

Goods of Various kinds furnished the Indians	£1200.14.2
Pay	£228.15.0

In all between 25 June and 24 December 1780   £1692.18.0

Disbursements between 25 December 1780 and 24 June 1781

Goods furnished Indians including the Boarding of Wounded Mohawks at the Hotel Dieu	£813.14.4
Medicines and Attendance on Sick Indians	£41.19.2
Rum	£26.15.3
Rent of Land	£15.0.0

Printing	£30.0.0
Wampum	£34.3.9
Hats	£13.13.4
Snow Shoes	£37.0.0
House Rent	£50.0
Stationary and pay of a School Master for the Indians	£25.0.1
Purchase of Utensils and for Milk and Vegetables and expenses attending the loss of a cow	£53.12.4 ¹/₂
Bark Canoes	£18.10.0
Reconnoitring Parties	£33.14.6
Pay	£307.2.6

NO TOTAL

Disbursements between 25 June and 24 December 1781

Furniture and Dress for Indians	£989.12.0
Blanket Coats, Deer Skins, Hogs for War Feasts and for the Chiefs	£55.12.10
Pay of Schoolmaster and for the Indians and Clerk of the Indian Church	£30.1.8
Batteau Hire, Bark Canoes, Ferriage and for Redeeming Prisoners	£29.9.10
Necessaries Furnished Indians on Scouting Parties	£57.8.11
Silversmiths Work	£65.17.9
Shoes	£40.8.7 ¹/₂
Blacksmiths Work	£14.12.3 ¹/₂
Armourers Work	£15.7.8
Pay	£308.16.3

In all between 25 June and 24 December 1781	£1708.16.6

Disbursements between 25 December 1781 and 24 June 1782

Various Articles furnished Indians	£887.15.7
Necessaries for Families of Mohawk Chiefs	£40.1.2
Snow Shoes and Belts of Wampum	£40
Schoolmaster and Clerk of Indian Church and for Printing and Binding Books	£25.17.7
Provisions, Hogs for War Feasts and Sundry Expenses	£44.5.4
Various expenses on a Scout and Wood destroyed by Mohawk for a Canoe and Inc.	£134.16.9
Coats and Hats	£76.19.9
Silversmiths Work	£46.15.6
Blacksmiths Work	£21.6.5
Armourers Work	£24.17.8
Pay for Officers, Assts, Rangers and Interpts.	£343.11.6
Boarding and Schooling for Mary Brants Children	£355.8. 1 ¹/₄

In all 25 December 1781 and 24 June 1782	£2150.11.8 ³/₄

Disbursements between 25 June and 24 December 1782

Various Goods furnished	£1128.12.1
Necessaries and Petty Articles	£50.8.3
Rum	£44.18.0
Scout, Mary Brants children, Wood Cows, Indian Corn and Sundries	£100
Redeeming Prisoners and furnishing Mohawk Chiefs with necessaries	£34.2.4
Pay for Officers, Assts, Interpreters and Rangers	£361.8.6
In all between 25 June and 24 December 1782	£1866.12.8 ¹/₂

For the Hire of a large Room to meet the
Indians in Council together with a room to
keep the Office in from Sept. 1778 to
December 1782 at £30 per Annum   £127.10.0

For Commission on purchasing Articles at
5% the Accountant being obliged to take
them upon Credit he having no Allowance from
General Haldimand   £821.9.10 ¹/₂

In all the Money paid by this Accountant
for services before mentioned Total Sum £16220.5.10 ³/₄

Also Accountant is Allowed Money by him
paid for purchase of Beef's and other Provisions
for use of Indians.

Total Sum   £5647.12.10

Total Discharge   £23890.13.8 ³/₄
                                                   (Halifax Currency)

SOURCE: PRO (London), Audit Office, declared Accounts, Indians of North America,
          AO 1, roll 8, bundle 1531.

Warriors

number brought forward	5410
Folavomes of Green Bay, & Baye des noquer	500
Winni bagoes, at the Fox River and Rivi à la Roche	200
Saa Kies on the East side of the River Mississippi & entry of River à la Roche	750
Miss qua Kies or Foxes on the East Bank of the Mississippi and them falling into the same	450
Chipaways & Ottawas of Saguina Bay Bay on Lake Huron	600
	8410

This forms a tolerably correct List of the Indian warriors on the frontier of the United States, extending from Sandusky on Lake Erie, to the River Mississippi, as they stood the first year of the late War. — They were all in arms for the British Goot and most of them joined the Armies in the field — but even those who did not were perhaps more serviceable to the Cause. — In this list I do not include the Sioux brought out by Mr Dickson. I believe their numbers did not at any time exceed 300 warriors but these were picked men

APPENDIX B

*List of Indian Warriors as they Stood in 1812
at the time war was declared*

State of the Indian tribes in The Territories of Michigan
Illinois and Indiana as calcu – viz

	Warriors
Wyandots or Hurons at Labout [?] Sandusky and neighbourhood of Detroit	450
Ottawas & Chipaways m Jagnina [?] and about River St. Clair	350
Miamis – on Miami River	80
Poass [Piakashaw ?]	180
Shawanons (Shawanese / at Their usual Towns on the Head Waters of the Wabash and other Shawanese falling into the Ohio-Tecumsehs tribe	550
Shawanons – on the west side of River Mississippi (a few only of these joined)	300
Potawatomies – at St. Joseph-Thea llake (?) Chicago – Millewakie and Illinois River	2000
Kikapoos and Mashcoutens, on the Illinois River	450
Ottawas of Arbre-Croche-grand River & other Rivers which fall into Lake Michigan	550
Chipaways of Michilimakinac-St. Marris and about the north side of Lake Michigan	400
	5410

	Warriors
numbers brought forward	5410
Folsavoins of Green Bay, & baye des noques	500
Winnibagoes, at the Fox River and River a la Roche	700
Saakies on the East side of the River Mississippi & entry of River a la Roche	750
Missquakies or Foxes – on the East Bank of the Mississippi and River falling into the same	450
Chipaways & Ottawas of Sagauna Bay Bay on Lake Huron	600
	8410

This forms a tolerably correct list of the Indian warriors on
the frontier of the United States extending from Sandusky on Lake
Erie to the River Mississippi, as they stood the first year of
the late War – They were all in Arms for the British Govt
and most of them joined the Armies in the Field-but even
those who did *not* were perhaps more ammicable to the
Cause. - In this list I do not include the
Scioux brought out by Mr. Dickson. I believe these
numbers did not [at] any time exceed 300 warriors
but those were picked men

The tribes above enumerated are which is generally
understood by the term *Western Indians* - but this description
also comprehends the Chipaways of the North & west side
of Lake Superior - as but few of these came to the
war. I have omited them although they are very brave.
       The Indians of Upper & Lower Canada, are but few
in numbers and entirely dependant upon Government –
They also hold reserve lands - and have greatly lost
their ancient Character by their intermixture with the
Whites - The following is nearly a correct enumeration of them _____

	Warriors
Mohawks on the Grand River. Lake Erie,	400
Ditto - of the Bay of Quinty	50
Mississaakies about York - & north & west of Lake Ontario	50
Chipaways of Matchesdash & Lake Simcoe	70
Iroquois of St. Regis	250
Ditto of Canawaga	670
Ditto - Lake 2 mountains	150
Nipisangs or Algonkans of the Lake of the 2 mountains	100

Ditto – about 3 Rivers etc.	50
Abinnaquis of St. Francis	100
	1590

the warriors of St. Regis were divided in Politiks and
owing chiefly to our own mismanagement one half of
them at least were with the Enemy.

Indians of upper & lower Canada – as	
Enumerated	1590
Western Indians	8,410
	10,000

Montreal 1814

SOURCE: OA, Strachan Papers.

My Children the Traders got to your Villages with Cloathing and Ammunition, and even a little Milk to gladden your Hearts. —

My Children. You are no Strangers to the War which the Big Knives have most unjustly began and carry on against the Indians: and my other Children:— Although placed as at a greater distance from the frontiers of their Country, You have long felt the effects of their wicked Policy. whenever they have had power, it has been uniformly exerted to distress the Indians — Joint or forcibly taking their lands; from those immediately in their vicinity, and depriving those at a distance of the Goods and Ammunition, which were absolutely necessary for the Support of their Families,

My Children, The Traders and the Indians have often complained to me of these acts of aggression, I advised to patience, and always spoke the words of peace — But when I found these words had no other effect than to increase the arrogance of the Big Knives, and that they had actually began the War with the Indians, I got angry and Ordered my Warriors to take their Arms—their Success in every rencounter with the Enemy has hitherto been complete. —

My Children, I speak the truth. Compare my words with your own experience — compare the situation of

Your

APPENDIX C

Speech of Robert Dickson Esquire to Indian tribes, 18 January 1813

To each of the Tribes of Indians whom Mr. Dickson may have occasion to Address – it would be [ordered] that with a few strings of Wampum to them respectively, he should open the business with a Short Speech saying,

Brothers, I have been to Quebec to see the great Chief Sir George Prevost, who holds there the place of your Father and ours, the Great King George, that I might know from him everything which relates to the War, which yours and our Enemies the Big Knives are Carrying on against you & us, and I am returning with his Talk to all the Indians Hear then what he says, and let these Strings of Wampum open your Ears to his voice The Ottawass or Others

My Children – It is now a longtime since you were adopted by me as my Children – Remember Sir William Johnson, he told you I never would forsake or abandon you, but on the Contrary, having pity on your wives and Children, I would send Traders amongst you with Cloathing, and with Arms and Ammunition, that they might be covered, and provisions provided by your Young Men for their sustenance.

My Children – I have not forgoten you, I have kept my word, and although many difficulties were thrown in their way, my Children the Traders got to your Villages with Cloathing and Ammunition, and even a little Milk to gladden your Hearts. –

My Children, You are no Strangers to the War which the Big Knives have most unjustly begun and carry on against the Indians and my other Children: – Although placed at a greater distance from the frontiers of their Country, You have long felt the effects of their wicked Policy, whenever they have had power, it has been uniformly exerted to distress the Indians – first in forcibly taking their lands from those immediately in their vicinity, and depriving those at a distance of the Goods and Ammunition which were absolutely necessary for the Support of their Families. My Children, The Traders and the Indians have often complained to me of these Acts of aggression, I advised to patience, and always spoke the words of peace - But when I found these words had no other effect than to increase the arrogance of the Big Knives, and that they had actually began the War with the Indians, I got angry and Ordered my Warriors to take their Arms - Our success in every rencounter with the Enemy has hitherto been complete. –

My Children, I speak the Truth. Compare my words with your own experience – compare the situation of Your country at this time with what it was 15 Winters ago when the Fort of Michilimackimac was given to the Big Knives - you then wanted for nothing - Your Country was full of Traders and Goods - You were happy - How is it now? These Traders have been ruined and chased away from amongst you, and you are reduced to the hard necessity of making use of your Bows and arrows for want of Powder to kill the Deer, But my Children, I have not nor will I lose hold of the Belt which has been so long among you from Sir William Johnson - on the contrary, I will now make it stronger by the Belt which I now present to you, and never will I leave you but as Your Father, see that Justice is done to you by the Big Knives and that your hunting Grounds shall be preserved for your use, and that of your Children agreeably to the Treaty made at Grenville with their General Wayne some years ago. - My Children, with this Belt I call upon you to rouse up your young Warriors and to join my Troops with the red Coats, and your ancient Bretherin the Canadians, who are also my Children, in order to defend your and our Country, Your and our Wives and Children from becoming Carriers of Water to these faithlefs people – they must be told in a Voice of Thunder that the object of the war is to secure to the Indian Nations the boundaries of their Territories, and that all those who may be found withing their boundaries, shall perish if they do not immediately remove – My Children, we have not attacked them, they have made war upon us and would remain at Peace – One of the reasons they give for that war is, that we have been kind to you and give you good advice – They offended the Great Spirit, and he gave us Victory - You know that Michilimackinac and Detroit were taken from them, for you were there and behaved Nobly in Arms, and not lefs so in humanity by sparing their lives after they were conquered –. You know also, that twice they have been thrown upon their backs at Niagara at this place also, you and my white Children fought together like Bretherin in Arms, and were again Victorious. – My Children, I have already said that the Big Knives would not remain at Peace – They will have War – Come then my red Children and join yourselves to me and my white Children, and let us Fight them together until they shall ask for Peace, but I intreat of you my red Children that in fighting You do not injure poor Women and helpless Children As you have neither Arms or Cloathing or yourselves, my Chiefs will take care to provide for you. – be kind to my Traders when they go among you, let them not return with empty Canoes, but let them come back joyful to pay their debts. – And now my Children, I invite you to the War Feast of your Father, be then Couragous and Stout hearted, and depend upon it that I shall hold firmly one end of the Belt whilst you hold the other which shall bind us to assist one another against our common Enemy. – Many Chiefs are dead since you became my Children, but others have grown up in their places – In the number is Sir John Johnson, Son of the Great Chief of that name, whom you can never forget, because he counselled you wisely, and his assurances of you having an English Father were not said in vain. – My Children, listen not to the Songs of wild birds who may tell you that the English will make Peace with the Enemy when it suits their own convenience without consulting your Interest. *My words* are pledged to you that this will never happen.

My Children, open you ears to my words, and do not throw them away – the Indian Nations united with my other Children are much Stronger than the Enemy, and wish four, them to demand Peace, but should any of the Nations be deaf to my words and think their distance will secure him from oppression, they will be miserably deceived. – The policy of the Big Knives, the Americans, which they never lose sight of and of which you have had so many proofs, is to possefs themselves of all the Indians lands and to destroy one Nation after an other until they get the Whole Country within the Rocky Mountains. – My Children, that you may bear in mind the Alliance now renewed between you and my White Children, I give you a Flag and a Medal to be preserved in your Nation forever: By looking at this Flag you will remember it came from your English Father, and when any of my Chiefs shall see it, they will be happy to take you by the hand and do you all the good they can. – And that you may see that I have the greatest regard for you, I have made your old friend the Red Head a Chief in order to carry to you my Speech, and have also given him a Flag as a pledge that I consider him as your Brother

/Signed/ Francis De Rottenburg
M General

Montreal 18 January 1813
/Signed/John Johnson

    I.G. & S.G.I.A.
        True copy
        W. Claus DIGS Ind. Affs

SOURCE: McCord Museum of Canadian History, M640

APPENDIX D

Lieut.-Governor Sir John Colborne to R.W. Hay, York, Upper Canada, 3 May 1829

Dear Sir,

Since the receipt of your letter of the 3rd of December, I have collected such information respecting the Indian Department, as now enables me to offer an opinion how far it may be expedient to carry reduction, and what measures should be adopted to diminish gradually the expense incurred in conveying the annual presents to the Indians settled in Upper Canada, and to those who have been accustomed to assemble at Drummond's Island, and Amherstburg, from the territory of the United States.

It appears I think, that a considerable decrease in the expense of the establishment of the Indian Department may be effected in a few years, if the course which has been pursued with the Mossissagas [Mississauga] of the Credit should be observed with the other tribes.

Under the superintendence of attentive resident agents, civilization may be extended to the whole of the Indians of the Province, and a fund created for their future support by granting leases of their lands, and selling part of them.

We have been involved, for many years, in a system which has occasioned an enormous expense without conferring any benefit on the Indians, or insuring their friendship. A great effort will now, I hope, be made to ameliorate their condition and to place their children under zealous instructors.

No alteration can yet take place with propriety, in the amount of the presents issued to the Indians who resort annually to Amherstburg from the United States, or to those who have been accustomed to visit Drummond's Island; but some expense may be saved by fixing the periods of issue at the former place...[a number of staff rearrangements in the Indian Department are recommended].

These four Superintendents should be actively employed in collecting the Indians in villages [reserves], and inducing them to cultivate their lands, and divide them into lots. They should encourage them to send their children to the schools which will be prepared for their reception. They will be able probably to persuade the Chiefs to give their consent, that the sums due to them for the lands sold to Government shall be expended on their houses, and in furnishing them with agricultural implements, cattle, etc. They can explain to them the benefit the tribes will received from their lands being leased, and in certain cases, from their being sold, with the sanction of the Lt. Governor and the usual Council ...

It is, however, highly important to let the Indians feel that they are indebted to our Government for the benefits which may be expected to result from establishing schools, and appointing religious teachers, and that all improvements proceed from us. The American Methodists are using great exertions to maintain their influence. They have taken Indian children into the States for the purpose of raising subscriptions, and they have a few days since requested that they may be allowed to import bibles, tracts and clothing for the Indians on the Rice Lakes ...

It will also be expedient to allow a charge of thirty of forty pounds a year at each station for medical attendance. A special Order will be required to authorize the Lt. Governor to consent to the Indian Reserves being disposed of, if in certain cases it should be desirable to alienate them. Several Chiefs have expressed their wish to have schools established, and to bring their tribes together.

The Americans have lately adopted a plan for civilizing the Indians in some parts of the United States; and have formed respectable establishments of missionaries, school masters, farmers, and mechanics. I think we should have similar establishments. The expense must be borne in the first instance by Government, but I have no doubt that we may depend on being able to make the Indians support themselves and all the establishments recommended, at no distant period ...

Source: NAC: MG 11, CO 42, vol. 388

NOTES

Abbreviations

AO	Audit Office, Public Record Office, London
ASPIA	American State Papers, Indian Affairs, U.S. Congress, Washington, D.C.
CHR	*Canadian Historical Review*
CO	Colonial Office Papers
DCB	*Dictionary of Canadian Biography*
Doc. History	*The Documentary History of the State of New York*
HLRO	House of Lords Record Office, London
MG	Manuscript Group, National Archives of Canada
MPHC	*Michigan Pioneer and Historical Collection*
NAC	National Archives of Canada
NDHQ	*North Dakota Historical Quarterly*
NYCD	*Documents Relative to the Colonial History of the State of New York*
OA	Ontario Archives, Toronto
OHSPR	*Ontario Historical Society Papers and Records*
PRO	Public Record Office, London
RG	Record Group, National Archives of Canada
WHC	*Wisconsin Historical Collections*
WO	War Office Papers, Public Record Office, London

Chapter 1: Forging the Chain of Friendship

1 National Archives of Canada (Ottawa), Record Group 10 (Records Relating to Indian Affairs), vol. 2287, file 57, 169 (also on microfilm reel C11195),. Royal Commission of Sir William Johnson, Court of St. James's, 11 March 1761, By His Majesty's Command. The official titles varied slightly in wording from April 1755. The 1761 version is the most complete in descriptive detail.

2 Jack Stagg, "Protection and Survival: Anglo-Indian Relations, 1748-1763 - Britain and the Northern Colonies" (Ph.D. dissertation, University of Cambridge, 1984), provides full details on this theme to the Proclamation of 1763.

3 The classic study of the People of the Longhouse is Lewis H. Morgan, *League of Ho-de-no-sau-nee or Iroquois* (New York: Sage and Brother, 1851). For more contemporary assessments, see Elisabeth Tooker, "The League of the Iroquois: History, Politics, and Ritual," in Bruce G. Trigger, vol. ed., *Handbook of North American Indians* (Washington, DC: Smithsonian Institution, 1978), vol. 15, *Northeast:* 418-41; and Barbara Graymont, *The Iroquois in the American Revolution* (Syracuse: Syracuse University Press, 1972), esp. chapter 1, 5-25, "The People of the Longhouse." An intriguing history of the Iroquois contemporary to the period of this study is Carl F. Klinck and James J. Talman, eds., *The Journal of Major John Norton, 1816* (Toronto: The Champlain Society, 1970), esp. pp. 198-370, "An Account of the Five Nations ... " The Scotch-

Cherokee Norton settled among the Iroquois along the Grand River in Upper
Canada (Ontario) where he became a "Chief of Renown." For the Mohawk, see
William N. Fenton and Elisabeth Tooker, "Mohawk," in Trigger, vol. ed.,
Handbook, vol. 15: 466-90; and for a distinctly Mohawk perspective, see David
Blanchard, *Seven Generations: A History of the Kanienkehaka* (Kahnawake:
Kahnawake Survival School, 1980).

4   Arthur C. Parker, *The Constitution of the Five Nations* (Albany: University of the
State of New York, 1916), esp. 30-49; and see also Paul A. Wallace, *The White
Roots of Peace* (Philadelphia: University of Pennsylvania Press, 1946). The Six
Nations Confederacy of Iroquois is based on the great Law of Peace, and there
is no confirmation or evidence of a constitution in Iroquois history. Today the
Six Nations, however, speak of a constitution, yet this assertion represents a
modern interpretation in the development of Iroquois social structure, rather
than the ancient version. Some discussion of this theme is found in Arthur C.
Parker and Duncan C. Scott, "Traditional History of the Six Nations," *Royal
Society of Canada. Transactions*, 3rd series, vol. 5 (1911), section 2: 195-246.

5   For the functioning of the clan system, see Alexander A. Goldenweiser, "The
Clan and Maternal Family of the Iroquois League," *American Anthropologist* 15
(October–December 1913): 696-99; Judith K. Brown, "Economic Organization
and the Position of Women among the Iroquois," *Ethnohistory* 17, no. 3 (1970):
151-67; and Elisabeth Tooker, "Women in Iroquois Society," in Michael K.
Foster et al, eds., *Extending the Rafters: Interdisciplinary Approaches to Iroquoian
Studies* (Albany: State University of New York, 1984), 109-23.

6   See Horatio E. Hale, ed., *The Iroquois Book of Rites* (Toronto: University of
Toronto Press, 1965; first publ. 1883); for the Condolence Council see Hale, "An
Iroquois Condoling Council," *Royal Society of Canada. Transactions*, 2nd series,
vol. 1, no. 2 (1895): 45-65; William N. Fenton, "The Roll Call of the Iroquois
Chiefs: A Study of a Mnemonic Cane from the Six Nations Reserve,"
Smithsonian Miscellaneous Collections 3, no. 15 (1950): 1-73; and for a brief,
critical, and recent summary, Tooker, "The League of the Iroquois," 437-40.

7   A good brief analysis of the use and meaning of wampum is Michael K. Foster,
"Another Look at the Function of Wampum in Iroquois-White Councils," in
Francis Jennings et al., eds., *The History and Culture of Iroquois Diplomacy: An
Interdisciplinary Guide to the Treaties of the Six Nations and Their League*
(Syracuse: University of Syracuse Press, 1985), 99-114; see also Tooker, "The
League of the Iroquois," 422-24.

8   Quoted in Tooker, "The League of the Iroquois," 422. The extent of the Mohawk
and Six Nations Iroquois territorial limits at the time of contact with the Dutch
is presented by Tooker, ibid., 419 (map). For the territorial evolution of the
Iroquois, see R. Cole Harris, ed., and Geoffrey J. Mathews,
cartographer/designer, *Historical Atlas of Canada* : vol. 1, *From the Beginning to
1800* (Toronto: University of Toronto Press, 1987), esp. plates 12, 33-35, 37-39,
40, and 69. Among the Mohawk and Six Nations today, there is a strong
conviction that their traditional lands extended north and west into Canada.
Although archaeological, anthropological, and historical research and
investigation has identified and documented the presence of ancient Iroquoian
sites in the regions of what became southern Quebec and southern Ontario
prior to the arrival and permanent settlement of Europeans, the Six Nations
Confederacy of Iroquois are generally considered to be indigenous to upper
New York, with their ancient castles or cantons located throughout the Finger
Lakes. This conclusion is realistic when faced with the complexities of the
constant fluctuations in tribal migrations and demographic patterns during the
pre-contact period. Further, any argument which attempts to support, for
instance, a Mohawk land claim in modern Quebec or Ontario by assuming a

direct ancestral link between themselves and Iroquoian people who lived along the St. Lawrence at the time of the arrival of Jacques Cartier in 1534-5 is quite specious. A claim of this sort appears even less creditable when placed beside the land claims of the Algonquin of Quebec or the Mississauga Ojibwa of southern Ontario, who have used and occupied those lands on a permanent basis far longer than the Six Nations League, and therefore consider these areas to be part of their traditional hunting grounds. In assessing this controversy, Bruce G. Trigger, *The Children of Aataentsic: A History of the Huron People to 1660*, 2 vols., (Montreal: McGill-Queen's University Press, 1976), 1: 79, warns that it is "important not to over-emphasize similarities among the northern Iroquoian-speaking peoples. Many presumed similarities may be an illusion resulting from inadequate sources and undue extrapolation." This thesis is supported by J.B. Jamieson, "Trade and Warfare: The Disappearance of the Saint Lawrence Iroquoians," *Man in the Northeast* 39 (1990): 79-86. These theoretical problems are covered in part by Bruce G. Trigger, *Natives and Newcomers: Canada's 'Heroic Age' Reconsidered* (Montreal: McGill-Queen's University Press, 1985). Finally, several British maps of the eighteenth century show Six Nations lands extending far north and west of upper New York, often with the remark "extirpated by the Iroquois." See, for instance, Edmund Berkeley and Dorothy Smith Berkeley, *Dr. John Mitchell: The Man who Made the Map of North America* (Chapel Hill: University of North Carolina Press, 1974). This fiction was created by the British in order to provide the Iroquois with an "empire" of conquests of other Indian nations. The policy was deliberate and calculated, for Britain assumed the Iroquois rights of conquests when the Six Nations put their lands under the protection of the British crown. The British, but not the Iroquois, applied the broadest possible meaning to this action, and asserted that what was claimed by the Iroquois, by extension, therefore belonged to Britain. In the struggle for imperial supremacy in North America between Britain and France, the British donated an empire to the Iroquois in order to claim extensive territory for themselves against similar French ambitions and claims. Francis Jennings, *The Ambiguous Iroquois Empire: The Covenant Chain Confederation of Indian Tribes with English Colonies from its beginnings to the Lancaster Treaty of 1744* (New York: W.W. Norton and Company, 1984), supports this contention and provides additional details.

9   Dutch Indian policy, with a focus on relations with the Mohawk and others of the Iroquois League, is detailed in Francis Jennings, "Dutch and Swedish Indian Policies," in Wilcomb E. Washburn, vol. ed., *Handbook of North American Indians*: vol. 4, *History of Indian-White Relations* (Washington, DC: Smithsonian Institution, 1988),: 13-19; Allen W. Trelease, "Dutch Treatment of the American Indian, with Particular Reference to New Netherlands," in Howard Peckham and Charles Gibson, eds., *Attitudes of Colonial Powers Toward the American Indian* (Salt Lake City: University of Utah Press, 1969), 47-59; and Trelease, *Indian Affairs in Colonial New York: The Seventeenth Century* (Ithaca, NY: Cornell University Press, 1960). Primary documentation is found in E.B. O'Callaghan and B. Fernow, eds., *Documents Relative to the Colonial History of the State of New York*, 15 vols. (Albany: Weed, Parsons and Co., 1856-87), vols. 1 and 2, *Holland Documents*, and vols. 13 and 14, *Dutch Patents*. This source will hereafter be cited as *NYCD*.

10 For the history of the Two Row Wampum and the Silver Covenant Chain of Friendship, see Jennings, *The Ambiguous Iroquois Empire*; the same author's "The Constitutional Evolution of the Covenant Chain," *Proceedings of the American Philosophical Society* 115, no. 2 (April 1971): 88-96; and *Iroquois Diplomacy*, 20-24, 37-45, 116, 121, 158, and 160. Also useful for background information and illustrative material is N. Jaye Fredrickson and Sandra Gibb, *The Covenant Chain: Indian Ceremonial and Trade Silver* (Ottawa: National

Museums of Canada, 1980). The extension of the Chain of Friendship, both between the Iroquois and other tribes and between the British and Indian tribes generally is detailed in Daniel K. Richter and James H. Merrell, eds., *Beyond the Covenant Chain: The Iroquois and Their Neighbors in Indian North America, 1600-1800* (Syracuse: Syracuse University Press, 1987); and Francis Jennings "Iroquois Alliances in American History," in Jennings et al, eds., *Iroquois Diplomacy*, 37-65. See also Paul Williams, "The Chain" (LL.M thesis, Osgoode Hall Law School, York University, 1982).

In Canada today, the Mohawk attach the strongest importance to the sovereignty symbol and principles embodied in the Two Row Wampum and the more enduring Silver Covenant Chain of Friendship. Notwithstanding, the current position of the government of Canada (July 1991) is that these vague seventeenth-century agreements were concluded between the Mohawk and Dutch and the Mohawk and British in what is now the State of New York in the United States. These agreements took place prior to the assertion of British sovereignty in Canada. Therefore, Canada argues that it has no legal responsibility to assume or honour these symbolic principles.

11 Quoted in Cotton Mather, *Magnalia Christi Americana: Or, the Ecclesiastical History of New-England; from its First Planting, in the Year 1620, unto the Year of Our Lord 1698* (London: T. Parkhurst, 1702), 664.

12 *NYCD*, 3: 393-4, Dongan to John Egerton, 2nd Earl of Bridgewater, President of the Board for Trade and Plantations, New York, 22 February 1687; see also NAC, RG10, vol. 2287, file 57, 169.

13 NAC, RG10,vol. 2287, file 57, 169, Richard, Earl of Bellomont, "Captn, Genl. and Governor in Cheife of his Majesties Provinces of New York ..." to Derick Wessells, mayor of Albany, Fort William Henry, 22 August 1698.

14 For a detailed analysis of the arguments and rationale for territorial acquisition in the new world, see John T. Juricek, Jr., "English Claims in North America to 1660: A Study in Legal and Constitutional History" (Ph.D. dissertation, University of Chicago, 1970).

15 Ibid.; see also Geoffrey S. Lester, *Aboriginal Land Rights: Some Notes on the Historiography of English Claims in North America* (Ottawa: Canadian Arctic Resources Committee, 1988) for a useful assessment of the various schools of thought on territorial acquisition.

16 Quoted in Roy Harvey Pearce, *The Savages of America: A Study of the Indian and the Idea of Civilization* (Baltimore: The Johns Hopkins Press, 1953), 12. A 1965 edition was published under the title *Savagism and Civilization*; see also Wilcomb E. Washburn, "The Moral and Legal Justifications for Dispossessing the Indians," in James Morton Smith, ed., *Seventeenth-Century America: Essays in Colonial History* (Chapel Hill: University of North Carolina Press, 1959), 15-32; and James Axtell, *The European and the Indian: Essays in the Ethnohistory of Colonial North America* (New York: Oxford University Press, 1981).

17 Quoted in *Johnson v. McIntosh* (1823): 681. This was a United States Supreme Court decision which reviewed European-Indian relations in America from the moment of "discovery." It concluded that Indian land could be taken irrespective of any moral or legal rights. Felix S. Cohen's *Handbook of Federal Indian Law* (Charlottesville, Virginia: The Michie Company, 1982), 486-90 provides a brief summary. For convenience a full text of the decision of *Johnson v. McIntosh* is offered in Wilcomb E. Washburn, ed., *The American Indian and the United States: A Documentary History*, 4 vols., (New York: Random House, 1973), 4: 2537-53. The decision, which placed decided limits on aboriginal title, has provided the rationale and authority upon which all similar court cases in Canada are founded. See, for example, *St. Catherine's Milling and Lumber Co.* v. *The Queen* (1888), *Calder et al.* v. *Attorney General of British Columbia* (1973) and *Guerin* v. *The Queen* (1985). The phrase "distinct society" has become today in

Canada an emotional and passionate expression of nationhood and sovereignty for both aboriginal people and for French Quebec.

18 Quoted in Wilcomb E. Washburn, "The Moral and Legal Justifications," 16. In colonial America, Francis Jennings, *The Invasion of America: Indians, Colonialism, and the Cant of Conquest* (Chapel Hill: University of North Carolina Press, 1975) details and assesses this theme by focusing on the Puritans of New England and their wars of conquest against the Pequot in 1637 and the Wampanoag in 1675-76 (King Philip's War).

19 For a narrative and analytical assessment of the Ojibwa-Iroquois wars, see Peter S. Schmaltz, "The Role of the Ojibwa in the Conquest of Southern Ontario, 1650-1701," *Ontario History*, 76, no.4 (December 1984): 328-32; Leroy V. Eid, "The Ojibwa-Iroquois War: The War the Five Nations Did Not Win," *Ethnohistory* 26, no. 4 (Fall 1979): 297-324; for a recent study, see Peter S. Schmaltz, *The Ojibwa of Southern Ontario* (Toronto: University of Toronto Press, 1991). Helen Hornbeck Tanner, *The Ojibwas: A Critical Bibliography* (Bloomington: Indiana University Press, 1976) provides an assessment of sources. The Ojibwa people (Anishnabwe) were part of the Council of "The Three Fires" which included the Ojibwa (Ojibwe), Ottawa (Odawa) and Potawatomi. Yet all were linguistically and culturally identified with Ojibwa. Other Ojibwa peoples were the Mississauga Ojibwa and the Saulteaux (Plains Ojibwa). In the United States the word Chippewa is applied to the Ojibwa people.

20 NAC, RG10, vol. 2287, file 57, 169, Five Nations Sachems to the Albany Commissioners of Indian Affairs, Albany, 30 June 1700.

21 Ibid., the Sachems of the Five Nations to Earl of Bellomont, Albany, 31 August 1700.

22 Ibid., Deed in Trust of the Five Nations of Indians to the King, Albany, 19 July 1701; reconfirmed at Albany, 14 September 1726 by Onondaga, Cayaga and Seneca Sachems.

23 Ibid., "Memorial of the Right of the British Crown over the New-York Indians," dated 2 June 1709, but prepared by the Commissioners of Trade and Plantations in 1697 relating to "the Right of the Crown of England, to the sovereignty over the Five Nations of Indians bordering upon the Province of New York."

24 For the Grand Alliance and neutrality agreements with the British at Albany and the French at Montreal in 1701, along with an assessment of Iroquois diplomacy and trade policies during this period, see Richard Haan, "The Problem of Iroquois Neutrality: Suggestions for Revision," *Ethnohistory* 27, no. 4 (Fall 1980): 317-29; and Richard Aquila, *The Iroquois Restoration. Iroquois Diplomacy on the Colonial Frontier, 1701-1754* (Detroit: Wayne State University, 1983).

25 NAC, RG10, vol. 2287, file 57, 169, Speech of Sachems of the Five Nations to Robert Hunter, "Captn Genll and governor in Cheife of her Majesties Provinces of New York ...," and to Robert Livingston, Secretary of Indian Affairs, Albany, 19 August 1710. A useful source for Indian policy in colonial New York is Lawrence H. Leder, ed., *The Livingston Indian Records, 1666-1723* (Gettysburg, Pa.: Pennsylvania Historical Association, 1956; facs., ed.). These records contain documents not duplicated in *NYCD*.

26 Reuben Gold Thwaites, ed., *The Jesuit Relations and Allied Documents*, 73 vols. (Cleveland: the Burrows Bros. Co., 1896-1901), 6: 296-8. Speech of Montagnais to Father Paul La Jeune in 1634. This superb collection details French-Indian relations throughout and beyond the period of New France.

27 Charles H. McIlwain, ed., *An Abridgement of the Indian Affairs Contained in Four Folio Volumes Transacted in the Colony of New York, from the Year 1678 to the Year 1751, by Peter Wraxall* (Cambridge: Harvard University Press, 1915), ix. This is volume 21 of Harvard Historical Studies.

28   NAC, RG10, vol. 2287, file 57, 169, Sachems of the Five Nations to Robert Hunter
     and Robert Livingston, Albany, 19 August 1710. The "faithful Mohawks"
     designation originated with the visit to England in 1710 of the "Four Indian
     Kings" (three Mohawk and one Mohican). As a result of their audience with
     Her Majesty, a Queen Anne silver communion set was delivered to the Fort
     Hunter Mohawk in the Mohawk Valley of upper New York, for their sole use
     forever. The details and political importance of the 1710 visit in solidifying the
     British-Iroquois alliance are provided in John Wolfe Lydekker, *The Faithful
     Mohawks* (Cambridge: Cambridge University Press, 1938); Richmond Bond,
     Queen Anne's American Kings (Oxford: Clarendon Press, 1952); and John G.
     Garrett, *The Four Indian Kings* (Ottawa: Minister of Supply and Services
     Canada, 1985). Following the American colonial rebellion, Mohawk Loyalists
     removed the communion set to Canada, where it was divided between the
     Grand River (Ohsweken) and Tyendinaga groups. The Tyendinaga people have
     been engaged in a gnawing conflict with the local diocese of the Church of
     England who contend that the Queen Anne set is church property and could
     be returned to the archbishop in London. As for the "faithful Mohawks" label,
     this proud legacy is no longer universally viewed as a positive condition by
     many Mohawk in Canada.

29   NAC, RG10, vol. 2287, file 57, 169, Lords of Trade and Plantations to the Duke of
     Newcastle, Secretary of State for the Southern Department, Whitehall, 21
     December 1727; see also Richard L. Hann, "The Covenant Chain: Iroquois
     Diplomacy on the Niagara Frontier, 1697-1730," (Ph.D. dissertation, University
     of California, 1976).

30   NAC, RG10, vol. 2287, file 57, 169, Minutes of a Speech in Conference of the Six
     Nations Iroquois to Marquis de la Galissonière, governor of New France, Castle
     of St. Louis of Quebec, 2 November 1748. The struggle over Iroquois lands is
     detailed in Georgiana C. Nammack, *Fraud, Politics, and the Dispossession of the
     Indians: The Iroquois Land Frontier in the Colonial Period* (Norman: University of
     Oklahoma Press, 1969). The European conflicts in which Britain and France
     were involved, such as the War of the League of Augsburg or "The Grand
     Alliance" (1689-97), the War of the Spanish Succession (1701-13), the War of
     the Austrian Succession (1740-48), and the Seven Years' War (1756-63), spilled
     over into America where they were called, in turn, King William's War, Queen
     Anne's War, King George's War (1740-48) and the French and Indian War
     (1754-63), known in Canada as *la guerre de la conquête*.

31   NAC, RG10, vol. 2287, file 57, 169, George Clinton, governor of New York, to the
     Marquis de la Jonquiere, governor of New France, Fort George in ye city of
     New York, 12 June 1751.

32   *NYCD*, 6: 781-8, Speech of Mohawk Sachem Hendrick to George Clinton and
     his Council, Fort George (city of New York), 12 June 1753. Hendrick, one of the
     "Four Indian Kings" who had visited England in 1710, was a powerful
     influence among his Mohawk people and with the British in New York for
     nearly forty years. His life is chronicled by Milton W. Hamilton in the
     Dictionary of Canadian Biography (Toronto: University of Toronto Press, 1974),
     3:622-24 (hereafter cited as *DCB*).

33   *NYCD*, 16: 869-70, Speech of Hendrick in Council to James Delancey,
     lieutenant-governor of New York, Albany, 2 July 1754.

Chapter 2: Sir William Johnson and the Indian Department

1   General biographies of Sir William Johnson include Milton W. Hamilton, *Sir
     William Johnson: Colonial American, 1715-1763* (Port Washington, NY: Kennikat
     Press, 1976); Arthur H. Pound, *Johnson of the Mohawks: A Biography of Sir
     William Johnson* (New York: Macmillan Co., 1930); James Thomas Flexner,

Mohawk Baronet: Sir William Johnson of New York (New York: Harper and Bros., 1959); and Arthur Pound (with Richard E. Day), *Johnson of the Mohawks* (New York: Macmillan Co., 1930). All of these works, however, border on hero worship, and none of them provides an insightful or satisfactory assessment of Johnson's importance in the scheme of British Indian policy. For a concise and balanced summary of Johnson's life, see Julian Gwyn's article in *DCB*, 4: 394-98. The most detailed and accurate reference source for understanding Indian policy and Indian relations in colonial New York during the Johnson years remains James J. Sullivan et al., eds., *The Papers of Sir William Johnson*, 14 vols. (Albany: University of the State of New York, 1921-1965). The papers are supplemented by Milton W. Hamilton, ed., "The Papers of Sir William Johnson: Addenda," *New York History* 60 (January 1979): 81-101.

2   For the Albany merchants and the New York economic and political rivalries, see David A. Armour, "The merchants of Albany, New York, 1686-1760," Ph.D. dissertation, Northwestern University, 1965); D.S. McKeith, "The Inadequacy of Men and Measures in English Imperial History: Sir William Johnson and the New York Politicians, a Case Study" (Ph.D. dissertation, Syracuse University, 1971); and Patricia U. Bonomi, *A Factious People: Politics and Society in Colonial New York* (New York: Columbia University Press, 1971).

3   For an assessment of Johnson's partial acculturation (politically motivated) to the Mohawk way of life, see Milton W. Hamilton, "Sir William Johnson: Interpreter of the Iroquois," *Ethnohistory* 10, no. 3 (1963): 270-86; and for a brief assessment, Robert S. Allen, *The British Indian Department and the Frontier in North America, 1755-1830* (Ottawa: Department of Indian and Northern Affairs Canada, 1975), 11-13, Canadian Historic Sites: Occasional Papers in Archaeology and History no. 14.

4   Quoted in Cadwallader Colden, *The History of the Five Nations of Canada: Which are Dependent on the Province of New York, and are a Barrier between the English and the French in that Part of the World*, 2 vols., New York: A.S. Barnes and Co., 1904; first publ. 1727, 1747), 2: 218-21. Cadwallader Colden, who became lieutenant-governor of New York, was considered an expert on Indian affairs. His book on the Five Nations emphasized and influenced the British propagandist argument that the Iroquois had conquered an empire over other tribes, and that since the Iroquois were subjects of the King of England, these extensive lands of the confederacy were therefore under British sovereignty.

5   Sullivan, ed., *Johnson Papers*, 1: 60-61, Commission and Instructions to William Johnson, by appointment of George Clinton, 28 August 1746.

6   This theme is developed in A. Mark Conrad, "The Christianization of Indians in Colonial Virginia" (Ph.D. dissertation, Union Theological Seminary, Richmond, Va., 1979), 203-10, esp. 204-205. The passage from the Old Testament is Genesis 12: 1-3.

7   These quotations are from William Byrd II of Westover, Virginia, "The History of the Dividing Line Betwixt Virginia and North Carolina Run in the Year of Our Lord 1728," in Louis B. Wright and Marion Tinling, eds., *William Byrd of Virginia: The London Diary (1717-1721) and Other Writings* (New York: Arno Press, 1972), 574.

8   Hamilton, *Sir William Johnson*, 34-35, provides details on the German woman, Catherine (Catty) "Wysenbergh." They had three children, viz Ann (Nancy), John and Mary (Polly). In William Johnson's will, published in W. Max Reid, *Old Fort Johnson* (New York: G.P. Putnam's Sons, 1906), 149-59, Johnson refers to Catharine as "my beloved wife," which fostered speculation that he may have married her formally near the time of her death. For Johnson's several liaisons with Iroquois women, see Milton W. Hamilton, "Myths and Legends of Sir William Johnson," *New York History* 34, no. 1 (1953): 3-26; and by the same author, "Sir William Johnson's Wives," *New York History* 38, no. 1 (1957): 18-28.

Johnson was quite open about his relationships with Iroquois women; see, for instance, Sullivan, ed., *Johnson Papers*, 12: 1062-75.

9   The life of Mary Brant is assessed by Barbara Graymont in *DCB*, 4: 416-19; Jean Johnston, "Ancestry and Descendants of Molly Brant," *Ontario History*, 63, no. 2 (June 1971): 87-92; and Gretchen Green, "Molly Brant, Catherine Brant, and their Daughters: A Study in Colonial Acculturation," *Ontario History* 81, no. 3 (September 1989): 236-50. The "prudent and faithful Housekeeper" was the expression used in the Johnson's will.

10 NAC, MG 21, Haldimand Collection, Series B, B114: 63, Daniel Claus to Frederick Haldimand, governor of Quebec.

11 E.B. O'Callaghan, ed., *The Documentary History of the State of New York*, 4 vols., (Albany: Weed, Parsons and Co., 1849-51), 2: 648-51. Minutes of a Council, held at the Camp, Alexandria, Virginia, 14 April 1755.

12 Sullivan, ed., *Johnson Papers*, 1: 465-66, Commission from Edward Braddock, Alexandria, 15 April 1755.

13 Public Record Office (London), Colonial Office Papers 5 (America and West Indies), 211, folio 134, "Secret Instructions."

14 For details of French and British activities in the Ohio Valley from 1749 to 1754, see Francis Jennings, *Empire of Fortune: Crowns, Colonies and Tribes in the Seven Years War in America* (New York: W.W. Norton and Co., 1988), 8-70; Francis Parkman, *Montcalm and Wolfe* (New York: Collier Books, 1966, ed.; first publ. 1884), 48-81 and 106-27; for a concise accounting, see Allen, *The British Indian Department*, 9-11.

15 British Library (London), Add. Mss. 32848, folios 85-87, letter of the Duke of Newcastle, who had been Secretary of State for the Southern Department, 1724-48 and responsible for American affairs, 15 January 1754. British imperial policy and diplomatic manoeuvring during these years are detailed in T.R. Clayton, "The Duke of Newcastle, the Duke of Halifax, and the American Origins of the Seven Years' War," *Historical Journal*, 24 (1981), 571-603. George Montague Dunk, Earl of Halifax, was President of the Board of Trade and Plantations from 1748 to 1761.

16 British Library, Add. Mss. 33029, folios 138-42, dated, 7 November 1754. Although "Methods" was presented by the president, it had been "passed through the hands" of the Duke of Newcastle. Both men worked in close harmony in the area of British-Indian relations and American affairs.

17 Fort Saint-Frédéric, built by the French in 1731, strategically commanded the narrow passage of the south-western portion of Lake Champlain. In 1755 the French pushed farther south and established Fort Carillon (Ticonderoga) at the confluence of Lake Champlain and Lake George. These French advances directly threatened Iroquoia, Albany, and all of upper New York. A fourth expedition was mounted against Fort Beauséjour on the Isthmus of Chignecto in Nova Scotia (Acadia). Following a two-week siege in June 1755 by British regulars and Massachusetts volunteers, the French surrendered. The British renamed the site Fort Cumberland. A detailed account of the British campaign against Fort Beauséjour is in Lawrence H. Gibson, *The British Empire before the American Revolution*, 15 vols. (New York: Alfred A. Knopf, 1936-70), 6: 212-42. A review of Gibson's volumes is useful for an understanding of British imperial policy in America prior to the outbreak of the Revolutionary War.

18 Paul E. Kopperman, *Braddock at the Monongahela* (Pittsburgh: University of Pittsburgh Press, 1977) provides a focused assessment; see also Parkman, *Montcalm and Wolfe*, 144-73; and Jennings, *Empire of Fortune*, 151-60. Jennings's concluding remarks on Braddock are that "there is absolutely no valid reason to condone this stupid brute of a man whose prime qualification for command was the political favour of the party of royal prerogative" (p. 158). Braddock died on 13 July 1755 of wounds received at the Monongahela

(also known as the Battle of the Wilderness). The candour and sarcasm throughout Jennings's academic analysis may be viewed as either refreshing or petty. But his assessment of Francis Parkman as "a liar" whose "work is fiction rather than history" (p. 480) is vitriolic and unfair. Parkman was writing in an age in which the social and moral climate regarding native people was quite different from that of today. His *France and England in North America*, 8 vols. (Boston: Little, Brown and Co., 1851-92) remains a rich mixture of history and literature which few contemporary scholars can hope to emulate.

19 *NYCD*, 6: 964-89, esp. p. 972. Council at Mount Johnson with Indians Assembled, 21 June to 4 July 1755.

20 NAC, RG10, vol. 2287, file 57, 169, Speech of the Onondaga sachem Kaghswrughtioni to William Johnson, Mount Johnson, 29 June 1755.

21 *Doc. History*, 2: 691-5, William Johnson to the Governors of the Several Colonies, Camp at Lake George, 9 September 1755, Report of the battle; see also Parkman, *Moncalm and Wolfe*, 207-27. Baron Dieskau complained that his carefully planned ambush of Johnson was spoiled when "Canadian" Mohawk from the Catholic mission of Caughnawaga (Kahnawake) near Montreal who were allied to the French, prematurely warned their brother New York Mohawk serving with the British. See *NYCD*, 10: 317-18, Dieskau to the Marquis de Vaudreuil, governor of New France, 15 September 1755. This sort of Six Nations factionalism was evident throughout the war.

22 The lengthy councils conducted by Johnson throughout these years are thoroughly detailed and assessed by Stagg, "Protection and Survival," 283-366. Thumbnail sketches are offered in Jennings, *Iroquois Diplomacy*, 188-90. For the military events of the war, see Douglas Edward Leach, *Arms for Empire: A Military History of the British Colonies in North America, 1607-1763* (New York: Macmillan Company, 1973); and Stanley McCory Pargellis, *Lord Loudon in North America* (New Haven, Conn.: Yale University Press, 1933), which is a particularly valuable scholarly account and analysis of colonial military problems throughout this period; for brief assessments of the French and British forces in North America during the 1754-63 period, see W.J. Eccles, " The French forces in North America during the Seven Years' War," *DCB*, 3: xv-xxiii and C.P. Stacey, "The British forces in North America during the Seven Years' War," ibid., xxiv-xxx. The aftermath of these French and Indian victories was often marked by bloody reprisals on the part of the Indian allies. At Fort William Henry, for instance, the garrison and civilians were "inconceivably frightened by the sight of the Indians" and panicked upon being marched out of the fort. This excitement stirred the Abenaki, who initiated a massacre. A horrified Louis Antoine de Bougainville, aide-de-camp to Montcalm, describes this episode in his journal; see Edward P. Hamilton, ed., *Adventures in the Wilderness: The American Journals of Louis Antoine de Bougainville 1756-1760* (Norman: University of Oklahoma Press, 1964), 172-3.

23 *NYCD*, 7: 76-77, Henry Fox, Secretary of State for the Southern Department, to Sir William Johnson, Whitehall, 13 March 1756.

24 PRO, CO 324, vol. 51, folio 301, The King's Commission, dated 13 May 1756. In May of 1755 Atkin submitted a proposal to Halifax entitled "Plan of a General Direction and Management of the Indian Affairs throughout North America," which in part outlined the establishment of a "Northern District" and a "Southern District." The proposal was well received, and influenced the final decision of senior crown officials at Whitehall in creating the Indian superintendencies. For details and an assessment, see Wilbur R. Jacobs, ed., *The Appalachian Indian Frontier: The Edmund Atkin Report and Plan of 1755* (Lincoln: University of Nebraska Press, 1967).

25 For the Indian tribes in the colonial south, see Charles Hudson, *The*

Southeastern Indians (Knoxville: University of Tennessee Press, 1976); R.S. Cotterill, *The Southern Indians: The Story of the Civilized Tribes Before Removal* (Norman: University of Oklahoma Press, 1954); and a classic contemporary account, James Adair, *The History of the American Indians: Particularly those Nations adjoining to the Mississippi, East and West Florida, Georgia, South and North Carolina, and Virginia* (London: Edward and Charles Dilly, 1775). For John Stuart, see John R. Alden, *John Stuart and the Southern Colonial Frontier: A Study of Indian Relations, War, Trade and Land Problems in the Southern Wilderness, 1754-1775* (Ann Arbor: University of Michigan Press, 1944).

26 The British administration of Indian Affairs in the Southern District is detailed in Helen Louise Shaw, *British Administration of the Southern Indians, 1756-1783* (Lancaster, Pa.: Lancaster Press, 1931). For the Northern District, see Ruth E. Pulfer, "The Administration of British Policy to the Indians in the Northern District of North America, 1760-1783" (MA thesis, University of Saskatchewan 1970). The long-term effect of the establishment of a Northern District responsible for Indian Affairs under the authority of the crown was a department which has in some continuous form endured for nearly 250 years. Today (July 1991), this conglomerate - the Department of Indian and Northern Affairs Canada - remains the senior department in the federal bureaucracy. Headquartered at Ottawa-Hull, but with regional branches scattered all over the land, the department employs about 4,300 people of whom 20 percent are native, and functions, under the mandate of the Indian Act, with an annual budget of $3.5 billion (see DINA, main estimates, 1990-91).

27 For Louisbourg, J.M. Hitsman with C.C.J. Bond, "The Assault Landing at Louisbourg, 1758," *Canadian Historical Review* 35 (1954): 314-30, is quite useful; see also Olive P. Dickason, *Louisbourg and the Indians: A Study in Imperial Race Relations, 1713-1760* (Ottawa: Department of Indian and Northern Affairs, 1976). National Historic Parks and Sites, History and Archaeology No. 6. The capture of Louisbourg cleared the way for the Royal Navy to transport troops up the St. Lawrence to Quebec, the heart of France in Canada. The successful attack on Cataraqui (Fort Frontenac) by Lieutenant-Colonel John Bradstreet severed the lifeline of the French empire in the Great Lakes and contributed to their loss of prestige among the "western Indians." For details, see National Library of Wales (Aberystwyth), Tredegar Park Muniments, box 128, file 43 (John Bradstreet Papers), Charles Gould to Bradstreet, 8 December 1758. The expedition is described in E.C. Kyte, *An Impartial Account of Lieut. Col. Bradstreets Expedition to Fort Frontenac* (Toronto: Rous and Mann Ltd., 1940). A useful biography of Bradstreet and the political machinations in eighteenth-century America is William G. Godfrey, *Pursuit of Profit and Preferment in Colonial North America: John Bradstreet's Quest* (Waterloo, Ont.: Wilfrid Laurier University Press, 1982).

The Treaty of Easton was "the most crucial, the most difficult, and the most significant" of the Indian conferences during the long period of French and British imperial rivalry in North America. Not only did the treaty end French domination in the Ohio Valley, it opened the way for the settlement of Indian lands to the west for Britain's northern colonies by largely eliminating the intrigue between the Pennsylvania Quakers and Teedyuscung, the "King the Delwares." A central figure in these treaty negotiations was Charles Thomson, future secretary to the Continental Congress, who took the council minutes and subsequently wrote an influential, but anonymously published, account of these events entitled *An Enquiry into the Causes of the Alienation of the Delaware and Shawanese Indians from the British Interest* (London: J. Wilkie, 1759) which was "a virulent attack on the proprietary dealings with Pennyslvania's Indians." For full details and an assessment of these complex and intriguing matters, see Boyd Stanley Schlenther, *Charles Thomson: A*

Patriot's Pursuit (Newark: University of Delaware Press, 1990), esp. 28–46 (the quotations are found on pp. 40 and 41); for a shorter and specific analysis of Indian relations, by the same author, see "Training for Resistance: Charles Thomson and Indian Affairs in Pennsylvania," *Pennsylvania History* 50, no. 3 (July 1983): 185–217. See also Anthony F.C. Wallace, *King of the Delawares: Teedyuscung 1700–1763* (Syracuse: Syracuse University Press, 1990). For Rogers' Rangers and irregular warfare during the French and Indian War, see Peter E. Russell, "Redcoats in the Wilderness: British Officers and Irregular Warfare in Europe and America, 1740 to 1760," *William and Mary Quarterly*, 3rd series, 35 (1978): 629–52; Robert Rogers, *Journals of Major Robert Rogers* (1765), reprinted facs., ed. (Readex Microprint, 1966); and John R. Cuneo, *Robert Rogers of the Rangers* (New York: Oxford University Press, 1959).

28   *Johnson Papers*, vol. 10: 53–55. Johnson to Major General James Abercromby, commander-in-chief of British forces in North America, 10 November 1758.

29   Quoted in Brian Leigh Dunnigan, *Siege - 1759: The Campaign against Niagara* (Youngstown, NY: Old Fort Niagara Association, Inc., 1986), 59.

30   Sullivan, ed., *Johnson Papers* 3: 108–10, Johnson to Major General Sir Jeffrey Amherst, commander-in-chief of British forces in North America, Niagara, 25 July 1759; and see also British Library, Add. Mss. 21670, Johnson to Lieutenant Colonel Frederick Haldimand, Niagara, 25 July 1759. The battle is detailed in Dunnigan, *Siege - 1759*, 69–80.

31   Full details of these conferences, including Indian speeches, are provided in Nicholas B. Wainwright, ed., "George Croghan's Journal 1759–1763," *Pennsylvania Magazine of History and Biography* 71, no. 4 (October 1947): 336–50, esp. 349 and 340. George Croghan had been appointed by Johnson on 24 November 1756 as his "official agent with special responsibility for the Shawnee and Delaware." See Sullivan, ed., *Johnson Papers*, 2: 656–57. A biography of Croghan is Nicholas B. Wainwright, *George Croghan: Wilderness Diplomat* (Chapel Hill: University of North Carolina, 1959).

32   *NYCD*, 7: 579–81, Johnson to the Lords of Trade and Plantations, Johnson Hall, 13 November 1763; and for the appointment of Daniel Claus to Canada, see NAC, MG 19, F1 (Claus Papers), 5–6, Appointment dated Montreal, 20 September 1760. Major Joseph Goreham, commander of Goreham's Rangers during the last war, was appointed deputy agent for Indian affairs in Nova Scotia, a subordinate position to Sir William Johnson in the Northern District. For Goreham, see Clarence E. Carter, ed., *The Correspondence of General Thomas Gage with the Secretaries of State, and with the War Office and the Treasury 1763-1755*, 2 vols. (New Haven: Yale University Press, 1931–33), 2: 42, Charles Lennox, Duke of Richmond, Secretary of State for the Southern Department, to Gage, Whitehall, 30 June 1766; and ibid., 48–9, Earl of Shelburne, Sec. of State, to Gage, Whitehall, 11 December 1766.

33   NAC, RG10, vol. 2287, file 57, 169, "Review of the Trade and Affairs of the Indians in the Northern District of America," by Sir William Johnson, Bart. (1767). This assessment of Wyandot influence among the western Indians proved true. Johnson, who possessed an undisguised bias toward the Mohawk, believed it was the result of the similarity in language and culture between Huron and Six Nations Iroquois.

34   In November 1763 Johnson enumerated all the Indian tribes within the Northern District. He classified them as: Six Nations Confederacy, Indians of Canada, Indians of Ohio, Ottawa Confederacy, and Miami (Confederacy). The total estimated number, not counting the tribes of the upper Mississippi, was 8,000 warriors. See *NYCD*, 7: 582–84. See also, Bruce G. Trigger, vol. ed., *Handbook*, vol. 15 (Northeast), for brief histories of all the tribes of the Great Lakes region; and *DCB*, 3: xxxi - xliii for a useful "Glossary of Indian Tribal Names."

35   Quotation from NAC, RG10, vol. 2287, file 57, 169, "Review ...," by Sir William
     Johnson, Bart. (1767); see also Lawrence Ostola, "The Seven Nations of Canada
     and the American Revolution 1774-1783" (MA thesis, Université de Montréal,
     1988). Today the Mohawk in Canada take great exception to this interpretation
     of their ancestral and territorial origins. Two well-documented assessments of
     the little-studied western Abenaki are Kenneth M. Morrison, *The Embattled
     Northeast: The Elusive Ideal of Alliance in Abenaki-Euramerican Relations* (Berkeley:
     University of California Press, 1984) and Colin G. Calloway, *The Western
     Abenakis of Vermont, 1600-1800* (Norman: University of Oklahoma Press, 1990).

36   Adam Shortt and Arthur G. Doughty, eds., *Documents Relating to the
     Constitutional History of Canada 1759-1791*, 2 vols. (Ottawa: King's Printer,
     1918), 1: 33. The *laisser-passer* and article XL provisions resulted in a 1990
     Supreme Court of Canada decision on the appeal of *Attorney General of Quebec
     v. Sioui* (1987) which unanimously held that the Huron of Lorreteville (Lorette)
     have "treaty" rights to practise their traditional customs under the 1760 above-
     noted two documents issued to their ancestors by the British military in time
     of crisis and chaos. Although a happy outcome for contemporary Huron in
     Quebec, many historians and lawyers in Canada remain puzzled and
     unconvinced by the legal arguments and logic which produced this decision.

37   British Library, Add. Mss. 21697, Instructions to Jeffrey Amherst Major General
     and General in Chief of Forces in North America, given at Court of St. James's,
     17 December 1760. Within the structure of command, the Indian Department
     was subordinate to the British military. See Clarence E. Carter, "The
     Significance of the Military Office in America, 1763-1775," *American Historical
     Review* 28, no. 4 (July 1923): 475-88. However, during wartime emergencies,
     the Indian Department often assumed an independence in the management of
     the tribes which caused friction between the department and British officers.

38   There was a decided arrogance in the manner and policies of Amherst toward
     the Indian tribes. This condition is well reflected in his post-1760 plan. See
     Harry Kelsey, "The Amherst Plan: A Factor in the Pontiac Uprising," *Ontario
     History* 45, no. 3 (September 1973): 149-58; and Sullivan, ed., *Johnson Papers*,
     10: 284 and 384, Amherst to Johnson, 11 June 1761 and 26 December 1761.

39   Sullivan, ed., *Johnson Papers*, 3: 588, Charles Wyndham, Earl of Egremont,
     Secretary of State for the Southern Department, to Amherst, Whitehall, 12
     December 1761. For the significance of presents, which the Indians regarded
     as symbols of friendship and as partial compensation for allowing the whites
     to enter their lands for the purpose of hunting, trading, and building forts, see
     Wilbur R. Jacobs, *Wilderness Politics and Indian Gifts: The Northern Colonial
     Frontier, 1748-1768* (Lincoln: University of Nebraska Press, 1966).

40   The reports propagated by the (French) Canadians at Detroit and in the Ohio
     country of a "French Armament coming up to Quebec" animated those tribes
     who had developed an "Inveteracy and Hatred" for the British. See Sullivan,
     ed., *Johnson Papers*, 4: 291, Major General Thomas Gage, commander-in-chief
     of Forces in North America, to Johnson, New York, 12 January 1764; see also C.-
     M. Boisonnault, "Les Canadiens et la révolte de Pontiac," *La Revue de
     l'université Laval* 2 (1947-48): 778-87.

41   Alexander Henry, *Travels and Adventures in Canada and the Indian Territories
     Between the Years 1760 and 1776* (Toronto: G.N. Morang, 1901), 44, Speech of
     Minavavana, Ojibwa chief, to Henry, Michilimackinac, spring of 1761; for the
     after effect, see David A. Armour, ed., *Attack at Michilimackinac 1763* (Mackinac
     Island, Michigan: Mackinac Island State Park Commission, 1971). Fort
     Michilimackinac was attacked on 4 June 1763 (the king's birthday) whilst a
     staged game of lacrosse or "le jeu de la crosse" was in progress between the
     local Ojibwa and the visiting Sauk. The garrison was killed or captured, but
     Alexander Henry escaped. In 1780 the fort was moved to the island of

Mackinac for better military security, but the British still called the place
Michilimackinac until the end of the War of 1812.

42 British Library, Add. Mss. 21648 (Bouquet Papers), Ensign Schlosser to Colonel
Henry Bouquet, commander of the western posts, Fort Ligonier, 24 January
1762.

43 See M. Quaife, ed., *The Siege of Detroit in 1763: The Journal of Pontiac's
Conspiracy and John Rutherfurd's Narrative of a Captivity* (Chicago: R.R.
Donnelley and Sons, 1958). Pontiac (Obwandiyag) was pro-French, and an
astute and persuasive war chief who grasped the significance of the "English"
takeover after 1760. In organizing the western tribes to revolt, he was
attempting, like Indian leaders throughout the history of Indian-White
relations, to protect the lands of his people against the advancing Europeans.
Louis Chevrette provides a balanced summary of Pontiac's life in *DCB*, 3:
525-31.

44 National Library of Wales, Tredegar Park Muniments (John Bradstreet Papers),
boxes 128/82 and 85, Bradstreet to Gould, Albany, 13 August and 7 October
1763; for general details and assessments of the Indian uprising, see Howard
H. Peckham, *Pontiac and the Indian Uprising* (Chicago: University of Chicago
Press, 1947); and Francis Parkman, *The Conspiracy of Pontiac* (New York: Collier
Books, 1966, ed.; first publ. 1851).

45 British Library, Add. Mss. 21364 (Bouquet Papers), Amherst to Bouquet, N.D.
Bouquet agreed to the suggestion in a letter to Amherst, dated Carlisle, 13 July
1763.

46 Ibid., Bouquet to Amherst, Camp at Bushy Run, 5 August and 6 August 1763,
reports of the battle; and for a descriptive narrative, see Niles Anderson, *The
Battle of Bushy Run* (Harrisburg, Pa.: Pennsylvania Historical and Museum
Commission, 1975).

47 For the Indian conferences and peace treaties of 1764, see British Library
(London): Add. Mss. 21655 (Bouquet Papers: Papers Relating to Indian Affairs,
1758-1765), 366 folios, scattered references; Paul K. Adams, "Colonel Henry
Bouquet's Ohio Expedition in 1764," *Pennsylvania History* 40, no. 2 (April
1973): 139-47; National Library of Wales, Tredegar Park Muniments (John
Bradstreet Papers), boxes 128/125, 126, 149 and 199; for a general annotated
listing, see Jennings, ed., *Iroquois Diplomacy*, 194-96.

48 This theme in British Indian policy in North America has been studied and
carefully documented by Peter Marshall, "Imperial Regulation of American
Indian Affairs, 1763-1774" (Ph.D. dissertation, Yale University, 1959); and Jack
M. Sosin, *Whitehall and the Wilderness: The Middle West in British Colonial Policy,
1760-1775* (Lincoln: University of Nebraska Press, 1961).

49 A true and accurate copy of the text of the Royal Proclamation of 7 October
1763 is Clarence S. Brigham, ed., *British Royal Proclamations Relating to America*
(Worcester, Mass.: American Antiquarian Society, 1911), vol. 12: 212-18.

50 Ibid.; 216-17. A complex and contentious issue which still remains unresolved
is whether the proclamation was "the object of mere provisional
arrangements," a necessary, but temporary, expedient to reduce the discontent
of the western tribes over encroachments upon their lands and abuses
committed by the traders and settlers. This was the considered opinion of the
Lords of Trade in a representation to the Earl of Hillsborough, Secretary of
State for the Colonies, and in response to queries posed by the Earl of
Shelburne, former Secretary of State responsible for colonial affairs. See PRO,
CO 5, vol. 69, folios 119 etc., "Lords of Trade to Principal Secretary of State,"
Whitehall, 7 March 1768. Equally arguable is the application of the territorial
and legal limits of the proclamation in recognizing aboriginal land rights. In
Canada, the Royal Proclamation of 1763 is regarded as the "magna carta" of
native rights, and has been duly entrenched in the Constitution Act, 1982. Yet

historians and lawyers continue to disagree over the full intent and meaning of this document. See, for instance, Jack Stagg, "Protection and Survival," 460-86; Brian Slattery, "The Land Rights of Indigenous Canadian Peoples, as Affected by the Crown's Acquisition of their Territories" (D.Phil. dissertation, University of Oxford, 1979), 191-349; and the forceful and convincing arguments of Geoffrey S. Lester, "The Territorial Rights of the Inuit of the Canadian Northwest Territories: A Legal Argument," 2 vols. (Doctor of Jurisprudence dissertation, York University, 1981).

51   *NYCD,* 7: 637-41, Plan of 10 July 1764. For Johnson's recommendations, see ibid., 572-84, Johnson to the Lords of Trade, Johnson Hall, 13 November 1763; for the observations of John Stuart on the plan, see Clarence E. Carter, ed., "Observations of Superintendent John Stuart and Governor James Grant of East Florida on the Proposed Plan of 1764 for the Future Management of Indian Affairs," *American Historical Review* 20, no. 4 (July 1915): 815-31.

52   British Library, Add. Mss. 21670, folios 17-34, Treaty of Fort Stanwix, 24 October-5 November 1768; for background details and an analysis, see Peter Marshall, "Sir William Johnson and the Treaty of Fort Stanwix, 1768," *Journal of American Studies* 1, no. 1 (April 1967): 149-79.

53   National Library of Wales, Tredegar Park Muniments (John Bradstreet Papers), box 128/154, Bradstreet to Gould, Albany, 2 June 1765; see also three works by Peter D.G. Thomas: *British Politics and the Stamp Act Crisis; The First Phase of the American Revolution 1763-1767* (Oxford: Clarendon Press, 1975); *The Townshend Duties Crisis: the Second Phase of the American Revolution* (Oxford: Clarendon Press, 1987), and *Tea Party to Independence: the Third Phase of the American Revolution, 1773-1776* (Oxford: Clarendon Press, 1991). The entire political-constitutional arguments are provided in Richard C. Simmons and Peter D.G. Thomas, eds., *Proceedings and Debates of the British Parliaments respecting North America, 1754-1783,* 5 vols. to date, (Millwood, NY: Kraus International Publications, 1982-).

54   This retreat is discussed in Peter Marshall, "Colonial Protest and Imperial Retrenchment: Indian Policy 1764-1768," *Journal of American Studies* 5, no. 1 (April 1971): 1-17. Imperial retrenchment included the abandonment of a plan to establish a "British" settlement at Detroit. See National Library of Wales. Tredegar Park Muniments (John Bradstreet Papers), box 128/151-82, Correspondence between Bradstreet and Gould in which Bradstreet promoted the idea with himself as governor. For an assessment of this scheme, see Peter Marshall, "Imperial Policy and the Government of Detroit: Projects and Problems 1760-1774," *Journal of Imperial and Commonwealth History* 2, no. 2 (January 1974): 153-89. The mounting colonial resistance to external authority is studied in the biography of Charles Thomson; see Schlenther, *Charles Thomson,* chapters 4-7; and "Training for Resistance," 185-217.

55   B.F. Stevens, ed., *Facsimiles of Manuscripts in European Archives Relating to America 1773-1783,* 25 vols., (Wilmington, Del.: Mellifont Press, Inc., 1970), 8: 133, Johnson to William Legge, Earl of Dartmouth, Secretary of State for the Colonies, Johnson Hall, 20 June 1774.

56   PRO, CO5, vol. 75, folio 139, Death of Sir William Johnson at Council, Johnson Hall, 11 July 1774; *NYCD,* 8: 471-72, Guy Johnson to Dartmouth, Johnson Hall, 12 July 1774; and Stevens, ed., *Facsimiles,* 8: 155, Cadwallader Colden, lieutenant-governor of New York, to Dartmouth, New York, 2 August 1774. The council proceedings are found in *NYCD,* 8: 474-84.

57   *NYCD,* 8: 485, Colden to Dartmouth, New York, 2 August 1774.

58   PRO, Audit Office, Declared Accounts (Indians of North America), AO, vol. 1, roll 2, bundle 1530, Account of Sir William Johnson.

59   For a more detailed perspective and analysis of the "bankruptcy" of British imperial policy in North America in the decade prior to the American

Revolution, see Marshall, "Imperial Regulation of American Indian Affairs."

Chapter 3: The American Rebellion and the Frontier

1 *NYCD*, 8: 471-72, Colonel Guy Johnson to Dartmouth, Johnson Hall, 12 July 1774.

2 PRO, CO 5, vol. 75, folio 99, Sir William Johnson to Dartmouth, Johnson Hall, 17 April 1774.

3 Carter, ed., *Gage Correspondence*, 1: 360, Gage to Dartmouth, Boston, 18 July 1774. Before a regular appointment was made, Whitehall wished to review fully the arrangements for the Indian Department. See PRO, CO 5, vol. 76, folios 238-39, Dartmouth to Gage, Whitehall, 8 September 1774. Guy Johnson was not given a full appointment until several months later.

4 Carter, ed., *Gage Correspondence*, 1: 360, Gage to Dartmouth, Boston, 18 July 1774.

5 Ibid.; see also PRO, 30/29/35 (Granville Papers), folios 422-26 and 426-32. "Indian Agents," letter of 13 February 1775 and Guy Johnson to Dartmouth, 16 March 1775. These letters provide a personal chronicling of events and intentions by Guy Johnson as superintendent.

6 For a discussion of this theme, see Irene B. Brand, "Dunmore's War," *West Virginia History* 40, no. 1 (Fall 1978): 28-46, esp. 28-29; and Jack M. Sosin, "The British Indian Department and Dunmore's War," *Virginia Magazine of History and Biography* 74, no. 1 (1966): 34-50.

7 For the military events of Dunmore's War, see Randolph C. Downes, *Council Fires on the Upper Ohio: A Narrative of Indian Affairs in the Upper Ohio Valley until 1795* (Pittsburgh: University of Pittsburgh Press, 1940), 152-78; Otis K. Rice, *The Allegheny Frontier, West Virginia Beginnings, 1730-1830* (Lexington: University of Kentucky Press, 1970), 55-61, 75 and 79-80; and especially Reuben G. Thwaites and Louise P. Kellogg, eds., *The Documentary History of Dunmore's War, 1774* (Madison: Wisconsin Historical Society, 1905).

8 Thwaites and Kellogg, eds., *Dunmore's War, 1774*, 371, Dunmore to Dartmouth, Williamsburg, 24 December 1774.

9 For a general discussion of this theme, see Ian R. Christie, *Crisis of Empire: Great Britain and the American Colonies, 1754-1783* (London: Edward Arnold, 1966), 83-93.

10 The text of the Quebec Act (22 June 1774) is printed in Shortt and Doughty, eds., *Documents Relating to the Constitutional History of Canada*, 1: 570-76. Two thorough assessments of the meaning and intention of the Quebec Act are Reginald Coupland, *The Quebec Act: A Study in Statesmanship* (Oxford: Clarendon Press, 1925) and A.L. Burt, *The Old Province of Quebec* (Toronto: Ryerson Press, 1933). Both authors contend that the Quebec Act was a necessary and justifiable conclusion to a pragmatic colonial policy and not designed as a blow at the old colonies. For a specific Quebec interpretation, see Gustave Lanctôt, *Canada and the American Revolution 1774-1783* (Toronto: Clarke, Irwin and Co., 1967), 17-42; and for a recent assessment, see P. Lawson, *The Imperial Challenge: Quebec and Britain in the Age of the American Revolution* (Montreal: McGill-Queen's University Press, 1989).

11 See, for instance, Julian Gwyn, "British Government Spending and the North American Colonies 1740-1775," *Journal of Imperial and Commonwealth History* 8, no. 2 (January 1980): 74-84. The British government spent £5,489,000 on the military effort in America between the years 1756 and 1763. This figure represented 63 percent of total expenses for American affairs from 1740 to 1775. This theme is further developed by Peter D.G. Thomas, "The Cost of the British Army in North America, 1763-1775," *William and Mary Quarterly* 45, no. 3 (1988): 510-16. For a critical assessment of the role and intent of the

British army in colonial America, with a particular focus on British and American attitudes towards the military, see John Shy, *Toward Lexington: The Role of the British Army and the Coming of the American Revolution* (Princeton: Princeton University Press, 1965), esp. 375-424.

12   The background and causes of the civil war and rebellion in colonial America can be gleaned from Robert S. Allen, *Loyalist Literature: An Annotated Bibliographic Guide to the Writings on the Loyalists of the American Revolution* (Toronto: Dundurn Press, 1982), 13-28; Jack M. Bumstead, "The American Revolution: Some Thoughts on Recent Bicentennial Scholarship," *Acadiensis* 6 (1977): 3-22; Jack P. Greene, ed., *The Ambiguity of the American Revolution* (New York: Harper and Row, 1969); Bernard B. Bailyn, *The Ideological Origins of the American Revolution* (Cambridge, Mass.: Harward University Press, 1967); Ian R. Christie, *Crisis of Empire*, and his, "The Imperial Dimension: British Ministerial Perspectives During the American Revolutionary Crisis, 1763-1776," in Esmond Wright, ed., *Red, White and True Blue: The Loyalists in the American Revolution* (New York: AMS Press, 1976), 149-66. Two solid biographical studies which focus in turn on the making of a "patriot" and the making of a "loyalist" are Schlenther, *Charles Thomson* and L.F.S. Upton, *The Loyal Whig: William Smith of New York and Quebec* (Toronto: University of Toronto Press, 1969).

13   PRO, CO5, vol. 253, folios 31-32, Gage to Carleton, Boston, 4 September 1774; for a sympathetic assessment of Gage during the opening months of the colonial rebellion, see John R. Alden, *Gage in America; Being Principally a History of His Role in the American Revolution* (Baton Rouge, La.: Louisiana State University Press, 1948).

14   PRO, 30/2934 (Granville Papers), folio 335, Gage to Dartmouth, Boston, 12 June 1775; see also, Carter, ed., *Gage Correspondence*, 1: 402-4, Gage to Dartmouth, Boston, 12 June 1775 (three letters relating to the need for and use of Indian allies).

15   PRO, CO5, vol. 92, folios 196-202, Dartmouth to Gage, Whitehall, 2 August 1775.

16   Ibid., vol. 76, folio 124, Dartmouth to Guy Johnson, Whitehall, 24 July 1775. These American Indian allies around Boston, as noted by Gage and Dartmouth, were actually "domiciled" Stockbridge Mission Indians (Mahican/Mohican) who had been for some time under the religious care of New England missionaries. The contention of the British crown, therefore, that it was justified in using the Six Nations Iroquois and other tribes against the Americans during the revolution because the colonial rebels had initiated the recruitment of Indian allies was misleading. Nonetheless, both the British and the Americans assiduously attempted to recruit Indian allies, with the colonists being quite successful in gaining promises of support in the first few months of the rebellion. For a general assessment of the Indian policy of the first Continental Congress, see James F. Vivian and Jean H. Vivian, "Congressional Indian Policy During the War for Independence: The Northern Department," *Maryland Historical Magazine* 63, no. 3 (September 1968): 241-74; for the early conferences between the Indians and the colonial rebels, including speeches, see PRO, War Office Papers 28 (Headquarters Records), vol. 10, folios 376-93.

17   PRO, CO5, vol. 76, folio 124, Dartmouth to Guy Johnson, Whitehall, 24 July 1775.

18   William L. Clements Library (Ann Arbor, Michigan), Gage Papers, American Series, vol. 125, Gage to Guy Johnson, Boston, 5 February 1775.

19   PRO, CO 42, vol. 34, folio 149, Ethan Allen to Councillors at Caughnawaga, Crown Point, Headquarters of the Army, 29 May 1775.

20   Quoted in Carl Berger, "The Campaign to Win the Indians' Allegiance," *Broadsides and Bayonets: The Propaganda War of the American Revolution* (Philadelphia: University of Pennsylvania Press, 1961), 55; see also, *NYCD*, 8:

605-31, Journal of Treaties at German Flats and Albany, 15 August-1 September 1775. See esp. pp. 621-4, speech of Mohawk sachem Abraham.

21 The Oneida and Tuscarora decision to forsake the unity of the league and the British crown is discussed in detail in John C. Guzzardo, "The Superintendent and the Ministers: The Battle for Oneida Allegiances, 1761-75," *New York History* 57, no. 3 (July 1976) : 255-83. The battle was between Sir William Johnson and New England missionaries. See also Ralph T. Pastore, "Congress and the Six Nations, 1775-1778," *Niagara Frontier* 20 (Winter, 1973): 80-95, for general details of the early relationships and dealings between the Continental Congress and the Iroquois.

22 PRO, WO 28, vol. 10, folios 376-93. Councils of the American Commissioners of Indian Affairs with the Delaware, Shawnee, Wyandot, Ottawa, and others, Pittsburgh, 11-17 October 1775; and Fort Pitt, 7 April 1777. Representatives of the Continental Congress also attempted to obtain the support of the Micmac and Malecite of Nova Scotia. This effort withered with the defeat of the invading colonial rebels at Fort Cumberland (Beauséjour) in November of 1776. The British subsequently concluded a treaty of peace and friendship with the "eastern Indians" at Fort Howe at the mouth of the St. John River in 1778. These events are detailed in Frederic Kidder, ed., *Military Operations in Eastern Maine and Nova Scotia during the American Revolution* (New York: Kraus .Reprint Co., 1971; first publ. 1867); L.F.S. Upton, *Micmacs and Colonists: Indian-White Relations in the Maritimes, 1713-1867* (Vancouver: University of British Columbia Press, 1979), 61-78; for a contemporary assessment, see British Library, Add. Mss. 21697, folio 181, Michael Francklin, superintendent of Indian Affairs, to Carleton, River St. John, Maugerville (Nova Scotia), 23 July 1777.

23 *Canadian Archives Report for 1904*, 345-46, Appendix 1, War of 1775-76, Guy Johnson to Dartmouth, Montreal, 12 October 1775.

24 PRO, 30/29/35 (Granville Papers), folio 460, Carleton to Gage, Quebec, 14 August 1775.

25 Ibid., CO 5, vol. 253, folio 79, "Extracts from the Records of Indian Transactions under the Superintendency of Colonel Guy Johnson during the year 1775."

26 A second American invasion force marched for Quebec via the Kennebec and Chaudière rivers.

27 *Canadian Archives Report for 1904* , 346, Guy Johnson to Darmouth, 12 October 1775.

28 For the siege of St. John, see *Canadian Archives Report for 1916*, 5-25, Appendix B, "Papers Relating to the Surrender of Fort St. Johns and Fort Chambly," narrative by officer commanding, Major Sir Charles Preston; and, George F.G. Stanley, *Canada Invaded, 1775-1776* (Toronto: Hakkert and Co., 1977), 49-62, Canadian War Museum Historical Publications No. 8.

29 Quote from Zephaniah Sheparson's "Journal," copy on file at the Vermont Historical Society (Montpelier), as cited in Robert McConnell Hatch, *Thrust for Canada: The American Attempt on Quebec in 1775-1776* (Boston: Houghton Mifflin Co., 1979), 198. For the Cedars (May 1776), see Stanley, *Canada Invaded*, 117-23; and Richard Cannon, *Historical Record of the King's Liverpool Regiment of Foot* (London: Harrison and Sons, 1883), 54-59.

30 The American retreat from Canada during the summer and autumn of 1776 is detailed in Stanley, *Canada Invaded*, 123-44, and R. Arthur Bowler, "Sir Guy Carleton and the Campaign of 1776 in Canada," *Canadian Historical Review* 55 (June 1974): 131-40.

31 For the Johnson-Carleton controversy over the use of Indians, see PRO, CO5, vol. 253, folios 79-86, "Extracts"; Graymont, *The Iroquois*: 66-69; and A.L. Burt, *Guy Carleton, Lord Dorchester, 1724-1808* (Ottawa: Canadian Historical Association, 1964), 7-8, Historical Booklet No. 5. The unwillingness of Carleton to use the

Indians to the full extent also produced friction between the governor and the secretary of state for the colonies, see A.L. Burt, "The Quarrel between Germain and Carleton: An Inverted Story," *Canadian Historical Review* 11 (1930): 202-22; and especially Gerald Saxon Brown, *The American Secretary: The Colonial policy of Lord George Germain, 1775-1778* (Ann Arbor: University of Michigan Press, 1963), chapters 4-5.

32 For the Carleton appointments see: Major John Campbell as superintendent of the Canadian Indians, Douglas Leighton, "John Campbell," *DCB*, 4: 129-31; and Captain Alexander Fraser as his deputy, Stephen G. Strach, "A Memoir of the Exploits of Captain Alexander Fraser and his Company of British Marksmen, 1776-1777," *Journal of the Society for Army Historical Research* 63, no. 254 (Summer 1985): 91-98 and ibid., 63, no. 255 (Autumn 1985): 164-79. Strach, apart from making some factual errors, offers an unconvincing defence of these appointments. For the Carleton years, see Paul Lawrence Stevens, "His Majesty's 'Savage' Allies: British Indian Policy during the Revolutionary War: The Carleton Years, 1774-1778" (Ph.D. dissertation, State University of New York at Buffalo, 1984). The dissertation, as printed by the University Microfilms International, consists of five volumes, totalling 2,496 pages and provides a minutely detailed study of the four years under review.

33 For the life of Joseph Brant, see William L. Stone, *The Life of Joseph Brant - Thayendanegea*, 2 vols. (New York: A.V. Blake, 1838); Isabel Thompson Kelsay, *Joseph Brant, 1743-1807: Man of Two Worlds* (Syracuse: Syracuse University Press, 1984); and Barbara Graymont's article in *DCB*, 5: 803-12.

34 James Dow McCallum, ed., *The Letters of Eleazer Wheelock's Indians* (Hanover, NH: Dartmouth College Manuscript Series, no. 1, 1932), 17, Wheelock to George Whitefield, 4 July 1761.

35 Sullivan, ed., *Johnson Papers*, 3: 556-57, Wheelock to Sir William Johnson, 2 November 1761.

36 PRO, CO 42 (Canada, Original Correspondence), vol. 18, folio 1, Appointment as "Interpreter for the Six Nations Language," 1775.

37 NAC, MG 11, CO 42, vol. 87, Germain to Brant, London, February 1776.

38 PRO, CO 42, vol. 39, folios 259-62, Frederick Haldimand, governor of Quebec, to Germain, Quebec, 13 September 1779; for Sayenqueraghta, see Thomas S. Adler, "Kalen' kwaanton," in *DCB*, 4: 404-6.

39 PRO, CO 42, vol. 36, folios 37-52, dated 28 February 1777. A copy of his "Thoughts" is also available in the Germain Papers at the William L. Clements Library (Ann Arbor, Michigan).

40 Full particulars are provided in John Burgoyne, *A State of the Expedition from Canada* (London: J. Almon, 1780). This publication, which is a reasonably argued defence of his campaign and conduct, was reprinted in 1969 by Arno Press of New York.

41 PRO, CO5, vol. 93, folios 304-5, Howe to Germain, 30 November 1776.

42 A good analysis of this confusion both at Whitehall and between the military commanders is William B. Willcox, "Too Many Cooks: British Planning Before Saratoga," *Journal of British Studies* 2 (November 1962): 56-90; and Brown, *The American Secretary*, 105-6.

43 Richard J. Hargrove, Jr., *General John Burgoyne* (Newark: University of Delaware Press, 1983) provides complete details on the campaign of 1777 and the life of Burgoyne. Other sources include William L. Stone, *The Campaign of Lieutenant Gen. John Burgoyne and the Expedition of Lieut. Col. Barry St. Leger* (Albany, NY: J. Munsell, 1877); Lieut. William Digby, *The British Invasion from the North: the Campaigns of Generals Carleton and Burgoyne from Canada, 1776-1777* (Albany, NY: J. Munsell, 1887); Lieut. James Hadden, *A Journal Kept in Canada and upon Burgoyne's Campaign in 1776 and 1777* (Albany, NY: J. Munsell, 1884); George F.G. Stanley, ed., *For Want of a Horse: Being a Journal of the*

Campaigns against the Americans in 1776 and 1777 conducted from Canada
(Sackville, NB: The Tribune Press Ltd., 1961); and Henry N. Muller and David A.
Donath, "The Road Not Taken - A Reassessment of Burgoyne's Campaign,"
Bulletin of the Fort Ticonderoga Museum 13, no. 4 (1973): 272-85.

44   PRO, CO 42, vol. 36, folios 571-74, "Substance of the Speech of Lieut. General
     Burgoyne to the Indians in Congress at the Camp upon the River Bouquet," 21
     June 1777, "and of their Answer"; and Hargrove, *General John Burgoyne*, 126.

45   *NYCD*, 8: 707, Alleged statement of Luc de La Corne, as noted in a letter,
     William Tryon, governor of New York, to William Knox, under-secretary of the
     colonies, 21 April 1777. See also Jean-Guy Pelletier, "Luc de La Corne," *DCB*, 4:
     429-31.

46   Digby, *The British Invasion from the North*, 120-21 and 228-29, from St. John, 5
     July 1776 and from Skeensborough [*sic*], 20 July 1777.

47   Ibid.

48   For the opinion that the impact of Jane McCrea's murder on the campaign
     which may have been minimal, see Brian Burns, "Massacre or Muster?
     Burgoyne's Indians and the Militia at Bennington," *Vermont History* 45, no. 3
     (Summer 1977): 133-44. For propaganda against the use of Indians in the
     American rebellion, see Jack M. Sosin, "The Use of Indians in the War of the
     American Revolution: A Re-Assessment of Responsibility," *Canadian Historical
     Review* 46, no. 2 (June 1965): 101-21; S.F. Wise, "The American Revolution and
     Indian History," in John S. Moir, ed., *Character and Circumstance: Essays in
     Honour of Donald Grant Creighton* (Toronto: Macmillan of Canada, 1970),
     182-200; and Norman Gell, "The Tomahawk Factor," *Less than Glory: A
     Revisionist's View of the American Revolution* (New York: G.P. Putnam's Sons,
     1984), 187-96.

49   For Saratoga, see Rupert Furneaux, *Saratoga: The Decisive Battle* (London:
     George Allen and Unwin Ltd., 1971); Max M. Mintz, *The Generals of Saratoga:
     John Burgoyne and Horatio Gates* (New Haven: Yale University Press, 1990); and
     for a final assessment, Michael Glover, *General Burgoyne in Canada and
     America: Scapegoat for a System* (London: Gordon and Cremonesi, 1976). A few
     details on what happened to Burgoyne's surrendered army are provided in J.A.
     Houlding and G. Kenneth Yates, "Corporal Fox's Memoir of Service,
     1776-1783: Quebec, Saratoga, and the Convention Army," *Journal of the Society
     for Army Historical Research* 68, no. 275 (Autumn 1990): 146-68.

50   Hargrove, *General John Burgoyne*, 128; and for general details of the St. Leger
     expedition, see Graymount, *The Iroquois*, 129-46; and R. Jenks, comp., *Siege of
     Fort Stanwix and Battle of Oriskany* (Rome, NY: Bropard Co., Inc., 1977). This
     source contains excerpts from William W. Campbell, *Annals of Tryon County*
     (1831) and William L. Stone, *Joseph Brant* (1838).

51   House of Lords Record Office (London), Main Papers (Burgoyne Campaign),
     "Extract of a Letter from Colonel Butler to Sir Guy Carleton dated Camp before
     Fort Stanwix," 15 August 1777; and ibid., St. Leger to Carleton, Oswego, 27
     August 1777.

52   Quoted in Brown, *The American Secretary*, 60; and taken from the Germain
     Papers at the William L. Clements Library.

53   Stevens, ed., *Facsimiles*, 1:31, "General Reflexions and Remarks ... tending to
     furnish Ideas and Hints towards a Plan for its speedy Reduction to the legal
     Authority of Parliament"; see also, PRO, CO 5, vol. 79, folio 73, Guy Johnson to
     Germain, New York, 12 March 1778. Referring to the Six Nations, "we cannot
     have them better occupied ... unless they are let loose to carry on the petite
     geurre in their own way." Johnson returned to America in the summer of
     1776, and remained at New York for three years. In England, he had managed
     to convince Germain of the importance of using the Indian allies to the fullest
     extent and in their traditional manner. Although his duties were reduced, and

he did not regain responsibility for the Canadian Indians, Johnson accepted a new appointment as superintendent of the Six Nations. In 1782 Sir John Johnson was appointed superintendent general and inspector general of Indian affairs. See NAC, MG 21 (Haldimand Collection), Series B, B116: 1-2.

54   This general theme has been assessed recently by Gregory Evans Dowd, *A Spirited Resistance: The North American Indian Struggle for Unity, 1745-1815* (Baltimore and London: The Johns Hopkins University Press, 1992). Dowd, although concentrating more on the Cherokee and Creek in the south, nonetheless demonstrates a decided lack of understanding and appreciation for the Indian resistance movement among the Shawnee and other tribes in the north by barely mentioning Canada. He largely ignores the vital fact that the Great Lakes tribes were involved in military alliances with the British from the Revolutionary War to the end of the War of 1812. These alliances against the common enemy prompted and motivated a British Indian policy which actively supported the pan-Indian movement and cause by offering counsel, provisions, arms, sundry supplies, and on occasion direct military involvement by British regulars and Canadians which in total not only strengthened and prolonged the "spirited resistance" of the Indian tribes, but at the same time preserved and protected Canada through the military use and assistance of His Majesty's Indian allies.

55   Good general accounts of these events are found in Graymont, *The Iroquois;* Mary Beacock Fryer, *King's Men: The Soldier Founders of Ontario* (Toronto: Dundurn Press, 1980); E.A. Cruikshank, *Butler's Rangers: The Revolutionary Period* (Owen Sound, Ont.: Richardson, Bond and Wright, 1975; first publ. 1893); and the same author's "The King's Royal Regiment of New York," *Ontario Historical Society Papers and Records*, 27 (1931): 1-131.

56   For the Sullivan expedition, see James Norris, "The Campaign of Major General Sullivan, May to October 1779," *Buffalo Historical Society Publications* 1 (1879): 217-52; and Donald R. McAdams, "The Sullivan Expedition: Success or Failure," *New York Historical Society Quarterly* 54, no. 1 (January 1970): 53-81. For Gnadenhutten and the retaliatory torturing and burning of Colonel Crawford, see Consul Willshire Butterfield, *History of the Girtys* (Columbus, Ohio: Lang's College Book Co., 1950; first publ. 1890), 154-89.

57   Details of these expenses can be gleaned by reviewing the accounts of the several senior officers of the British Indian Department. See, for instance, PRO, "Declared Accounts" of Guy Johnson, John Campbell, and Daniel Claus, AO 1, rolls 5, 6, and 8, bundle 1530. For an example of a full auditing, including specifics and notations, see Appendix A, "The Declaration of the Account of Daniel Claus Esquire for Public Expenses as Agent for the Indian Department of the Six Nations in Canada from 1777 to 1782," Total Discharge £23,890.13.8 3/4 (Halifax currency). No accounts have been canvassed for the "western Indians." In the Southern District, which was divided into the Eastern Department and the Western Department after 1779 with the death of John Stuart, the "Declared Accounts" of Thomas Brown, John Graham and John Douglas are found in AO 1, rolls 9, 10 and 11, bundle 1531. For the Indian allies in the colonial south during the American rebellion, see James H. O'Donnell, III, *Southern Indians in the American Revolution* (Knoxville: University of Tennessee Press, 1973); and Edward J. Cashin, *The King's Ranger: Thomas Brown and the American Revolution on the Southern Frontier* (Athens: University of Georgia Press, 1989), 58-158 and 219-28.

58   NAC, MG 21, Haldimand Collection, Series B, B54: 144, Haldimand to Germain, Quebec, 13 September 1779. For the Haldimand years, see John Oliver Dendy, "Frederick Haldimand and the Defence of Canada, 1778-1784" (Ph.D. dissertation, Duke University, 1972).

59   NAC , MG 11, CO 42, vol. 41, Guy Johnson to Germain, Niagara, 20 November 1780.

60   M.M. Quaife, "The Ohio Campaigns of 1782," *Mississippi Valley Historical Review* 18 (1931): 515-29.

61   NAC, MG 21, Haldimand Collection, Series B, B55: 233, Haldimand to Thomas Townshend, the future Lord Sydney, secretary of state at the Home Department and responsible for colonial affairs, Quebec, 23 October 1782.

62   Ibid., B116: 8-9, Haldimand to Johnson, Quebec, 6 February 1783. Johnson subsequently held a successful conference with the Indian allies at Sandusky where he delivered his "Tomahawk Speech" in which he assured the tribes that the peace treaty had not extinguished their aboriginal title or right of soil to the lands north and west of the Ohio River which had been preserved for them at the Treaty of Fort Stanwix in 1768. For the Sandusky conference, see NAC, MG 11, CO 42, vol. 45, "Journal of the Minutes of Transactions with the Indians at Sandusky," 26 August-8 September 1783.

63   NAC, MG 21, Haldimand Collection, Series B, B103: 175, Brigadier General Allan Maclean, post commander at Niagara, to Haldimand, Niagara, 18 May 1783.

64   Series B, B100: 157. The Indian allies in the south had the same reaction. See PRO, CO 5, vol. 82, folios 403-10, Alexander McGillivray to Lt. Col. Thomas Brown, superintendent of the Eastern Department of the Southern District, Little Tallassie [sic], 30 August 1783. McGillivray complained that "after helping the British we have now been betrayed to our enemies." Alexander McGillivray, of French-Creek and Scotch ancestry, was the southern equivalent of Joseph Brant and had ably led the Creek on behalf of the British crown throughout the rebellion years: see J.H. O'Donnell, "Alexander McGillivray: Training for Leadership, 1777-1783," *Georgia Historical Quarterly* 49, no. 2 (1965): 172-86.

65   NAC, MG 11, CO 42, vol. 46, Haldimand to Lord North, Quebec, 27 November 1783.

Chapter 4: The Struggle for the Ohio Valley

1   Shortt and Doughty, eds., *Documents Relating to the Constitutional History of Canada, 1759-1791*, 2: 775, Petition of Sir John Johnson and Loyalists, London, 11 April 1785.

2   PRO, CO 42, vol. 46, Thomas Townshend, Lord Sydney, Sec. of State at the Home Dept., to Haldimand, 8 April 1784.

3   NAC, MG 19, F1 (Claus papers), vol. 3: 277, Haldimand to Claus, Quebec, 17 December 1783; and especially ibid., RG 10, vol. 8: 8124-811 for general correspondence relating to the establishment of the Mohawk settlement at Grand River under Joseph Brant.

4   For general details on this theme, see Robert J. Surtees, "Indian Land Cessions in Ontario, 1763-1862: The Evolution of a System" (Ph.D dissertation, Carleton University, 1982); Donald B. Smith, "The Dispossession of the Mississauga Indians: A Missing Chapter in the Early History of Upper Canada," *Ontario History* 73, no. 2 (June 1981): 67-87; for the "Sale of Grand River Lands by the Mississaugas to the Crown, 22 May 1784," see Charles M. Johnston, ed., *The Valley of the Six Nations: A Collection of Documents on the Indian Lands of the Grand River* (Toronto: University of Toronto Press, 1964), 48.

5   For details, see E.A. Cruikshank, "The Coming of the Loyalist Mohawks to the Bay of Quinté," *OHSPR*, 26 (1930): 390-403; C.H. Torok, "The Tyendinaga Mohawks," *Ontario History* 57, no. 2 (June 1965): 69-77; and M. Eleanor Herrington, "Captain John Deserontyou and the Mohawk Settlement at Deseronto," *Queen's Quarterly* 29 (1921): 165-80.

6   For the Grand River Mohawk and Haldimand's Proclamation of 25 October 1784, see Johnston, ed., *The Valley of the Six Nations*, 50; Wilbur H. Siebert, "The Loyalists and Six Nations Indians in the Niagara Peninsula," *Proceedings and*

Transactions of the Royal Society of Canada 9 (1915): 79–128; and Charles M. Johnston, "An Outline of Early Settlement in the Grand River Valley," in J.K. Johnson, ed., *Historical Essays on Upper Canada* (Toronto: McClelland and Stewart Ltd., 1975), 1–31 (Carleton Library No. 82). This extensive land grant to the dispossessed was not tantamount to recognizing the Mohawk as a sovereign nation. In an analysis of the Grand River controversy, Peter Marshall, "First Americans and Last Loyalists: An Indian Dilemma in War and Peace," in Wright, ed., *Red, White and True Blue*, 33–53, argues that the non-indigenous Mohawk and other similarly situated native groups had no valid claim to land title in the province in the aboriginal sense of prior occupancy. Furthermore, by accepting the protection of the British, they owed allegiance to the crown. Therefore, concludes Marshall, the status of the Iroquois who settled on the Grand River changed from faithful allies to loyal subjects. This assessment has been traditionally refuted, and with some success by the Mohawk Nation in Canada. This theme is also assessed by Malcolm Montgomery, "The Legal Status of the Six Nations Indians in Canada," *Ontario History* 60, no. 2 (1963): 93–105.

7   NAC, MG 19, F1 (Claus Papers), Letter dated 19 October 1787. This was the first Protestant church in the province and remains today the only royal chapel outside the British Isles. In 1984 Queen Elizabeth II declared the building a national historic site; and ibid., MG 21, B 103: 457, A Census of the Six Nations on the Grand River, 1785.

8   Ontario Archives (Toronto), Anne Powell Diary, Montreal to Detroit 1789, in the Jarvis-Powell Papers.

9   For a thematic study of British-Indian relations following the American Revolutionary War, see Colin G. Calloway, *Crown and Calumet: British-Indian Relations, 1783–1815* (Norman: University of Oklahoma Press, 1987). Calloway regards military and commercial considerations as the key twin components of British-Indian relations during this critical period. He assesses both the British and Indians as military allies and commercial partners in fur in terms of how they regarded each other and what advantages could be derived by both sides in this "uneasy alliance" (p.189). Calloway demonstrates a transparent fascination with native people and their attitudes and draws examples from across North America. He correctly emphasizes that the chiefs and warriors critically evaluated British promises and actions and determined their own and distinct responses which best suited the welfare of their people. Although the book is well researched and broad in scope, the focus, although not as blatant as Dowd, is too "American"-based, and there is little discussion or analysis of the military use and assistance of Indian allies in the defence of Canada.

10   NAC, MG 21, B 119: 322–4, Haldimand to Sydney, London, 16 March 1785; see also Orpha E. Leavitt, "British Policy on the Canadian Frontier, 1782–92: Mediation and an Indian Barrier State," *Publications of the State Historical Society of Wisconsin for 1916*, 151–85.

11   These views are expressed in Reginald Horsman, "United States Indian Policies, 1776–1815," in Wilcomb E. Washburn, vol., ed., *Handbook of North American Indians*, vol. 4, *History of Indian-White Relations*, 29–30; see also Downes, *Council Fires*, 284–85; for a general assessment, see Francis Paul Prucha, *United States Indian Policy: A Critical Bibliography* (Bloomington: Indiana University Press, 1977).

12   Reginald Horsman, "American Indian Policy in the Old Northwest, 1783–1812," *William and Mary Quarterly* 18 (1961): 35–53.

13   US Congress, American State Papers: Indian Affairs (hereafter cited as ASPIA), 1: 10–11, Treaty of Fort Stanwix, 22 October 1784.

14   Ibid., 1: 12, and 6–8, Treaty with the Wyandot and others, Fort McIntosh 21 January 1785.

15 *Montreal Gazette*, 4 October 1785, letter from Fort McIntosh. See also Dale Van Every, *The Frontier People of America*, 4 vols. (New York: W. Morrow and Co., 1961-64), 3, *Ark of Empire*.

16 *MPHC*, 25 (1894): 692; see also Horsman, *Matthew Elliott*, 53, Speech of Captain Johnny to Americans, Wakatomica, 18 May 1785.

17 ASPIA, 1: 12; and Kappler, ed., *Indian Treaties*, 16-18, Treaty with the Shawnee at the Mouth of the Great Miami, 31 January 1786 (also known as the Treaty of Fort Finney).

18 NAC, MG 11, CO 42, vol. 51, vol. 87, Simon Girty to McKee, Upper Sandusky, 11 October 1786.

19 Ibid., vol. 49. Brant to Sydney, London, 4 January 1786; see also Stone, *Joseph Brant*, 2: 248-49.

20 NAC, MG 11, CO 42, vol. 49, Sydney to Brant, Whitehall, 6 April 1786; and Shortt and Doughty, eds., *Constitutional History*, 2: 809.

21 Shortt and Doughty, eds., *Constitutional History*, 2: 807-8, Sydney to Hope, Whitehall, 6 April 1786.

22 Ibid., 807

23 Ibid., 827, Instructions to Lord Dorchester, Court of St. James's, 23 August 1786.

24 NAC, MG 11, CO 42, vol. 50, Dorchester to Sir John Johnson, Quebec, 27 November 1786.

25 Ibid., Dorchester to Sydney, Quebec, 11 December 1786.

26 Ibid., Sydney to Dorchester, Whitehall, 5 April 1787.

27 NAC, MG19, F1 (Claus Papers), Letter to Daniel Claus, at the Hurontown near Detroit, 14 December 1786; and see also Robert F. Berkhofer, Jr., "Barrier to Settlement: British Indian Policy in the Old Northwest, 1783-1794," in David M. Ellis, ed., *The Frontier in American Development* (Ithaca: Cornell University Press, 1969), 249-76, esp. p. 267.

28 NAC, MG11, CO 42, vol. 87, Speech of the United Indian Nations at the Confederated Council held near the Mouth of the Detroit River, sent to the Congress of the United States, Detroit, 18 December 1786.

29 Quoted in Stone, ed., *Joseph Brant*, 2: 270-72, Matthews to Brant, Niagara, 29 May 1787.

30 NAC, MG11, CO 42, vol. 51, Sydney to Dorchester, Whitehall, 14 September 1787.

31 C.E. Carter, ed., *The Territorial Papers of the United States*, 26 vols., (Washington, DC: United States Government Printing Office, 1934-62), 2, *The Territory Northwest of the River Ohio, 1781-1803*, 47.

32 Ibid., 78-79, Charles Thomson, Sec. of the Continental Congress, to St. Clair, Philadelphia, 26 October 1787, Instructions to St. Clair Relative to an Indian Treaty in the Northern Department; see also Schlenther, *Charles Thomson*, 183. For the life and career of Arthur St. Clair, a revolutionary war veteran and president of the Continental Congress, see William Henry Smith, ed., *The St. Clair Papers*, 2 vols. (Cincinnati: R. Clarke and Co., 1882).

33 Kappler, ed., *Indian Treaties*, 18-25, Treaty with the Six Nations, Fort Harmar, 9 January 1789; and Treaty with the Wyandot et al., Fort Harmar, 9 January 1789.

34 Joseph Gales, ed., *Annals of Congress 1789-1824* (Washington, DC: Gales and Seaton, 1834-56) 1: 40, Senate, Monday, 25 May 1789.

35 ASPIA, 1: 12, Washington to the Senate, New York, 7 August 1789; see also Alan S. Brown, "The Role of the Army in Western Settlement: Josiah Harmar's Command, 1785-1790," *Pennsylvania Magazine of History and Biography* 18 (1969): 161-78.

36 The life of Little Turtle is detailed in Harvey Lewis Carter, *The Life and Times of Little Turtle: First Sagamore of the Wabash* (Urbana: University of Illinois Press, 1987); see also Herbert C.W. Goltz, "Michikinakoua" *DCB*, 5: 593-95; for general details on the Miami confederacy, see R. David Edmunds, "Wea Participation

in the Northwest Indian Wars, 1790-1795," *Filson Club History Quarterly* 66 (1972): 241-53.

37 NAC, MG11, CO 42, vol. 73, Report of Matthew Elliot, Detroit 28 October 1790. Indian losses were about twenty-five; see also the lurid report in *Gentleman's Magazine* (London), 61 (1791): 668.

38 NAC, MG11, CO 42, vol. 73, Major John Smith to Francis Le Maistre, Mil. Sec. at Quebec, Detroit, 5 November 1790, Report on Speeches of Little Turtle and Blue Jacket at Detroit, November 1790.

39 OA, "British Military Correspondence Relating Principally to Indian Affairs on the U.S.-Canadian Frontier, October 1789-October 1807," A Speech from the Delaware Nation, The Glaize, 29 November 1790.

40 NAC, MG11, CO 42, vol.73, Grenville to Dorchester, Whitehall, 7 March 1791; and Dorchester to Sir John Johnson, Quebec, 10 February 1791.

41 OA, "British Military Correspondence," McKee to Major Smith at Detroit, Foot of the Miamis Rapids, 18 August 1791; and Dorchester to Sir John Johnson, Quebec, 10 February 1791.

42 ASPIA, 1: 36-138, Report of St. Clair; ibid., 2: 1106-14, Defeat of General St. Clair; Gales, ed., *Annals of Congress*, vol. 2: 1052-59, Letters and details of the St. Clair campaign and defeat of 4 November 1791; and NAC, MG11, CO 42, vol. 89, McKee to Sir John Johnson, Detroit, 5 December 1791, Report on the St. Clair campaign and battle.

43 NAC, CO 42, vol. 88, A Letter From Niagara, Niagara, 24 November 1791-News from Detroit.

44 OA, "British Military Correspondence," Speech of the Shawnee, Delaware and Miami, Grand Glaize, 15 April 1792.

45 E.A. Cruikshank, ed., *The Simcoe Papers*, 5 vols. (Toronto: Ontario Historical Society, 1923-31), 1: 208, John Graves Simcoe, Lt. Gov. of Upper Canada, to McKee, Navy Hall [Niagara], 30 August 1792.

46 Bernard Mayo, ed., *Instructions to the British Ministers to the United States, 1791-1812* (Washington, DC: American Historical Association, 1941), 25-27, Henry Dundas, Sec. of State at the Home Department, to Hammond, Whitehall, 17 March 1792.

47 NAC, MG11, CO 42, vol. 89, Dorchester to Dundas, London, 23 March 1792.

48 Cruikshank, ed., *Simcoe Papers*, 1: 202, Simcoe to Alured Clarke, Lt. Gov. of Lower Canada, Niagara, 20 August 1792; for a brief analysis of the life and career of John Graves Simcoe, see S.R. Mealing's article in *DCB*, 5: 754-59.

49 For Simcoe's enthusiams and Indian policy in Upper Canada, see S.R. Mealing, "The Enthusiasms of John Graves Simcoe," *Canadian Historical Association Report for 1958*, 50-62; S.F. Wise, "The Indian Diplomacy of John Graves Simcoe," *Canadian Historical Association Report for 1953*, 36-44; H.K. Letcher, "The Imperial Designs of John Graves Simcoe: First Lieutenant Governor of Upper Canada, 1792-1796" (MA thesis, Wayne State University, 1930); and Malcolm MacLeod, "Fortress Ontario or Forlorn Hope? Simcoe and the Defence of Upper Canada," *Canadian Historical Review* 53, no. 2 (June 1972): 149-78.

50 Cruikshank, ed., *Simcoe Papers*, 1: 207-8, Simcoe to McKee, Navy Hall, 30 August 1792; and for the later career of Alexander McKee, see Walter R. Hoberg, "A Tory in the Northwest," *Pennsylvania Magazine of History and Biography* 59, no. 1 (January 1935): 32-41.

51 The nature, extent, and composition of the Glaize at this time is detailed and assessed by Helen Hornbeck Tanner, "The Glaize in 1792: A Composite Indian Community," *Ethnohistory* 25, no. 1 (Winter 1978): 15-40.

52 OA, "British Military Correspondence," George Ironside, British trader and agent for the Indian Department, to Major E.B. Littlehales, Miamis, 14 July 1792.

53 Cruikshank, ed., *Simcoe Papers*, 1: 224, Indian Council at the Glaize 30

September–9 October 1792.

54 Ibid., 317, Simcoe to Alured Clarke, Niagara, 21 April 1793.

55 NAC, MG11, CO 42, vol. 96, McKee to Simcoe, Foot of the Miami Rapids, 1 July 1793.

56 Ibid., Simcoe to Alured Clarke, Navy Hall, 10 July 1793; and Cruikshank, ed., Simcoe Papers, 1: 377–82, Minutes of a council with the Indians, 7–9 July 1793, Free Mason's Hall, Niagara.

57 Cruikshank, ed., Simcoe Papers, 1:405–9, esp. 408, Speech of the Commissioners of the United States to the Deputies of the Confederated Indian Nations Assembled at Rapids of the Miamis River, at Captain [Matthew] Elliott's at the mouth of Detroit River, 31 July 1793.

58 Ibid., 2: 17–20, esp. 19, Message from the Western Indians to the Commissioners of the United States, Done in General Council at the Foot of the Miamis Rapids, 13 August 1793; for a general assessement of these events, see Reginald Horsman, "The British Indian Department and the Abortive Treaty of Lower Sandusky, 1793," Ohio Historical Quarterly 70, no. 3 (July 1961): 189–213; for the influence of American missionaries among the Six Nations in New York, see Joseph Ibbotson, "Samuel Kirkland, the treaty of 1792 and the Indian Barrier State," New York History 19, no. 4 (October 1938): 374–91. With the Treaty of Fort Stanwix in 1784, the Six Nations in New York remained pacifistic and did not participate in the battles for the Ohio Valley. The United States, assisted by American missionaries, maintained among these people a policy of peace-making. Several treaties of peace, which included land cessions, were subsequently concluded. See Jennings, ed., Iroquois Diplomacy, 202–4, for a list.

59 Cruishank, ed., Simcoe Papers, 2: 44, Simcoe to Hammond, York, UC, 24 August 1793.

60 Ibid., 83–84. Dorchester to Simcoe, Quebec, 7 October 1793; and ibid., 100, Simcoe to Henry Dundas, Sec. of State at the Home Department, York, UC, 10 November 1793.

61 Ibid., 187, Dundas to Simcoe, Whitehall, 16 March 1794.

62 Ibid., 149–50, Dorchester to the Seven Nations of Canada, Quebec, 10 February 1794.

63 For Anthony Wayne, see R.C. Knopf, ed., Anthony Wayne, a Name in Arms: Soldier, Diplomat, Defender of Expansion Westward of a Nation; The Wayne-Knox-Pickering-McHenry Correspondence (Pittsburgh: University of Pittsburgh Press, 1959); for details of Wayne's campaign, see Reginald Horsman, "The British Indian Department and the Resistance to General Anthony Wayne, 1793-1795," Mississippi Valley Historical Review 49, no. 2 (1962): 269–90.

64 Cruikshank, ed., Simcoe Papers, 3: 8, McKee's account of the battle, Camp near Fort Miami, 27 August 1794.

65 Ibid., 2: 396, Major William Campbell to Colonel Richard England at Detroit, Fort Miami, 20 August 1794. Following the battle of Fallen Timbers, Wayne exchanged notes with the British commander at Fort Miami and then promptly withdrew. Neither officer wished to provoke an Anglo-American war.

66 A detailed discussion of the negotiations is provided by Samuel F. Bemis, Jay's Treaty: A Study in Commerce and Diplomacy (New Haven: Yale University Press, 1962); see also Burt, The United States, 141–66, for a criticism.

67 Quoted in Vincent T. Harlow and Frederick Madden, eds., British Colonial Developments: Select Documents, 1774-1834 (Oxford: Clarendon Press, 1967), 477–80, Considerations on the Propriety of Great Britain Abandoning the Indian Posts and Coming to a Good Understanding with America, July 1794; see also G.S. Graham, "The Indian Menace and the Retention of the Western Posts," CHR 15 (1934): 46–48.

68 For the crown's perspective on the Jay Treaty and especially Article III, see John
    Leslie, *The Treaty of Amity, Commerce and Navigation, 1794-1796: The Jay Treaty*
    (Ottawa: Department of Indian and Northern Affairs Canada, 1979); for a
    Mohawk perspective, see Kahn-Tineta Horn, *The Jay Treaty 1794: Where the Jay
    Treaty Issue Presently Stands* (Ottawa: Department of Indian and Northern
    Affairs Canada, 1984); and Elizabeth C. Duran and James Duran, Jr., "Indian
    Rights in the Jay Treaty," *The Indian Historian* 6, no. 1 (Winter 1973): 33-37.
    Although many contemporary Indian leaders in Canada and the United States
    would disagree, the Jay Treaty was nonetheless not an Indian treaty. Article III
    stipulated that Indians crossing between Canada and the United States, with
    their own proper goods and effects, could do so duty free. Although both
    Canada and the United States considered the Jay Treaty abrogated by the War
    of 1812, subsequent enabling legislation in the United States reaffirmed the
    conditions of article III. This has not been done in Canada.
        Repeated requests by the native people to secure a formal exemption
    from the payment of customs duties culminated in the 1956 Supreme Court of
    Canada decision of *Louis Francis v. the Queen*. In this decision, the court
    concluded that neither the Jay Treaty nor any provision of the 1951 Indian Act
    had the cumulative effect of exempting Indian people living in Canada from
    payment of duty on goods brought into Canada from the United States; and
    that rights expressed in the Jay Treaty were not ratified and enacted into
    competent Canadian legislation and thus are no longer valid. The Supreme
    Court further stated that the specific privileges afforded Indian people under
    article III of the Jay Treaty were the result of the circumstances and exigencies
    of the times – that is, the British retention of the western posts south of the
    international border, contrary to the terms of 1783 – and were therefore not
    intended to be perpetual. This opinion was upheld in the British Columbia
    provincial court in *R. v. Gravelle* (1985).
69 Cruikshank, ed., *Simcoe Papers*, 4:286, Beckwith to the Commanders of the
    Western Posts, Quebec, General Order of 1 June 1796.
70 Ibid., 3: 252-53, Wayne to the Indians of Sandusky, Greenville, 1 January 1795;
    and ASPIA, 1: 528.
71 NAC, RG 8, series C, vol. 248, Joseph Brant to Colonel John Butler, Grand River,
    23 July 1795; and ASPIA, 1: 562, The Treaty of Greenville, 3 August 1795.

Chapter 5: Renewing the Chain of Friendship

1   For a general assessment of this theme on ethnic identities on the frontier,
    see James A. Clifton, ed., *Being and Becoming Indian: Biographical Studies of
    North American Frontiers* (Chicago: The Dorsey Press, 1989), and especially his
    own introductory article, "Alternate Identities and Cultural Frontiers," 1-37.
    For specific examples which relate to Canada, see Tanner, "The Glaize," esp.
    15-17, 25-29 and 34-35; James A. Clifton, "Personal and Ethnic Identity on the
    ˚Great Lakes Frontier: the Case of Billy Caldwell, Anglo-Canadian,"
    Ethnohistory 78 (1978): 69-94; and his "Merchant, Soldier, Broker, Chief: A
    Corrected Obituary of Captain Billy Caldwell," *Journal of the Illinois State
    Historical Society* 71 (1978): 185-210. Billy Caldwell (1780-1841) was the son of
    William Caldwell, an ex-captain of Butler's Rangers, and a Mohawk woman.
    The young Caldwell served subsequently in the British Indian Department
    and in the War of 1812. He followed the "custom of the country" and married
    Indian women, his first wife being Potawatomi and his second an Ojibwa. He
    died in the United States.
2   Isaac Weld, *Travels through the States of North America, and the Provinces of
    Upper and Lower Canada, during the Years 1795, 1796, and 1797*, 2 vols. (London:
    J. Stockdale, 1807), 2: 205.

3   Cruikshank, ed., *Simcoe Papers*, 3: 29, William Jarvis, Secretary and Registrar of the Records of the Province of Upper Canada, to his father-in-law, the Rev. Dr. Samuel Peters, Niagara, 3 September 1794. Charles Smith was on the staff of the provincial secretary.

4   Ibid., 3:8, Alexander McKee to Joseph Chew, Secretary of the Indian Department, Camp, Near Fort Miamis, 27 August 1794.

5   NAC, RG 8, series C, vol. 1206, Peter Russell, Lieutenant-Governor of Upper Canada to Lieutenant-General Robert Prescott, Administrator of Lower Canada and Commander of the Forces, York, 20 August 1796; for details and assessments of these frontier posts, see Robert S. Allen, "A History of Fort George, Upper Canada," *Canadian Historic Sites* (Ottawa: Department of Indian and Northern Affairs Canada, 1974), 61-93, Occasional Papers in Archaeology and History No. 11; Dennis Carter-Edwards, "Defending the Straits: The Military Base at Amherstburg," in K. Pryke and L. Kulisek, eds., *The Western District* (Windsor: Essex County Historical Society, 1983), 33-43; and Elizabeth Vincent, *Fort St. Joseph: A History* (Ottawa: Department of Environment Canada, 1978), Parks Canada, Manuscript Report Series 335.

6   NAC, RG 8, Series C, vol. 249; and Cruikshank, ed., *Simcoe Papers*, 4: 293-95, McKee to Dorchester, 7 June 1796 (Proposed Plan for the Future Government of the Indian Department).

7   Cruikshank, ed., *The Simcoe Papers*, vol. 4: 295.

8   Ibid., 294, McKee to Dorchester, 7 June 1796.

9   OA, British Military Correspondence Relating Principally to Indian Affairs on the United States-Canadian Frontier, October 1789-October 1807, Return of Provisions Shipped for the Indians at Swan Creek, From 1 October to 8 December 1794.

10 Cruikshank, ed., *Simcoe Papers*, 4: 323, McKee to Joseph Chew, Detroit, 1 July 1796. In 1797 the "Requisition for Stores Proposed as Presents for Indians Resorting to the Post of Amherstburg" totalled £5785, see NAC, RG 8, series C, vol. 250. By order of the Commander-in Chief, Montreal, 9 February 1797. Major items included: ball and shot, blankets, plain broaches, buttons, ear bobs, gun flints, gun powder, brass, copper and tin kettles, needles, scissors, tea, tobacco, and black and white wampum. In a "Return of Provisions and Rum Issued at Amhersburg and Chenail Ecarté," from 25 June 1797 to 24 June 1798, the commodities of rations, rum and corn, although "being a demenution since last year," were considerable, see NAC, RG 8, series C, vol. 251. Thereafter, there was a gradual but steady reduction in expenditures. For details on the general Indian settlement at Chenail Ecarté, see Nin.Da.Waab.Jig, *Minishenhying Anishnaabe-aki: Walpole Island; the Soul of Indian Territory* (Walpole Island, Ontario, 1987), 21-25.

11 Some examples of these Mississauga land cessions include the Niagara Purchase of 1781, the Crawford "Gunshot" treaties of 1783-84 along the north shore of the upper St. Lawrence, the Grand River tract and Niagara peninsula purchases of 1784, the Lake Simcoe-Matchedash purchases of 1785, and the Johnson-Butler purchases of 1787-88 along the north shore of Lake Ontario. For texts of these agreements, see *Indian Treaties and Surrenders* 3 vols. (Toronto: Coles Publishing Co., 1971; first publ. 1891 and 1912), 1: 1-7; and for an assessment of these agreements, see Surtees, "Indian Land Cessions in Ontario," 45-98.

12 Cruikshank, ed., *Simcoe Papers*, 3: 24, William Chewett, Deputy Surveyor of Upper Canada, to E.B. Littlehales, Brigade Major, Newark, 31 August 1794.

13 E.A. Cruikshank and A.F. Hunter, eds., *The Correspondence of the Honourable Peter Russell*, 3 vols. (Toronto: Ontario Historical Society, 1932-36), 1: 49-50, Peter Russell, Administrator of Upper Canada, to Simcoe, Niagara, 28 September 1796.

14 This unit, now the Queen's (York) Rangers of Toronto, was initially raised in 1776 as a Loyalist provincial corps and fought throughout the Revolutionary War, following which it was disbanded in 1783. From mid-October 1777 the corps was commanded by John Graves Simcoe. The regiment was re-formed in 1792 for pioneer and garrison service in Upper Canada, and was disbanded again in 1802. For the distribution of the Queen's Rangers in garrison at various posts throughout Upper Canada during the time of the Wabukanyn incident, see Cruikshank, ed., *Simcoe Papers*, 4: 344, State of the Troops in the Province of Upper Canada, Headquarters, Niagara, 1 August 1796. For brief histories of the corps, see H.M. Jackson, "The Queen's Rangers, 1st American Regiment," *Journal of the Society for Army Historical Research* 14 (1935): 143–54; and Robert S. Allen, "Mr. Secretary Javis: William Jarvis of Connecticut and York," in Phyllis R. Blakeley and John N. Grant, eds., *Eleven Exiles: Accounts of Loyalists of the American Revolution* (Toronto: Dundurn Press, 1982), 292–95.

15 Cruikshank and Hunter, eds., *Russell Papers*, 1: 49–50; for details and discussion of this event, see Donald B. Smith, *Sacred Feathers: The Reverend Peter Jones (Kahkewaquonaby) and the Mississauga Indians* (Toronto: University of Toronto Press, 1987), 27–29, and also his "The Dispossession of the Mississauga Indians," 76–78.

16 Cruikshank and Hunter, eds., *Russell Papers*, 1: 98, Speech from Indian Chiefs of Lake Simcoe, York, 25 November 1796; for details and a discussion of these events, see Leo A. Johnson, "The Mississauga-Lake Ontario Land Surrender of 1805," *Ontario History* 83, no. 3 (September 1990): 233–53, esp. pp. 236–37.

17 Cruikshank and Hunter, eds., *Russell Papers*, 1: 117, Russell to Simcoe, Niagara, 31 December 1796.

18 NAC, RG 8, series C, vol. 247, Brant to Chew, 25 March 1794; and ibid., vol. 249, Brant to Chew, Grand River, 19 January 1796.

19 PRO, CO 42, vol. 321, Brant's Power of Attorney to Sell the Indian Lands, Grand River, 2 November 1796.

20 Ibid., Brant's Address to William Claus on the Subject of the Indian Lands, Indian Council House, Fort George, 24 November 1796; and Johnston, ed., *The Valley of the Six Nations*, 81–84.

21 This argument has been developed by Peter Marshall, "First Americans and Last Loyalists," 33–53; and Montgomery, "The Legal Status of the Six Nations," 93–105. For additional assessments on the Grand River controversy, see C.M. Johnston, "Joseph Brant, the Grand River Lands and the Northwest Crisis," *Ontario History* 55 (1963): 267–82; and Andrea E. Green, "Land, Leadership and Conflict: The Six Nations' Early Years on the Grand River," (MA thesis, University of Western Ontario, 1984).

22 Brigham, ed., *British Royal Proclamations*, 216–17, para 4, The Royal Proclamation of 7 October 1763.

23 PRO, CO 42, vol. 321, Liston to Robert Prescott, Administrator and soon Governor-in-Chief of Canada, Philadelphia, 8 April 1797.

24 NAC, RG 8, series C, vol. 250, Liston to James Green, Mil. Sec. to Prescott, Philadelphia, 28 March 1797.

25 Metropolitan Toronto Library, Russell Papers, Russell to Prescott, Niagara, 17 July 1797; and Johnston, ed., *The Valley of the Six Nations*, 87–89, Minutes of the Executive Council, York, 1 July 1797.

26 Cruikshank and Hunter, eds., *Russell Papers*, 1: 277–78, Portland to Russell, Whitehall, 11 September 1797, Instructions marked "Secret and Confidential."

27 Ibid., Portland to Russell, Whitehall, 4 November 1797.

28 Ibid., 2: 122–23. Russell to Portland, York, 21 March 1798; and Metropolitan Toronto Library, James Givins Papers, Confirmation of appointment by Order in Council, 31 August 1798.

29 Johnston, ed., *The Valley of the Six Nations*, 97–98, The Formal Transfer of the

Grand River Tracts, York, 5 February 1798.

30 Weld, *Travels*, 2: 272.

31 For details of Brant's integration-acculturation policy, see Green, "Land, Leadership and Conflict"; Metropolitan Toronto Library, Russell Papers, Brant to Sir John Johnson, Grand River, 15 December 1797; PRO, CO 42, vol. 322, Russell to Brant, York, 14 May 1798; NAC, MG 19, FI (Brant Papers), scattered references; and esp. Carl F. Klinck and James J. Talman, eds., *The Journal of Major John Norton 1816* (Toronto: The Champlain Society, 1970), liv-lv, letter of 12 August 1806.

32 For the life and career of John Norton and his impact on the Grand River Mohawk, see Klinck and Talman, eds., *Journal of Major John Norton 1816*; OA, John Norton Papers; J. McE. Murray, "John Norton," OHSPR 37 (1945): 7-16; and W.N. Fenton, "Cherokee and Iroquois connections revisited," *Journal of Cherokee Studies* 3 (1978): 239-49.

33 *London Magazine: or Gentleman's Monthly Intellingencer* 45 (1776): 339, from James Boswell, "An Account of the chief of the 'Mohock Indians' who lately visited England."

34 Quoted in Stone, *Joseph Brant*, 2: 499; and in Klinck and Talman, eds., *Journal of Major John Norton 1816*, lxi.

35 Knopf, ed., *Anthony Wayne*, 405, Pickering to Wayne, Philadelphia, 15 April 1796.

36 See Francis Paul Prucha, ed., *Documents of United States Indian Policy*, 2nd ed. (Lincoln: University of Nebraska Press, 1990), 16-17, An Act for establishing Trading Houses, 18 April 1796; for an assessment of this theme, see Francis Paul Prucha, *American Indian Policy in the Formative Years: The Indian Trade and Intercourse Acts, 1790-1834* (Cambridge, Mass.: Harvard University Press, 1962) and Royal B. Way, "The United States Factory System for Trading with the Indians, 1796-1822," *Mississippi Valley Historical Review* 6 (1919): 220-35. For background details to the policy of removal, see Grant Foreman, *Indian Removal: The Emigration of the Five Civilized Tribes of Indians*, 2nd ed. (Norman: University of Oklahoma Press, 1953).

37 For the Indian as the natural man and the efforts to enlighten through programs of civilization and Christianization, see Klinck and Talman, eds., *Journal of Major John Norton 1816*, xlii-lvii and esp. liv-lv, letter of 12 August 1806, outlining a plan to improve the Indians at Grand River; Roy Harvey Pearce, *Savagism and Civilization: A Study of the Indian and the American Mind* (Baltimore: The Johns Hopkins Press, 1953); and R. Pierce Beaver, "Protestant Churches and the Indians," in Wilcomb E. Washburn vol., ed., *Handbook of North American Indians* (Washington: Smithsonian Institution, 1988), 4: *History of Indian-White Relations*: 430-58, esp. 432-40.

38 Prucha, ed., *Documents*, 21-23, Jefferson to Congress, 18 January 1803 and Jefferson to Harrison, 27 February 1803. For a detailed and intellectual analysis of Thomas Jefferson and the Indians, see Bernard W. Sheehan, *Seeds of Extinction: Jeffersonian Philanthropy and the American Indian* (New York: W.W. Norton, 1974).

39 The life of the Prophet has been assessed in R. David Edmunds, *The Shawnee Prophet* (Lincoln: University of Nebraska Press, 1983); see also his "Tenskwatawa," *DCB*, 7: 847-50. The religious doctrine of the Prophet paralleled that of the Seneca chief Handsome Lake (Ganiodaio) who had a vision in June 1799 that led to a revival of traditional practices and religion among the Six Nations Iroquois. For the religion of Handsome Lake, see F.C. Wallace, *The Death and Rebirth of the Seneca* (New York: A.A. Knopf, 1970). These life concepts found similar expression in the teachings of the Paiute, Wovoka, in 1889-90. See Robert M. Utley, *The Last Days of the Sioux Nation* (New Haven: Yale University Press, 1963), esp. pp. 60-63.

40 NAC, MG19, F11 (Johnson Papers), From a talk by the Indian chief Le Maggonis, as coming from the first man God created now in the Shawnee Country, addressed to all Different Tribes of Indians, 4 August 1807; and also quoted in Herbert C.W. Goltz, Jr., "Indian Revival Religion and the Western District, 1805-1813," in *Association of Iroquois and Allied Indians and the Native Perspective - Western District Historical Conference 1979* (Walpole Island, Ontario, December 1979), 1. For an assessment of the Prophet's Confederacy, see H.C.W. Goltz, "Tecumseh, the Prophet, and the rise of the Northwest Indian Confederation" (Ph.D. dissertation, University of Western Ontario, 1973).

41 For assessments of the causes of the War of 1812 from a predominantly maritime perspective, see Burt, *The United States, Great Britain and British North America*, 207-316; Bradford Perkins, *Prologue to War: England and the United States, 1805-1812* (Berkeley: University of California Press, 1961); Reginald Horsman, *The Causes of the War of 1812* (New York: A.S. Barnes and Co., 1962); and J.C.A. Stagg, *Mr. Madison's War: Politics Diplomacy, and Warfare in the Early American Republic, 1783-1830* (Princeton: Princeton University Press, 1983).

42 For assessments of the causes of the War of 1812 from the perspective of western war aims and Canada, see Julius W. Pratt, *Expansionists of 1812* (New York: Macmillan Co., 1925); George F.G. Stanley, *The War of 1812: Land Operations* (Ottawa: National Museums of Canada, 1983), 16-51, Canadian War Museum Historical Publication No. 18; and Reginald Horsman, "Western War Aims, 1811-12," *Indiana Magazine of History* 53 (March 1957): 1-18. For a fairly recent discussion of the historiography of the War of 1812, see Clifford L. Egan, "The Origins of the War of 1812: Three Decades of Historical Writing," *Military Affairs* 38 (April 1974): 72-75.

43 Logan Esarey, ed., *Messages and Letters of Governor William Henry Harrison*, 2 vols. (Indianapolis: Indiana Historical Commission, 1922), 1: 229-36, Harrison to the Legislature of the Indiana Territory, 17 August 1807.

44 Joseph Gales, ed., *Annals of Congress*, 709, 12th Congress, 2nd session, 11 January 1813, from the speech of Congressman Thomas Robertson of Louisiana. For brief details of the composition and arguments of the "War Hawks," see Horsman, *The Causes of the War of 1812*, 225-26, 229-32 and 235-36. Horsman concluded that for the "War Hawks" the conquest of Canada was an obvious method of injuring Britain; see also Stanley, *The War of 1812*, 35-44, who considered them as merely "hungry for power and for war."

45 Gales, ed., *Annals of Congress*, 657, 12th Congress, 1st session, 4 January 1812, from the speech of congressman John A. Harper of New Hampshire.

46 PRO, CO 43, vol. 22, Castlereagh to Craig, Whitehall, 1 September 1807.

47 Ibid., CO 42, vol. 136, Craig to Gore, Quebec, 6 December 1807.

48 MPHC, 25 (1894): 232-33, Craig to Gore, Quebec, 28 December 1807.

49 NAC, RG10, A4, vol. 11, Gore to Claus, York, 29 January 1808, enclosing "Secret Instructions." For an assessment of British Indian policy in Canada from 1807 until the War of 1812, see Reginald Horsman, "British Indian Policy in the Northwest, 1807-1812," *Mississippi Valley Historical Review* 45 (1958): 51-66.

50 NAC, MG11, CO 42, vol. 136, Craig to Gore, Quebec, 10 March 1808.

51 In December 1797 Elliott had been dismissed for certain irregularities - including peculation - concerning the expenditures and the distribution of goods to the visiting Indians. For details, see Horsman, *Matthew Elliott*, 119-41. He was replaced by Thomas McKee, who was initially acceptable to the Indians. But by 1807 the Wyandot were complaining that he was "too young and inexperienced, he loved to frolick too much and neglected our affairs." For a brief assessment of his life, see John Clarke, "Thomas McKee," *DCB*, 5:

535-36.

52 NAC, RG10, vol. 11, unnumbered, Gore to Craig, 27 July 1808.

53 There are a host of studies on the life and times of Tecumseh, many of which are quite romanticized; useful assessments include Goltz, "Tecumseh, the Prophet, and the Rise of the Northwest Indian Confederation"; R. David Edmunds, *Tecumseh and the Quest for Indian Leadership* (Boston: Little, Brown and Co., 1984); and for a brief analysis, Goltz's article in *DCB*, 5: 795-801. For the Creek-Shawnee connection, see Charles Callendar, "Shawnee," in Bruce G. Trigger, vol., ed., *Handbook of North American Indians* (Washington: Smithsonian Institution, 1978), vol. 15: 622-35. In British correspondence prior to the War of 1812, Tecumseh was referred to only as "the Prophet's brother."

54 NAC, RG10, A4, vol. 11, Indian Council at Amherstburg, 11 and 13 July 1808; and ibid., RG10, vol. 11, unnumbered, Gore to Craig, 27 July 1808.

55 W.C.H. Wood, ed., *Select British Documents of the Canadian War of 1812*, 3 vols. (Toronto: The Champlain Society, 1920-28), 2: 90. Major General Roger Hale Sheaffe to Sir George Prevost, Captain-General and Governor-in-Chief of British North America, Kingston, 5 May 1813.

56 E.A. Cruikshank, ed., *Records of Niagara in the Days of Commodore Grand and Lieut. Governor Gore, 1805-1811* (Niagara-on-the Lake: Niagara Historical Society, 1931): 63. Claus to Prideaux Selby, Asst. Sec. of the Indian Department, Indian Council House, Fort George, 10 August 1808; and ibid., 84-89, Proceedings of Councils with the Six Nations at the Council House, Fort George, 10 and 13 March 1809.

57 NAC, MG11, CO42, vol. 143, Elliott to Claus, Amherstburg, 9 July 1810, Speech of Tecumseh to Major Taylor, Commandant at Fort Amherstburg, at Amherstburg, 15 November 1810; and Elliott to Claus, Amherstburg, 16 November 1810.

58 For details and an analysis of this period and theme, see Robert S. Allen, "His Majesty's Indian Allies: Native Peoples, the British Crown and the War of 1812," *Michigan Historical Review* 14, no. 2 (Fall 1988): 1-24, esp. 6-11; and George C. Chalou, "The Red Pawns Go to War: British-Indian relations, 1810-1815" (Ph.D. dissertation, Indiana University 1971).

59 Full details of the battle of Tippecanoe are provided in R. David Edmund, *The Shawnee Prophet*, 94-116. But for a rather different perspective, see E.A. Cruikshank, ed., *Documents Relating to The Invasion of Canada and the Surrender of Detroit 1812* (Ottawa: Government Printing Bureau, 1913), 6-8, Colonel Matthew Elliott to Major-General Isaac Brock, Administrator of Upper Canada, Amherstburg, 12 January 1812. For conflicting personal accounts of the battle, see Richard G. Carlson, ed., "George P. Peters' Version of the Battle of Tippecanoe (November 7, 1811)," *Vermont History* 45, no. 1 (Winter 1977): 38-43; and J.W. Whickar, ed., "Shabonee's Account of Tippecanoe," *Indiana Magazine of History* 17 (1921): 356-63. The battle virtually ended the Indian faith in the Prophet's revival religion. Since about 1809, when he could not stop the signing of the Treaty of Fort Wayne in Indiana which forced the cession of huge tracts of Indian land, the influence of the Shawnee Prophet had been waning. He subsequently participated to a degree in support of the British during the War of 1812, and received a pension – "His Majesty' Bounty." After the war he remained in Canada for about ten years, before following the Shawnee to Kansas as part of the Indian removal policy of the United States in the 1830s.

60 *Scioto Gazette* (Chillicothe, Ohio), 27 November 1811.

61 *Western Intelligencer* (Worthington, Ohio), 25 December 1811.

62 Quoted in Stanley, *The War of 1812*, 37, From a speech by Felix Grundy, congressman from Tennessee, relating to and in support of a report of the House Committee on Foreign Affairs, November 1811.

63 Gales, ed., *Annals of Congress*, 457-58, 12th Congress, 1st session, 11 December
    1811, Speech in Congress relating to war with Great Britain.
64 Andrew A. Lipscomb and Albert E. Bergh, eds., *The Writings of Thomas Jefferson*,
    20 vols., (Washington, DC: Thomas Jefferson Memorial Association, 1905), 13:
    168-72, Jefferson to Thaddeus Kosciusko, 28 June 1812.
65 Gales, ed., *Annals of Congress*, 579, 11th Congress, 1st session, 22 February
    1810, Speech of Henry Clay to House of Representatives.
66 For an excellent assessment of American thought and strategy in relation to
    Canada prior to the War of 1812, see Reginald Horsman, "On to Canada:
    Manifest Destiny and United States Strategy in the War of 1812," *Michigan
    Historical Review* 13, no. 2 (Fall 1987): 1-24.
67 Ferdinand Brock Tupper, ed., *The Life and Correspondence of Major-General Sir
    Isaac Brock, K.B.* (London: Simpkin, Marshall and Co., 1847), 124, Brock to
    Prevost, York, 2 December 1811.
68 The best single source for the study of the life and military career of Sir Isaac
    Brock is Tupper, ed., *Brock Correspondence*. C.P. Stacey gives a brief but
    insightful assessment in his article in *DCB*, 5: 109-15; see also NAC, MG 24 (19th
    century pre-Confederation Papers), Brock Papers 1806-12.
69 Tupper, ed., *Brock Correspondence*, 125 and 134, Brock to Prevost, York, 2
    December 1811; and Prevost to Brock, Quebec, 24 December 1811.
70 PRO, CO 43, vol. 23, Prince Regent's Instructions to Prevost, St. James's, 22
    October 1811.
71 Tupper, ed., *Brock Correspondence*, 134-35, Prevost to Brock, Quebec, 24
    December 1811.
72 PRO, CO42, vol. 146, Prevost to Liverpool, Quebec, 18 May 1812, and referring to
    the despatch of 13 February 1812.
73 Ibid.; see also NAC, MG12, WO 17, vol. 1516, "Strength Returns, Canada, Quebec,
    25 November 1811; and HLRO, Main Papers, "Return of the Effective Strength of
    the British Land Forces in North America on the 25th May 1812," prepared in
    pursuance of an Order of the House of Lords, dated 12th April 1813.
74 PRO, CO 42, vol. 146, Prevost to Liverpool Quebec, 18 May 1812; see also J.
    MacKay Hitsman, *The Incredible War of 1812* (Toronto: University of Toronto
    Press, 1965), 243-49, who has printed the despatch in the appendix.
75 PRO, CO 42, vol. 146, Prevost to Sir John Johnson, Quebec 1 May 1812,
    "Instructions."
76 For assessments of the Indians in the War of 1812, see Cruikshank, "The
    Employment of Indians in the War of 1812," *American Historical Association
    Report for 1895*, 321-35; Reginald Horsman, "The Role of the Indian in the
    War," in Philip P. Mason, ed., *After Tippecanoe: Some Aspects of the War of 1812*
    (Toronto: Ryerson Press, 1963), 60-77; and George F.G. Stanley, "The Indians in
    the War of 1812," in Morris Zaslow, ed., *The Defended Border: Upper Canada and
    the War of 1812* (Toronto: Macmillan Co., 1964), 174-88.
77 PRO, CO 42, vol. 146, Prevost to Liverpool, Quebec, 18 May 1812.
78 For details on American military strength in 1812, see John K. Mahon, *The War
    of 1812* (Gainsville: University of Florida Press, 1972), 4-5.
79 For William Hull and the North Western Army, see Alex R. Gilpin, *The War of
    1812 in the Old Northwest* (East Lansing: Michigan State University, 1958),
    23-65.
80 OA, Strachan Papers, "List of Indian Warriors ...," dated Montreal 1814. A
    reproduction of the original document is presented in Appendix B.
81 NAC, RG8, series C, vol. 676, Claus to Brock, Amherstburg, 20 June 1812; for
    details and an assessment of Amherstburg and the Detroit front during the
    War of 1812, see Dennis Carter-Edwards, "The War of 1812 along the Detroit
    Frontier: A Canadian Perspective," *Michigan Historical Review* 13, no. 2 (Fall

1987), 25-50.

Chapter 6: The War of 1812: Michilimackinac and Upper Canada

1   For background details, see "The Declaration of War," in Stanley, *The War of 1812*, 3-9, esp. p. 4.
2   Tupper, ed., *Brock Correspondence*, 197-98, Proclamation, dated York, UC, 6 July 1812.
3   Ibid., 194; and NAC, RG 8, series C, vol. 676, Brock to Prevost, Fort George, 3 July 1812.
4   For assessments of Prevost and his strategy for the defence of Canada in the War of 1812 see Peter Burroughs, "Sir George Prevost," *DCB*, 5: 693-98; J.M. Hitsman, "Sir George Prevost's conduct of the Canadian War of 1812," *Canadian Historical Association Report for 1962*, 34-43; and Maxwell Sutherland, "The Civil Administration of Sir George Prevost, 1811-1815: A Study in Conciliation" (MA thesis, Queen's University, 1959).
5   Tupper, ed., *Brock Correspondence*, 200-1, Prevost to Brock, Montreal, 10 July 1812; see also John K. Mahon, "British Command Decisions in the Northern Campaigns of the War of 1812," *CHR* 46, no. 3 (1965): 219-37.
6   NAC, RG 8, series C, vol. 256, Captain J.B. Glegg, aide-de camp to Brock, to Dickson, dated 27 February 1812.
7   Ibid., Dickson to Glegg, 18 June 1812.
8   Queen's University Archives (Kingston), Richard Cartwright Papers, coll. 96, box 2, Letterbooks, 1785-1802, Richard Cartwright to Robert Hamilton, Cataraqui (Kingston), 10 July 1786; see also Robert S. Allen, "Robert Dickson," *DCB*, 6: 209-11; L.A. Tohill, "Robert Dickson, British fur trader on the upper Mississippi," *NDHQ* 2 (1928): 5-49 and 3 (1929): 83-128 and 182-203; E.A. Cruikshank, "Robert Dickson, the Indian trader," *WHC* 12 (1892): 133-53; and Reuben G. Thwaites, ed., "Dickson and Grignon Papers, 1812-1815," ibid, 11 (1888): 271-315.
9   Cruikshank, ed., *Simcoe Papers*, 1: 387-91, Dickson to Robert Hamilton, Michilimackinac, 14 July 1793. In this lengthy and detailed letter, Dickson discussed the various water and trade routes from Michilimackinac to the Mississippi; described the "rich black soil," hills and level plains of this fertile and vast country in which Indian corn, squash, potatoes, melons, cucumbers and a "very well flavoured tobacco" were grown in abundance; pinpointed the various locations of Spanish and American forts on the Mississippi; and assessed the hunting and fighting skills of the numerous and fractious Indian tribes of the region. The acute observations of Dickson provided such useful information for the civil and military authorities in Upper Canada that the contents were subsequently delivered to Simcoe for study and assessment.
10   L.A. Tohill, "Robert Dickson," *NDHQ* 2 (1928), 14-15; Gontran Laviolette, *The Sioux in Canada* (Regina: Marion Press, 1944), 24; see also Elijah Black Thunder et al., *Ehanna Woyakapi: History of the Sisseton Wahpeton Sioux Tribe* (Sisseton, SD: Sisseton-Wahpeton Tribe Inc., 1972).
11   Quoted in Cruikshank, "Robert Dickson," 138.
12   NAC, RG 8, series C, vol. 257, Statement of Robert Dickson, Montreal, 3 December 1812.
13   *Western Spy* (Cincinnati), 23 May 1812.
14   256, Dickson to Brock, St. Joseph, 13 July 1812; and Cruikshank, "Robert Dickson," 140.
15   NAC, RG 8, series C, vol. 688A, Roberts to Glegg, 29 July 1812.
16   Tupper, ed., *Brock Correspondence*, 223-24. Brock to Roberts, 26 June 1812; Brock to Roberts, Fort George, 28 June 1812; and Prevost to Roberts, Quebec, 25 June 1812.

17 Wood, ed., *Select British Documents,* 1: 425, Speeches of Indian Chiefs
    assembled in Council. Speech of Wabasha; for general details see also Pierre
    Berton, *The Invasion of Canada, 1812-1813* (Toronto: McClelland and Stewart,
    1980), 108.
18 NAC, RG 8, series C, vol. 676. Roberts to Brock, Fort of Michilimackinac, 17 July
    1812; see also Tupper, ed., *Brock Correspondence,* 224, Brock to Roberts, 4 July
    1812.
19 Cruikshank, ed., *Detroit Documents,* 67-69, Lt. Porter Hanks to Brig. Gen.
    William Hull, Detroit, 4 August 1812; NAC, RG 8, series C, vol. 676, Articles of
    Capitulation, Heights above Michilimackinac, 17 July 1812; for the British
    occupation during the War of 1812, see Brian Leigh Dunnigan, *The British
    Army at Mackinac 1812-1815,* (Mackinac Island, Michigan: Mackinac Island
    State Park Commission, 1980), 12, Reports in Mackinac History and
    Archaeology No. 7.
20 NAC, RG 8, series C, vol. 676, Roberts to Brock, Fort of Michilimackinac, 17 July
    1812.
21 Ibid., Askin to Claus, Michilimackinac, 18 July 1812.
22 Ibid., vol. 676, Roberts to Baynes, Fort Michilimackinac, 17 July 1812.
23 Cruikshank, ed., *Detroit Documents,* 37 and 57, William Eustis, Sec. of War, to
    Hull, War Department, 24 June 1812; and Hull to Eustis, Sandwich, in Upper
    Canada, 13 July 1812.
24 NAC, RG 8, series C, vol. 676, A Proclamation By William Hull, Brigadier General
    and Commander of the North Western Army of the United States, Head
    Quarters at Sandwich, 13 July 1812.
25 Cruikshank, ed., *Detroit Documents,* 60, Hull to Eustis, Sandwich, 15 July 1812.
26 NAC, RG 8, series C, vol. 676, A Proclamation, dated Sandwich, 13 July 1812.
27 Cruikshank, ed., *Detroit Documents,* 43-44 and 60, Hull to Secretary of War,
    Headquarters, Detroit, 7 July 1812; Hull to Secretary of War, Sandwich, 15 July
    1812; and Hull to Secretary of War, Headquarters of the North Western Army,
    Sandwich, 21 July 1812.
28 NAC, RG 8, series C, vol. 676, Lt. Col. the Hon. James Baby to Glegg, Dundas Street
    30 miles from York, 27 July 1812; Cruikshank, ed., *Detroit Documents,* 71, Lt. Col.
    Lewis Cass to Hull, Sandwich, Upper Canada, 17 July 1812; A.C. Casselman, ed.,
    Richardson's War of 1812 (Toronto: Coles Publishing Co., 1974; first publ. 1842),
    21-22; Berton, *The Invasion of Canada,* 138-40. The desperate defence at the
    bridge on 16 July 1812 by John Dean and James Hancock of the Welch
    Regiment, now the Royal Regiment of Wales (24th/41st Foot), is depicted in the
    form of a diorama at the Welch Regiment Museum in Cardiff Castle.
29 Cruikshank, ed., *Detroit Documents,* 115-16, Hull to Secretary of War,
    Sandwich, UC, 4 August 1812.
30 Ibid., 126, Hull to Secretary of War, Detroit, 8 August 1812.
31 NAC, RG 8, series C, vol. 676, Lt. Col. St. George to Brock, Amherstburg, 15 July
    1812; and ibid., Col. Elliott to Col. Claus.
32 Quoted in D.A.N. Lomax, *A History of the Services of the 41st (Welch) Regiment ...
    from its Formation in 1719 to 1895* (Devonport, England: Hiorns and Miller,
    1899), 369; for background details on Procter's life, see A.M.J. Hyatt, "Henry
    Procter," *DCB,* 6: 616-18.
33 NAC, RG 8, series C, vol. 676, Procter to Brock, Amherstburg, 26 July 1812; ibid.,
    vol. 677, Procter to Brock, Amherstburg, 11 August 1812; Cruikshank, ed.,
    Detroit Documents, 125-26, Hull to Secretary of State, Sandwich, 7 August 1812;
    ibid., 139-41, Hull to Secretary of State, 13 August 1812; and see M.M. Quaife,
    "The Story of Brownstown," *Burton Historical Collection Leaflet* 4 (1926): 65-80.
34 Casselman, ed., *Richardson's War of 1812,* 27-30. Richardson said that the name
    of the chief was Logan, "a great favourite with the Officers," in part because he
    understood some English; and M.M. Quaife, ed., *War on the Detroit: The*

Chronicles of Thomas Verchères de Boucherville (Chicago: The Lakeside Press, 1940), 89-93.

35 Cruikshank, ed., *Detroit Documents*, 225, Heald to Secretary of War, Pittsburg [sic], 23 October 1812; and see Mentor L. Williams, ed., "John Kinzie's Narrative of the Fort Dearborn Massacre," *Journal of the Illinois State Historical Society* 46 (1953): 343-62.

36 NAC, RG 8, series C, vol. 676, Brock to Baynes,York, 29 July 1812; see also C.P. Stacey, "The Defence of Upper Canada, 1812," in Morris Zaslow, ed., *The Defended Border: Upper Canada and the War of 1812* (Toronto: Macmillan Co., 1964), 11-20, esp. p. 13.

37 Tupper, ed., *Brock Correspondence*, 216-17, Brock to Prevost, Fort George, 25 July 1812; and for an account of the Grand River Iroquois in the War of 1812, see David J. Glenney, "An Ethnohistory of the Grand River Iroquois and the War of 1812" (MA thesis, University of Guelph, 1973).

38 Ibid., 125, Brock to Prevost, York, 2 December 1811. This reference may have been to the Prophet.

39 Cruikshank, ed., *Detroit Documents*, 192, Brock to Liverpool, now Prime Minister, York, Upper Canada, 29 August 1812.

40 NAC, RG 8, series C, vol. 677. Brock to Prevost, Headquarters, Detroit, 16 August 1812; and PRO, CO 42, vol. 147, Brock to Prevost, Headquarters, Detroit, 17 August 1812; for general details of the events of 15-16 August, see Stanley, *The War of 1812*, 107-11. A good American account of the Detroit campaign is M.M. Quaife, ed., *War on the Detroit: The Capitulation, or A History of the Expedition Conducted by William Hull, Brigadier-General of the North-Western Army. By an Ohio volunteer*, 179-320; see also Benson J. Lossing, *The Pictorial Field-Book of the War of 1812* (New York: Harper and Bros., 1868), 283-96.

41 Cruikshank, ed., *Detroit Documents*, 184-90, Hull to Secretary of War, Fort George, 26 August 1812.

42 NAC, RG 8, series C, vol. 688A, Major Peter Chambers to Procter, Detroit, 24 August 1812.

43 Tupper, ed., *Brock Correspondence*, 327, Brock to Procter, undated: probably 11 or 12 October 1812.

44 The 49th Regiment of Foot, Brock's old regiment, was sent to Upper Canada in August by Prevost to bolster the defences. The best description of 13 October 1812 remains Ernest A. Cruikshank, "The Battle of Queenston Heights," in Zaslow, ed., *The Defended Border*, 21-44. The article first appeared in 1888. Two detailed and intriguing studies of Brock are Ludwig Kosche, "Relics of Brock: An Investigation," *Archivaria* 9 (Winter 1979-80): 33-103; and his "Contemporary Portraits of Isaac Brock: An Analysis," *Archivaria* 20 (Summer 1985): 22-66.

45 NAC, RG 8, series C, vol. 677, Brock to Prevost, Fort George, 7 September 1812.

46 PRO, CO 42, vol. 147, Major-General Roger Hale Sheaffe to Prevost, Fort George, 13 October 1812; for the participation of the Grand River Iroquois in the battle under John Norton, see Klinck and Talman, eds., *Journal of Major John Norton 1816*, 304-10.

47 Some examples are T.G. Marquis, *Brock the Hero of Canada* (1912); W.R. Nursey, *The Story of Isaac Brock (General Sir Isaac Brock, K.B.) Hero, Defender and Saviour of Upper Canada in 1812* (1923); Cruikshank, *Queenston Heights: A Thrilling Narrative of the Famous Battle where General Brock died Defending his Country* (1890); and W.K. Lamb, *The Hero of Upper Canada* (1962).

48 NAC, RG 8, series C, vol. 1220, Appointment of Mr. Robert Dickson. Prevost to Earl Bathurst, Sec. of State for War and the Colonies, Quebec, 26 January 1813; and McCord Museum Archives (Montreal), Office of the Mil. Sec., Quebec, 14 January 1813, signed by Noah Freer, Mil. Sec. to Prevost, Copies sent to Sir John Johnson and William Claus.

49 OA, MS-109 (Microcopy No. T-836), British Military Correspondence, 16 July

1812-10 September 1813, Instructions for Robert Dickson, Esq., Quebec, 14 January 1813.

50 McCord Museum Archives, Copy of a Speech to be delivered by Robert Dickson Esq. to such of the Indian Nations whom he may have occasion to address, dated, Montreal, 18 January 1813. This rare document, found by the present author, has not hitherto been used nor assessed by historians of the War of 1812. Therefore, and with the permission of the McCord Museum Archives, the speech is reproduced in Appendix C. For additional physical descriptions of Dickson, see L.A. Tohill, "Robert Dickson," *NDHQ* 3 (1929): 85; Cruikshank, "Robert Dickson:," *WHC* 12 (1982): 138; and Augustin Grignon, "Seventy-two Years Recollections of Wisconsin," *WHC* 3 (1904): 280.

51 Statement of Wahpeton Sioux tribal historian Robert Goodvoice of Prince Albert, Saskatchewan, as quoted in Peter Douglas Elias, *The Dakota of the Canadian Northwest: Lessons for Survival* (Winnipeg: University of Manitoba Press, 1988), 8.

52 NAC, RG 8, series C, vol. 257, Dickson to Procter, Michilimackinac, 21 June 1813. List of Warriors sent to Detroit; and OA, MS-109 (Microcopy No. T-836), Dickson to Procter, La Baye [Green Bay], Lake Michigan, 31 May 1813.

53 OA, MS-109 (Microcopy No. T-836), Procter to Sheaffe, Detroit, 28 November 1812.

54 Wood, ed., *Select British Documents*, 2: 7-9, Procter to Sheaffe, Sandwick, 25 January 1813; for the massacre of 23 January 1813, see Dennis M. Au, *War on the Raisin: A Narrative Account of the War of 1812 in the River Raisin Settlement, Michigan Territory* (Monroe: Monroe County Historical Commission, 1981), 50-61.

55 Wood, ed., *Select British Documents*, 2: 33-40, Procter to Prevost, Sandwich, 14 May 1813; ibid., 37-40, General Order, signed by Edward Baynes, Adj. Gen., Kingston, 21 May 1813; and Alex R. Gilpin, *The War of 1812 in the Old Northwest* (East Lansing: Michigan State University Press, 1958), 183-93.

56 Wood, ed., *Select British Documents*, 2: 35.

57 Ibid., 44-46, Procter to Prevost, Sandwich, 9 August 1813; and see Shadrach Byfield, "A Common Soldier's Account," in *Recollections of the War of 1812* (Toronto: Baxter Publishing Co., 1964; first publ. between 1828-58), 20-23.

58 Wood, ed., *Select British Documents*, 2: 269, Procter to Noah Freer, Mil. Sec. to Prevost, Sandwich, 6 September 1813.

59 Quoted in Casselman, ed., *Richardson's War of 1812*, 206, Speech of Tecumseh in Council, Amherstburg, 18 September 1813.

60 NAC, RG 8, series C, vol. 680, Procter to Major-General Francis de Rottenburg, Ancaster, 23 October 1813; see also C.O.Z. Ermatinger, "The retreat of Procter and Tecumseh," *OHSPR* 17 (1919): 11-21; Katherine B. Coutts, "Thamesville and the Battle of the Thames," in Zaslow, ed., *The Defended Border*, 114-20; and "The War in Canada, 1812-15," by an unidentified officer (probably James Cochran), property of the Welch Regiment Museum (Cardiff), n.d. and unpublished.

61 NAC, RG 8, series C, vol. 680, Procter to de Rottenburg, Ancaster, 23 October 1813; see also Charles A. Wickliffe, "Tecumseh and the Battle of the Thames," *Register of the Kentucky Historical Society*, 60 (1962): 45-49, first publ. 1859; Robert McAfee, *History of the Late War in the Western Country...* (Lexington, Ky.: Worsley and Smith, 1816), 348-51; and esp. John Sugden, *Tecumseh's Last Stand* (Norman: University of Oklahoma Press, 1985), 105-135 and 136-181. The British lost about fifty killed and wounded and perhaps four hundred captured. Indian losses were thirty-three killed. The Americans lost but thirty-four out of a force of some three thousand. Eventually 246 officers and men of the Right Division assembled at Ancaster, near the Grand River.

62 The battle at the Longwoods in March 1814 and the raid up the Thames of

Brigadier-General Duncan McArthur with a force of eight hundred riflemen, composed entirely of mounted "Kentuckians and undisciplined," in October and November 1814, were two notable exceptions. For these events, see J.I. Poole, "The Fight at Battle Hill," in Zaslow, ed., *The Defended Border*, 130-42; and E.A. Cruikshank, "The County of Norfolk in the War of 1812," ibid., 224-40, esp. 236-9.

63 PRO, WO 71, vol. 243, Court Martial of Major-General Henry Procter. Some assessments of Procter are Victor Lauriston, "The Case for General Procter," in Zaslow, ed., *The Defended Border*, 121-29; S. Antal, "Myths and Facts Concerning General Procter," *Ontario History* 79, no. 3 (September 1987): 251-62; and *DCB*, 6: 616-18.

64 Two recent assessments of Tecumseh by R. David Edmunds are "'Tecumseh, The Shawnee Prophet, and American History: A Reassessment," *Western Historical Quarterly* 14, no. 3 (July 1983): 261-76; and "The Thin Red Line: Tecumseh, the Prophet, and Shawnee Resistance," *Timeline* 4, no. 6 (December 1987 - January 1988): 2-19.

65 Accounts of the battle of Beaver Dams, 24 June 1813 can be gleaned from Charles M. Johnston, ed., *The Valley of the Six Nations*, lxxv and footnote, and 199-206; see also Klinck and Talman, eds., *Journal of Major John Norton 1816*, 330-32.

66 Cruikshank, ed., *Documentary History* 6: 283, General Peter B. Porter to John Armstrong, Sec. of War, Black Rock, 27 July 1813.

67 NAC, RG 8, series C, vol. 682, Major-General Phineas Riall to Lieutenant-General Gordon Drummond, Commander of the Forces in Upper Canada, 7 January 1814; for events along the Niagara River in December 1813, see Stanley, *The War of 1812*, 216-24; and Louis L. Babcock, *The War of 1812 on the Niagara Frontier* (Buffalo: Buffalo Historical Society, 1927), 115-138, esp. 128.

68 Johnston, ed., *The Valley of the Six Nations*, 206, General Orders Affecting the Awards of Presents to Indian Warriors, 7 August 1813; Wood, ed., *Select British Documents* 3: 726-27, Col. William Caldwell to Western Indians Assembled, 14 June 1814; see also E.A. Cruikshank, ed., "Campaigns of 1812-1814; Contemporary Narratives by Captain W.H. Merritt, Lieutenant-Colonel Matthew Elliott, Colonel William Claus and Captain John Norton," *Niagara Historical Society* 9 (1902): 3-20; and C.M. Johnston, "William Claus and John Norton: a struggle for power in old Ontario," *Ontario History* 57, no. 2 (June 1965): 101-8.

69 For British Indian policy in the American South during the War of 1812, and for the Creek War of 1813-1814, see John K. Mahon, "British Strategy and Southern Indians: War of 1812," *Florida Historical Quarterly* 45 (April 1966): 285-302; John Sugden, "The Southern Indians in the War of 1812: The Closing Phase," *Florida Historical Quarterly* 60, no. 3 (1982): 273-312; F.L. Owsley, "The Fort Mims Massacre," *Alabama Review* 24 (1971): 194-204; and Henry S. Halbert and T.H. Ball, *The Creek War of 1813 and 1814* (Chicago: Donohue and Henneberry, 1895).

70 N.C. Lord, ed., "The War on the Canadian Frontier, 1812-14: Letters Written by Sergt. James Commins, 8th Foot, August 1815," *Journal of the Society for Army Historical Research* 18 (1939): 200.

Chapter 7: The War of 1812: The Northwest

1 The Quebec Act, 14 Geo. III, cap. 83, sect. 12-18, is reprinted, with a description of the geographical boundaries, in Shortt and Doughty, eds., *Documents Relating to the Constitutional History of Canada, 1759-1791*, 1: 570-76; see also, Helen Hornbeck Tanner, ed., *Atlas of Great Lakes Indian History* (Norman: University of Oklahoma Press, 1987), 105-21.

2   This theme is detailed in Sylvia Van Kirk, *Many Tender Ties: Women in Fur Trade Society in Western Canada 1670-1870* (Winnipeg: Watson and Dwyer, 1980); Jennifer S.H. Brown, *Strangers in Blood: Fur Trade Company Families in the Indian Country* (Vancouver: University of British Columbia Press, 1980); for a good brief general discussion, see Frits Pannekoek, *The Fur Trade and Western Canadian Society 1670-1870* (Ottawa: Canadian Historical Association, 1987), Historical Booklet No. 43.

3   Variants of this theme are advanced by G.F.G. Stanley, "British Operations in the American Northwest, 1812-15," *Journal of the Society for Army Historical Research*, 22 (1943): 91-106; and Julius W. Pratt, "Fur Trade Strategy and the American Left Flank in the War of 1812," *American Historical Review* 40 (1935): 246-73.

4   NAC, RG 8, series C, vol 257, 31, McGill to Prevost, Montreal, 19 December 1812; for the fur trade and the North West Company, see H.A. Innis, *The Fur Trade in Canada* (New Haven: Yale University Press, 1930; reprinted in several editions).

5   *WHC*, 11 (1888): 291, Dickson to his fur trade partner Lt. John Lawe, Winnibago Lake, 4 February 1814.

6   OA, MS-109 (microcopy No. T-836), "British Military Correspondence, 16 July 1812-10 September 1813," Henry Procter, n.d.

7   *WHC*, 12 (1892): 111-12, Dickson to Noah Freer, Mil. Sec to Prevost, Michilimackinac, 23 October 1813.

8   Ibid., 11 (1888): 279, Dickson to Lawe, Winnibago Lake, 19 December 1813.

9   Ibid., 282, Dickson to Lawe, 25 December 1813.

10   Ibid., 10 (1883-85): 111-12, Dickson to Lawe, 15 March 1814.

11   *MPHC*, 25 (1896): 573-74. Prevost to Earl Bathurst, Sec. of State for War and the Colonies, Quebec, 8 February 1814.

12   Ibid., 391-92, Captain Richard Bullock to Procter, Michilimackinac, 25 September 1813; see also Brian Leigh Dunnigan, "The Michigan Fencibles," *Michigan History* 57, no. 4 (Winter 1973): 277-95.

13   Robert S. Allen, "McDouall," *DCB*, 7: 556-57; and "Major-General McDouall, C.B.," Free Church of Scotland, Pub. Committee, *Monthly Series of Tracts* (Edinburgh), No. 58 (July 1849).

14   OA, MS-35 (reel 1), Strachan Papers, scattered correspondence.

15   Ibid., McDouall to McGillivray, Michilimackinac, 15, 19 August 1814; 15, 25 September 1814; and 25 October 1814.

16   NAC, MG. 11, CO 42, vol. 157, 7-10, Prevost to Bathurst, Quebec, 10 July 1814.

17   Ibid., RG 8, series C, vol. 257, Speech of Sioux chief Wabasha at the Michilimackinac Council, 5 June 1814; he repeated these words to Prevost at Quebec later that summer.

18   Wood, ed., *Select British Documents* 3: 270, Prevost to Bathurst, Quebec, 10 August 1814.

19   Alex R. Gilpin, *The War of 1812 in the Old Northwest* (East Lansing: Michigan State University Press, 1958), 246, *Kingston Gazette* (Upper Canada), 26 August 1814, reported that "nine or ten trunks" of property belonging to Robert Dickson was taken, among which was correspondence dating back to 1786.

20   NAC, RG 8, series C, vol. 685, McDouall to Lt. Gen. Gordon Drummond, Michilimackinac, 16 July 1814.

21   *WHC* 13 (1895): 122, McDouall to Captain Andrew Bulger, Michilimackinac, 20 March 1815; see also Robert S. Allen, "William McKay," *DCB*, 6: 464-66; McCord Museum Archives, Lt. Col. William McKay Papers; and NAC, MG 30, D1, vol. 21, 143-52 (biog. notes).

22   *WHC* 11 (1888): 260-63, McDouall to Drummond, Michilimackinac, 16 July 1814.

23   NAC, RG 8, series C, vol. 685, William McKay, *Report* of the capture of Prairie du Chien, 27 July 1814.

24   Ibid., McKay Report, Supplement, 29 July 1814.

25 Captain Thomas G. Anderson, "Anderson's Journal at Fort McKay, 1814," *WHC* 9 (1882): 207-61.

26 M.M. Quaife, "An Artilleryman of Old Fort Mackinac," *Burton Historical Collection Leaflet* 6, no. 3 (January 1928): 33-48, with Report of Zachary Taylor.

27 *Kingston Gazette* (Upper Canada), 9 September 1814, provided full details of these events; see also OA, MS-35 (reel 1), Strachan Papers, McDouall to McGillivray, 15 August 1814, which describes the North West Company losses.

28 NAC, RG 8, series C, vol. 685, McDouall to Drummond, Michilimackinac, 28 July 1814.

29 Wood, ed., *Select British Documents* 2: 275, McDouall to Prevost, Michilimackinac, 14 August 1814; see also Brian Leigh Dunnigan, "The Battle of Mackinac Island," *Michigan History* 59, no. 4 (Winter 1975): 239-54.

30 *MPHC*, vol. 25 (1896): 500-1, McDouall to Bulger, Michilimackinac, 1 March 1815.

31 *WHC* 12 (1892): 123-25, McKay to Prevost, undated but probably early November 1814.

32 NAC, MG 11, CO 42, vol. 258, Invoice of Sundry Indian Stores delivered Robert Dickson Esq. ... , 29 October 1814. Items included, ball and shot, blankets, flints, muskets, gunpowder, laced hats, butcher knives, needles, flour, thread, ribbon, vermillion, and ear bobs.

33 Ibid., MG 19, E5 (Bulger Papers), 1: 50-63, Instructions, McDouall to Bulger, Michilimackinac, 29 October 1814; see also Robert S. Allen and Carol M. Judd, Andrew Bulger, *DCB*, 8: 111-13; NAC, MG 30, D1, vol. 6: 566-84 (biog. notes); ibid., MG 19, E5 (Bulger Papers), vol. 1; and *An Autobiographical Sketch of the services of the late Captain Andrew Bulger of the Royal Newfoundland Regiment* (Bangalore, India: Regimental Press, Second Battalion Tenth Regiment, 1865).

34 NAC, MG 19, E5 (Bulger Papers), vol. 1: 86 and 194; and vol. 7: 3, 8-10 and 87, Proclamation of Martial Law and Proceedings of a Garrison Court Martial.

35 NAC, MG 19, E5 (Bulger Papers), vol. 1: 135, McDouall to Bulger, Michilimackinac, 20 February 1815.

36 *WHC* 10 (1883-85): 131, Graham to Lawe, Prairie du Chien, 14 March 1815.

37 Bulger, *Autobiographical Sketch*, 21; and *Kingston Gazette*, 29 April 1815.

38 Benjamin Drake, *The Life and Adventures of Black Hawk* (Cincinnati: E. Morgan and Co., 1850), 85-89; see also Frank E. Stevens, *The Black Hawk War* (Chicago: Stevens, 1903), 55-57.

39 NAC, MG 24, F19 (Anderson's Journal), Fort McKay 1814; ibid., MG 19, E5 (Bulger Papers), vol. 1: 604-13 and 614-17, Declaration of Peace to the Indians on the Mississippi, 23 May 1815.

40 NAC, RG 8, series C, vol. 688, McDouall to Bulgar, Michilmackinac, 5 May 1815.

41 Wood, ed., *Select British Documents,* 3: 538, McDouall to Maj. Gen. Frederick Robinson, 21 July 1815.

Chapter 8: From Warriors to Wards

1 PRO, CO 43, vol. 23, Earl Bathurst, Secretary of State for War and the Colonies, to Prevost, Downing St., 3 June 1814.

2 John K. Mahon, *The War of 1812* (Gainsville: University of Florida Press, 1972). 375-86, provides an analysis of the Treaty of Ghent.

3 *The Times* (London), 2 February 1815; see also Robert S. Allen, "The End of an Era, "*The British Indian Department* (1975): 86-93; and Colin G. Calloway, "The End of an Era: British Indian Relations in the Great Lakes Region after the War of 1812," *Michigan Historical Review* 12 (Fall 1986): 3-4.

4 Wood, ed., *Select British Documents,* 3: 524; see also Vincent Harlow and Frederick Madden, eds., *British Colonial Developments, 1774-1834* (Oxford: Clarendon Press, 1967), 481. The full text of the Treaty of Ghent is quoted in

Fred L. Israel, ed., *Major Peace Treaties of Modern History 1648-1967* (New York: Chelsea House Publs., 1967), 697-705.

5   Robert L. Fisher, "The Treaties of Portage des Sioux," *MPHR*, 19 (1933): 495-508.

6   Charles J. Kappler, ed., *Indian Treaties 1778-1883* (New York: Interland Publ. Inc., 1973), 110-19.

7   Harlow and Madden, eds., *British Colonial Developments*, 483-84, quote this particular section of the Convention of 1818. By the Oregon Treaty (15 June 1846), the boundary line was extended along the 49th parallel to the Pacific Ocean. This treaty line was a compromise, as President James K. Polk, an ardent expansionist, had successfully campaigned in 1844 on the slogan of "54' 40 or fight." But by 1846 the annexation of Texas, the Mexican War and the general interest of the United States in the affairs of central and South America had become urgent priorities.

8   Over two thousand Indians, for instance, were issued rations and presents at Amherstburg in 1816. See Detroit Public Library. Burton Historical Collection (George Ironside Papers), letter dated Amherstburg, 14 December 1816.

9   Detroit Public Library, Burton Historical Collection (Silas Farmer Papers), Cass to John C. Calhoun, Sec. of War, Detroit, 3 August 1819; see also James A. Clifton, "Visiting Indian" in Canada, unpubl. ms. on file at Fort Malden National Historic Park (Amherstburg).

10 Detroit Public Library, Burton Historical Collection (Silas Farmer Papers), Cass to Calhoun, Detroit 3 August 1819.

11 NAC, RG 8, series C, 258, Lt. Col. Reginald James, commanding officer at Fort Malden, to Lewis Cass, Governor of Michgan, Sandwich, 5 October 1815; see also evidence of the Kickapoo, Chemango, at the inquest of the murder of Akochis, Indian Reserve, Malden, 6 October 1815. Following a brief investigation, no charges were laid.

12 For Amercian Indian policy and objectives in the post-1815 years, see Francis Paul Prucha, "United States Indian Policies, 1815-1860," in Wilcomb E. Washburn, vol. ed., *Handbook*: vol. 4, *History of Indian-White Relations,* 40-47; Reginald Horsman, *The Origins of Indian Removal 1815-1824* (East Lansing: Michigan State University Press, 1970); for a major excerpt from the Report of 1831 by Elbert Herring, Commissioner of Indian Affairs, dated 19 November 1831 which assesses the supposed benefits of the "humane policy," see Wilcomb E. Washburn, ed., *The American Indian and the United States: A Documentary History*, 4 vols. New York: Random House, 1973), 1: 18-21.

13 Washburn, ed., *The American Indian*, 1:18-23, Reports of Commissioner of Indian Affairs, Elbert Herring, 19 November 1831 and 22 November 1832.

14 Prucha, ed., *Documents*, 52-53, provides a text for the Indian Removal Act which is properly cited as "An Act to provide for an exchange of lands with the Indians residing in any of the states or territories, and for their removal west of the river Mississippi."

15 Grant Foreman, *Indian Removal: The Emigration of the Five Civilized Tribes of Indians* (Norman: University of Oklahoma Press, 1953, ed.), provides a detailed and sympathetic assessment. A full text of the Marshall decision is printed in Washburn, ed., *The American Indian*, 4: 2554-2602. This decision was one of the fundamental legal arguments which defined the relationship between the Indian and the non-Indian in the United States.

16 The Bureau of Indian Affairs, initially a part of the War Department, was created by John C. Calhoun, secretary of war, without special congressional authorization. Congress only confirmed the position "Commissioner of Indian Affairs" in 1832. See Prucha, ed., *Documents*, 37-38; for a full history of government-Indian relations, see Francis Paul Prucha, *The Great Father: The United States Government and the American Indians*, 2 vols. (Lincoln: University of Nebraska Press, 1984).

17 Carter, ed., *Territorial Papers*, 17: 526, Letter of Gov. Lewis Cass, 21 July 1817; see also Lewis Cass, "British Policy in Respect to the Indians, 1840," reproduced in *The North American Review* (Winter 1973): 24-25.

18 PRO, CO 43, vol. 24, Earl Bathurst to Drummond, 14 March 1816.

19 NAC, MG 11, CO 42, vol. 370, Sir Peregrine Maitland, Lieutenant Governor of Upper Canada, to Wilmot Horton, Par. Undersecretary to Earl Bathurst, 20 November 1823; see also John F. Leslie, "Commissions of Inquiry into Indian affairs in the Canadas, 1828-1858: Evolving a corporate memory for the Indian department," (MA thesis, Carleton University, 1984), 18.

20 Ibid., RG 10, vol. 12, 10557-69, Indian Council at Burlington Bay, Upper Canada, 24-27 April 1815.

21 *MPHC*, 16 (1890): 284 and 367-69, McDouall to Maj. Gen. Frederick Robinson, Drummond Island, 22 September and 4 October 1815; see also Detroit Public Library, Burton Historical Collection (Robert McDouall orderly book, Drummond Island, 1815).

22 *MPHC*, 16 (1890): 464, McDouall to Mil. Sec, Drummond Island, 17 June 1816; the speech of the Winnebago chief is quoted in Burt, *United States*, 378, n. 16.

23 McCord Museum Archives, Lt. Col. William McKay Papers, box 1, M7090, Date of appointment, 25 December 1814, by order of Sir George Prevost.

24 *MPHC*, 16 (1890): 479-80, Indian Council at Drummond Island, 29-30 June 1816; the speech of Little Crow is quoted in Virginia Irving Armstrong comp., *I Have Spoken: American History Through the Voices of the Indians* (New York: Pocket Books, 1972), 57-58.

25 NAC, MG 19, F29 (William McKay Papers); McCord Museum Archives, Lt. Col. William McKay Papers, box 5 (Minutes of Indian Councils, Drummond Island), Indian Council at Drummond Island, 3 August 1817 and for several days, Speech of Black Hawk.

26 McCord Museum Archives, Lt. Col. William McKay Papers, box 5, M5640, Statistical data and enumeration of Indians visiting at Drummond Island, 1814-1828.

27 For graphic details and a sympathetic assessment of Black Hawk and the Sauk, see Cecil Eby, *"That Disgraceful Affair," The Black Hawk War* (New York: W.W. Norton, 1973). One revised edition of the 1833 dictation and recording is Donald Jackson, ed., *Black Hawk (Ma-ka-tai-me-she-kia-kiak): An Autobiography* (Urbana: University of Illinois Press, 1955, ed.).

28 NAC, RG 19 (Finance), series E5 and series E2 (War of 1812) contains information and statistical data on war losses, claims, and pensions, with scattered references to Indian allies; see also NAC, RG 9 (Militia and Defence) for War of 1812 pensions and Indian recepients. A general source which touches on this theme is Fred Gaffen, *Forgotten Soldiers; An Illustrated History of Canada's Native Peoples in Both World Wars* (Penticton, BC: Theytus Books, 1984). The quotation is taken from the files of the Claims and Historical Research Centre of the Department of Indian and Northern Affairs Canada under the title "Revised Schedule of Equipment, as Presents for Indians of Upper Canada," Indian Office, Toronto, 29 November 1837, approved Francis Bond Head, Lieutenant Governor of Upper Canada.

29 The surrender is assessed in Robert J. Surtees, "Indian Land Cessions in Ontario," 173-80; see also Anthony J. Hall, "Aisance," *DCB*, 7: 11-12; and "Yellowhead," ibid., 9: 589-90, paragraph one.

30 Canada: *Indian Treaties and Surrenders*, 3 vols. (Toronto: Coles Publishing Co., 1971; first publ. 1891 and 1912), 1: 42-43; see also *DCB*, 7: 11; ibid., 9: 589; and Robert J. Surtees, "Indian Land Cessions in Upper Canada, 1815-1830," in Ian A.L. Getty and Antoine S. Lussier, eds., *As Long as the Sun Shines and Water Flows: A Reader in Canadian Native Studies* (Vancouver: University of British Columbia Press, 1983), 70-72.

31 NAC, MG 19, F1 (Claus Papers), vol. 11: 101-4, Minutes of an Indian Council, 17 October 1818; and see also *Indian Treaties and Surrenders*, 1: 47.

32 The life of Sir Peregrine Maitland is detailed by Hartwell Bowsfield in *DCB*, 8: 596-605. His Indian policy in Canada is assessed by F.M. Quealey, "The Administration of Sir Peregrine Maitland, Lieutenant-Governor of Upper Canada, 1818-1828," 2 vols. (Ph.D. dissertation, University of Toronto, 1968): 300-27.

33 PRO, CO 42, vol. 266. Maitland to Bathurst, 29 November 1821, provides full details of the proposed "civilization" programme.

34 NAC, RG 10, vol. 37, Minutes of a Council with the Mississauga, York, 28 February 1820.

35 David Shanahan, *The Indian Land Management Fund* (Ottawa: Department of Indian and Northern Affairs Canada, 1991) has prepared a background history and detailed assessment of the Indian trust fund accounts and contributions made by the various groups and bands. Established in the 1820s from the sale of Indian lands, a board was appointed to administer and manage the Indian fund in 1858. The board was dissolved in 1913, and the monies in the trust fund accounts were distributed among the various contributors.

36 NAC, MG 11, CO 42, vol. 388, Colborne to R.W. Hay, Sec. to Sir George Murray, Sec. for War and the Colonies, York, 3 May 1829. A typed copy of this proposal, which initiated the formal beginning of the reserve system in Canada, is presented in Appendix D.

37 Ibid., MG 11, CO 42, vol. 223, Kempt to Murray, 16 May 1829.

38 *Journal of the Legislative Assembly. Canada* (1844-45), "Report on Affairs of Indians in Canada," Section III. This report reviewed Indian conditions in the province of Canada from the end of the War of 1812.

39 NAC, RG 10, vol. 116, Murray to Kempt, 25 January 1830. For a continuation of this theme, see John S. Milloy, "The Era of Civilization - British Policy for the Indians of Canada, 1830-1860" (D.Phil. dissertation, University of Oxford, 1978).

40 Smith, *Sacred Feathers*, provides a thoroughly researched assessment of the life and work of Peter Jones.

41 Quoted from *British Parliamentary Papers* (Shannon: Irish University Press, 1969), vol. 13: 125, Bond Head to Baron Glenelg, Sec. of State for War and the Colonies, - 1836; and S.F. Wise, "Bond Head," *DCB* 10 : 342-45.

42 *Indian Treaties and Surrender*, 1: 112-13; and NAC, MG 11, CO 42, vol. 431, Bond Head to Glenelg, 20 August 1836.

43 PRO, CO 42, vol. 451: 257-58, William Johnson Kerr to John Macaulay, Civil Sec. to Sir George Arthur, lieutenant governor of Upper Canada, Brant House, Wellington Square, 3 October 1838.

44 Ibid., 262. William Johnson Kerr to John Macaulay, 3 October 1838.

45 Ibid., Glenelg to Arthur, Downing Street, 5 December 1838; also quoted in Johnston, ed., *The Valley of the Six Nations*, 231.

46 NAC, MG 19, F29 (William McKay Papers), Speech of Ocaito, Drummond Island, 7 July 1818; for a shortened version, see Penny Petrone, ed., *First People, First Voices* (Toronto: University of Toronto Press, 1984), 42-46.

Chapter 9: Epilogue: Recasting the Chain of Friendship

1   James A. Clifton, *A Place of Refuge for All Time: Migration of the American Potawatomi into Upper Canada, 1835 to 1850* (Ottawa: National Museum of Man, 1975), 100.

2   David Murray, *Modern Indians: Native Americans in the Twentieth Century* (British Association for American Studies, 1982), 13.

3   Quoted in *The Economist* (29 June 1991), 5.

4   Notes for an address by Prime Minister Brian Mulroney to the First Nation Congress, Victoria, British Columbia, 23 April 1991.

5   This view is expressed and detailed in Jacques Monet, *The Last Cannon Shot: A Study of French-Canadian Nationalism* (Toronto: University of Toronto Press, 1976).

BIBLIOGRAPHY

MANUSCRIPT COLLECTIONS
British Library (London)
Department of Manuscripts:
    Add. Mss. 21631-21660 (Bouquet Papers)
    Add. Mss. 21661-21892 (Haldimand Papers)
    Add. Mss. 32848
    Add. Mss. 33029
Detroit Public Library
    Burton Historical Collection:
    Farmer Papers
    Ironside Papers
    McDouall Orderly Book (Drummond Island, 1815)
House of Lords Record Office (London)
    Burgoyne Campaign, 1777-78
    Journals of the House of Lords, 1775-76
    Return of British Land Forces in North America (May 1812)
McCord Museum Archives (Montréal)
    McKay Papers
    War of 1812 (box)
Metropolitan Toronto Library
    Givins Papers
    Norton Papers
    Russell Papers
National Archives of Canada (Ottawa)
    Manuscript Groups (MG):
    MG 4, Archives de la Guerre, Colonies B, vol. 87
    MG 11, Colonial Office Papers (CO),
        CO 42 (Canada, Original Correspondence), vols. 41,
        45, 46, 47, 51, 73, 87, 88, 89, 96, 98, 136, 143, 157,
        167, 223, 226, 258, 319, 370, 388, 431
    MG 13, War Office Papers (WO),
        WO 17 (Monthly Returns), vols. 1516, 1523
    MG 19, Fur trade and Indians
        E5, Bulger Papers
        F1, Claus Papers
        F6, Brant Papers
        F29, McKay Papers
    MG 21, Haldimand Collection (series B)
        B54, B55, B100, B103, B114, B116, B119
    MG 23, Late Eighteenth-century Papers
    MG 24, Nineteenth-century pre-confederation Papers
        A1, Brock Papers
        F19, Anderson Journal (1814)
    MG 30, Manuscripts of the first half of the twentieth century, vol. 21
    Record Groups (RG):
    RG 8, British military and naval records (Series C),
        vols. 247-71 (Indians of North America), 676, 677, 680,
        682, 687, 688, 688A, , 695A, 1206, 1220
    RG 9, Militia and Defence
        War of 1812

RG 10, Records Relating to Indian Affairs
　　vols. 8, 11, 12, 37, 116, 2287 (Colonial Documents: Six Nations)
RG 19, Finance (series E2 and series E5)
　　War of 1812
National Library of Wales (Aberystwyth)
Tredegar Park Muniments:
　　Bradstreet Papers (Bradstreet-Gould Correspondence)
Ontario Archives (Toronto)
　　British Military Correspondence, 1789-1807 (Indian Affairs)
　　Jarvis-Powell Papers
　　Strachan Papers
　　War of 1812 (MS-74 and MS-109)
Public Record Office (London)
Audit Office (AO): Declared Accounts (Indians of North America)
　　AO 1, roll 2, bundle 1530 (Sir William Johnson)
　　AO 1, roll 5, bundle 1530 (Guy Johnson)
　　AO 1, roll 6, bundle 1530 (John Campbell)
　　AO 1, roll 8, bundle 1530 (Daniel Claus)
　　AO 1, roll 9, bundle 1531 (Thomas Brown)
　　AO 1, roll 10, bundle 1531 (John Graham)
　　AO 1, roll 11, bundle 1531 (John Douglas)
Colonial Office Papers (CO):
　　CO 5 (America and West Indies), vols. 69, 75, 76, 78, 79, 82, 92, 93, 211, 253
　　CO 42 (Canada, Original Correspondence), vols. 18, 34, 36, 38, 39, 42, 78, 136,
　　　　146, 147, 266, 321, 322, 347, 352, 451
　　CO 43 (Canada, Entry Books), vols. 22, 23, 24
　　CO 324 (Entry Books), vol. 51
Granville Papers (Indian Agents)
　　PRO 30/2933
　　PRO 30/2934
　　PRO 30/2935
War Office Papers (WO)
　　WO 28 (Headquarters Records), vol. 10
　　WO 71 (Courts Martial), vol. 243
Queen's University Archives (Kingston)
　　Cartwright Papers
Welch Regiment Museum (Cardiff)
　　The War of 1812 (files)
　　The War in Canada, 1812-1815 (handwritten/undated)
William L. Clements Library (Ann Arbor, Michigan)
　　Gage Papers
　　Germain Papers

SELECT PRINTED MATERIAL

Adair, James. *The History of the American Indians: Particularly those Nations adjoining the Mississippi, East and West Florida, Georgia, South and North Carolina, and Virginia.* London: Edward and Charles Dilly, 1775.

Adams, Paul K. "Colonel Henry Bouquet's Ohio Expedition in 1764," *Pennsylvania History* 40, no. 2 (April 1973): 139-47.

Alden, John Richard. *General Gage in America.* Baton Rouge: Louisiana State University Press, 1948.

———. *John Stuart and the Southern Colonial Frontier: A Study of Indian Relations, War, Trade, and Land Problems in the Southern Wilderness, 1754-1755.* Ann Arbor: University of Michigan Press, 1944.

Allen, Robert S. "A History of Fort George, Upper Canada," *Canadian Historic Sites*: 61-93. Ottawa: Department of Indian and Northern Affairs Canada, 1974. Occasional Papers in Archaeology and History No. 11.

———. "Canadians on the Upper Mississippi: The Capture and Occupation of Prairie du Chien during the War of 1812," *Military Collector and Historian* 31, no. 3 (Fall 1979): 118-23.

———. "His Majesty's Indian Allies: Native Peoples, the British Crown and the War of 1812," *Michigan Historical Review* 14, no .2 (Fall 1988): 1-24.

———. *Loyalist Literature: An Annotated Bibliographic Guide to the Writings of the Loyalists of the American Revolution.* Toronto: Dundurn Press, 1982.

———. "Red and White: The Indian Tribes of the Ohio Valley and Anglo-American Relations, 1783-96." MA thesis, Dalhousie University, 1970.

———. *The British Indian Department and the Frontier in North America, 1755-1830.* Ottawa: Department of Indian and Northern Affairs Canada, 1975. Canadian Historic Sites: Occasional Papers in Archaeology and History no. 14.

———, ed. *The Loyal Americans: The Military Role of the Loyalist Provincial Corps and their Settlement in British North America, 1775-1784.* Ottawa: National Museums of Canada, 1983.

———. "Mr. Secretary Jarvis: William Jarvis of Connecticut and York," in Phyllis R. Blakeley and John N. Grant, eds. *Eleven Exiles: Accounts of Loyalists of the American Revolution,* 288-317. Toronto: Dundurn Press, 1982.

Anderson, Niles. *The Battle of Bushy Run.* Harrisburg, Pa.: Pennsylvania Historical and Museum Commission, 1975.

Anderson, Thomas G. "Anderson's Journal at Fort Mackay, 1814," *Wisconsin Historical Collection* 9 (1882): 207-61.

Antal, S. "Myths and Facts Concerning General Procter," *Ontario History* 79, no. 3 (September 1987): 251-62.

Aquila, Richard. *The Iroquois Restoration. Iroquois Diplomacy on the Colonial Frontier, 1701-1754.* Detroit: Wayne State University, 1983.

Armour, David A., ed. *Attack at Michilimackinac 1763.* Mackinac Island, Michigan: Mackinac Island State Parks Commission, 1971.

Armstrong, Virginia Irving, comp. *I Have Spoken: American History Through the Voices of the Indians.* New York: Pocket Books, 1972.

Axtell, James. *The European and the Indian: Essays in the Ethnohistory of Colonial North America.* New York: Oxford University Press, 1981.

Au, Dennis. *War on the Raisin: A Narrative Account of the War of 1812 in the River Raisin Settlement, Michigan Territory.* Monroe: Monroe County Historical Commission, 1981.

Barron, F.L. and J.B. Waldram, eds. *1885 and After: Native Society in Transition.* Regina: Canadian Plains Research Centre, 1986.

Beaver, R. Pierce. "Protestant Churches and the Indians," in Wilcomb E.
    Washburn, vol. ed., *Handbook of North American Indians*, vol. 4, *History of
    Indian-White Relations*: 430-58. Washington: Smithsonian Institution, 1988.
Bemis, Samuel F. "Canada and the Peace Settlement of 1782-1783,"*Canadian
    Historical Review* 14 (1933): 265-84.
——. *Jay's Treaty: A Study in Commerce and Diplomacy*. New Haven: Yale University
    Press, 1962.
Benn, Carl. "The Military Context of the Founding of Toronto," *Ontario History* 81,
    no. 277, 4 (December 1989): 303-22.
Berger, Carl. "The Campaign to Win the Indians' Allegiance," *Broadsides and
    Bayonets: The Propaganda War of the American Revolution*: 52-83.
    Philadelphia: University of Pennsylvania Press, 1961.
Berkeley, Edmund and Dorothy Smith Berkeley. *Dr. John Mitchell: The Man Who
    Made the Map of North America*. Chapel Hill: University of North Carolina
    Press, 1974.
Berkhofer, Robert F., Jr. *The White Man's Indian: Images of the American Indian from
    Columbus to the Present*. New York: A.A. Knopf, 1978.
Berton, Pierre. *Flames across the Border, 1813-1814*. Toronto: McClelland and
    Stewart, 1981.
——. *The Invasion of Canada, 1812-1813*. Toronto: McClelland and Stewart, 1980.
Black Thunder, Elijah et al. *Ehanna Woyakapi: History of the Sisseton Wahpeton
    Sioux Tribe*. Sisseton, South Dakota: Sisseton-Wahpeton Tribe Inc., 1972.
Blanchard, David. *Seven Generations: A History of the Kanienkehaka*. Kahnawake:
    Kahnawake Survival School, 1980.
Boisonnault, C.-M. "Les Canadiens et la révolte de Pontiac," *La Revue de l'université
    Laval* 2 (1947-48): 778-87.
Bonomi, Patricia U. *A Factious People: Politics and Society in Colonial New York*. New
    York: Columbia University Press, 1971.
Bowler, R. Arthur. "Sir Guy Carleton and the Campaign of 1776 in Canada,"
    Canadian Historical Review 55 (June 1974): 131-40.
Brigham, Clarence S., ed. *British Royal Proclamations Relating to America*: vol. 12:
    212-18. Worcester, Mass.: American Antiquarian Society, 1911.
British Critic. London, 1763-96.
Brown, Alan S. "The Role of the Army in Western Settlement: Josiah Harmar's
    Command, 1785-1790," *Pennsylvania Magazine of History and Biography* 18
    (1969): 161-78.
Brown, Gerald Saxon. *The American Secretary: The Colonial Policy of Lord George
    Germain, 1775-1778*. Ann Arbor: University of Michigan Press, 1963.
Brown, Jennifer. *Strangers in Blood: Fur Trade Company Families in the Indian
    Country*. Vancouver: University of British Columbia Press, 1980
Brown, Judith K. "Economic Organization and the Position of Women among the
    Iroquois," *Ethnohistory* 17, no. 3 (1970): 151-67.
Bryce, Peter H. "Sir John Johnson Baronet; Superintendent-General of Indian
    Affairs, 1743-1830," *New York State Historical Association Quarterly Journal* 9,
    no. 3 (July 1928): 233-71.
Bulger, Andrew. *An Autobiographical Sketch of the services of the late Captain Andrew
    Bulger of the Royal Newfoundland Regiment*. Bangalore, India: Regimental
    Press, Second Battalion Tenth Regiment, 1865.
Bumstead, Jack M. "The American Revolution: Some Thoughts on Recent
    Bicentennial Scholarship," *Acadiensis* 6 (1977): 3-22.
Burgoyne, Lt. Gen. John. *A State of the Expedition from Canada as laid before the
    House of Commons*. London: J. Almon, 1780; reprinted New York: Arno
    Press, 1969.
Burns, Brian. "Massacre or Muster? Burgoyne's Indians and the Militia at

Bennington," *Vermont History* 45, no. 3 (Summer 1977): 133–44.

Burt, A.L. *Guy Carleton, Lord Dorchester, 1724-1808.* Ottawa: The Canadian Historical Association, 1964. Historical Booklet no. 5.

——. *The Old Province of Quebec.* Toronto: Ryerson Press, 1933.

——. "The Quarrel between Germain and Carleton: An Inverted Story," *Canadian Historical Review* 11 (1930): 202–22.

——. *The United States, Great Britain and British North America from the Revolution to the Establishment of Peace after the War of 1812.* Toronto: Ryerson Press, 1940.

Butterfield, Consul Willshire. *History of the Girtys.* Columbus, Ohio: Long's College Book Co., 1950; first published 1890.

Byfield, Shadrach. "A Common Soldier's Account," in *Recollections of the War of 1812.* Toronto: Baxter Publishing Co., 1964; first publ. between 1828 and 1854.

Callendar, Charles. "Shawnee," in Bruce G. Trigger, vol. ed., *Handbook of North American Indians*: vol. 15, Northeast: 622–35. Washington: Smithsonian Institute, 1978.

Calloway, Colin G. *Crown and Calumet: British-Indian Relations, 1783-1815.* Norman: University of Oklahoma Press, 1987.

——. "The End of an Era: British-Indian Relations in the Great Lakes Region after the War of 1812," *Michigan Historical Review* 12, no. 2 (Fall 1986): 1–20.

——. *The Western Abenakis of Vermont, 1600-1800.* Norman: University of Oklahoma Press, 1990.

Canada. *Indian Self-Government in Canada; Report of the Special Committee* (The Penner Report). Ottawa, 1983.

——. *Living Treaties: Lasting Agreements: Report of the Task Force to Review Comprehensive Claims Policy* (The Coolican Report). Ottawa: Department of Indian and Northern Affairs, 1985.

——. *Indian Treaties and Surrenders.* 3 vols., Toronto: Coles Publishing Co., 1971; first publ. 1891 and 1912.

——. *Journal of the Legislative Assembly* (1844–45). "Report on Affairs of Indians in Canada," section III.

——. National Archives. *Canada Archives Reports,* 1884-1893, 1896-1904, 1914, and 1916.

Carlson, Richard G., ed. "George P. Peters' Version of the Battle of Tippecanoe (November 7, 1811)," *Vermont History* 45, no. 1 (Winter 1977): 38–43.

Carter, Clarence E. "British Policy towards the American Indians in the South, 1763-8," *English Historical Review* 33 (1918): 37–56.

——. *The Correspondence of General Thomas Gage, with the Secretaries of State, and with the War Office and the Treasury 1763-1755.* 2 vols., New Haven: Yale University Press, 1931-33.

——. "The Significance of the Military Office in America, 1763-1775," *American Historical Review* 28, no. 4 (July 1923): 475–87.

——. *The Territorial Papers of the United States.* 26 vols., Washington, DC: United States Government Printing Office, 1934-62.

Carter, Harvey Lewis. *The Life and Times of Little Turtle: First Sagamore of the Wabash.* Urbana: University of Illinois Press, 1987.

Carter-Edwards, Dennis. "Defending the Straits: The Military Base at Amherstburg," in K. Dryke and L. Kulisek, eds. *The Western District*: 33–43. Windsor: Essex County Historical Society, 1983.

——. "The War of 1812 Along the Detroit Frontier: A Canadian Perspective," *Michigan Historical Reveiw* 13, no. 2 (Fall 1987): 25–50.

Cashin, Edward J. *The King's Ranger: Thomas Brown and the American Revolution on the Southern Frontier.* Athens: University of Georgia Press, 1989.

Cass, Lewis. "British Policy in Respect to the Indians, 1840," *North American Review*

(Winter 1973): 24-25.

Casselman, A.C., ed. *Richardson's War of 1812*. Toronto: Coles Publishing Co., 1974; first publ. 1842.

Centinel of the Northwest. Cincinnati, 1793-97.

Chalou, George C. "The Red Pawns Go to War: British-Indian Relations, 1810-1815." Ph.D. dissertation, Indiana University, 1971.

Christie, Ian R. *Crisis of Empire: Great Britain and the American Colonies, 1754-1783*. London: Edward Arnold, 1966.

——. "The Imperial Dimension: British Ministerial Perspectives during the American Revolutionary Crisis, 1763-1776," in Esmond Wright, ed. *Red, White and True Blue: The Loyalists in the American Revolution*, 149-66. New York: AMS Press, 1976.

Church of Scotland. "Major General McDouall, CB," Free Church of Scotland, Pub. Committee, *Monthly Series of Tracts* 58 (July 1849).

Clayton, T.R. "The Duke of Newcastle, the Duke of Halifax, and the American Origins of the Seven Years' War," *Historical Journal* 24 (1981): 571-603.

Clifton, James A., ed. *Being and Becoming Indian: Biographical Studies of North American Frontiers*. Chicago: The Dorsey Press, 1989.

——. "Merchant, Soldier Broker, Chief: A Corrected Obituary of Captain Billy Caldwell," *Journal of the Illinois State Historical Society* 71 (1978): 185-210.

——. "Personal and Ethnic Identity on the Great Lakes Frontier: The Case of Billy Caldwell, Anglo-Canadian," *Ethnohistory* 78 (1978): 69-94.

Cohen, Felix S. *Handbook of Federal Indian Law*. Charlottesville, Virginia: The Michie Company, 1982.

Colden, Cadwallader. *The History of the Five Nations of Canada: Which are Dependent on the Province of New York, and are a Barrier between the English and the French in that Part of the World*. 2 vols., New York: A.S. Barnes and Co., 1904.

Conrad, Mark A. "The Christianization of Indians in Colonial Virginia." Ph.D. dissertation, Union Theological Seminary, Richmond, Va., 1979.

Cotterill, R.S. *The Southern Indians: The Story of the Civilized Tribes Before Removal*. Norman: University of Oklahoma Press, 1954.

Coupland, Reginald. *The Quebec Act: A Study in Statesmanship*. Oxford: Clarendon Press, 1925.

Coutts, Katherine B. "Thamesville and the Battle of the Thames," in Morris Zaslow, ed. *The Defended Border: Upper Canada and the War of 1812*: 114-20. Toronto: Macmillan Co., 1964.

Cruikshank, E.A., ed. "Campaigns of 1812-1814; Contemporary Narratives by Captain W.H. Merritt, Lieutenant Colonel Matthew Elliott, Colonel William Claus and Captain John Norton," *Niagara Historical Society Publications* 9 (1902): 3-20.

——, ed. *Correspondence of Lieutenant-Governor John Graves Simcoe*. 5 vols., Toronto: Ontario Historical Society, 1923-31.

——. *Documents Relating to the Invasion of Canada and the Surrender of Detroit 1812*. Ottawa: Government Printing Bureau, 1913.

——, ed. *Records of Niagara in the Days of the Commodore Grand and Lieut. Governor Gore, 1805-1811*. Niagara-on-the-Lake: Niagara Historical Society, 1931.

——. "Robert Dickson, the Indian Trader," *Wisconsin Historical Collections* 12 (1892): 133-53.

——. "The Battle of Queenston Heights," in Morris Zaslow, ed. *The Defended Border: Upper Canada and the War of 1812*: 21-44. Toronto: Macmillan Co., 1964.

——. "The Coming of the Loyalist Mohawks to the Bay of Quinté," *Ontario Historical Society Papers and Records* 26 (1930): 390-403.

——. "The County of Norfolk in the War of 1812," in Morris Zaslow, ed. *The Defended Border: Upper Canada and the War of 1812.*: 224-40. Toronto: Macmillan Co., 1964.

——, ed. *The Documentary History of the Campaigns upon the Niagara Frontier, in the Years 1812, 1813 and 1814.* 9 vols., Welland: Tribune Office, 1896-1908.

——. "The King's Royal Regiment of New York, "*Ontario Historical Society Papers and Records* 27 (1931): 1-131.

Cruikshank, E.A. and A.F. Hunter, eds. *Correspondence of the Honourable Peter Russell.* 3 vols., Toronto: Ontario Historical Society, 1932-6.

Cutcliffe, Stephen H. "Colonial Indian Policy as a Measure of Rising Imperialism: New York and Pennsylvania, 1700-1755," *Western Pennsylvania Historical Magazine* 64, no. 3 (July 1981): 237-68.

Daniel, R. *A History of Native Claims Processes in Canada, 1867-1979.* Ottawa: Department of Indian and Northern Affairs, 1980.

Davies, K.G., ed. *Documents of the American Revolution 1770-1783.* 21 vols., Shannon: Irish University Press, 1976.

Dendy, John Oliver. "Frederick Haldimand and the Defence of Canada, 1778-1784." Ph.D. dissertation, Duke University, 1972.

Digby, Lt. William. *The British Invasion from the North: The Campaigns of Gens. Carleton and Burgoyne from Canada, 1776-1777.* Albany: J. Munsell, 1887.

Dictionary of Canadian Biography. Toronto: University of Toronto Press, 1974-88; vol. 3 (1974), vol. 4 (1979), vol. 5 (1983), vol. 6 (1987), and vol. 7 (1988).

Dowd, Gregory Evans. *A Spirited Resistance: The North American Indian Struggle for Unity, 1745-1815.* Baltimore and London: The Johns Hopkins University Press, 1992.

Downes, Randolph C. *Council Fires on the Upper Ohio: A Narrative of Indian Affairs in the Upper Ohio Valley until 1795.* Pittsburgh: University of Pittsburgh Press, 1940.

Drake, Benjamin. *The Life and Adventures of Black Hawk.* Cincinnati: E. Morgan and Co., 1850.

Dunnigan, Brian Leigh. *Siege - 1759: The Campaign Against Niagara.* Youngstown, NY: Old Fort Niagara Association, Inc., 1986.

——. "The Battle of Mackinac Island," *Michigan History* 59, no.4 (Winter 1975): 239-54.

——. *The British Army at Mackinac 1812-1815.* Mackinac Island, Michigan: Mackinac Island State Park Commission, 1980. Reports in Mackinac History and Archaeology no. 7.

——. "The Michigan Fencibles," *Michigan History* 57, no. 4 (Winter 1973): 277-95.

Duran, Elizabeth C. and James Duran, Jr. "Indian Rights in the Jay Treaty," *Indian Historian* 6, no.1 (Winter 1973): 33-37.

Eby, Cecil. *"That Disgraceful Affair," The Black Hawk War.* New York: W.W. Norton, 1973.

Edmunds, R. David. *Tecumseh and the Quest for Indian Leadership.* Boston: Little, Brown and Co., 1984.

——. "Tecumseh, The Shawnee Prophet, and American History: A Reassessment," *Western Historical Quarterly* 14, no. 3 (July 1983): 261-76.

——. *The Shawnee Prophet.* Lincoln: University of Nebraska Press, 1983.

——. "The Thin Red Line: Tecumseh, the Prophet, and Shawnee Resistance," *Timeline* 4, no.6 (December 1987 - January 1988): 2-19.

——. "Wea Participation in the Northwest Indian Wars, 1790-1795," *Filson Club History Quarterly* 46 (1972): 241-53.

Egan, Clifford L. "The Origins of the War of 1812: Three Decades of Historical Writing," *Military Affairs* 38 (April 1974): 72-75.

Eid, Leroy V. "The Ojibwa-Iroquois War: The War the Five Nations Did Not Win," *Ethnohistory* 26, no. 4 (Fall 1979): 297-324.

Ermatinger, C.O.Z. "The Retreat of Procter and Tecumseh," *Ontario Historical Society Papers and Records* 17 (1919): 11-21.

Esarey, Logan, ed. *Messages and Letters of Governor William Henry Harrison.* 2 vols., Indianapolis: Indiana Historical Commission, 1922.

Fenton, Willim N. "Cherokee and Iroquois Connections Revisited," *Journal of Cherokee Studies* 3 (1978): 239-49.

——. "The Roll Call of the Iroquois Chiefs: A Study of A Mnemonic Cane from the Six Nations Reserve," *Smithsonian Miscellaneous Collections* 3, no. 15 (1950): 1-73.

Fenton, William N. and Elisabeth Tooker. "Mohawk," in Bruce G. Trigger, vol., ed., *Handbook of North American Indians*: vol. 15, Northeast: 466-90. Washington, D.C.: Smithsonian Institution, 1978.

Fisher, Robert L. "The Treaties of Portage des Sioux," *Mississippi Valley Historical Review* 19 (1933): 495-508.

Fitzpatrick, John C., ed. *The Writings of George Washington, from the Original Manuscript Sources, 1745-1799.* 39 vols., Washington: US Government Printing Office, 1931-44.

Flick, A.C. "New Sources on the Sullivan-Clinton Campaign in 1779," *New York State Historical Association Quarterly Journal* 10, no.3 (July 1929): 185-224; and no. 4 (October 1929): 265-317.

Foreman, Grant. *Indian Removal: The Emigration of the Five Civilized Tribes of Indians.* 2nd ed. Norman: University of Oklahoma Press, 1953.

Fortescue, Hon. John W. *A History of the British Army.* 13 vols., London: Macmillan and Co. Ltd., 1899-1930; vol. 3, *1763-93.*

Foster, Michael K. "Another Look at the Function of Wampum in Iroquois-White Councils," in Francis Jennings et al., eds., *The History and Culture of Iroquois Diplomacy: An Interdisciplinary Guide to the Treaties of the Six Nations and Their League*: 99-114. Syracuse: University of Syracuse Press, 1985.

Fredrickson, N. Jaye and Sandra Gibb. *The Covenant Chain: Indian Ceremonial and Trade Silver.* Ottawa: National Museum of Canada, 1980.

Furneaux, Rupert. *Saratoga: The Decisive Battle.* London: George Allen and Unwin Ltd., 1971.

Gaffen, Fred. *Forgotten Soldiers; An Illustrated History of Canada's Native Peoples in Both World Wars.* Penticton, BC: Theytus Books, 1984.

Gales, Joseph, ed. *Annals of Congress 1789-1824.* 42 vols., Washington, DC: Gales and Seaton, 1834-56.

Gentleman's Magazine. London, 1783-96.

Gilpin, Alex R. *The War of 1812 in the Old Northwest.* East Lansing: Michigan State University Press, 1958.

Gipson, Lawrence H. *The British Empire Before the American Revolution.* 15 vols., New York: Alfred A. Knopf, 1936-70.

Glenney, Daniel J. "An Ethnohistory of the Grand River Iroquois and the War of 1812." MA thesis, University of Guelph, 1973.

Glover, Michael. *General Burgoyne in Canada and America: Scapegoat for a System.* London: Gordon and Cremonesi, 1976.

Godfrey, William G. *Pursuit of Profit and Preferment in Colonial North America: John Bradstreet's Quest.* Waterloo, Ont.: Wilfrid Laurier University Press, 1982.

Goldenweiser, Alexander A. "[Review of] The Constitution of the Five Nations, by Arthur C. Parker." *American Anthropologist* 18, no. 3 (1916): 431-36.

——. "The Clan and Maternal Family of the Iroquois League," *American Anthropologist*, 15 (October–December 1913): 696-99.

Goltz, H.C.W., Jr. "Indian Revival Religion and the Western District, 1805-1813," in *Association of Iroquois and Allied Indians and the Native Perspective-Western District Historical Conference 1979.* Walpole Island, Ontario, December 1979.

———. "Tecumseh, The Prophet and the Rise of the Northwest Indian Confederation." Ph.D. dissertation, University of Western Ontario, 1973.

Graham, G.S. "The Indian Menace and the Retention of the Western Posts (extracts from the Chatham Papers)," Canadian Historical Review 15 (March 1934): 46-48.

Graymont, Barbara. The Iroquois in the American Revolution. Syracuse: Syracuse University Press, 1972.

Great Britain. British Parliamentary Papers. vol. 13, Shannon: Irish University Press, 1969.

Green, Andrea E. "Land, Leadership and Conflict: The Six Nations Early Years on the Grand River." MA thesis, University of Western Ontario, 1984.

Green, Gretchen. "Molly Brant, Catherine Brant, and their Daughters: A Study in Colonial Administration," Ontario History 81, no. 3 (September 1989): 236-50.

Greene, Jack P., ed. The Ambiguity of the American Revolution. New York: Harper and Row, 1969.

Grignon, Augustin. "Seventy-two Years Recollections of Wisconsin, "Wisconsin Historical Collections 3 (1904).

Gwyn, Julian. "British Government Spending and the North American Colonies 1740-1775," Journal of Imperial and Commonwealth History 8, no. 2 (January 1980): 74-84.

Guzzardo, John C. "Sir William Johnson's Official Family: Patron and Clients in an Anglo-American Empire, 1742-1777." Ph.D. dissertation, Syracuse University, 1975.

———. "The Superintendant and the Ministers: The Battle for Oneida Alliances, 1761-1775," New York History 57, no. 3 (July 1976): 255-83.

Haan, Richard. L. "The Problem of Iroquois Neutrality: Suggestions for Revision," Ethnohistory 27, no. 4 (Fall 1980): 317-29.

———. "The Covenant Chain: Iroquois Diplomacy on the Niagara Frontier, 1697-1730." Ph.D. dissertation, University of California, 1976.

Hadden, Lt. James M. A Journal Kept in Canada and upon Burgoyne's Campaign in 1776 and 1777. Freeport, NY: Books for Libraries Press, 1970; first publ. 1884.

Halbert, Henry S. and T.H. Ball. The Creek War of 1813 and 1814. Chicago: Donohue and Henneberry, 1895.

Hale, Horatio, E. "An Iroquois Condoling Council," Royal Society of Canada. Transactions, 2nd series, vol. 1, no. 2 (895): 45-65.

———, ed. The Iroquois Book of Rites. Toronto: University of Toronto Press, 1965.

Hamer, Philip M. "John Stuart's Indian Policy during the Early Months of the American Revolution," Mississippi Valley Historical Review 17 (1930-31): 351-66.

———. "The British in Canada and the Southern Indians, 1790-1794," East Tennessee Historical Society's Publications 2 (1930): 107-34.

Hamilton, Edward P., ed. Adventures in the Wilderness: The American Journals of Louis Antoine de Bougainville 1756-1760. Norman: University of Oklahoma Press, 1964.

Hamilton, Milton W. "Myths and Legends of Sir William Johnson," New York History 34, no.1 (1953): 3-26.

———. Sir William Johnson: Colonial American, 1715-1763. Port Washington, NY: Kennikat Press, 1976.

———. "Sir William Johnson: Interpreter of the Iroquois," Ethnohistory 10, no. 3 (1963): 270-86.

———. "Sir William Johnson's Wives," New York History 38, no.1 (1957): 18-28.

———. "The Papers of Sir William Johnson: Addenda," New York History 60 (January 1979): 81-101.

Hargrove, Richard J., Jr. General John Burgoyne. Newark: University of Delaware

Press, 1983.

Harlow, Vincent T. and Frederick Madden, eds. *British Colonial Developments: Select Documents, 1774-1834*. Oxford: Clarendon Press, 1967.

Harris, R. Cole, ed. and Geoffrey J. Mathews (cartographer/designer). *Historical Atlas of Canada*. 3 vols., Toronto: University of Toronto Press, 1987: vol. 1, *From the Beginning to 1800*.

Hatch, Robert McConnell. *Thrust for Canada: The American Attempt on Quebec in 1775-1776*. Boston: Houghton Mifflin Company, 1979.

Hatheway, G.G. "The Neutral Barrier State: A Project in British North American Policy, 1754-1815." Ph.D. dissertation, University of Minnesota, 1957.

Hawthorn, H.B., ed. *A Survey of the Contemporary Indians of Canada: Economic, Political, Educational Needs and Policies*. 2 vols., Ottawa: Department of Indian and Northern Affairs, 1966-67.

Henry, Alexander. *Travels and Adventures in Canada and the Indian Territories Between the Years 1760 and 1776*. Toronto: G.N. Morang, 1901.

Herrington, M. Eleanor. "Captain John Deserontyou and the Mohawk Settlement at Deseronto," *Queen's Quarterly* 29 (1921): 165-80.

Hitsman, J.M. "Sir George Prevost's Conduct of the Canadian War of 1812," *Canadian Historical Association for 1962*; 34-43.

Hoberg, Walter R. "A Tory in the Northwest," *Pennsylvania Magazine of History and Biography* 59, no. 1 (January 1935): 32-41.

———. "Early History of Colonel Alexander McKee," *Pennsylvania Magazine and Biography* 58, no. 1 (1934): 26-36.

Horn, Kahn-Tineta. *The Jay Treaty 1794: Where the Jay Treaty Issue Presently Stands*. Ottawa: Department of Indian and Northern Affairs Canada, 1984.

Horsman, Reginald. "American Indian Policy in the Old Northwest, 1783-1812," *William and Mary Quarterly* 18 (1961): 35-53.

———. "British Indian Policy in the Northwest, 1807-1812," *Mississippi Valley Historical Review* 45, no. 1 (June 1958): 51-66.

———. *Expansion and American Indian Policy, 1783-1812*. East Lansing: Michigan State University Press, 1967.

———. *Matthew Elliott, British Indian Agent*. Detroit: Wayne State University, 1964.

———. "On To Canada: Manifest Destiny and United States Strategy in the War of 1812," *Michigan Historical Review* 13, no. 2 (Fall 1987): 1-24.

———. "The British Indian Department and the Abortive Treaty of Lower Sandusky, 1793," *Ohio Historical Quarterly* 70, no. 3 (July 1961): 189-213.

———. "The British Indian Department and the Resistance to General Anthony Wayne, 1793-1795," *Mississippi Valley Historical Review* 49, no. 2 (1962): 269-90.

———. *The Causes of the War of 1812*. New York: A.S. Barnes, 1962.

———. *The Origins of Indian Removal 1815-1824*. East Lansing: Michigan State University Press, 1970.

———. "The Role of the Indian in the War," in Philip P. Mason, ed., *After Tippecanoe, Some Aspects of the War of 1812*: 60-77. Toronto: Ryerson Press, 1963.

———. "United States Indian Policies, 1776-1815," in Wilcomb E. Washburn, vol. ed., *Handbook of North American Indians*: vol. 4, *History of Indian-White Relations*: 29-39. Washington, DC: Smithsonian Institution, 1988.

Houlding, J.A. and G. Kenneth Yates. "Corporal Fox's Memoir of Service, 1776-1783: Quebec, Saratoga and the Convention Army," *Journal of the Society for Army Historical Research* 68, no. 275 (Autumn 1990): 146-68.

Hudson, Charles. *The Southeastern Indians*. Knoxville: University of Tennessee Press, 1976.

Hunt, George T. *The Wars of the Iroquois: A Study in Intertribal Trade Relations*. Madison: University of Wisconsin Press, 1960.

Hurley, J.D. "Children or Brethren: Aboriginal Rights in Colonial Iroquoia." Ph.D.

dissertation, University of Cambridge, 1985.

Ibbotson, Joseph D. "Samuel Kirkland, the Treaty of 1792, and the Indian Barrier State," *New York History* 19, no. 4 (October 1938): 374-91.

Innis, H.A. *The Fur Trade in Canada*. New Haven: Yale University Press, 1930.

Inouye, Frank T. "Sir William Johnson and the Administration of the Northern Indian Department." Ph.D. dissertation, University of Southern California, 1951.

Israel, Fred L., ed. *Major Peace Treaties of Modern History 1648-1967*. New York: Chelsea House Publs., 1967.

Jackson, Donald, ed. *Black Hawk (Ma-ka-tai-me-she-kia-kiak): An Autobiography*. Urbana: University of Illinois Press, 1955, ed.

Jacobs, Wilbur R. "British-Colonial Attitudes and Policies Toward the Indian in the American Colonies," in Howard Peckham and Charles Gibson, eds., *Attitudes of Colonial Powers Towards the American Indian*, 81-106. Salt Lake City: University of Utah Press, 1969.

——. *The Appalachian Indian Frontier: The Edmund Atkin Report and Plan of 1755*. Lincoln, University of Nebraska Press, 1967.

——. *Wilderness Politics and Indian Gifts: The Northern Colonial Frontier, 1748-1763*. Lincoln: University of Nebraska Press, 1966.

Jamieson, J.B. "Trade and Warfare: The Disappearance of the St. Lawrence Iroquoians," *Man and the Northeast* 39 (1990): 79-86.

Jenks, R., comp. *Siege of Fort Stanwix and Battle of Oriskany*. Rome, NY: Bropard and Co., Inc., 1977.

Jennings, Francis. "Dutch and Swedish Indian Policies," in Wilcomb E. Washburn, vol. ed. *Handbook of North American Indians: vol. 4, History of Indian-White Relations*: 13-19. Washington, DC: Smithsonian Institution, 1988.

——. *Empire of Fortune: Crowns, Colonies and Tribes in the Seven Years War in America*. New York: Collier Books, 1988.

——. *The Ambiguous Iroquois Empire: The Covenant Chain Confederation of Indian Tribes with English Colonies from its beginnings to the Lancaster Treaty of 1744*. New York: W.W. Norton and Company, 1984.

——. "The Constitutional Evolution of the Covenant Chain," *Proceedings of the American Philosophical Society* 15. no. 2 (April 1971): 88-96.

——. *The History and Culture of Iroquois Diplomacy: An Interdisciplinary Guide to the Treaties of the Six Nations and Their League*. Syracuse: Syracuse University Press, 1985.

——. *The Invasion of America: Indians, Colonialism and the Cant of Conquest*. Chapel Hill: University of North Carolina Press, 1975.

Johnson, Leo A. "The Mississauga-Lake Ontario Land Surrender of 1805," *Ontario History* 83, no. 3 (September 1990): 233-53.

Johnston, Charles M., ed. *The Valley of the Six Nations: A Collection of Documents on the Indian Lands of the Grand River*. Toronto: University of Toronto Press, 1964.

——. "Joseph Brant, The Grand River Lands and the Northwest Crisis," *Ontario History* 55, no. 4 (1963): 267-82.

——. "William Claus and John Norton: A Struggle for Power in Old Ontario," *Ontario History* 57, no. 2 (June 1965): 101-8.

Johnston, Jean. "Ancestry and Descendents of Molly Brant," *Ontario History* 63, no. 2 (June 1971): 87-92.

Josephy, Alvin M., Jr., ed. *America in 1492: The World of the Indian Peoples Before the Arrival of Columbus*. New York: Alfred A. Knopf, 1992.

Juricek, John T. Jr. "English Claims in North America to 1660: A Study in Legal and Constitutional History." Ph.D. dissertation, University of Chicago, 1970.

Kappler, Charles J., ed. *Indian Treaties 1778-1883*. New York: Interland Publishing

Inc., 1973.

Kelsay, Isabel Thompson. *Joseph Brant 1743-1807: Man of Two Worlds.* Syracuse: Syracuse University Press, 1984.

Kelsey, Harry. "The Amherst Plan: A Factor in the Pontiac Uprising," *Ontario History* 65, no. 3 (September 1973): 149-58.

Kentucky Gazette. Lexington, 1764.

Kingston Gazette. Kingston, Upper Canada, 1812-14.

Klink, Carl F. and James J. Talman, eds. *The Journal of Major John Norton 1816.* Toronto: The Champlain Society, 1970.

Knopf, R.C., ed. *Anthony Wayne, a Name in Arms: Soldier, Diplomat, Defender of Expansion Westward of a Nation; The Wayne-Knox-Pickering-McHenry Correspondence.* Pittsburgh: University of Pittsburgh Press, 1959.

Kopperman, Paul E. *Braddock at the Monongahela.* Pittsburgh: University of Pittsburgh Press, 1977.

Kosche, Ludwig. "Contemporary Portraits of Isaac Brock: An Analysis," *Archivaria* 20 (Summer 1985): 22-66.

——. "Relics of Brock: An Investigation," *Archivaria* 9 (Winter 1979-80): 33-103.

Lanctôt, Gustave. *Canada and the American Revolution, 1774-1783,* transl. Margaret M. Camerson. Toronto: Clark, Irwin and Co., 1967.

Lauriston, Victor. "The Case for General Procter," in Morris Zaslow, ed., *The Defended Border: Upper Canada and the War of 1812:* 121-29. Toronto: Macmillan Co., 1964.

Laviolette, Gontran. *The Sioux in Canada.* Regina: Marion Press, 1944.

Lawson, P. *The Imperial Challenge: Quebec and Britain in the Age of the American Revolution.* Montreal: McGill-Queen's University Press, 1989.

Leavitt, Orpha E. "British Policy on the Canadian Frontier, 1782-92: Mediation and an Indian Barrier State," *Publications of the State Historical Society of Wisconsin for 1916*: 151-85.

Leder, Lawrence H., ed. *The Livingston Indian Records, 1666-1723.* Gettysburg, Pa.: Pennsylvania Historical Association, 1956.

Leslie, John F. "Commissions of Inquiry into Indian Affairs in the Canadas, 1828-1858: Evolving a Corporate Memory for the Indian Department." MA thesis, Carleton University, 1984.

——. *The Treaty of Amity, Commerce and Navigation, 1794-1796: The Jay Treaty.* Ottawa: Department of Indian and Northern Affairs Canada, 1979.

Lester, Geoffrey S. *Aboriginal Land Rights: Some Notes on the Historiography of English Claims in North America.* Ottawa: Canadian Arctic Resources Committee, 1988.

——. "The Territorial Rights of the Inuit of the Canadian Northwest Territories: A Legal Argument." Doctor of Jurisprudence dissertation, York University, 1981.

Letcher, H.K. "The Imperial Designs of John Graves Simcoe: First Lieutenant Governor of Upper Canada, 1792-1796." MA thesis, Wayne State University, 1930.

Lipscomb, Andrew A. and Albert E. Bergh, eds. *The Writings of Thomas Jefferson.* 20 vols., Washington: Thomas Jefferson Memorial Association, 1905: vol. 13: 168-72.

Lomax, D.A.N. *A History of the Services of the 41st (Welch) Regiment ..., from its formation in 1719 to 1895.* Devonport, England: Hiorns and Miller, 1899.

London Magazine. London, 1776.

Lord, N.C., ed. "The War on the Canadian Frontier, 1812-14: Letters Written by Sergt. James Commins, 8th Foot August 1815," *Journal of the Society for Army Historical Research* 18 (1939): 199-211.

Lurie, Nancy Oestreich. "Indian Cultural Adjustment to European Civilization," in James Morton Smith, ed. *Seventeeth-Century America: Essays in Colonial*

History: 33-60. Chapel Hill: University of North Carolina Press, 1959.

Lydekker, John W. *The Faithful Mohawks*. Cambridge, Mass.: Cambridge University Press, 1938.

Mackesy, Piers. *The War for America, 1775-1783*. Cambridge, Mass.: Harvard University Press, 1965.

MacLeod, Malcolm. "Fortress Ontario or Forlorn Hope ? Simcoe and the Defence of Upper Canada," *Canadian Historical Review* 53, no. 2 (June 1972): 149-78.

Mahon, John K. "British Command Decisions in the Northern Campaigns of the War of 1812," *Canadian Historical Review* 46, no. 3 (1965): 219-37.

——. "British Strategy and Southern Indians: War of 1812," *Florida Historical Quarterly* 45 (April 1966): 285-302.

——. *The War of 1812*. Gainsville: University of Florida Press, 1972.

Marshall, Peter. "Colonial Protest and Imperial Retrenchment: Indian Policy 1764-1768," *Journal of American Studies* 5, no. 1 (April 1971): 1-17.

——. "First Americans and Last Loyalists: An Indian Dilemma in War and Peace," in Esmond Wright, ed. *Red White and True Blue: The Loyalists in the American Revolution*: 33-53. New York: AMS Press, 1976.

——. "Imperial Policy and The Government of Detroit: Projects and Problems, 1760-1774," *Journal of Imperial and Commonwealth History* 2, no. 2 (January 1974): 153-89.

——. "Imperial Regulation of American Indian Affairs, 1763-1774." Ph.D. dissertation, Yale University, 1959.

——. "Sir William Johnson and the Treaty of Fort Stanwix, 1768," *Journal of American Studies* 1, no. 1 (April 1967): 149-79.

Mather, Cotton. *Magnalia Christi Americana: Or, the Ecclesiastical History of New England: from its First Planting, in the Year 1620, unto the Year of Our Lord 1698*. London: T. Pankhurst, 1702.

Mayo, Bernard, ed. *Instructions to the British Ministers to the United States, 1791-1812*. Washington, DC: American Historical Association, 1941.

McAdams, Donald R. "The Sullivan Expedition: Success or Failure?," *New York Historical Society Quarterly Bulletin* 54, no. 1 (January 1970): 53-81.

McAfee, Robert. *History of the Late War in the Western Country* ... Lexington, Kentucky: Worsley and Smith, 1816.

McCallum, James Dow, ed. *The Letters of Eleazer Wheelock's Indians*. Hanover, NH: Dartmouth College Manuscript Series, no. 1, 1932.

McIlwain, Charles H., ed. *An Abridgement of the Indian Affairs Contained in Four Folio Volumes Transacted in the Colony of New York, from the Year 1678 to the Year 1751, by Peter Wraxall*. Cambridge, Mass.: Harvard University Press, 1915. Vol. 21 of Harvard Historical Studies.

McKeith, D.S. " The Inadequacy of Men and Measures in English Imperial History: Sir William Johnson and the New York Politicians, a Case Study." Ph.D. dissertation, Syracuse University, 1971.

Mealing, S.R. "The Enthusiasms of John Graves Simcoe," *Canadian Historical Association Report for 1958*: 50-62.

Miller, J.R. *Skyscrapers Hide the Heavens: A History of Indian-White Relations in Canada*. Toronto: University of Toronto Press, 1989.

Milloy, John S. "The Era of Civilization - British Policy for the Indians of Canada, 1830-1860." D.Phil. dissertation, University of Oxford, 1978.

Mintz, Max M. *The Generals of Saratoga: John Burgoyne and Horatio Gates*. New Haven: Yale University Press, 1990.

Mohr, Walter H. *Federal Indian Relations, 1774-1788*. Philadelphia: University of Pennsylvania Press, 1933.

Montgomery, Malcolm. "The Legal Status of the Six Nations Indians in Canada," *Ontario History* 60, no. 2 (1963): 93-105.

Montreal Gazette. Montreal, 1785-97.

Morgan, Lewis H. *League of Ho-de-no-sau-nee or Iroquois.* New York: Sage and Brother, 1851.

Morris, Alexander. *The Treaties of Canada with the Indians.* Toronto: Belfords, Clarke, 1880.

Morrison, Kenneth M. *The Embattled Northeast: The Elusive Ideal of Alliance in Abenaki-Euramerican Relations.* Berkeley: University of California Press, 1984.

Muller, Henry N. and Daniel A. Donath. "The Road Not Taken – A Reassessment of Burgoyne's Campaign," *Bulletin of the Fort Ticonderoga Museum* 13, no. 4 (1973): 272-85.

Murray, David. *Mordern Indians: Native Americans in the Twentieth Century.* British Association for American Studies, 1982.

Murray, J. McE. "John Norton," *Ontario History Society Papers and Records* 37 (1945): 7-16.

Nammack, Georgiana C. *Fraud, Politics, and the Dispossession of the Indians: The Iroquois Land Frontier in the Colonial Period.* Norman: University of Oklahoma Press, 1969.

Nin. Da. Waab. Jig. *Minishenhying Anishnaabe-aki: Walpole Island; The Soul of Indian Territory.* Walpole Island, Ontario, 1987.

Norris, James. "The Campaign of Major General Sullivan, May to October 1779," *Buffalo Historical Society Publications* 1 (1879): 217-52.

Oaks, Robert F. "The Impact of British Western Policy on the Coming of the Revolution in Pennsylvania," *Pennsylvania Magazine of History and Biography* 101, no. 2 (April 1977): 171-89.

O'Callaghan, E.B., ed. *Documents Relative to the Colonial History of the State of New York.* 15 vols., Albany: Weed, Parsons and Co., 1853-87.

———. *The Documentary History of the State of New York.* 4 vols., Albany: Weed Parsons and Co., 1849-51.

O'Donnell, James H., III. "Alexander McGillivray: Training for Leadership, 1777-1783," *Georgia Historical Quarterly* 49, no. 2 (1965): 172-86.

———. *Southern Indians in the American Revolution.* Knoxville: University of Tennessee Press, 1973.

———. "The Southern Indians in the War for American Independence, 1775-1783," in Charles M. Hudson, ed. *Four Centuries of Southern Indians*: 46-64. Athens: University of Georgia Press, 1975.

Ostola, Lawrence. "The Seven Nations of Canada and the American Revolution 1774-1783." MA thesis, Université de Montréal, 1988.

Owsley, Frank L. *Struggle for the Gulf Borderlands: The Creek War and the Battle of New Orleans.* Gainsville: University of Florida Press, 1981.

———. "The Fort Mims Massacre," *Alabama Review* 24 (1971): 194-204.

Pannekoek, Frits. *The Fur Trade and Western Canadian Society 1670-1870.* Ottawa: Canadian Historical Association, 1987. Historical Booklet no. 43.

Pargellis, Stanley McCory. *Lord Loudon in North America.* New Haven, Conn.: Yale University Press, 1933.

Parker, Arthur C. *The Constitution of the Five Nations or the Iroquois Book of the Great Law.* Albany: University of the State of New York, 1916.

Parkman, Francis. *France and England in North America.* 8 vols., Boston: Little, Brown and Co., 1851-92.

———. *Montcalm and Wolfe.* New York: Collier Books, 1966; first publ. Boston 1884.

———. *The Conspiracy of Pontiac.* New York: Collier Books, 1962; first publ. Boston 1851.

Pastore, Ralph T. "Congress and the Six Nations, 1775-1778," *Niagara Frontier* 20, no. 4 (Winter 1973): 80-95.

Pearce, Roy H. *The Savages of America: A Study of the Indian and the Idea of Civilization*. Baltimore: The Johns Hopkins Press, 1953; republ. as *Savagism and Civilization* (1965).

Peckham, H. *Pontiac and the Indian Uprising*. Chicago: University of Chicago Press, 1947.

Perkins, Bradford. *Prologue to War: England and the United States, 1805-1812*. Berkeley: University of California Press, 1961.

Perkins, Bradford, ed. "Lord Hawkesbury and the Jay-Grenville Negotiations," *Mississippi Valley Historical Review* 40 (1953): 291-304.

Petrone, Penny, ed. *First People, First Voices*. Toronto: University of Toronto Press, 1984.

Pittsburgh Gazette. Pittsburgh, 1791-94.

Pratt, Julius W. "Fur Trade Strategy and the American Left Flank in the War of 1812," *American Historical Review* 40 (1935): 246-73.

Prucha, Francis Paul. *American Indian Policy in the Formative Years: The Indian Trade and Intercourse Acts, 1790-1834*. Cambridge, Mass.: Harvard University Press, 1962.

——, ed. *Documents of United States Indian Policy*. Lincoln: University of Nebraska Press, 1990.

——. *Indian Policy in the United States: Historical Essays*. Lincoln: University of Nebraska Press, 1981.

——. *Lewis Cass and American Indian Policy*. Detroit: Wayne State University, 1967.

——. *The Great Father: The United States Government and the American Indians*: 2 vols., Lincoln: University of Nebraska Press, 1984.

——. *The Sword of the Republic: The United States Army on the Frontier, 1783-1846*. Bloomington: Indiana University Press, 1977.

——. "United States Indian Policies, 1815-1860," in Wilcomb E. Washburn vol. ed., *Handbook of North American Indians*: vol. 4 *History of Indian-White Relations*: 40-47. Washington, DC: Smithsonian Institution, 1988.

——. *United States Indian Policy: A Critical Bibliography*. Bloomington: Indiana University Press, 1977.

Pulfer, Ruth E. "The Administration of British Policy to the Indians in the Northern District of North America, 1760-1783." MA thesis, University of Saskatchewan, 1970.

Quaife, M.M. "An Artilleryman of Old Fort Mackinac," *Burton Historical Collection Leaflet* 6, no. 3 (January 1928): 33-48.

——. "The Ohio Campaigns of 1782," *Mississippi Valley Historical Review* 18 (1931): 515-29.

——, ed. *The Siege of Detroit in 1763: The Journal of Pontiac's Conspiracy and John Rutherford's Narrative of a Captivity*. Chicago: R.R. Donnelley and Sons, 1958.

——. "*The Story of Brownstown*," Burton Historical Collection Leaflet 4 (1926): 65-80.

——, ed. *War on the Detroit: The Chronicles of Thomas Verchères de Boucherville* and *The Capitulation, by an Ohio Volunteer*. Chicago: The Lakeside Press, 1940.

Quealy, F.M. "The Administration of Sir Peregrine Maitland, Lieutenant-Governor of Upper Canada, 1818-1828." 2 vols., Ph.D. dissertation, University of Toronto, 1968.

Richter, Daniel K. and Merrell, James H., eds. *Beyond the Covenant Chain: The Iroquois and Their Neighbours in Indian North America, 1600-1800*. Syracuse: Syracuse University Press, 1987.

Scioto Gazette. Chillicothe, 1811-12.

Schlenther, Boyd Stanley. *Charles Thomson: A Patriot's Pursuit*. Newark: University of Delaware Press, 1990.

——. "Training for Resistance: Charles Thomson and Indian Affairs in Pennsylvania," *Pennsylvania History* 50, no. 3 (July 1983): 185-217.

Schmaltz, Peter S. *The Ojibwa of Southern Ontario*. Toronto: University of Toronto Press, 1991.

——. "The Role of the Ojibwa in the Conquest of Southern Ontario, 1650-1701," *Ontario History* 76, no. 4 (December 1984): 328-52.

Scots Magazine. Edinburgh, 1783-96.

Severance, Frank H. "The Niagara Peace Mission of Major Ephraim Douglas in 1783," *Buffalo Historical Society Publications* 18 (1914): 115-41.

Shanahan, David. *The Indian Land Management Fund*. Ottawa: Department of Indian and Northern Affairs Canada, 1991.

Shaw, Helen Louise. *British Administration of the Southern Indians, 1756-1783*. Lancaster, Pa.: Lancaster Press. 1931.

Sheehan, Bernard W. *Seeds of Extinction: Jeffersonian Philanthropy and the American Indian*. New York: W.W. Norton and Co., 1974.

——. "The Famous Hair Buyer General: Henry Hamilton, George Rogers Clark, and the American Indian," *Indiana Magazine of History* 76, no. 1 (March 1983): 1-28.

Shortt, A. and A.G. Doughty, eds. *Documents Relating to the Constitutional History of Canada, 1759-1791*. 2 vols., Ottawa: King's Printer, 1918.

Shy, John. *Toward Lexington: The Role of the British Army and the Coming of the American Revolution*. Princeton. NJ: Princeton University Press, 1965.

Simmons, Richard C. and Peter D.G. Thomas, eds. *Proceedings and debates of the British Parliaments respecting North America, 1754-1783*. 5 vols. to date. Millwood, NY: Kraus International Publications, 1982- .

Slattery, Brian J. "The Land Rights of Indigenous Canadian Peoples, as affected by the Crown's Acquisition of their Territories." D.Phil. dissertation, University of Oxford, 1979.

Smith, Donald B. *Sacred Feathers: The Reverend Peter Jones (Kahkewaquonaby) and the Mississauga Indians*. Toronto: University of Toronto Press, 1987.

——. "The Dispossession of the Mississauga Indians: a Missing Chapter in the Early History of Upper Canada," *Ontario History* 73, no. 2 (June 1981): 67-87.

Smith, Paul H., ed. *Letters of Delegates to Congress*. 16 vols. (to date), Washington, DC: United States Government Printing Office, 1976-89.

Smith, William Henry, ed. *The St. Clair Papers*. 2 vols., Cincinnati: R. Clarke and Co., 1882.

Sosin, Jack M. "The British Indian Department and Dunmore's War," *Virginia Magazine of History and Biography* 74, no. 1 (1966): 34-50.

——. "The Use of Indians in the War of the American Revolution: A Re-Assessment of Responsibility," *Canadian Historical Review* 46, no. 2 (June 1965): 101-21.

——. *Whitehall and the Wilderness: the Middle West in British Colonial Policy, 1760-1775*. Lincoln: University of Nebraska Press, 1961.

Stacey, C.P. "The Defence of Upper Canada, 1812," in Morris Zaslow, ed., *The Defended Border: Upper Canada and the War of 1812*: 11-20. Toronto: Macmillan Co., 1964.

Stagg, Jack. "Protection and Survival: Anglo-Indian Relations, 1748-63 - Britain and the Northern Colonies." Ph.D. dissertation, University of Cambridge, 1984.

Stagg, J.C.A. *Mr. Madison's War: Politics, Diplomacy, and Warfare in the Early American Republic, 1783-1830*. Princeton: Princeton University Press, 1983.

Stanley, George F.G. "British Operations in the American Northwest, 1812-15," *Journal of the Society for Army Historical Research* 22 (1943): 91-106.

——. *Canada Invaded 1775-1776*. Toronto and Sarasota: Hakkert and Company,

1977. Canadian War Museum Historical Publication no. 8.

——. "Displaced Red Men: The Sioux in Canada," in Ian A.L. Getty and Donald B. Smith, eds., *One Century Later: Western Canadian Reserve Indians Since Treaty 7.* Vancouver: University of British Columbia Press, 1978.

——, ed. *For Want of a Horse: being a Journal of the Campaigns against the Americans in 1776 and 1777 conducted from Canada.* Sackville, NB: The Tribune Press Ltd., 1961.

——. *The War of 1812: Land Operations.* Ottawa: National Museums of Canada, 1983. Canadian War Museum Historical Publication no. 18.

Stevens, Paul Lawrence. "His Majesty's 'Savage' Allies: British Indian Policy during the Revolutionary War: The Carleton Years, 1774-78." Ph.D. dissertation, State University of New York at Buffalo, 1984.

Stevens, S.K. and D.H. Kent, eds. *The Papers of Col. Henry Bouquet.* 19 vols., Harrisburg: Pennsylvania Historical and Museum Commission, 1940-43.

Stone, W.L. *The Campaign of Lieut. Gen. John Burgoyne and the Expedition of Col. Barry St. Leger.* Albany, NY: J. Munsell, 1877.

——. *The Life of Joseph Brant-Thayendanegea.* 2 vols., New York: A.V. Blake, 1838.

Strach, Stephen G. "A Memoir of the Exploits of Captain Alexander Fraser and his Company of British Marksmen, 1776-1777," *Journal of the Society for Army Historical Research* 63, no. 254 (Summer 1985): 91-98, and no. 255 (Autumn 1985): 164-79.

Sugden, John. " The Southern Indians in the War of 1812: The Closing Phase," *Florida Historical Quarterly* 60, no. 3 (1982): 273-312.

——. *Tecumseh's Last Stand.* Norman: University of Oklahoma Press, 1985.

Sullivan, J.J., ed. *The Papers of Sir William Johnson.* 14 vols., Albany: University of the State of New York, 1921-65.

Surtees, Robert J. "Indian Land Cessions in Ontario, 1763-1862: The Evolution of a System." Ph.D. dissertation, Carleton University, 1982.

——. "Indian Land Cessions in Upper Canada, 1815-1830," in Ian A.L. Getty and Antoine S. Lussier, eds. *As Long As the Sun Shines and Water Flows: A Reader in Canadian Native Studies.* Vancouver: University of British Columbia Press, 1983.

——. "The Development of an Indian Reserve Policy in Canada," *Ontario History* 61 (June 1969):87-98.

Sutherland, Maxwell. "The Civil Administration of Sir George Prevost, 1811-1815: A Study in Conciliation." MA thesis, Queen's University, 1959.

Tanner, Helen Hornbeck, ed. *Atlas of Great Lakes Indian History.* Norman: University of Oklahoma Press, 1987.

——. "The Glaize in 1792: A Composite Indian Community," *Ethnohistory* 25, no. 1 (Winter 1978): 15-40.

Taylor, Theodore W. *The Bureau of Indian Affairs.* Boulder, Colorado: Westview Press, 1984.

The Times. London, 1811-15.

Thomas, Peter D.G. *British Politics and the Stamp Act crisis: the First Phase of the American Revolution 1763-1767.* Oxford: Clarendon Press, 1975.

——. *Tea Party to Independence: the Third Phase of the American Revolution, 1773-1776.* Oxford: Clarendon Press, 1991.

——. "The Cost of the British Army in North America, 1763-1775," *William and Mary Quarterly* 45, no. 3 (1988): 510-16.

——. *The Townshend Duties Crisis: the Second Phase of the American Revolution, 1767-1773.* Oxford: Clarendon Press, 1987.

Thwaites, Reuben G., ed. "Dickson and Grignon Papers, 1812-1815," *Wisconsin Historical Collections* 9 (1882), and 11 (1888).

——. *The Jesuit Relations and Allied Documents.* 73 vols., Cleveland: the Burrows

Bros. Co., 1896–1901.

Thwaites, Reuben G. and Louise P. Kellogg, eds. *The Documentary History of Dunmore's War, 1774.* Madison: Wisconsin Historical Society, 1905.

Titley, Brian E. *A Narrow Vision: Duncan Campbell Scott and the Administration of Indian Affairs in Canada.* Vancouver: University of British Columbia Press, 1986.

Tobias, John. "Protection, Civilization, Assimilation: An Outline History of Canada's Indian Policy," *Western Canadian Journal of Anthropology* 6, no. 2 (1976).

Tohill, L.A. "Robert Dickson, British Fur Trade on the Upper Mississippi," *North Dakota Historical Quarterly* 2 (1928): 5–49, and 3 (1929): 83–128 and 182–203.

Tooker, Elisabeth. "The League of the Iroquois: History Politics, and Ritual" in Bruce G. Trigger, vol. ed., *Handbook of North American Indians*: vol. 15, *Northeast*: 418–41. Washington, DC: Smithsonian Institution, 1978.

——. "Women in Iroquois Society," in Michael K. Foster et al., eds. *Extending the Rafters: Interdisciplinary Approaches to Iroquoian Studies*, 109–23. Albany: State University of New York, 1984.

Tootle, J. "Anglo-Indian Relations in the Northern Theatre of the French and Indian War, 1748–1761." Ph.D. dissertation, Ohio State University, 1972.

Torok, C.H. "The Tyendinaga Mohawks," *Ontario History* 57, no. 2 (June 1965): 69–77.

Trelease, Allen W. *Indian Affairs in Colonial New York: The Seventeenth Century.* Ithaca, NY: Cornell University Press, 1960.

Trigger, Bruce, vol. ed. *Handbook of North American Indians*: Vol. 15, *Northeast*. Washington DC: Smithsonian Institution, 1978.

——. *Natives and Newcomers: Canada's 'Heroic Age' Reconsidered.* Montreal: McGill-Queen's University Press, 1985.

——. *The Children of Aataentsic: A History of the Huron People to 1660.* 2 vols., Montreal: McGill-Queen's University Press, 1976.

Tupper, Ferdinand Brock, ed. *The Life and Correspondence of Major General Sir Isaac Brock, K.B.* London: Simpkin and Marshall, 1847.

United States. *American Indians Today.* Washington, DC: Bureau of Indian Affairs, 1988.

——. *American State Papers: Indian Affairs, 1789–1814.* 2 vols., Washington, DC: US Government Printing Office, 1832–61.

——. *Final Report and Legislative Recommendations - A Report of the Special Committee on Investigations of the Select Committee on Indian Affairs. United States Senate.* Washington, DC: US Government Printing Office, 1989.

Updyke, Frank Arthur. *The Diplomacy of the War of 1812.* Baltimore: The Johns Hopkins Press, 1915.

Upper Canada Gazette. Newark, 1793–1813.

Upton, L.F.S. *Micmacs and Colonists: Indian-White Relations in the Maritimes, 1713–1867.* Vancouver: University of British Columbia Press, 1979.

——. *The Loyal Whig: William Smith of New York and Quebec.* Toronto: University of Toronto Press, 1969.

Van Every, Dale. *The Frontier People of America.* 4 vols., New York: W. Morrow and Co., 1961–64.

Van Kirk, Sylvia. *Many Tender Ties: Women in Fur Trade Society in Western Canada 1670–1870.* Winnipeg: Watson and Dwyer, 1980.

Vincent, Elizabeth. *Fort St. Joseph: A History.* Ottawa: Department of Environment Canada, 1978. Parks Canada, Manuscript Report Series 335.

Vivian, James F. and Jean H. Vivian. "Congressional Indian Policy During the War for Independence: The Northern Department," *Maryland Historical*

  Magazine 63, no. 3 (September 1968): 241-74.

Wade, Mason. "French Indian Policies," in Wilcomb E. Washburn, vol.ed.,
  Handbook of North American Indians: vol. 4, *History of Indian-White Relations*:
  20-28. Washington, DC: Smithsonian Institution, 1988.

Wainwright, Nicholas B., ed. "George Croghan's Journal, 1759-1763," *Pennsylvania
  Magazine of History and Biography* 71, no. 4 (October 1947): 305-444.

——. *George Croghan: Wilderness Diplomat*. Chapel Hill: University of North
  Carolina, 1959.

Wallace, Anthony F.C. *King of the Delawares, Teedyuscung, 1700-1763*. Philadelphia:
  University of Pennsylvania Press, 1949.

——. *The Death and Rebirth of the Seneca*. New York: A.A. Knopf, 1970.

Wallace, Paul A. *The White Roots of Peace*. Philadelphia: University of Pennsylvania
  Press, 1946.

Warrick, W. Sheridan. "The American Indian Policy in the Upper Old Northwest
  following the War of 1812," *Ethnohistory* 3 (Summer 1956):109-10.

Washburn, Wilcomb E., vol.ed. *Handbook of North American Indians*: vol. 4, *History
  of Indian-White Relations*. Washington, DC: Smithsonian Insititution, 1988.

——, ed.*The American Indian and the United States: A Documentary History*. 4 vols.,
  New York: Random House, 1973.

——. "The Moral and Legal Justifications for Dispossessing the Indians," in James
  Morton Smith, ed. *Seventeeth Century America: Essays in Colonial History*,
  15-32. Chapel Hill: University of North Carolina Press, 1959.

Weaver, Sally M. *Making Canadian Indian Policy: The Hidden Agenda, 1968-1970*.
  Toronto: University of Toronto Press, 1981.

Weld, Isaac. *Travels through the States of North America, and the Provinces of Upper
  and Lower Canada during the Years 1795, 1796 and 1797*. 2 vols., London: J.
  Stockdale, 1807.

Western Intelligencer. Worthington, Ohio, 1811-15.

Western Spy. Cincinnati, 1811-15.

Whickar, J.W., ed. "Shabonee's Account of Tippecanoe," *Indiana Magazine of
  History* 17 (1921): 356-63.

Wickliffe, Charles A. "Tecumseh and the Battle of the Thames," *Register of the
  Kentucky Historical Society* 60 (1962): 45-49.

Willcox, William B. "Too Many Cooks: British Planning Before Saratoga," *Journal
  of British Studies* 2 (November 1962): 56-90.

Williams, Mentor L., ed. "John Kinzie's Narrative of the Fort Dearborn Massacre,"
  Journal of the Illinois State Historical Society 46 (1953): 343-62.

Williams, Paul. "The Chain." LL.M. thesis, Osgoode Hall Law School, 1982.

Wise, S.F. "The American Revolution and Indian History," in John S. Moir, ed.
  Character and Circumstance. Essays in Honour of Donald Grant Creighton:
  182-200. Toronto: Macmillan of Canada, 1970.

——. "The Indian Diplomacy of John Graves Simcoe," *Canadian Historical
  Association Report for 1953*: 36-44.

Wood, William, ed. *Select British Documents of the Canadian War of 1812*. 3 vols.,
  Toronto: The Champlain Society, 1920-28.

Wright, J. Leitch, Jr. *Britain and the American Frontier, 1783-1815*. Athens:
  University of Georgia Press, 1975.

——. *Creeks and Seminoles*. Lincoln: University of Nebraska Press, 1986.

Wright, Louis B. and Marion Tinling, eds. *William Byrd of Virginia: The London
  Diary (1717-1721) and Other Writings*. New York: Arno Press, 1972.

Zaslow, Morris, ed. *The Defended Border: Upper Canada and the War of 1812*.
  Toronto: Macmillan Co., 1964.

INDEX